the perfect planet
and other stories

BY

James Kochalka

act I
the perfect planet

act II
nonironic futuropolis

act III
frog & fly

top shelf productions

write to James Kochalka
PO Box 8321, Burlington Vt 05402

Published by top shelf productions
PO Box 1282, Marietta Ga 30061-1282
top shelf productions and the top shelf logo tm and © 1999
top shelf productions, inc.

Publication design by Brad (Highball) Engle and Brett Warnock
(a tip-o-the hat to Michel Vrana.) Heaps of praise to Gray Matter Design.
"the Perfect Planet" first appeared as *James Kochalka Superstar* #9.
"nonironic futuropolis" first appeared as a weekly strip in Burlington, Vt's *Vox*.
printed with style and finesse in Canada by Quebecor

Kochalka, James
the Perfect Planet/James Kochalka
1st top shelf productions ed.
ISBN 1-891830-08-2
1. Humor 2.Cartoons 3. Graphic novels

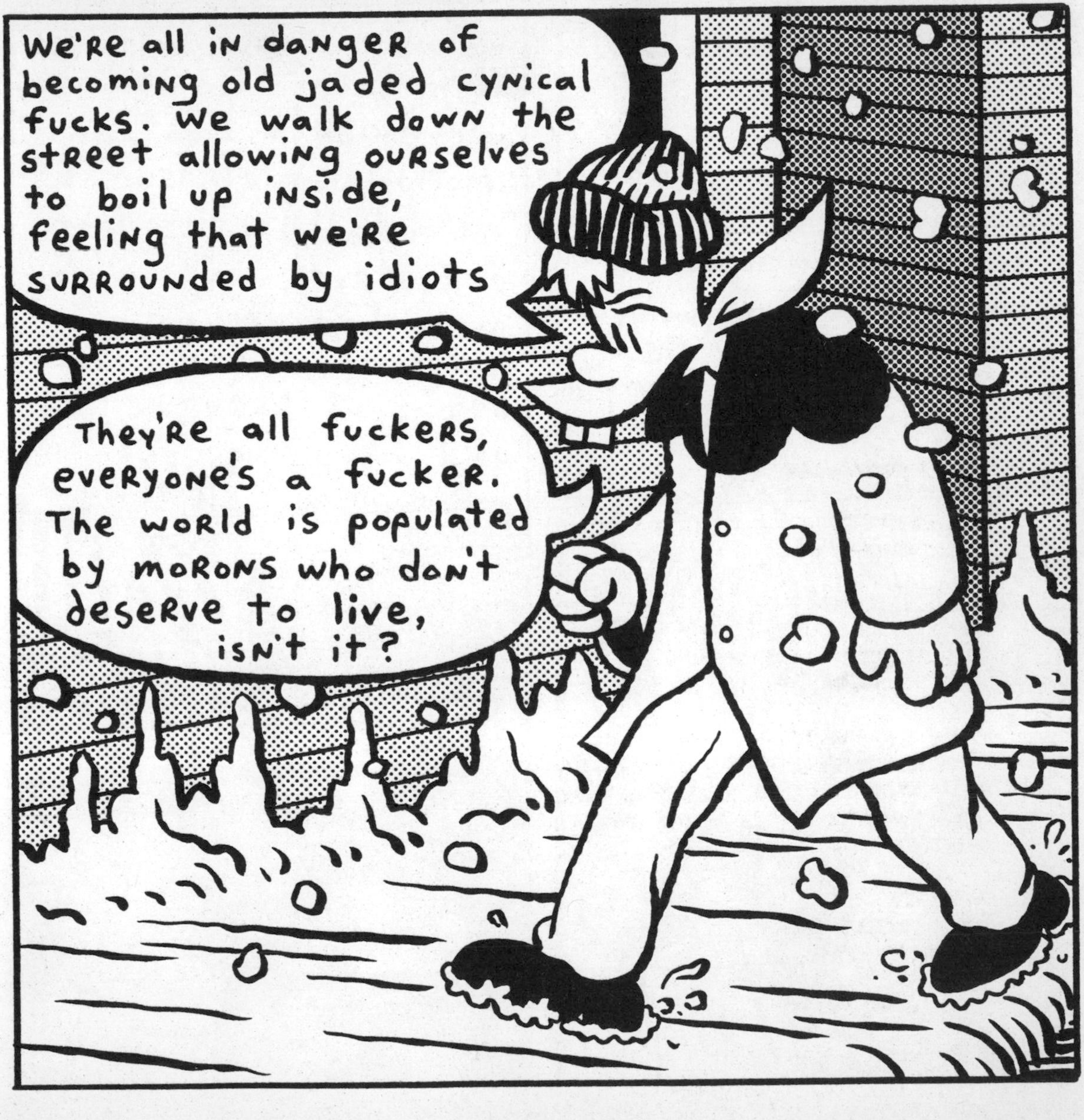
We're all in danger of becoming old jaded cynical fucks. We walk down the street allowing ourselves to boil up inside, feeling that we're surrounded by idiots
They're all fuckers, everyone's a fucker. The world is populated by morons who don't deserve to live, isn't it?

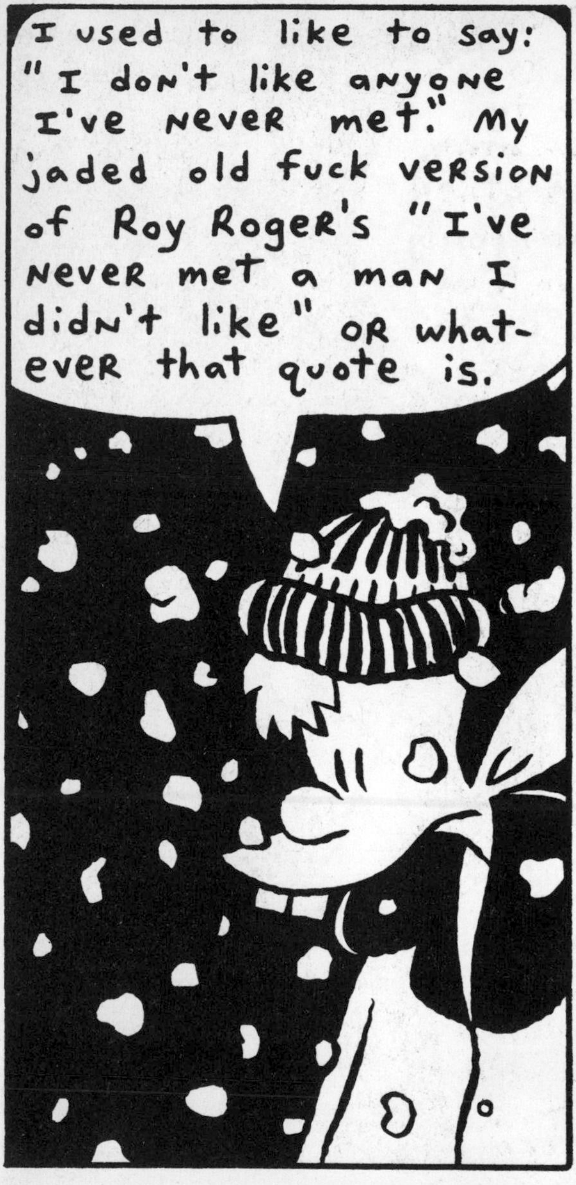
I used to like to say: "I don't like anyone I've never met." My jaded old fuck version of Roy Roger's "I've never met a man I didn't like" or whatever that quote is.

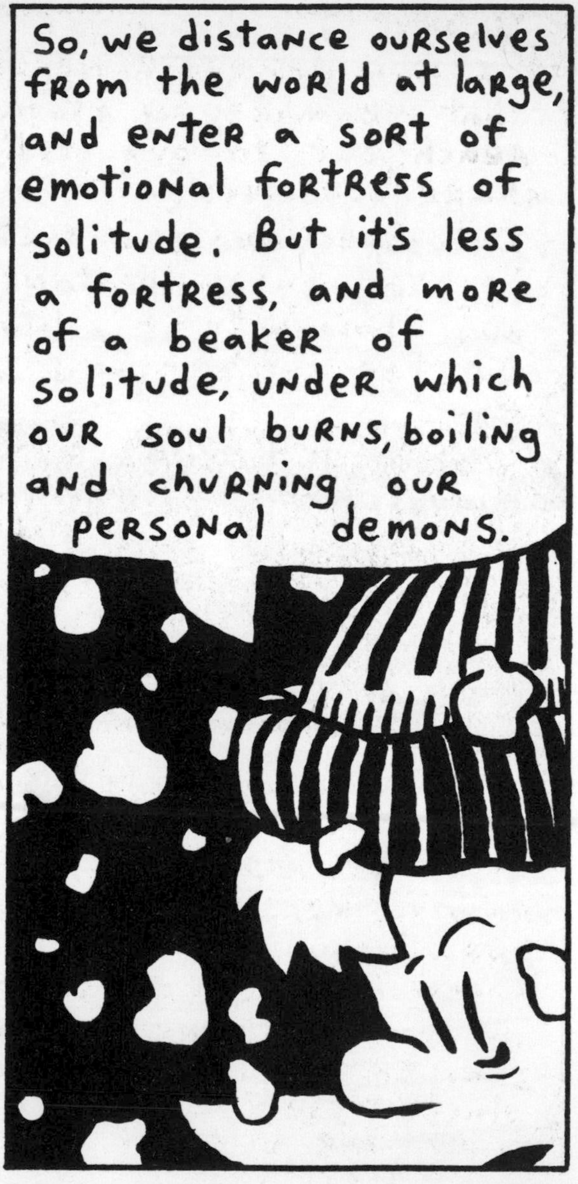
So, we distance ourselves from the world at large, and enter a sort of emotional fortress of solitude. But it's less a fortress, and more of a beaker of solitude, under which our soul burns, boiling and churning our personal demons.

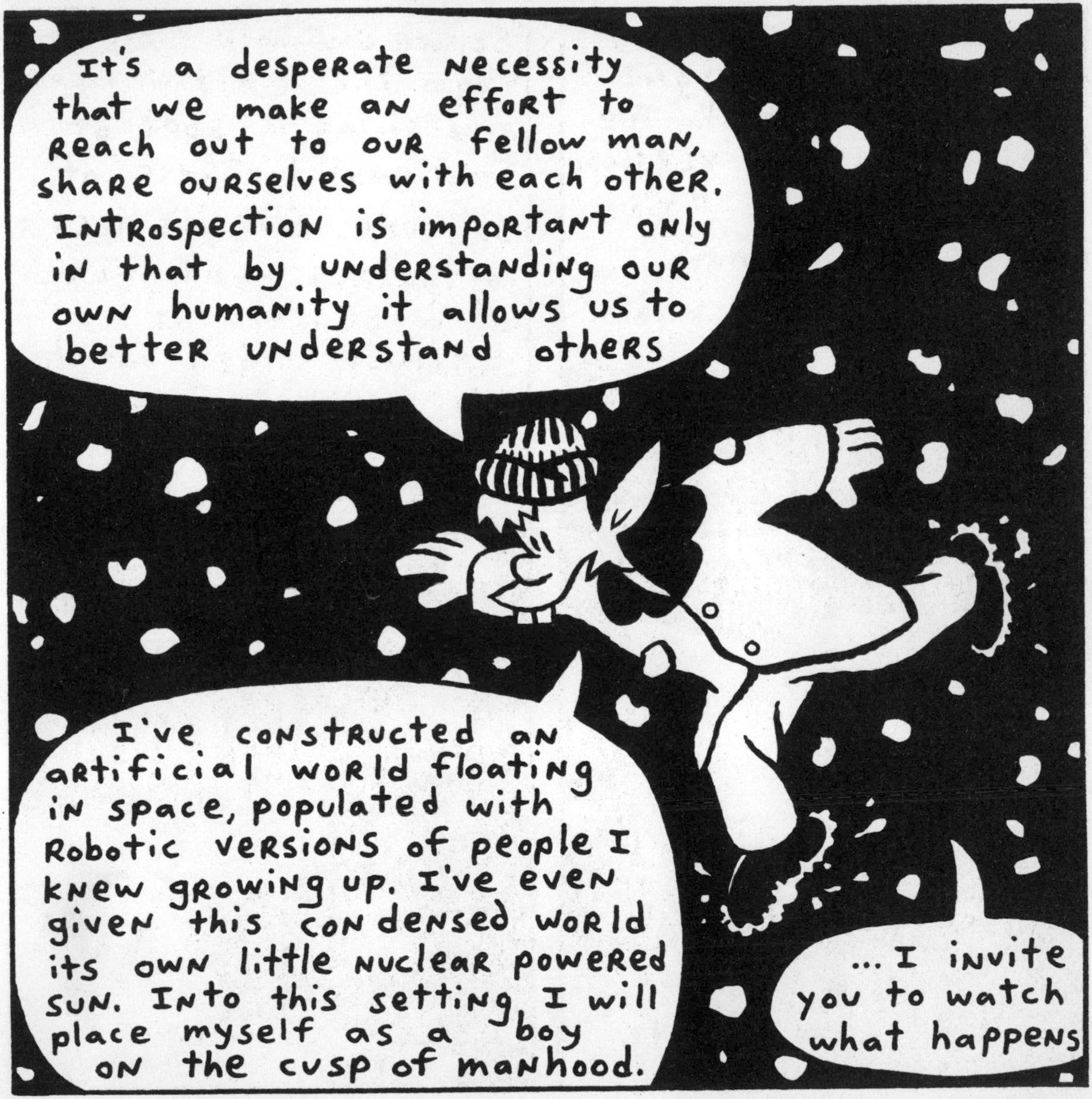
It's a desperate necessity that we make an effort to reach out to our fellow man, share ourselves with each other. Introspection is important only in that by understanding our own humanity it allows us to better understand others
I've constructed an artificial world floating in space, populated with robotic versions of people I knew growing up. I've even given this condensed world its own little nuclear powered sun. Into this setting I will place myself as a boy on the cusp of manhood.
...I invite you to watch what happens

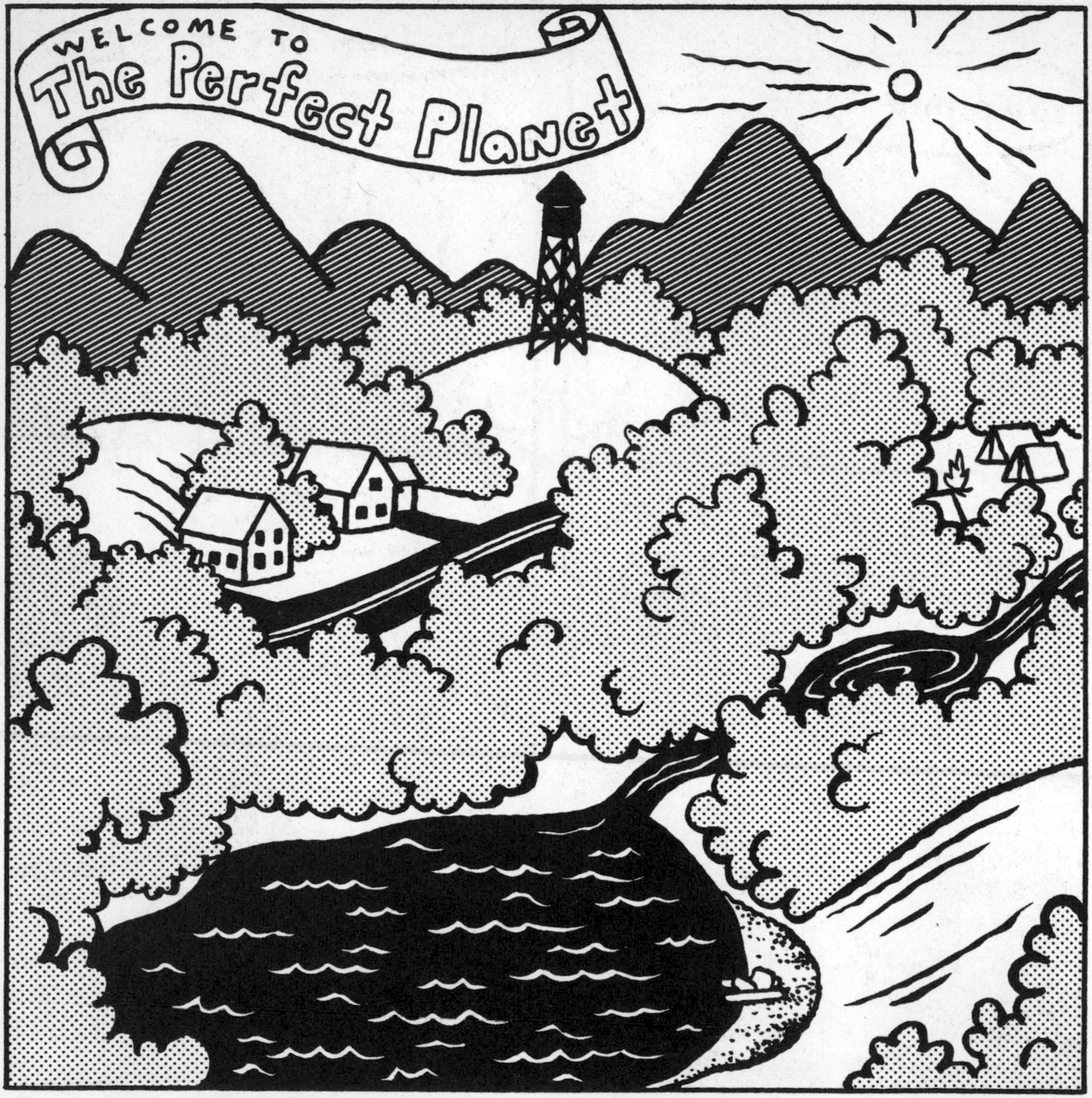
WELCOME TO
The Perfect Planet

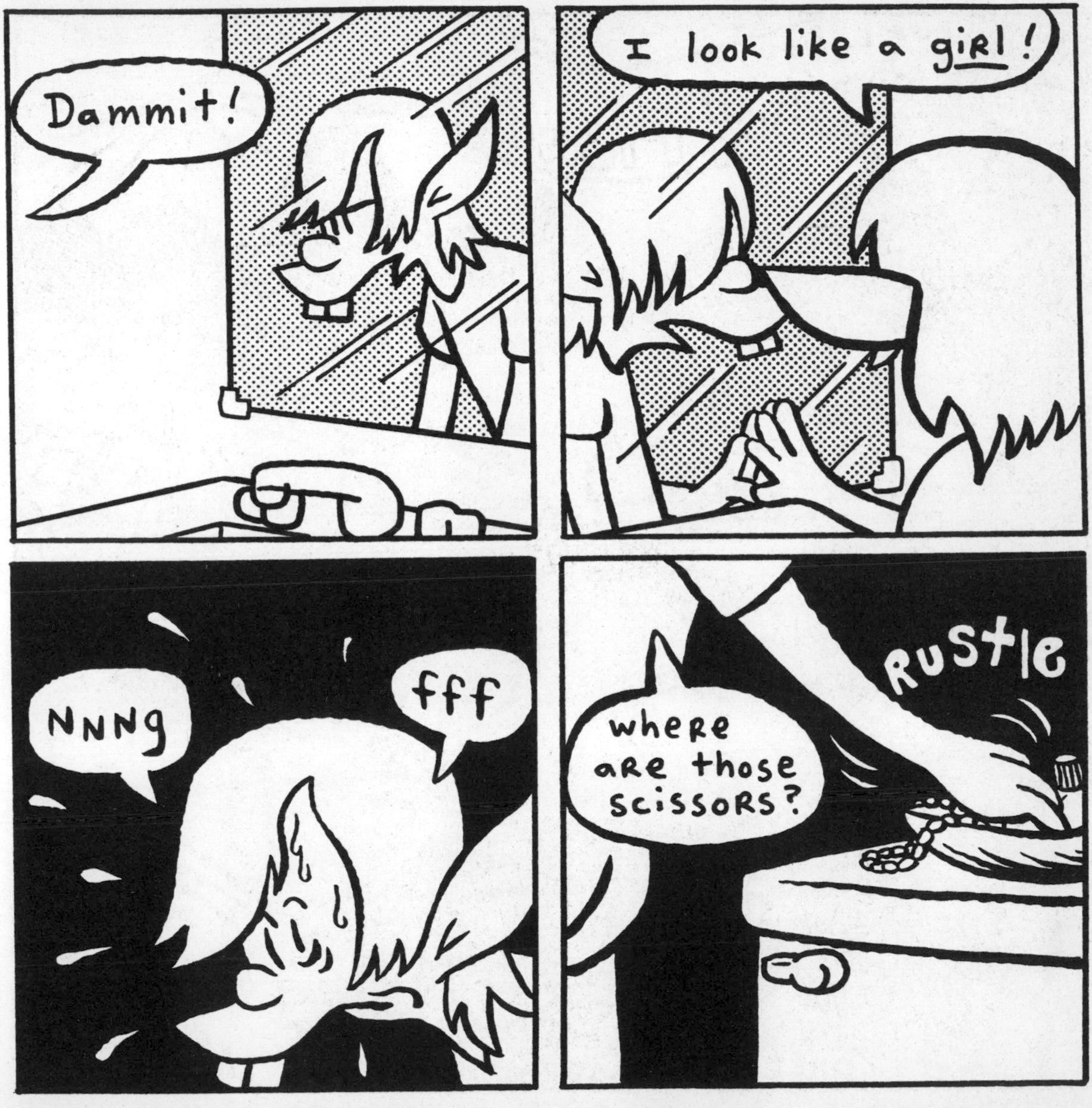
Dammit!
I look like a girl!
NNNg
fff
where are those scissors?
RUStle

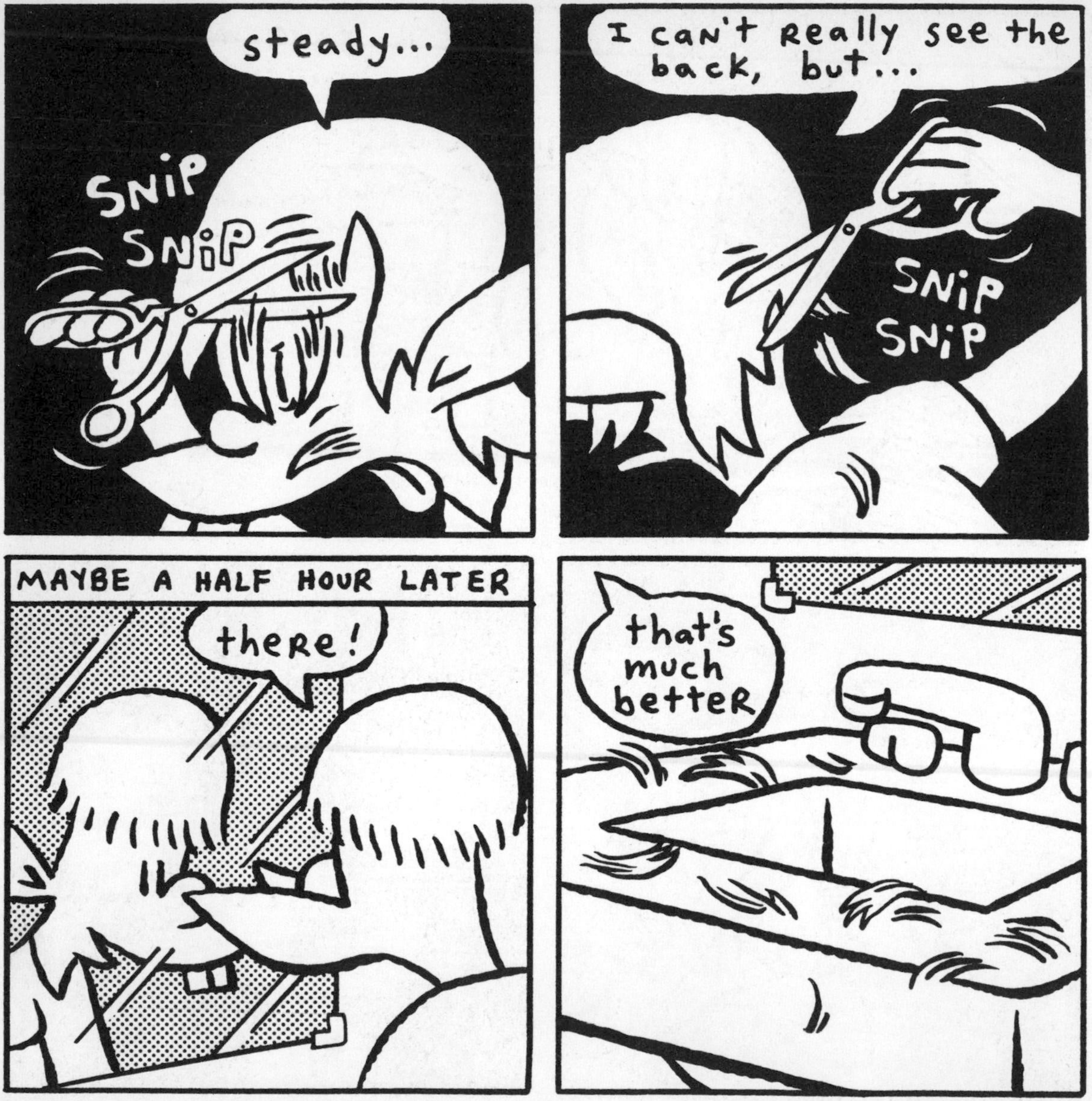
steady...
SNIP
SNIP
I can't really see the back, but...
SNIP
SNIP
MAYBE A HALF HOUR LATER
there!
that's much better

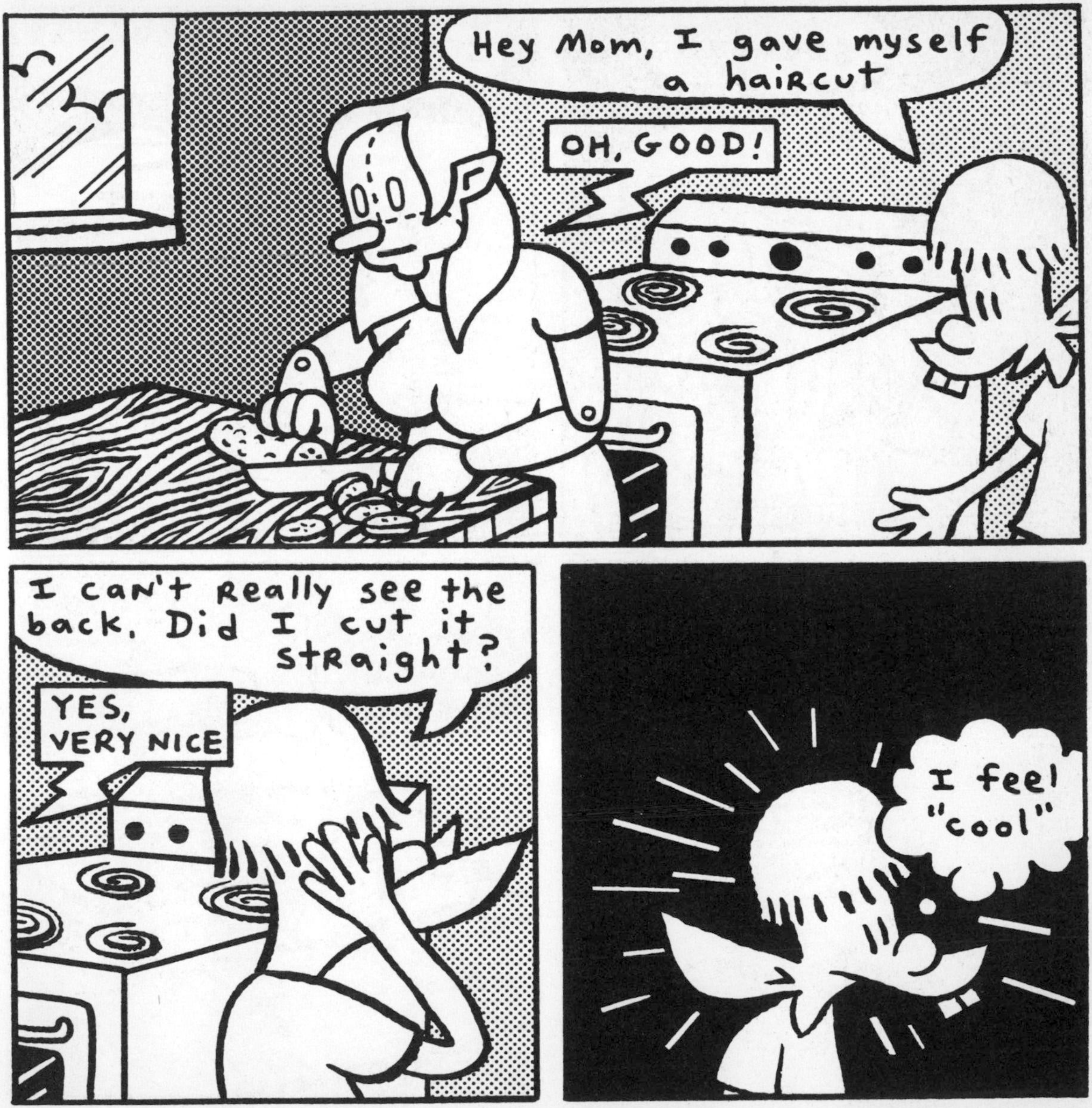
Hey Mom, I gave myself a haircut
OH, GOOD!
I can't really see the back. Did I cut it straight?
YES, VERY NICE
I feel "cool"

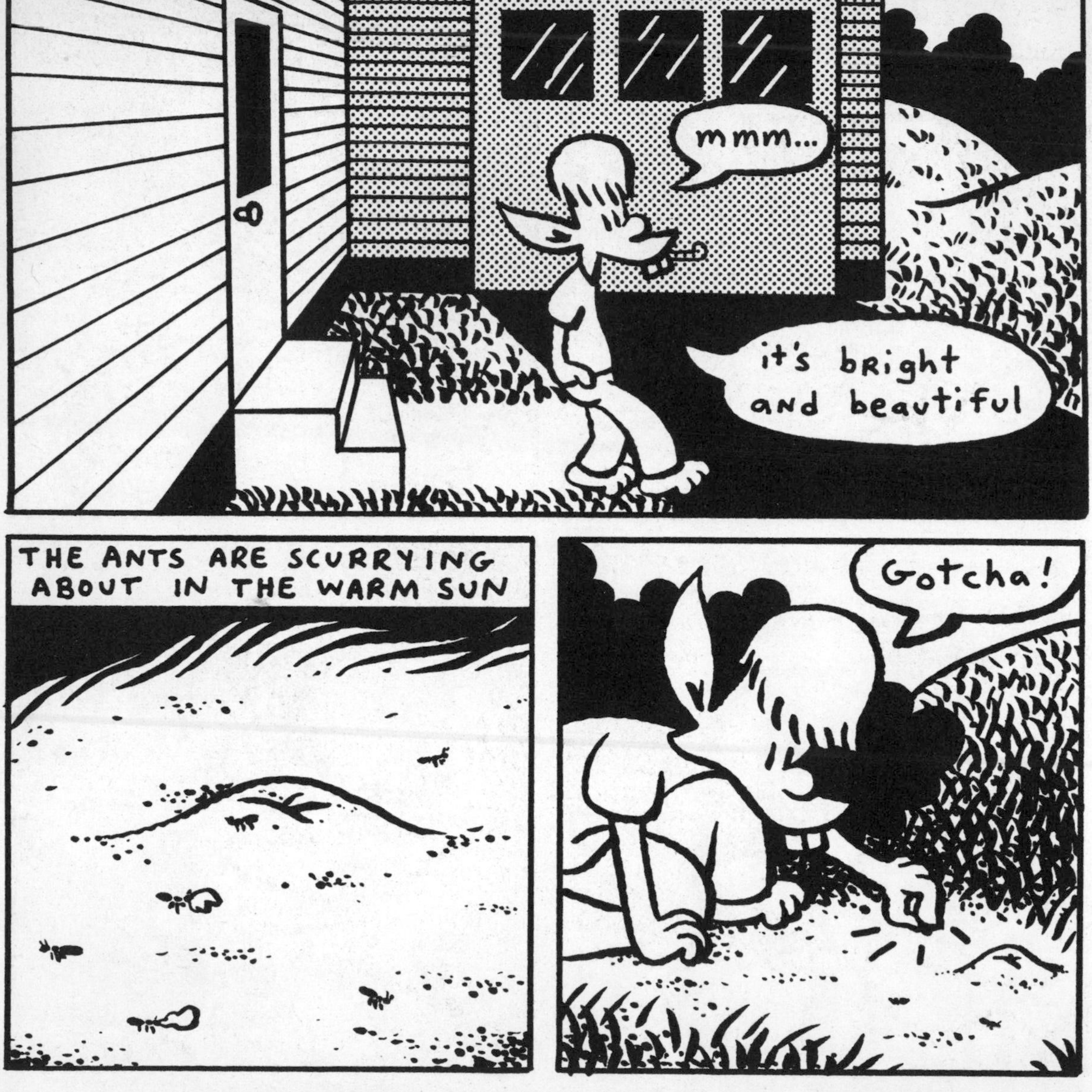
mmm...
it's bright and beautiful
THE ANTS ARE SCURRYING ABOUT IN THE WARM SUN
Gotcha!

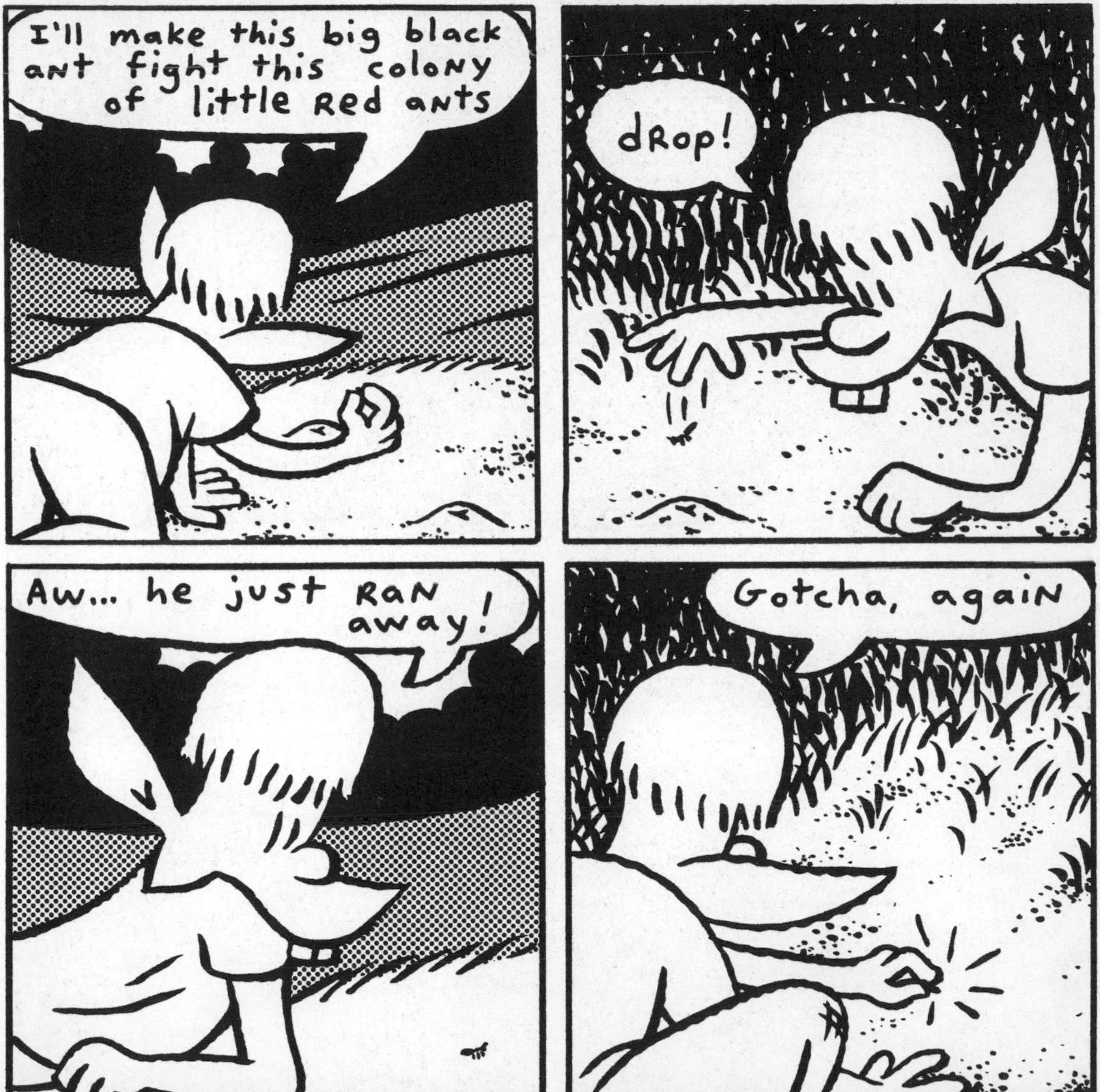
I'll make this big black ant fight this colony of little Red ants
dRop!
Aw... he just RaN away!
Gotcha, again

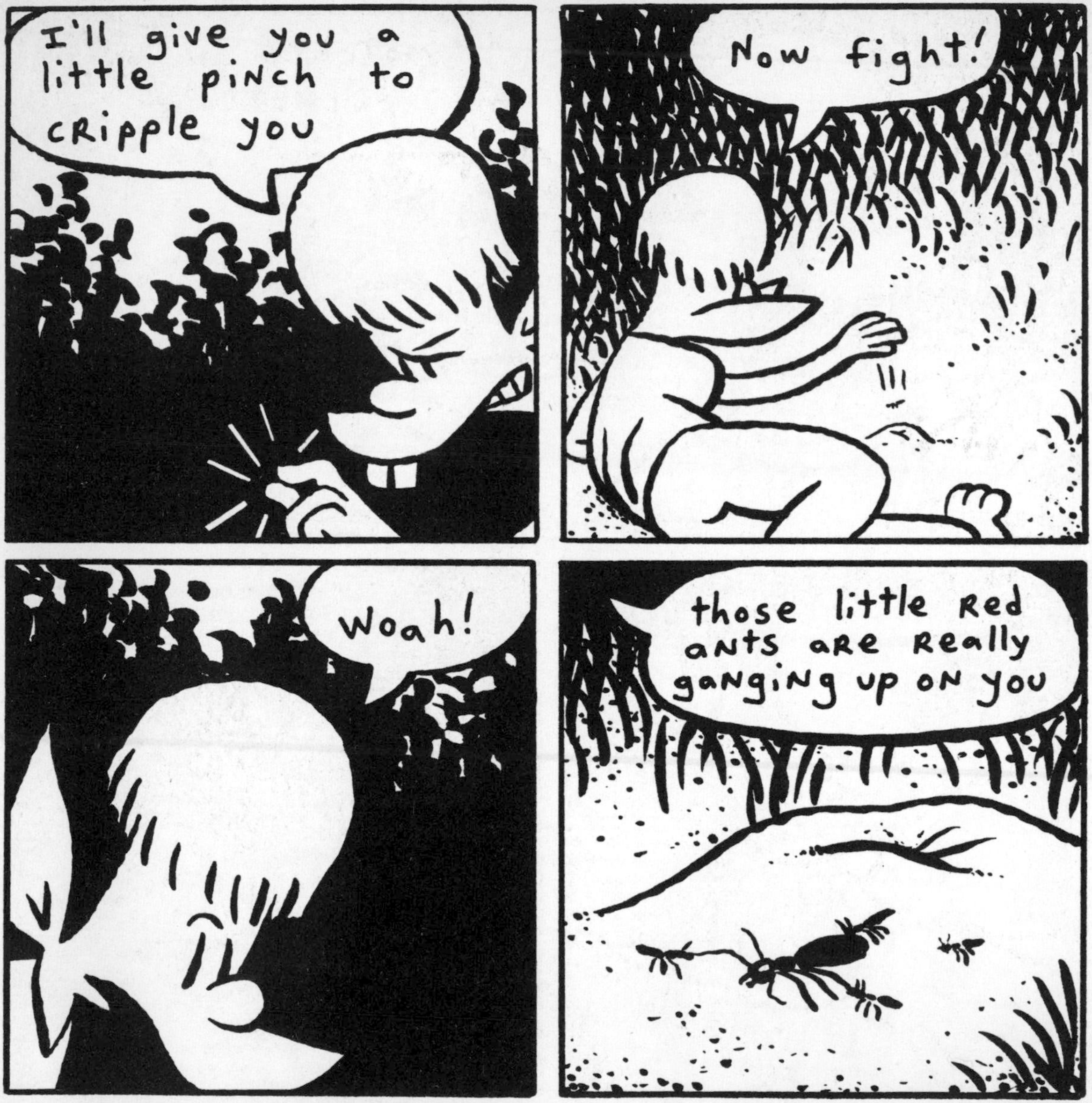
I'll give you a little pinch to cripple you
Now fight!
Woah!
those little Red ants are really ganging up on you

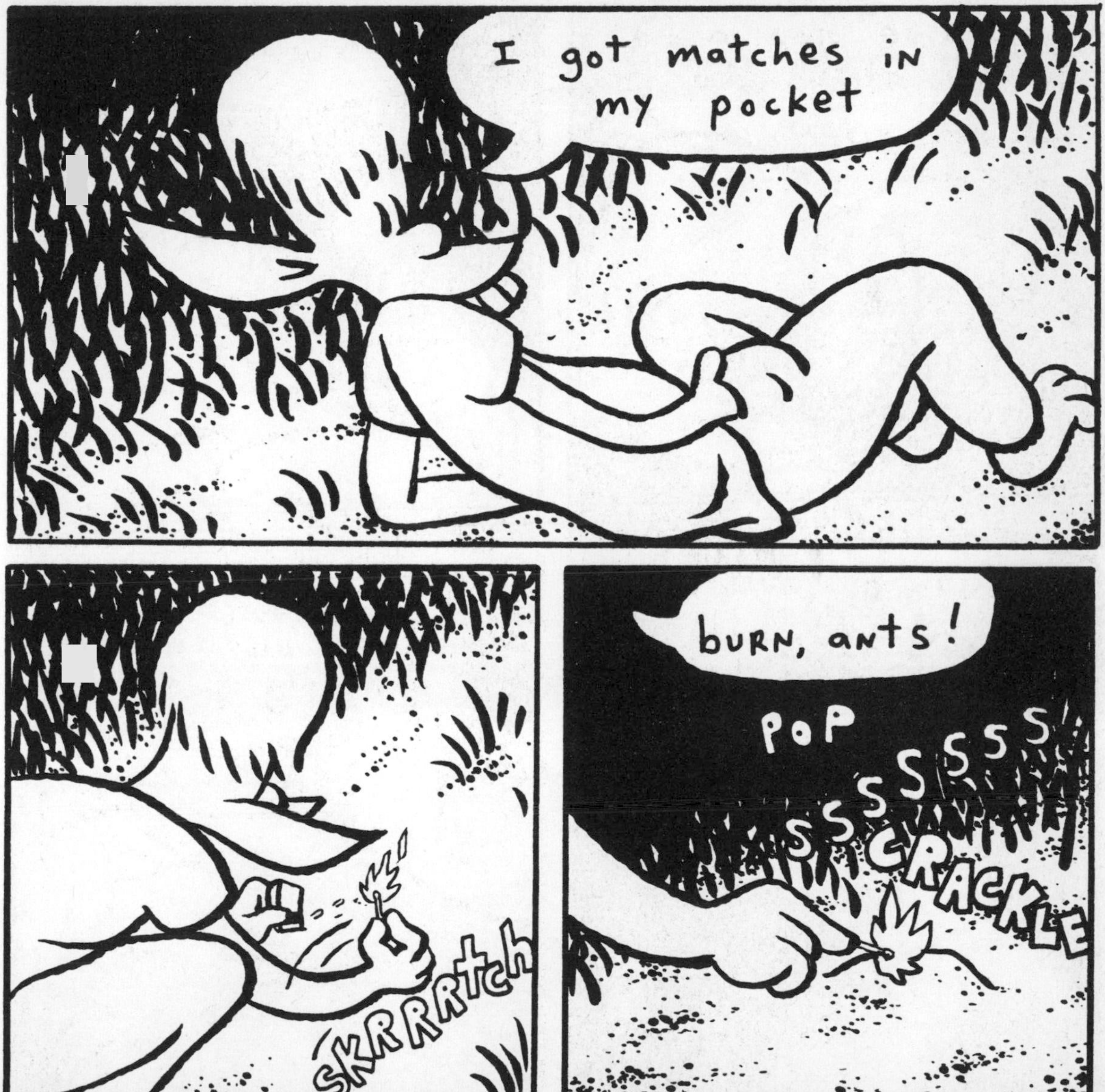
I got matches in my pocket
SKRRRtch
burn, ants!
POP
SSSSSSSS
CRACKLE

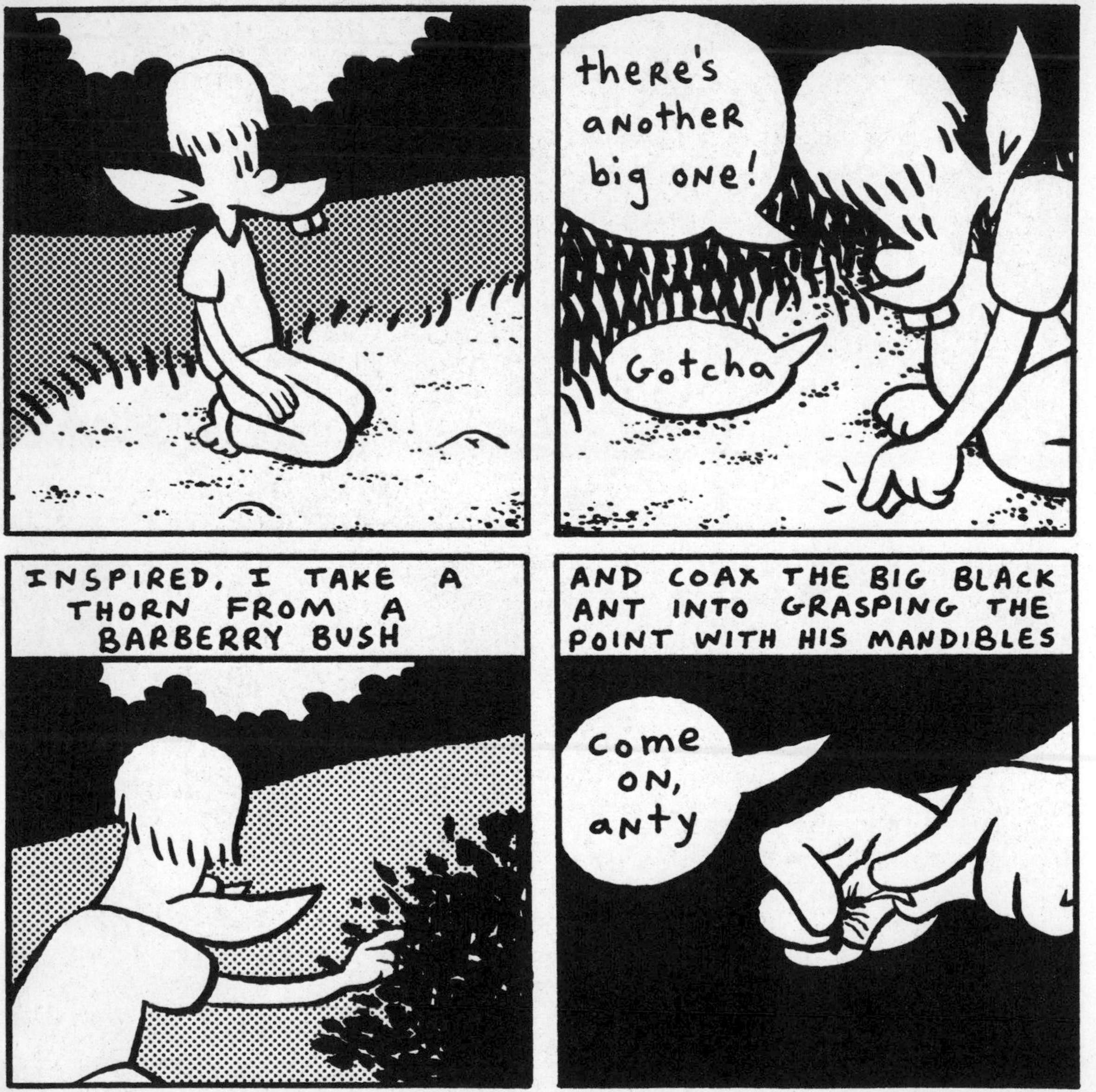
there's another big one!
Gotcha
INSPIRED, I TAKE A THORN FROM A BARBERRY BUSH
AND COAX THE BIG BLACK ANT INTO GRASPING THE POINT WITH HIS MANDIBLES
come ON, anty

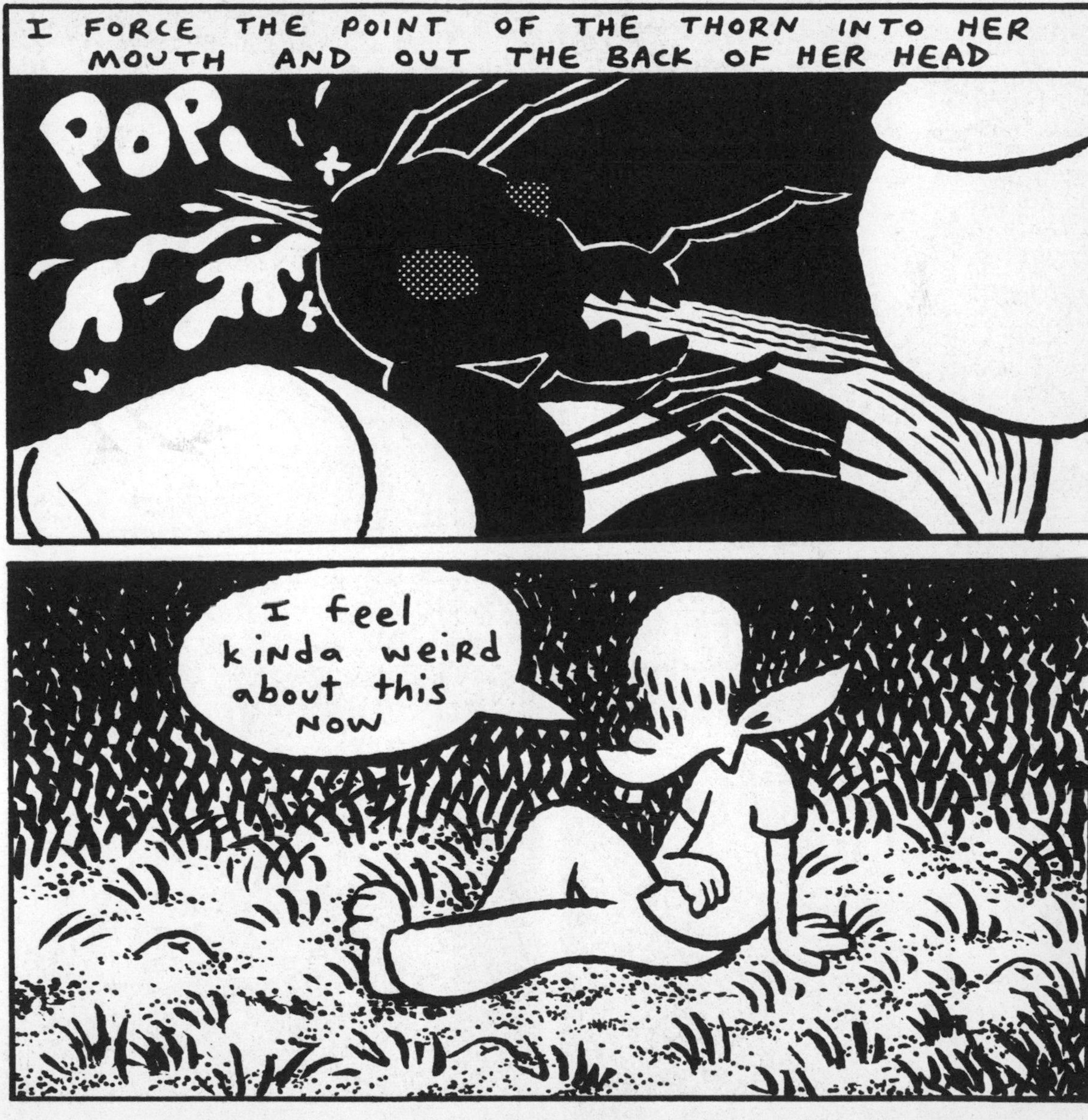
I FORCE THE POINT OF THE THORN INTO HER MOUTH AND OUT THE BACK OF HER HEAD
POP
I feel kinda weird about this now

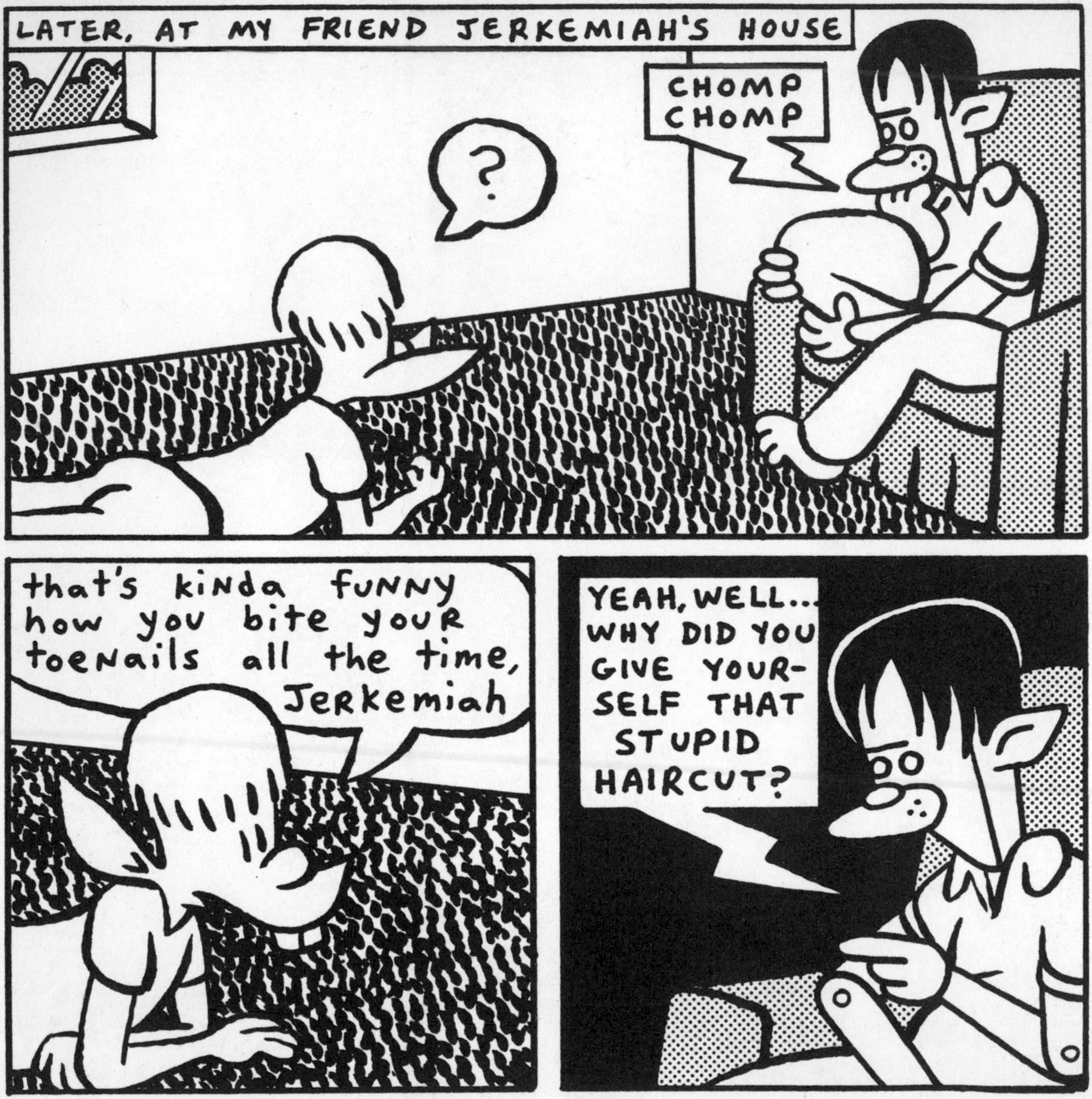
LATER, AT MY FRIEND JERKEMIAH'S HOUSE
CHOMP CHOMP
?
that's kinda funny how you bite your toenails all the time, Jerkemiah
YEAH, WELL... WHY DID YOU GIVE YOURSELF THAT STUPID HAIRCUT?

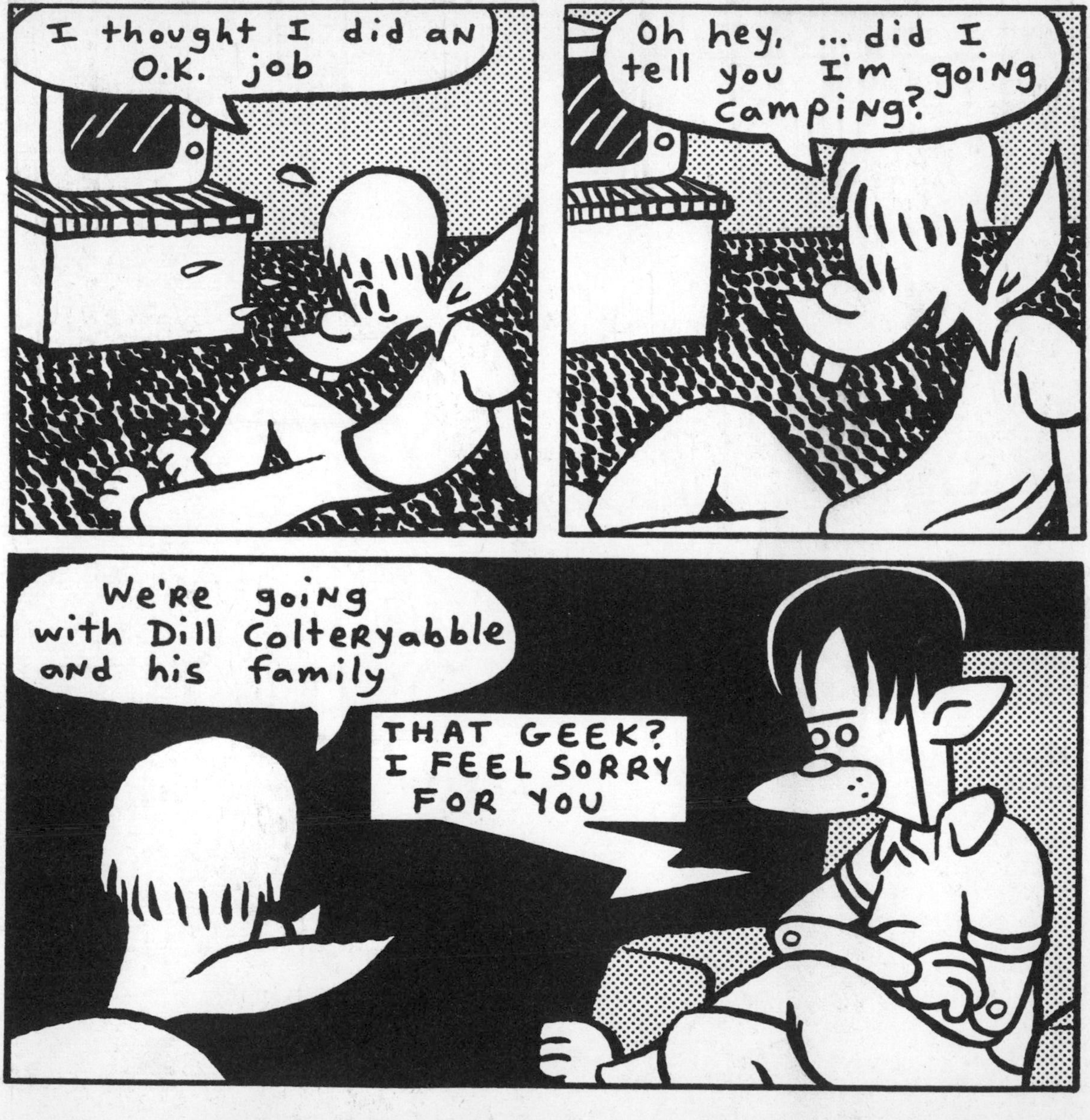
I thought I did aN O.K. job
Oh hey, ... did I tell you I'm going camping?
We're going with Dill Colteryabble and his family
THAT GEEK? I FEEL SORRY FOR YOU

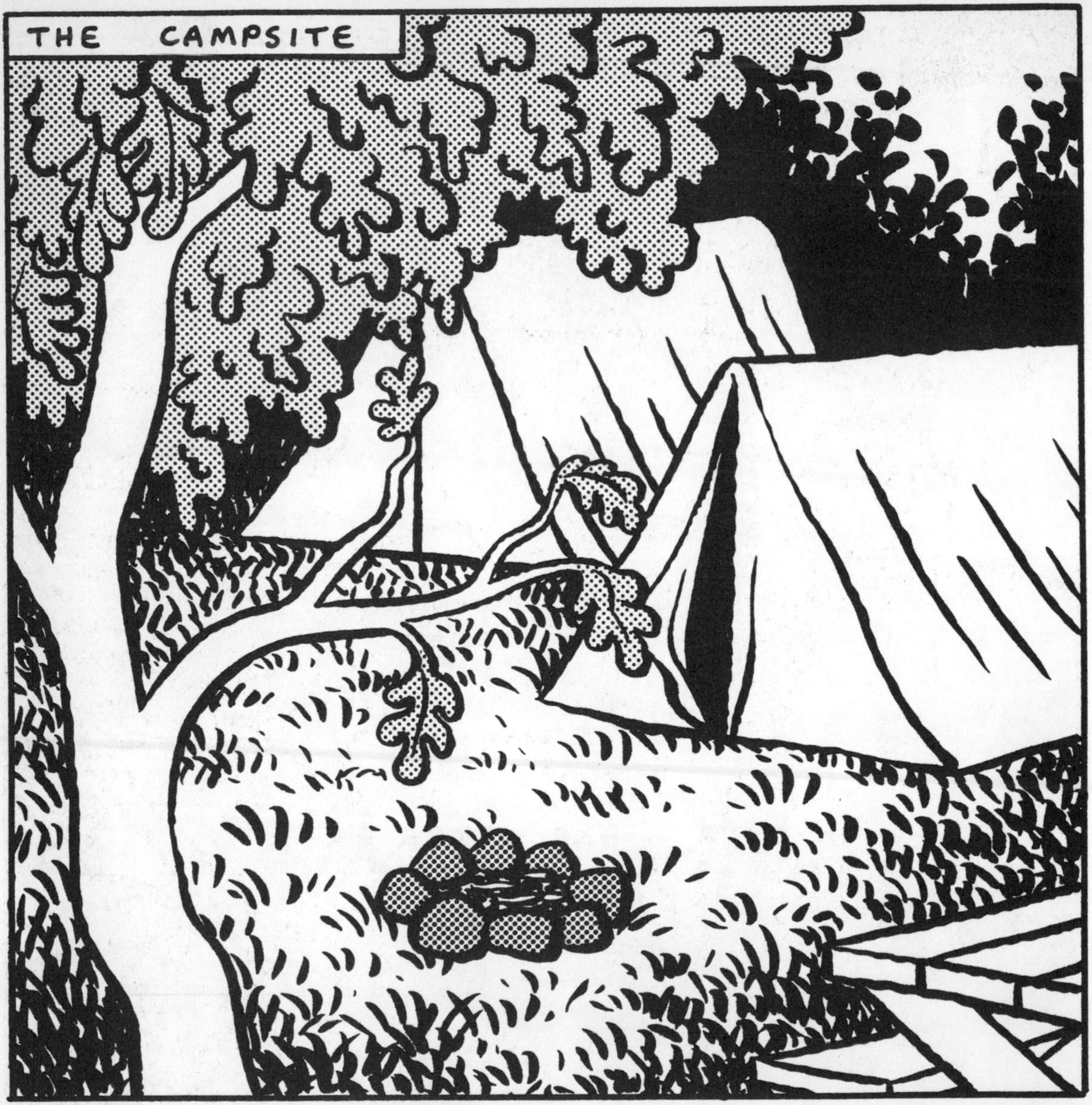
THE CAMPSITE

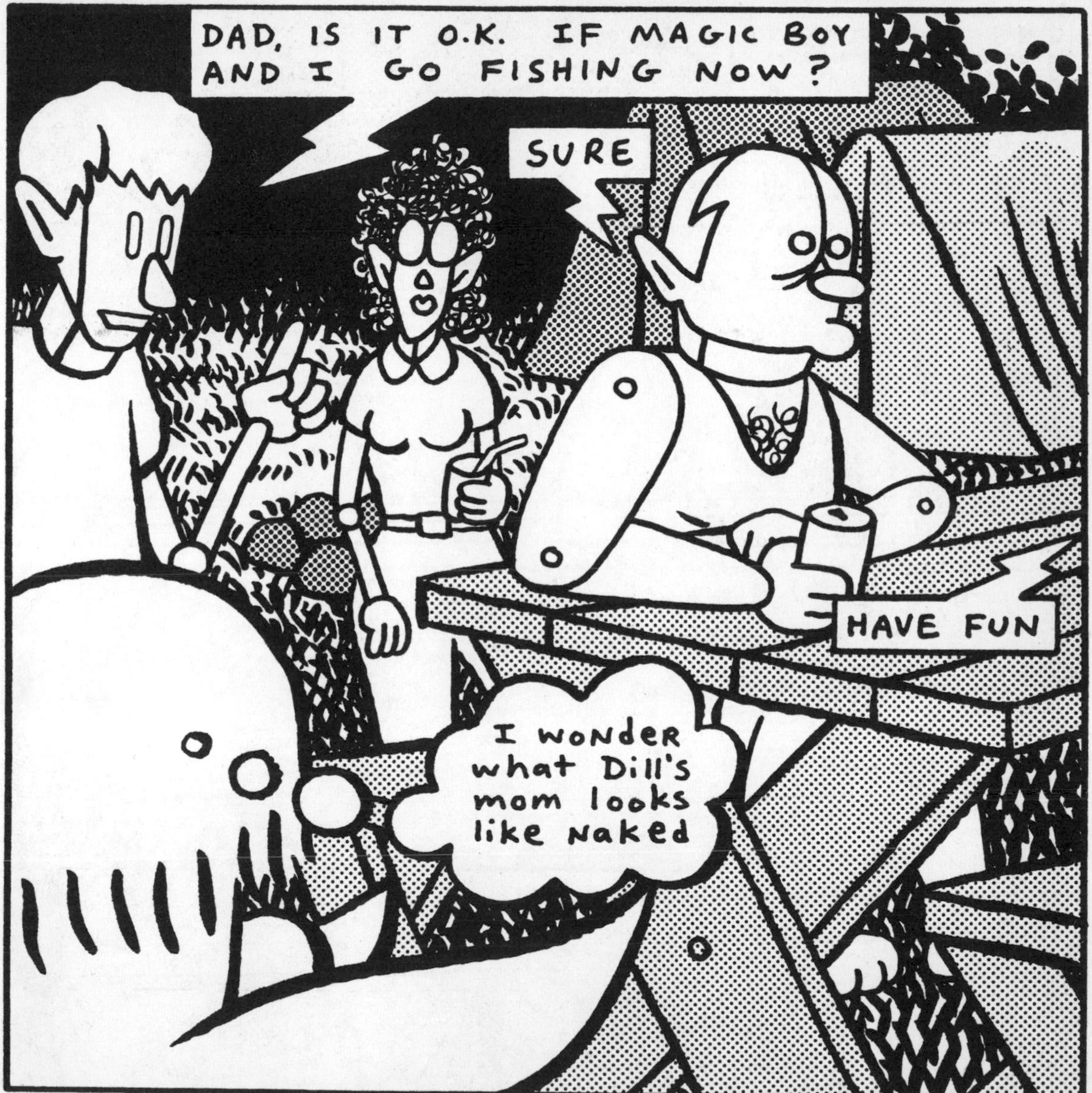
DAD, IS IT O.K. IF MAGIC BOY AND I GO FISHING NOW?
SURE
HAVE FUN
I wonder what Dill's mom looks like naked

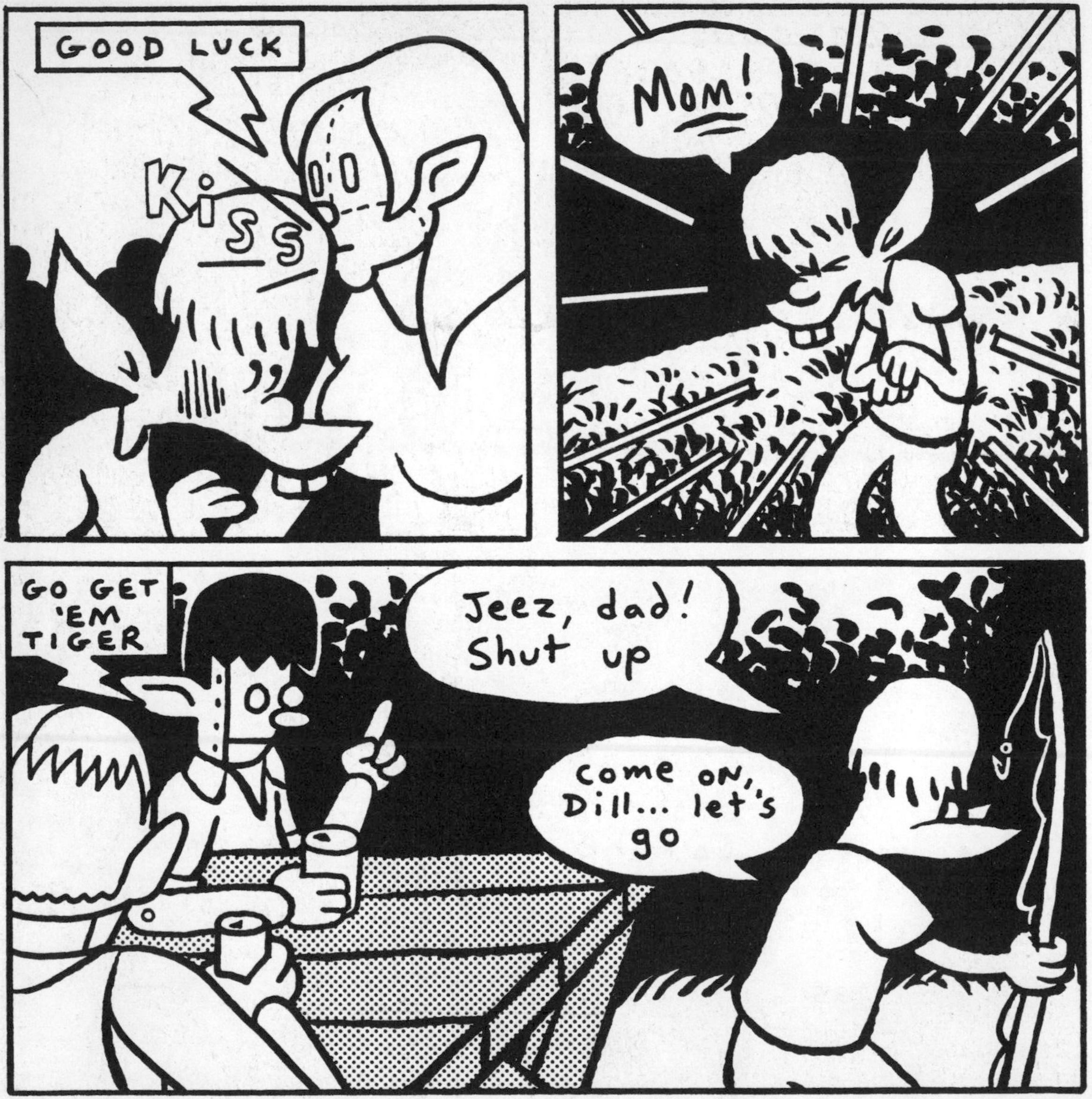
GOOD LUCK
KiSS
MOM!
GO GET 'EM TIGER
Jeez, dad! Shut up
come on, Dill... let's go

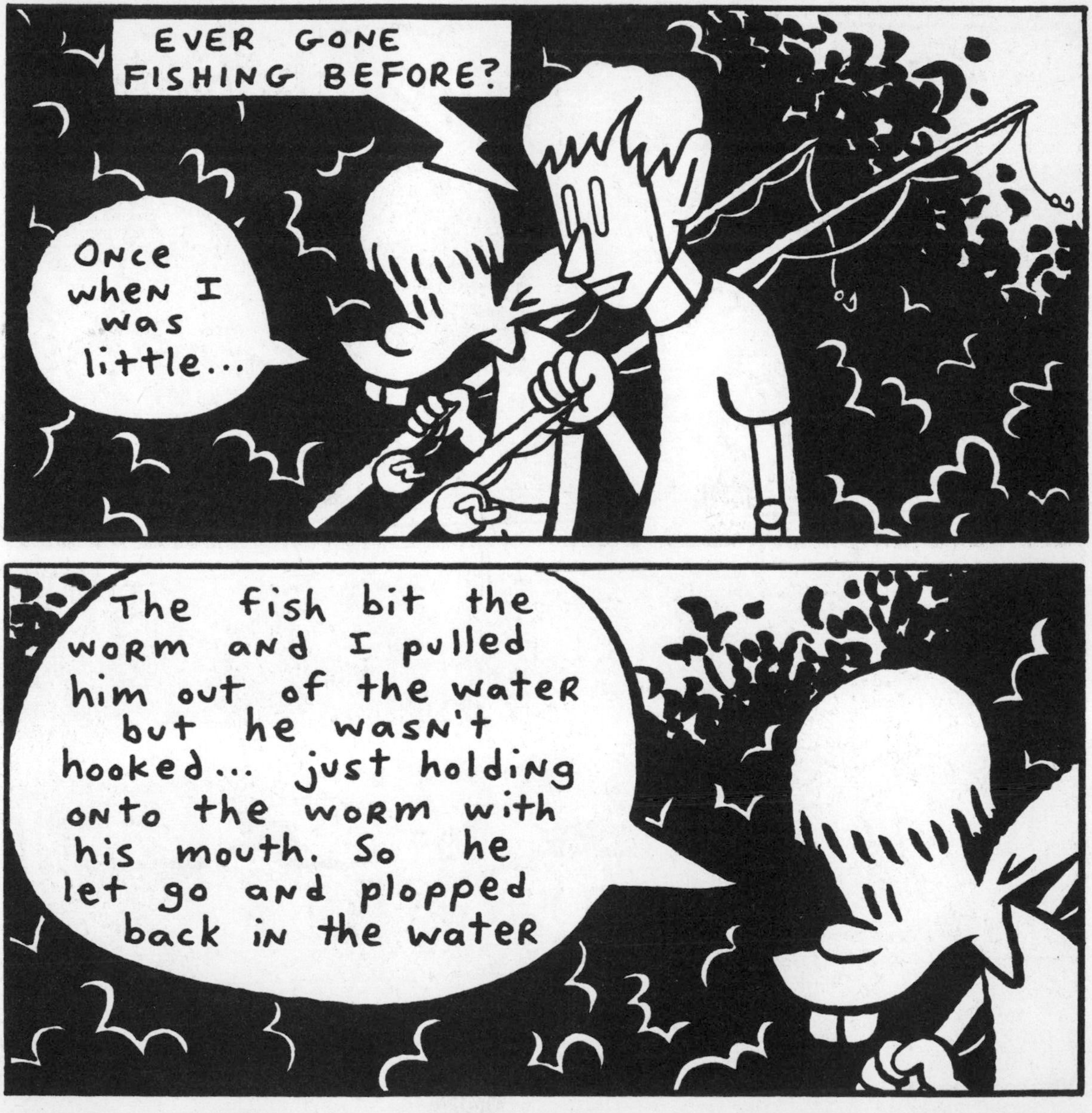
EVER GONE FISHING BEFORE?
Once when I was little...
The fish bit the worm and I pulled him out of the water but he wasn't hooked... just holding onto the worm with his mouth. So he let go and plopped back in the water

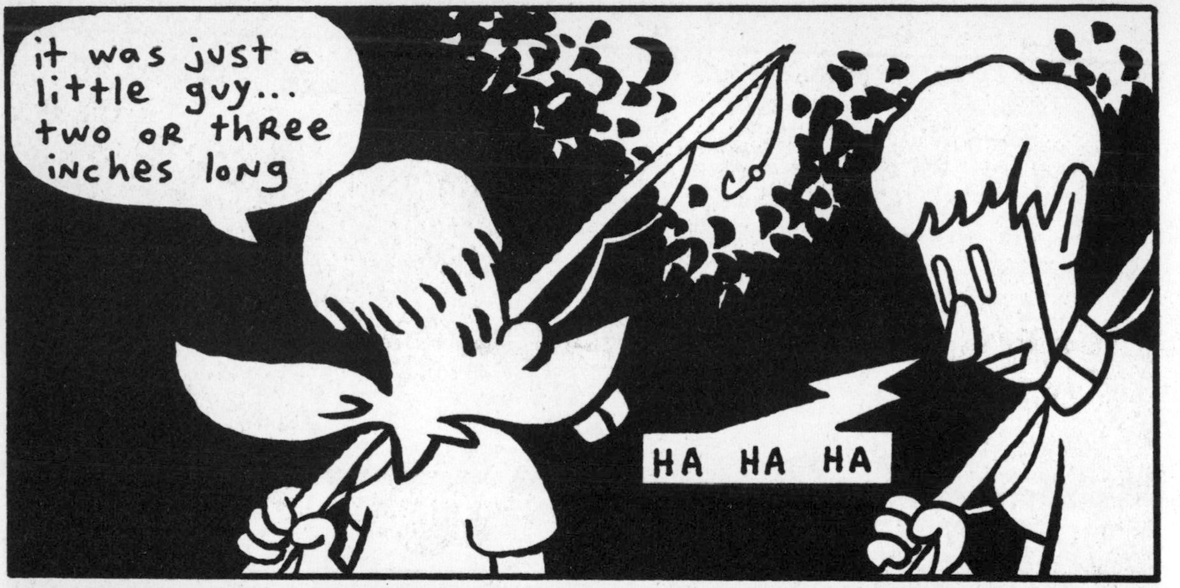
it was just a little guy... two or three inches long
HA HA HA
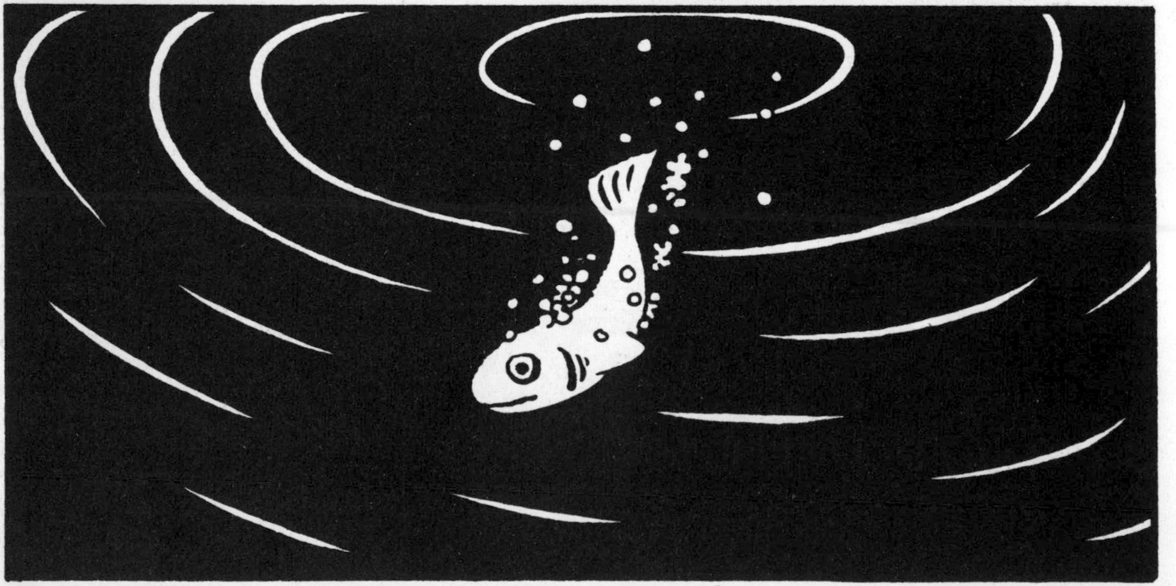

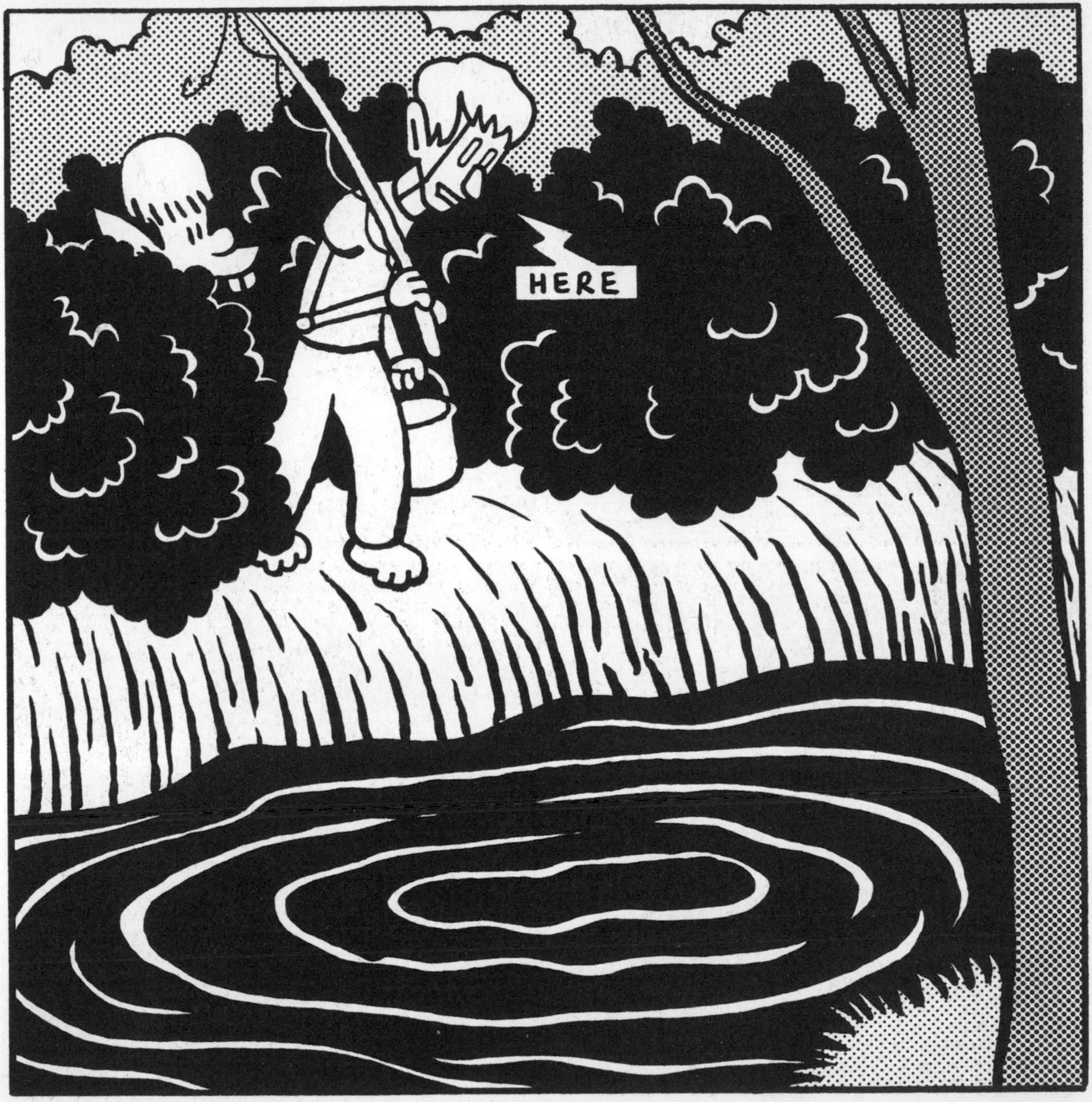
HERE

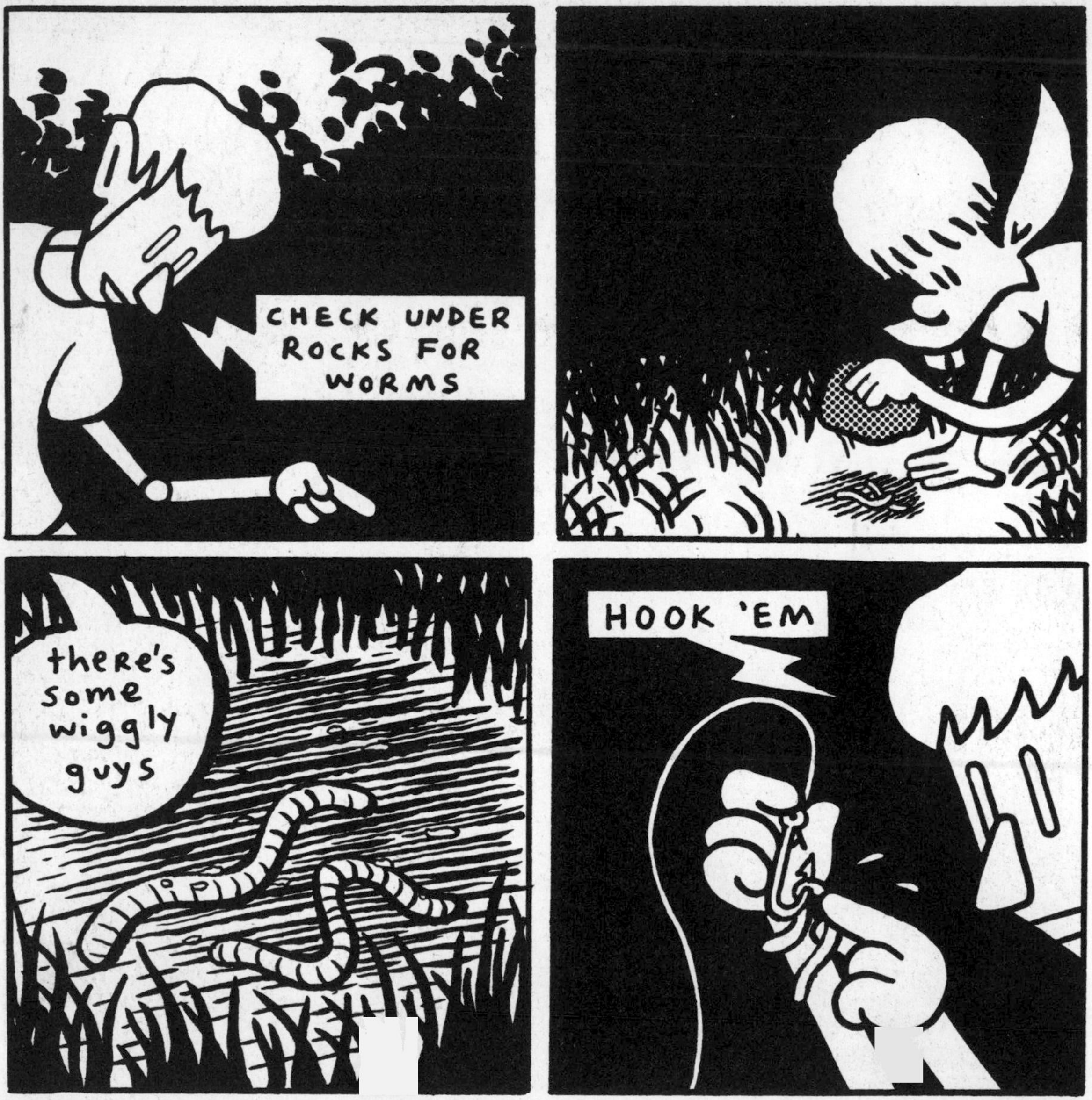
CHECK UNDER ROCKS FOR WORMS
there's some wiggly guys
HOOK 'EM

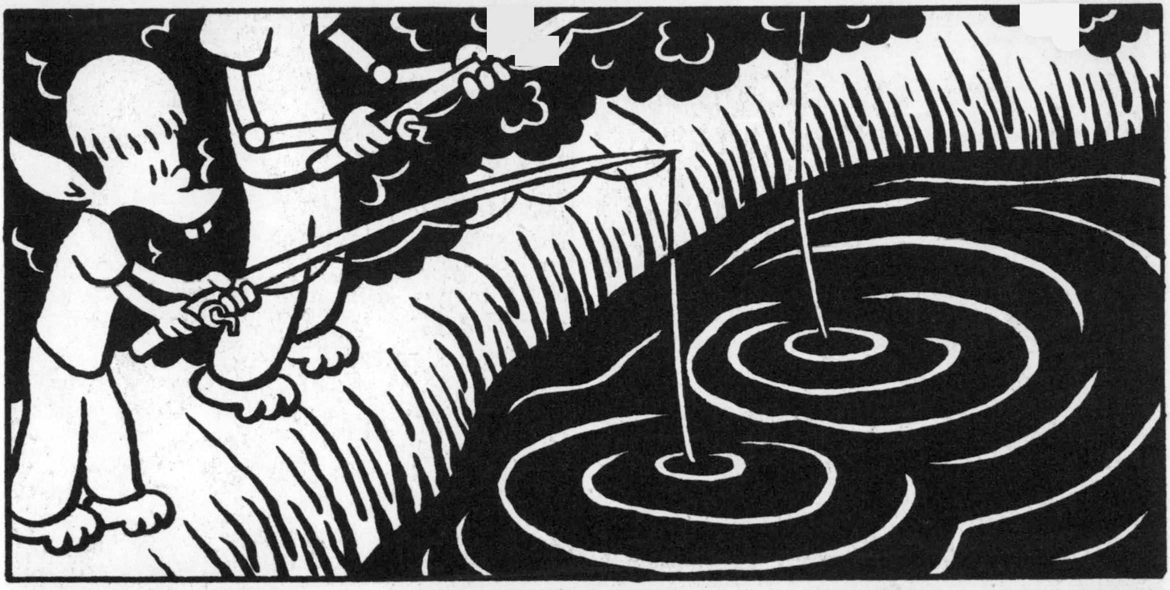

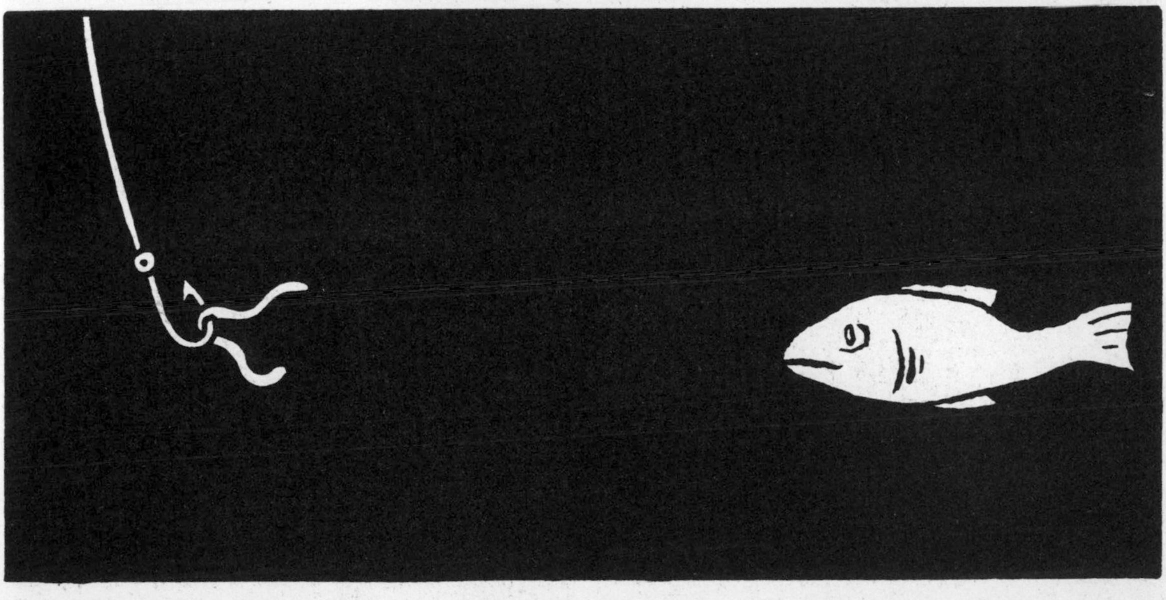

THIS IS TAKING TOO LONG

THE WATER IS SHALLOW AND CLEAR SO WE CAN USE MY SECRET TECHNIQUE

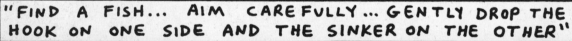

"FIND A FISH... AIM CAREFULLY... GENTLY DROP THE HOOK ON ONE SIDE AND THE SINKER ON THE OTHER"

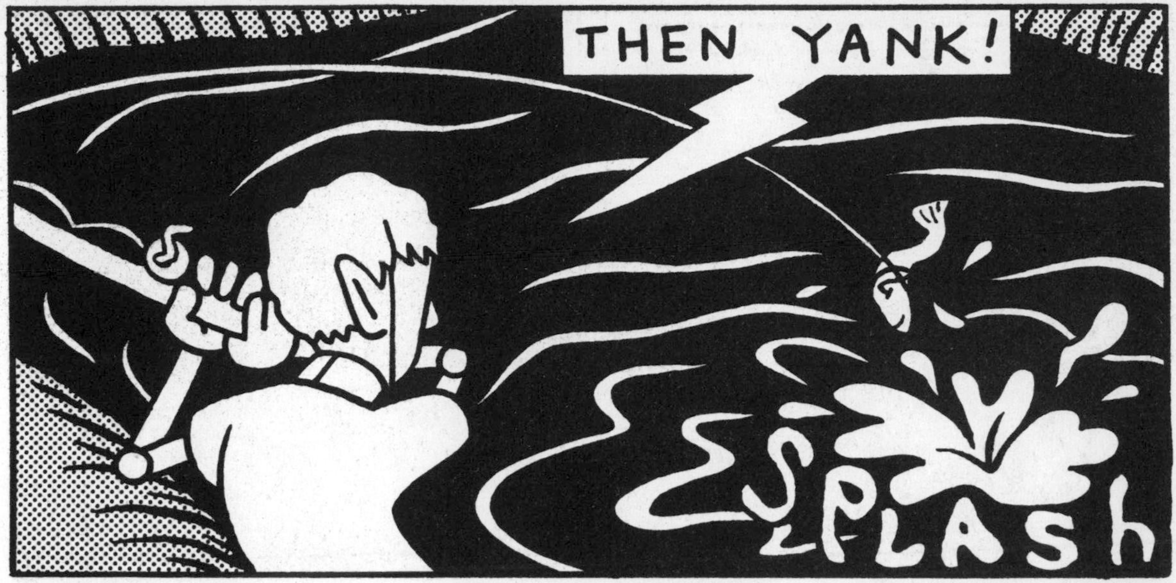
THEN YANK!
SPLASH

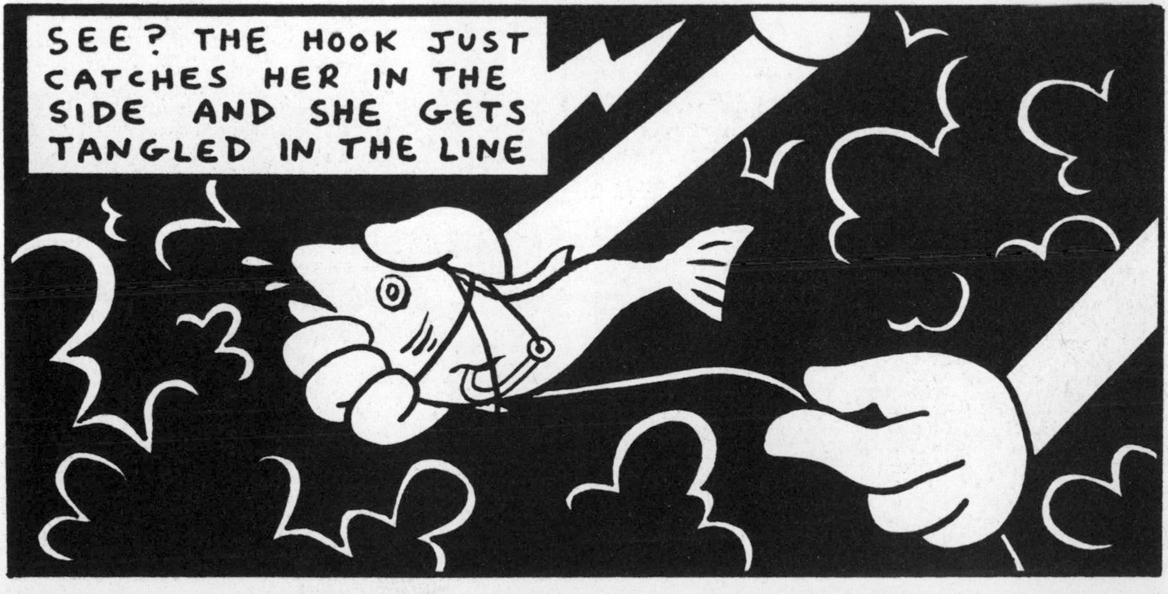
SEE? THE HOOK JUST CATCHES HER IN THE SIDE AND SHE GETS TANGLED IN THE LINE

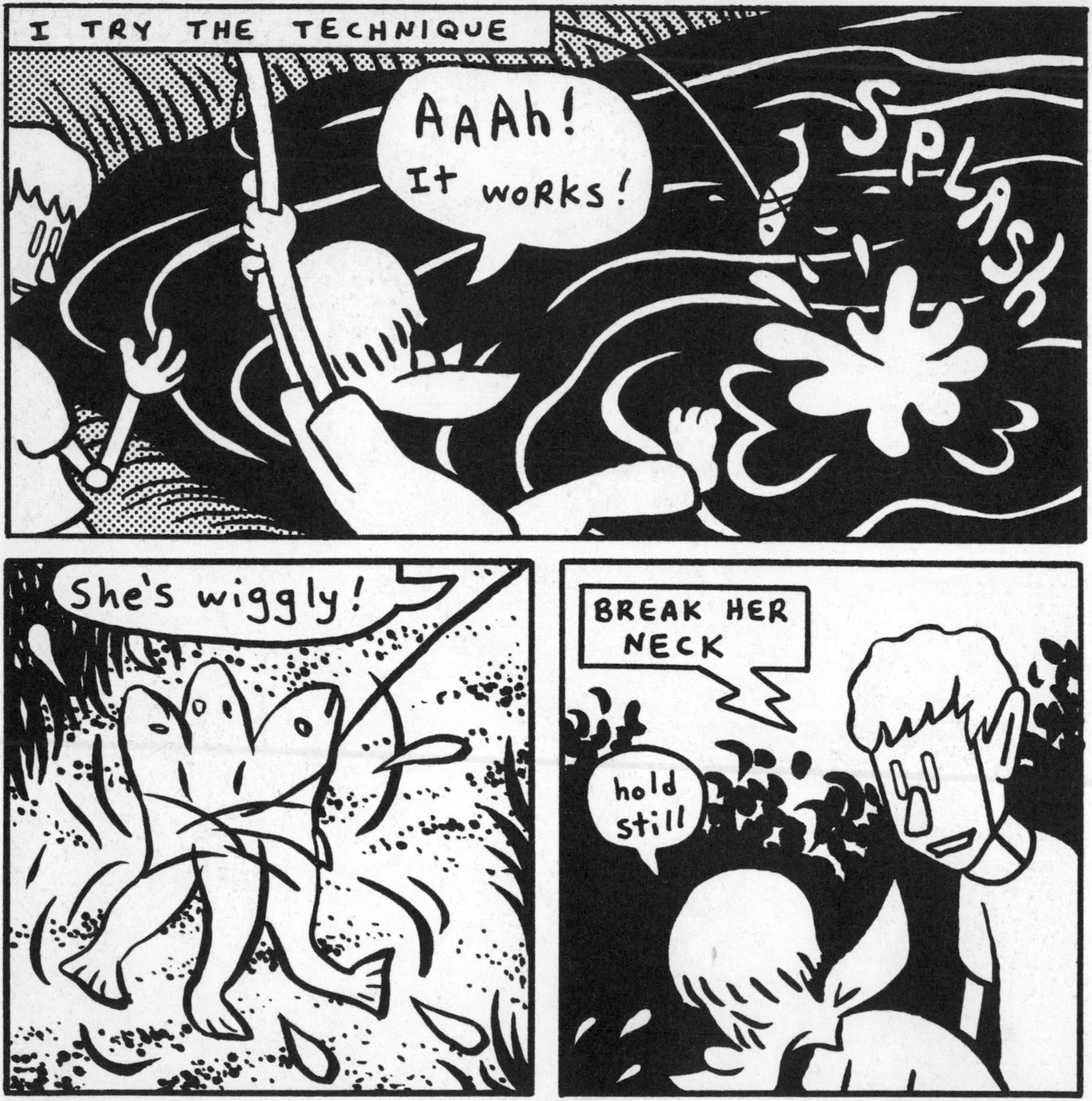
I TRY THE TECHNIQUE
AAAh! It works!
SPLASH
She's wiggly!
BREAK HER NECK
hold still

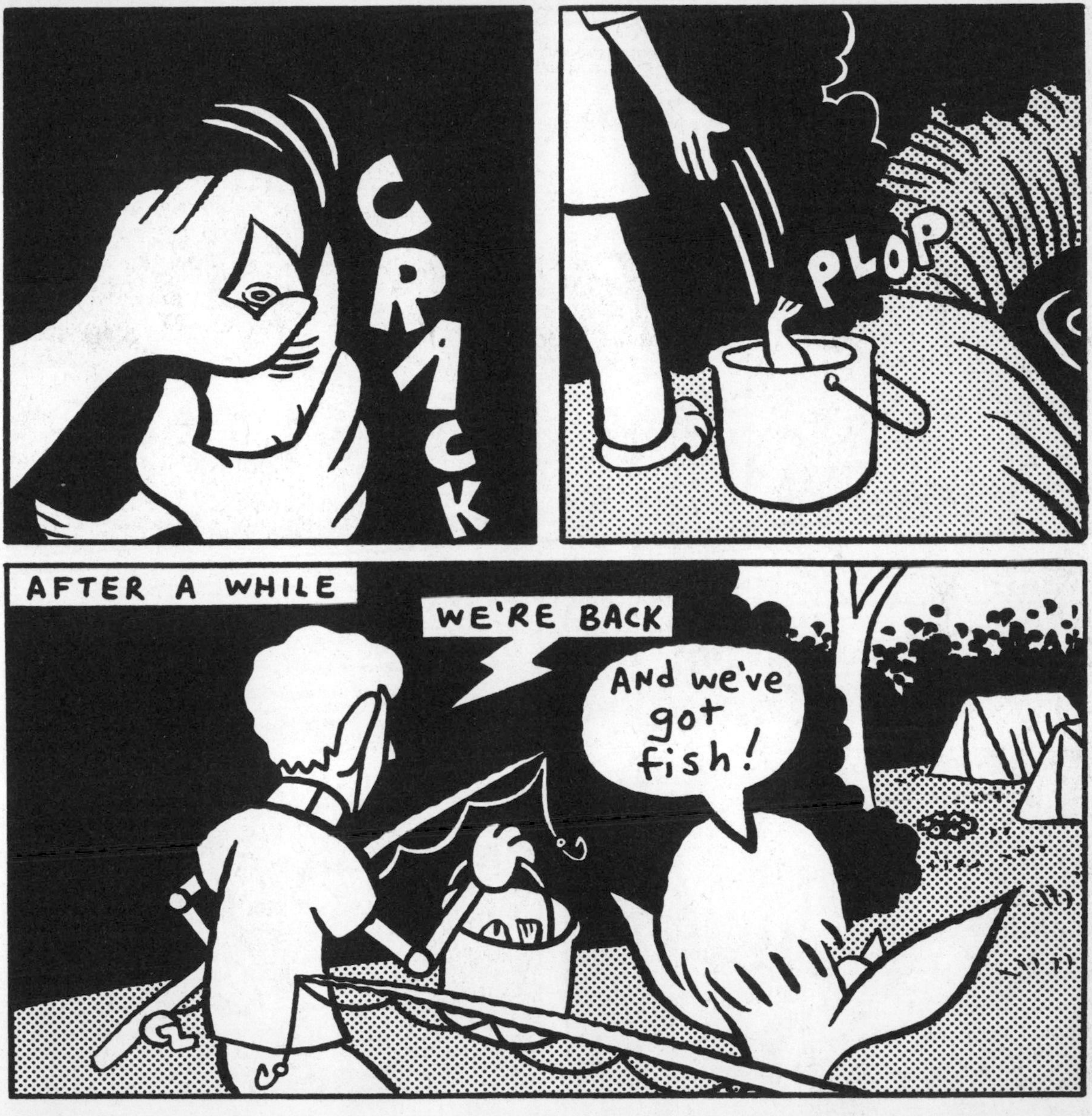
CRACK
PLOP
AFTER A WHILE
WE'RE BACK
And we've got fish!

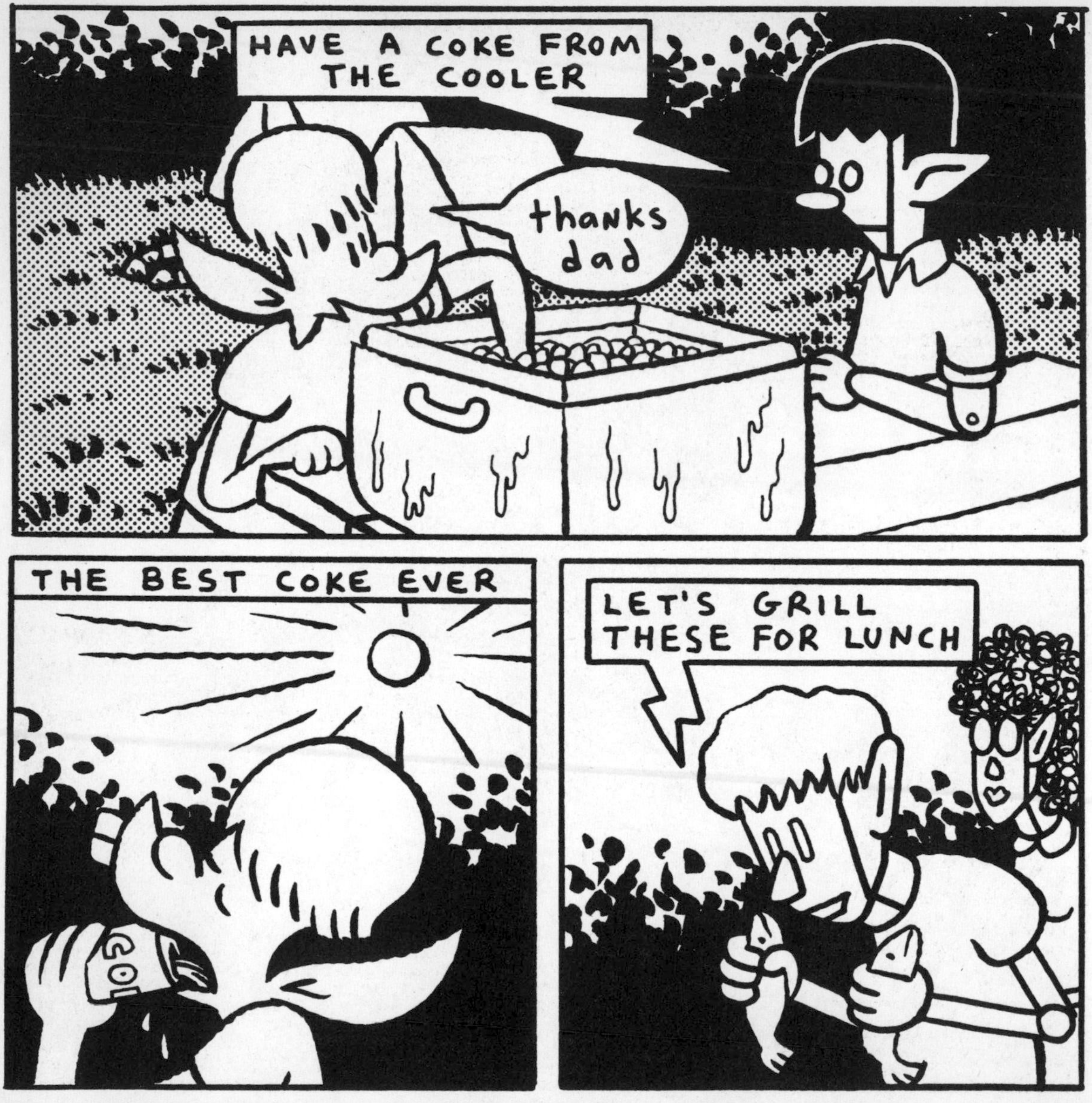
HAVE A COKE FROM THE COOLER
thanks dad
THE BEST COKE EVER
COK
LET'S GRILL THESE FOR LUNCH

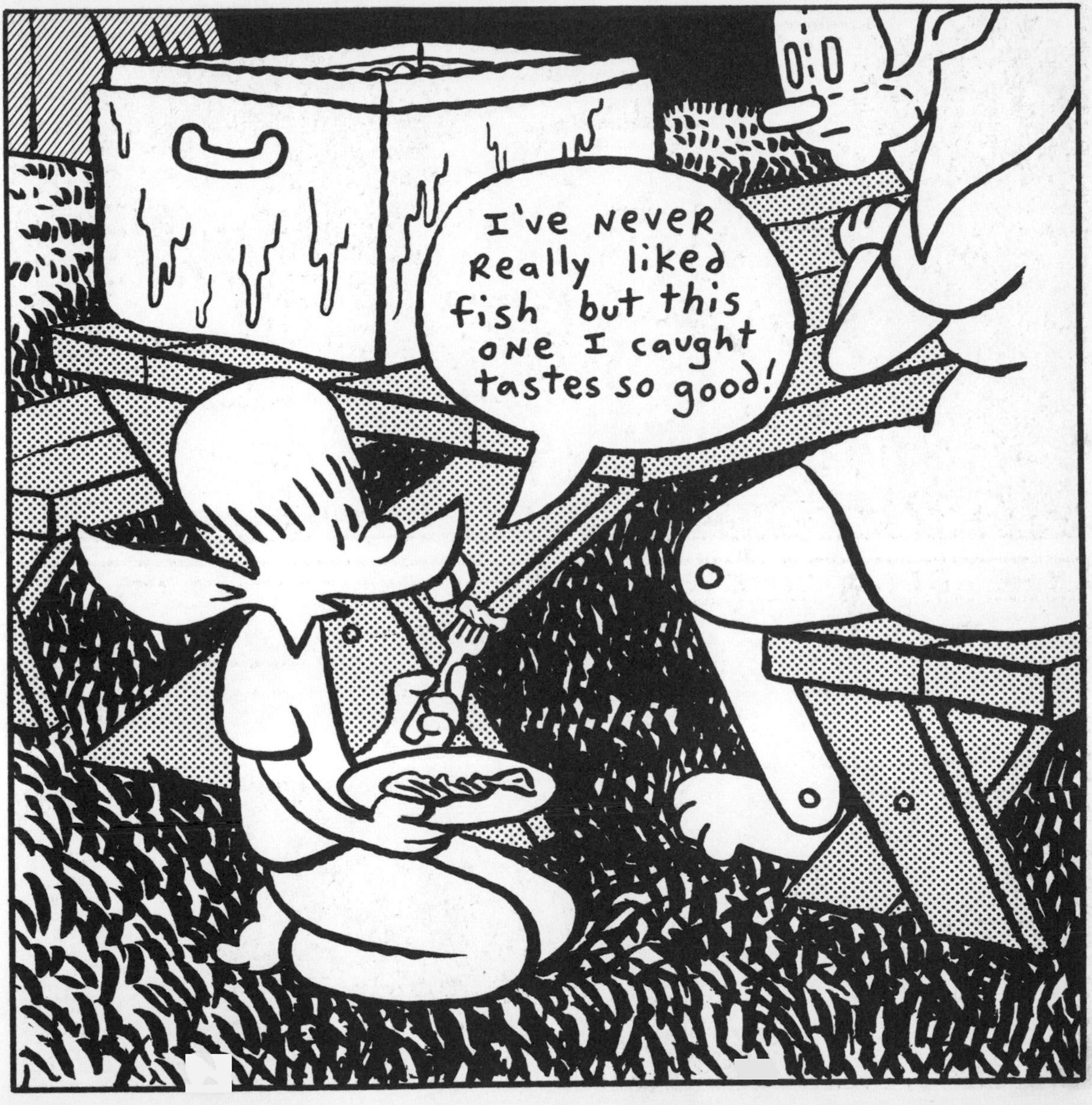
I've never really liked fish but this one I caught tastes so good!

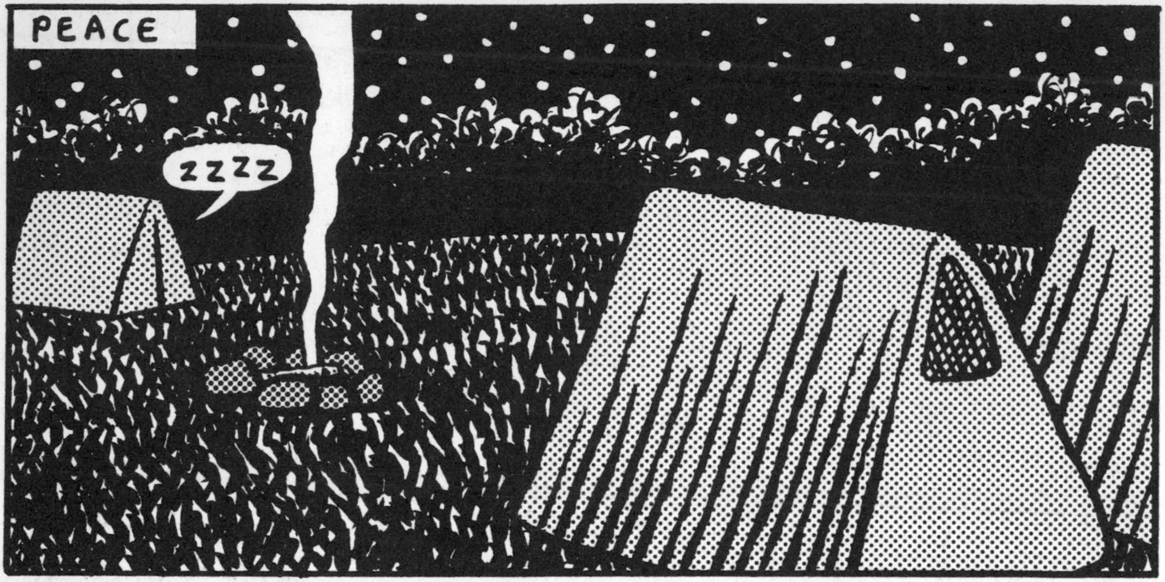
PEACE
ZZZZ

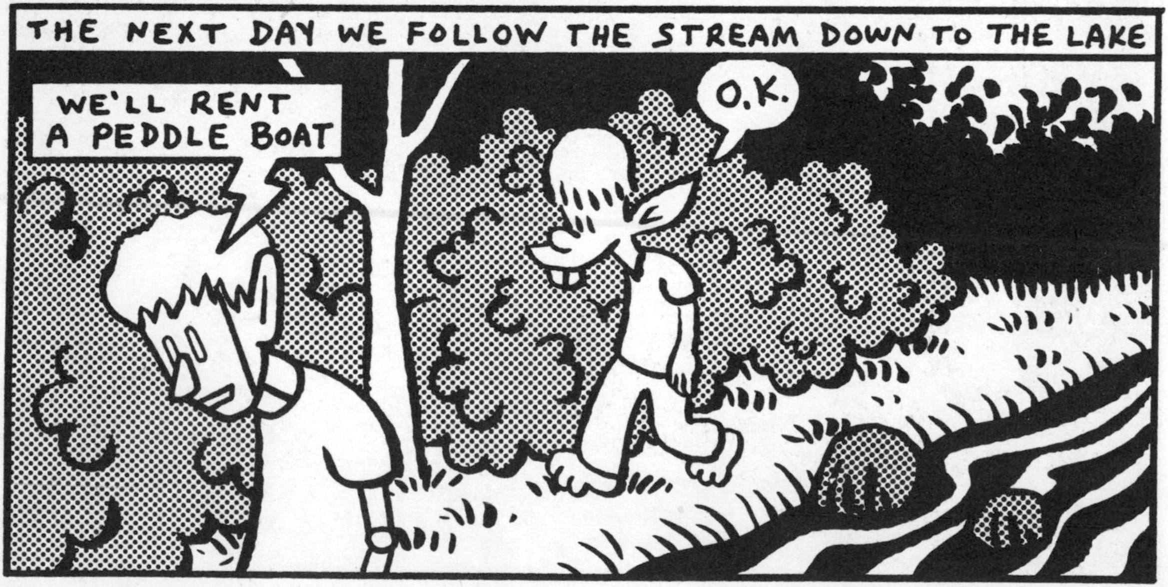
THE NEXT DAY WE FOLLOW THE STREAM DOWN TO THE LAKE
WE'LL RENT A PEDDLE BOAT
O.K.

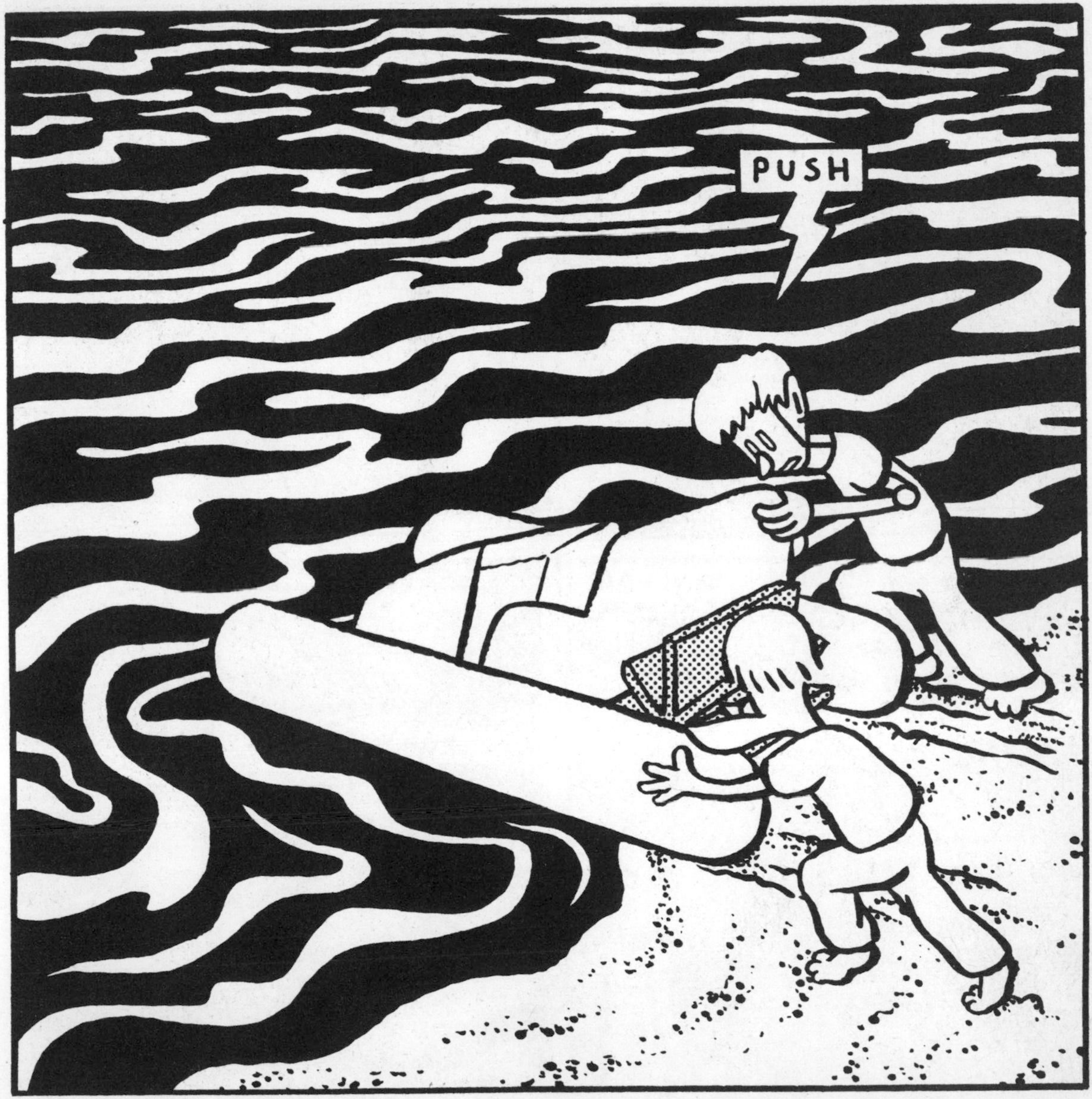
PUSH

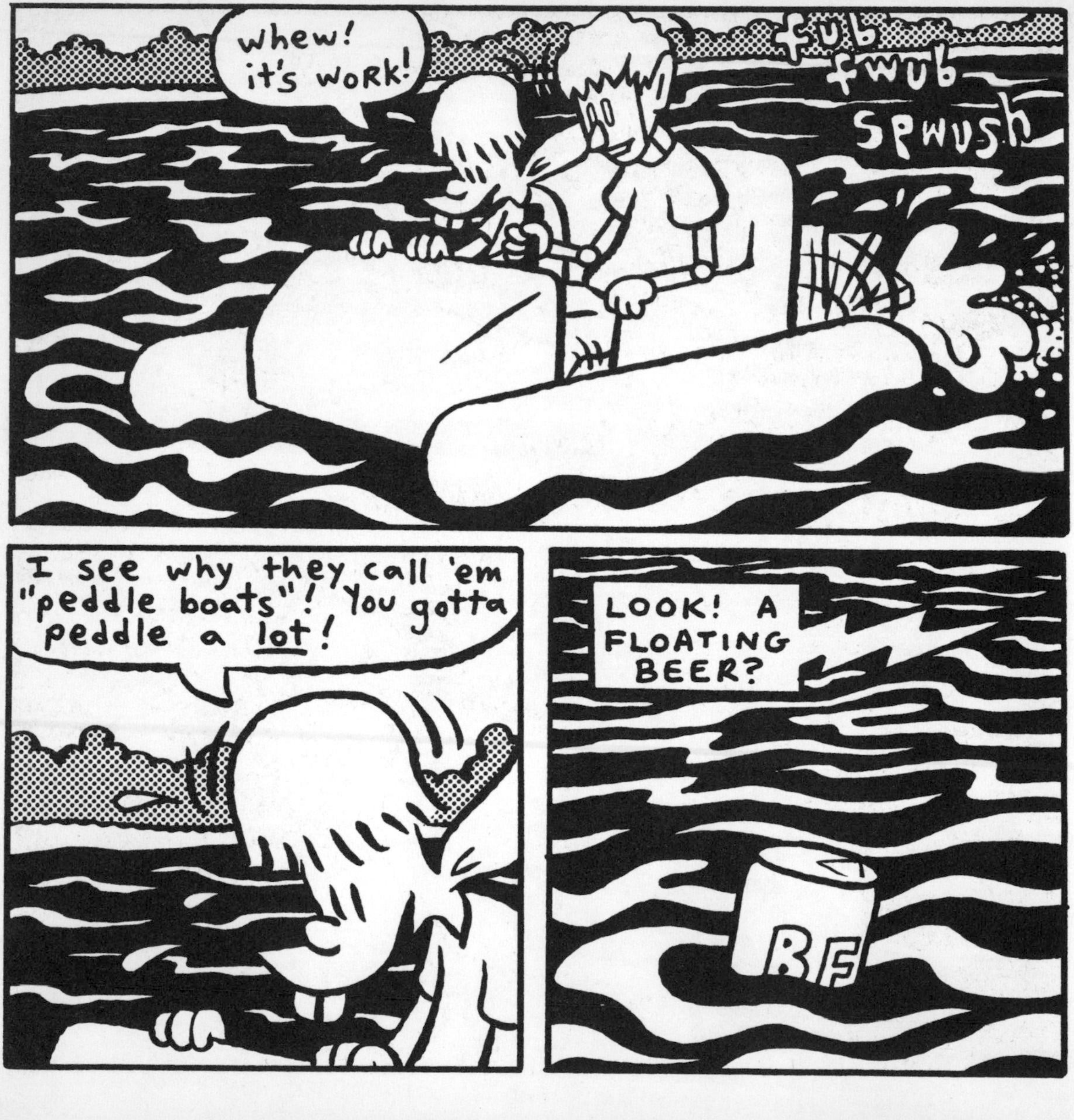
whew! it's WORK!
fub fwub spwush
I see why they call 'em "peddle boats"! You gotta peddle a lot!
LOOK! A FLOATING BEER?
BF

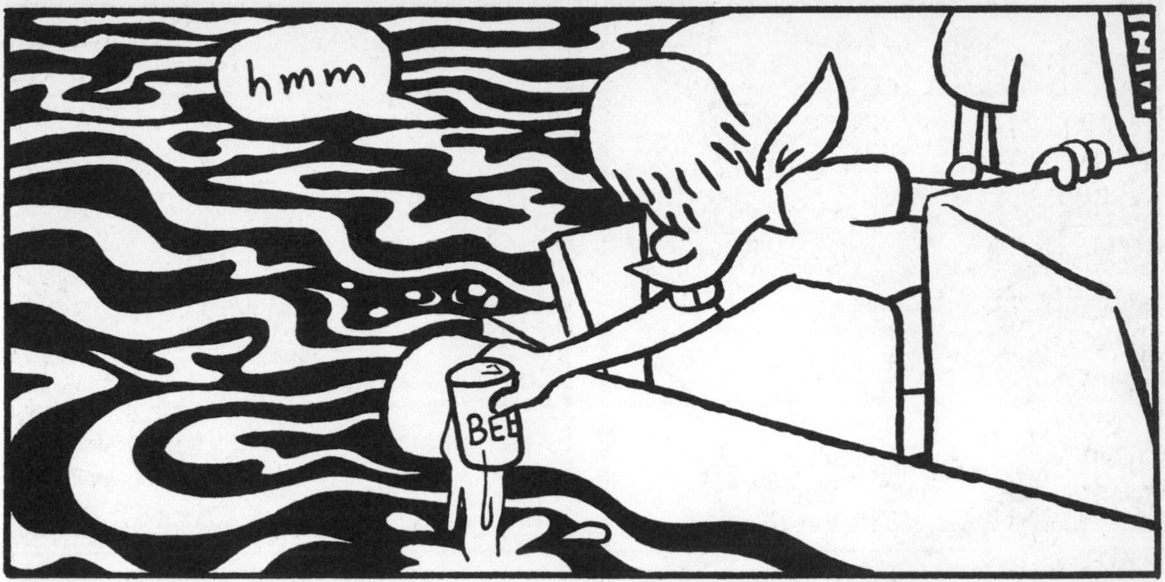
hmm
BEE

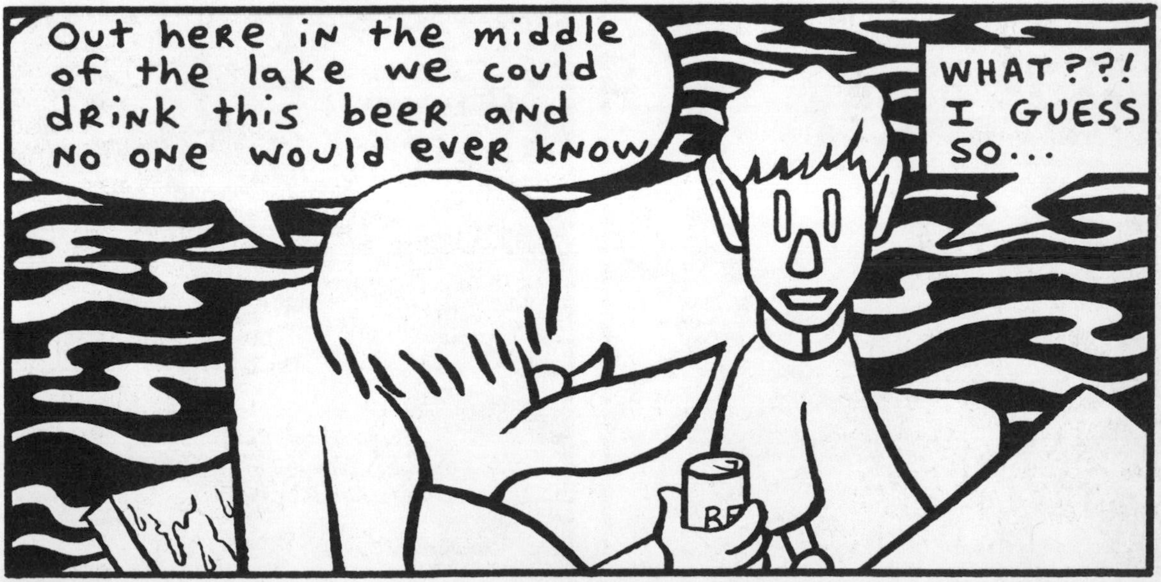
Out here in the middle of the lake we could drink this beer and no one would ever know
WHAT??! I GUESS SO...

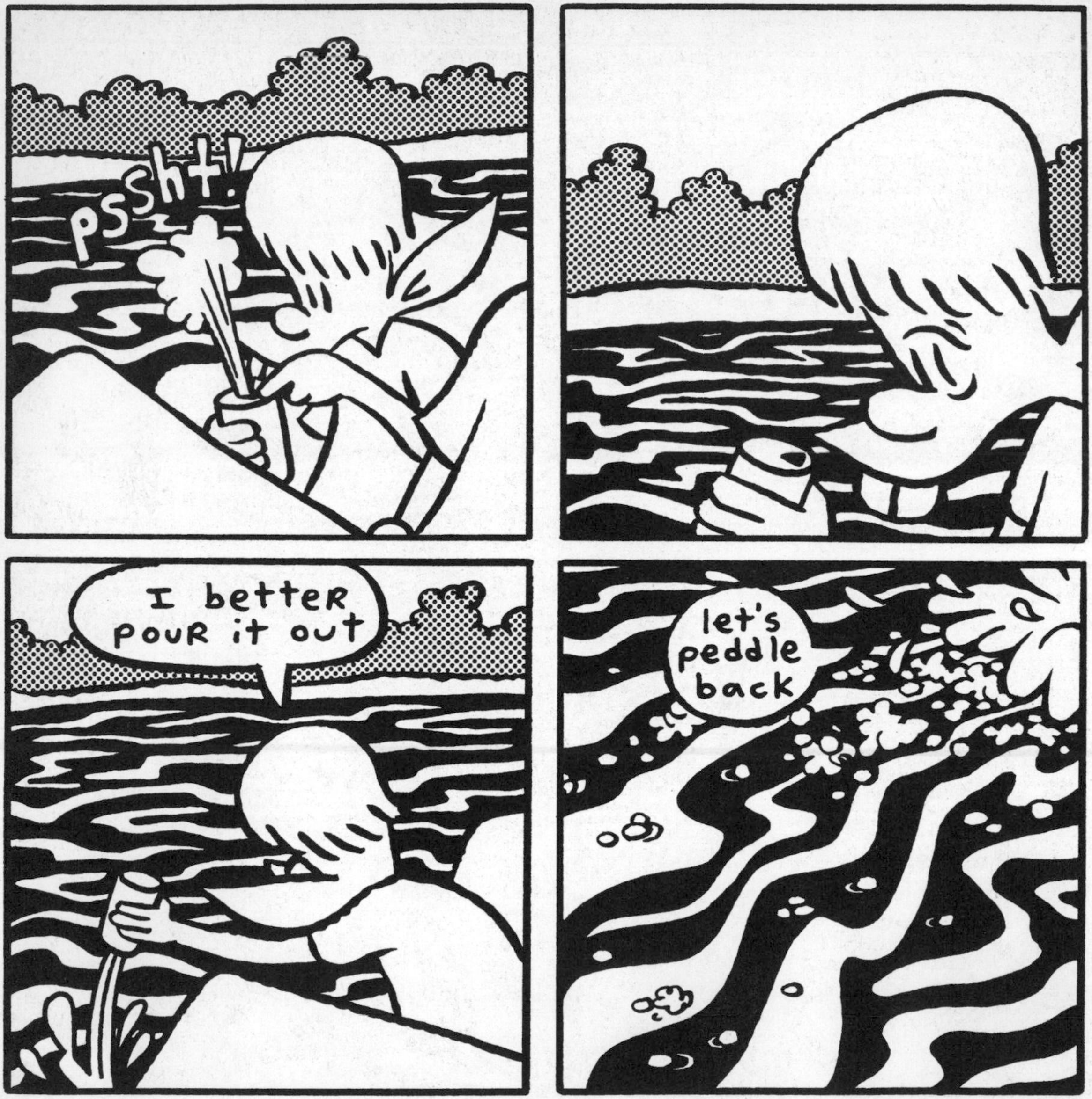
psSht!
I better pour it out
let's peddle back

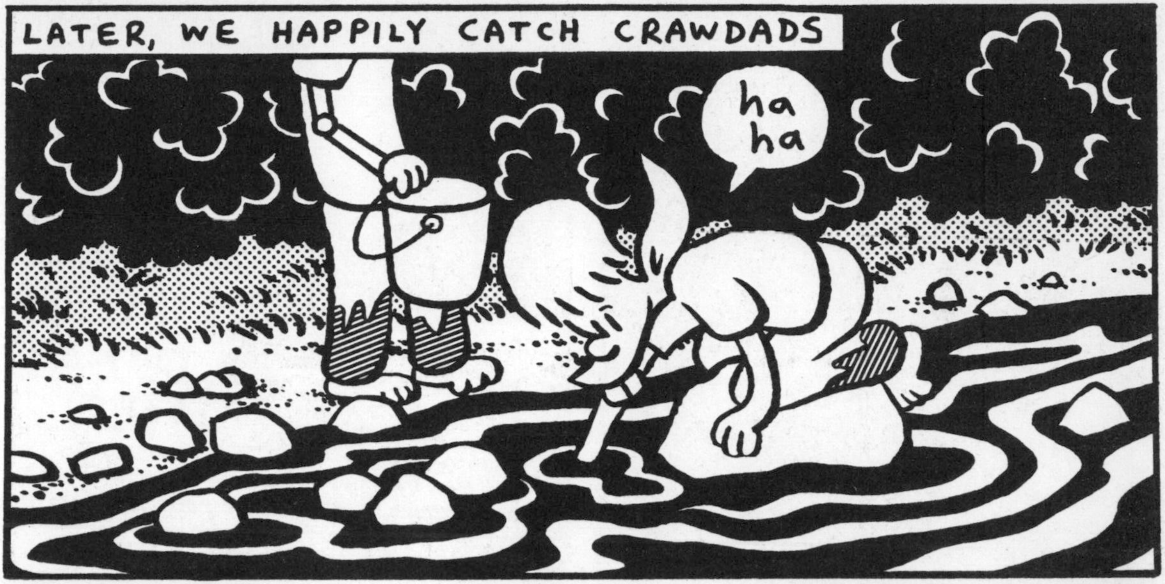
LATER, WE HAPPILY CATCH CRAWDADS
ha ha

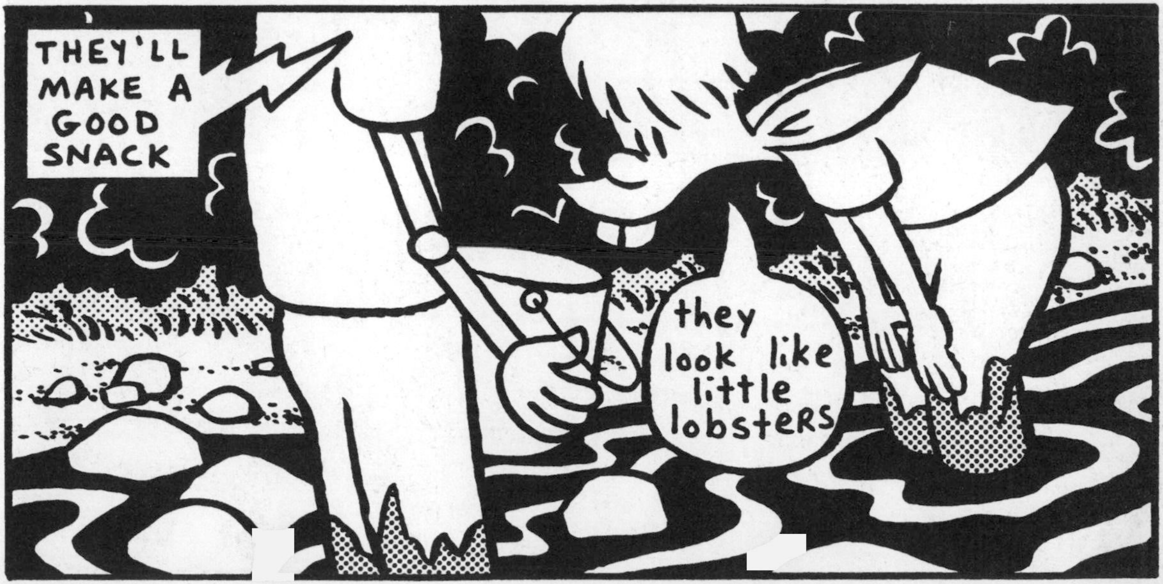
THEY'LL MAKE A GOOD SNACK
they look like little lobsters

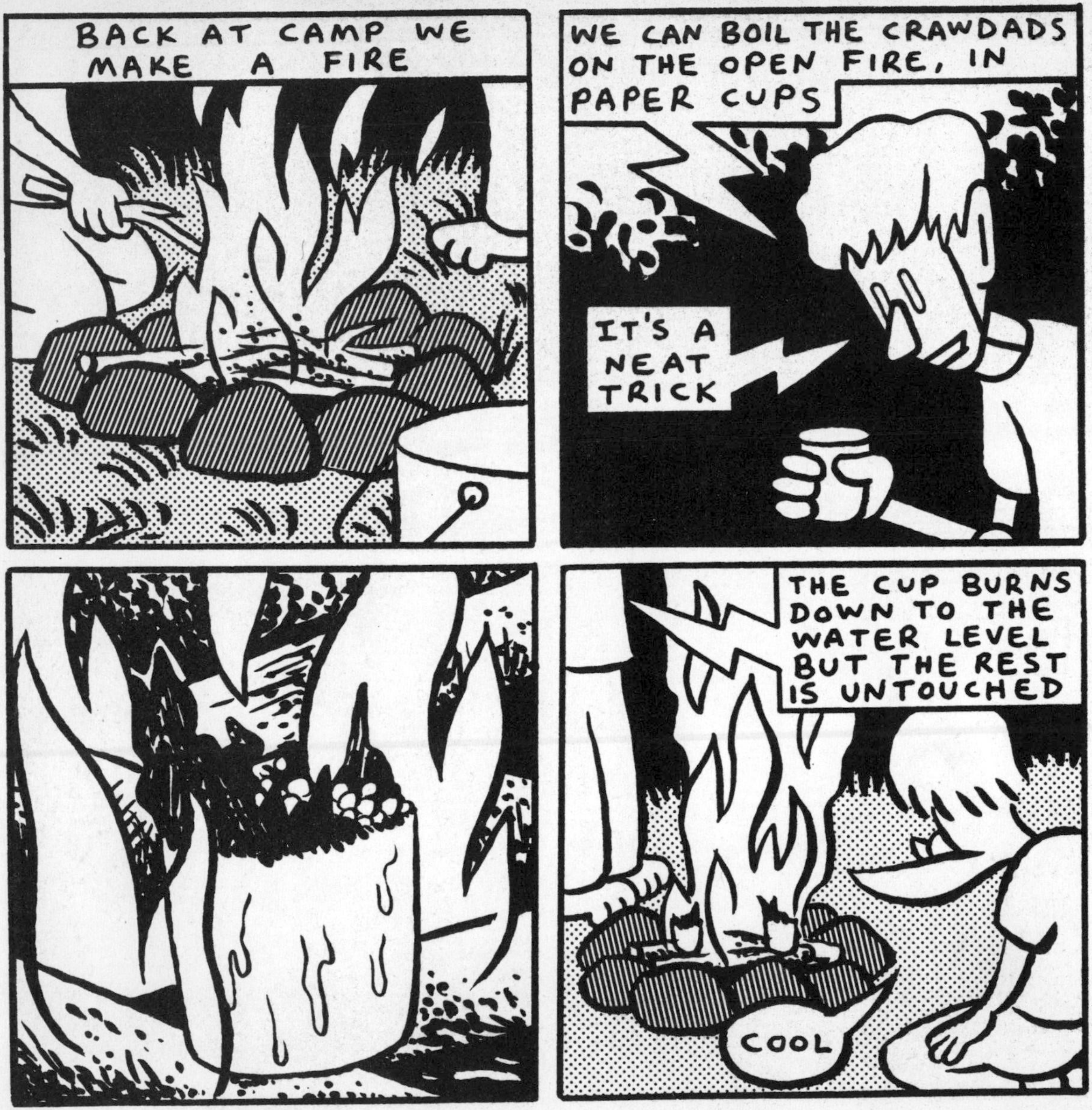
BACK AT CAMP WE MAKE A FIRE
WE CAN BOIL THE CRAWDADS ON THE OPEN FIRE, IN PAPER CUPS
IT'S A NEAT TRICK
THE CUP BURNS DOWN TO THE WATER LEVEL BUT THE REST IS UNTOUCHED
COOL

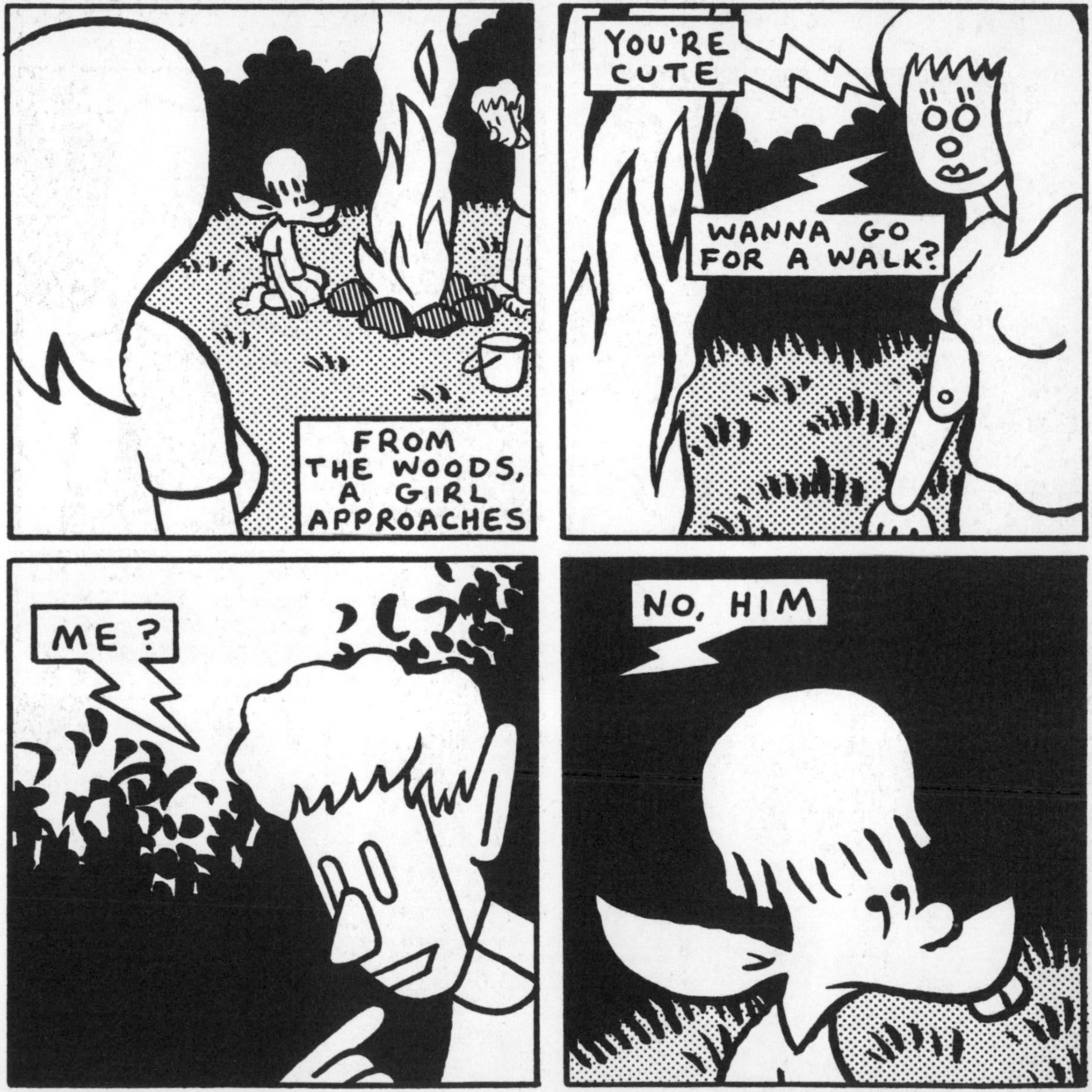
FROM THE WOODS, A GIRL APPROACHES
YOU'RE CUTE
WANNA GO FOR A WALK?
ME ?
NO, HIM

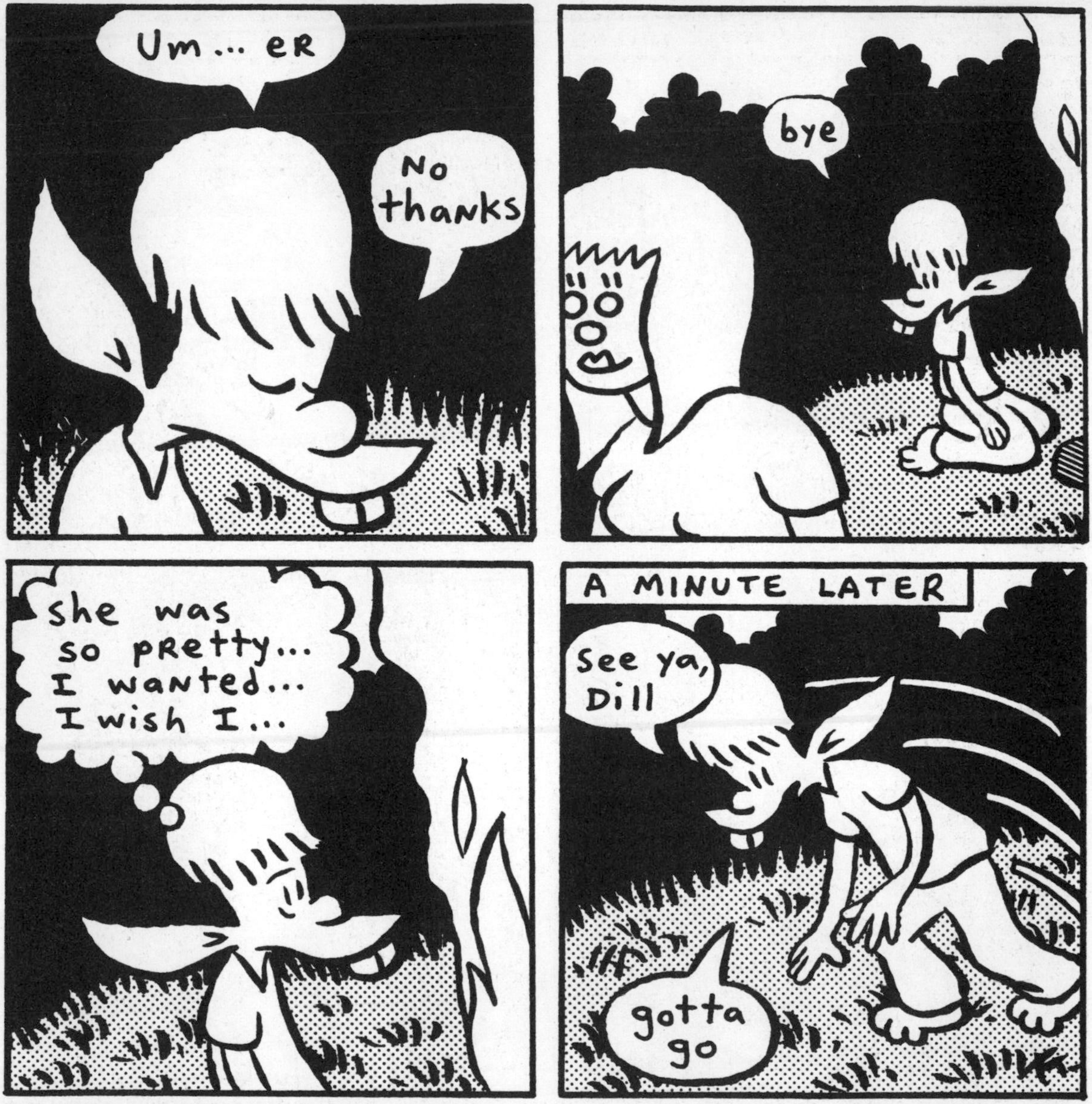

Um... eR
No thanks
bye
she was so pretty... I wanted... I wish I...
A MINUTE LATER
See ya, Dill
gotta go

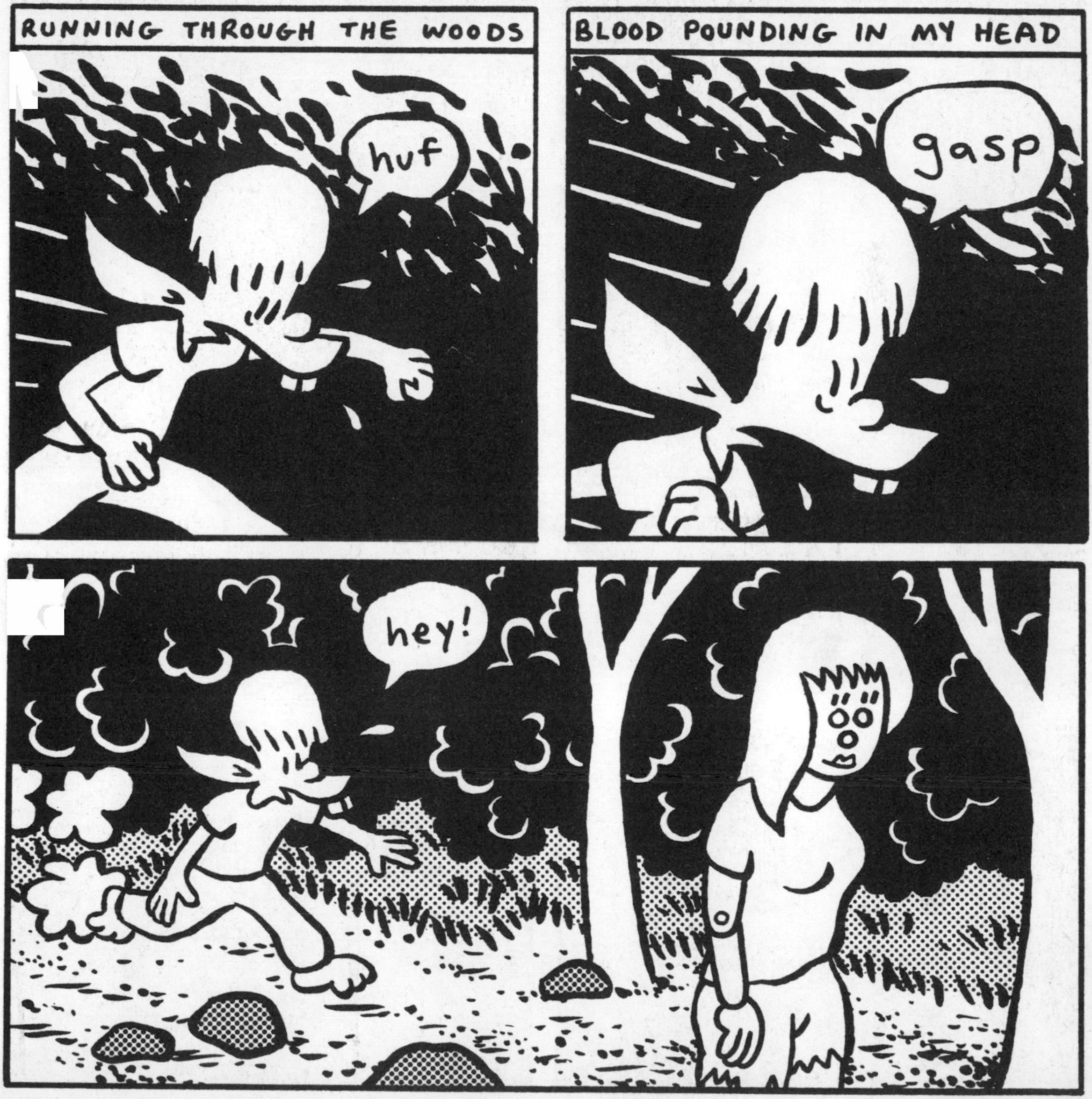
RUNNING THROUGH THE WOODS
huf
BLOOD POUNDING IN MY HEAD
gasp
hey!

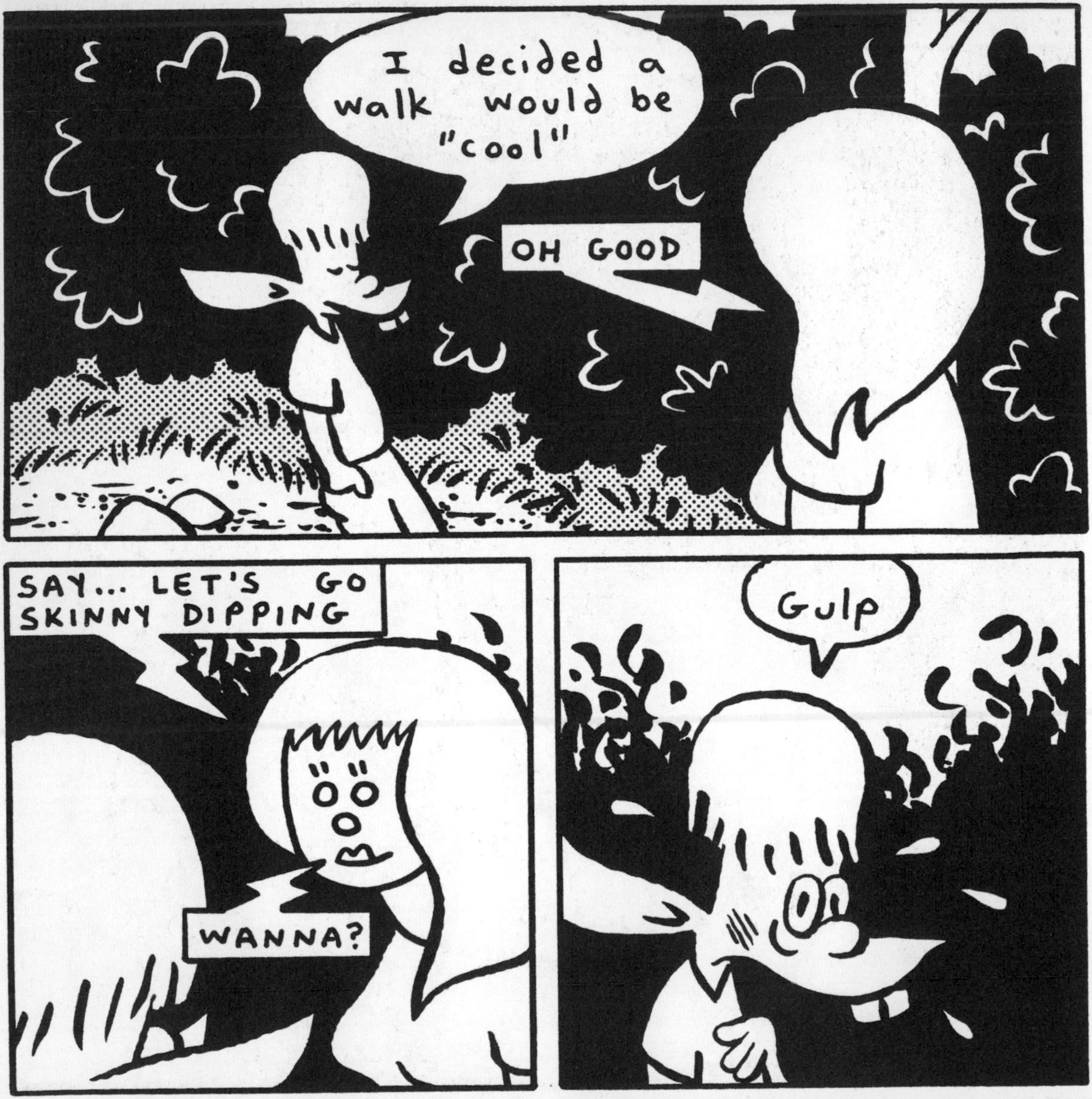
I decided a walk would be "cool"
OH GOOD
SAY... LET'S GO SKINNY DIPPING
WANNA?
Gulp

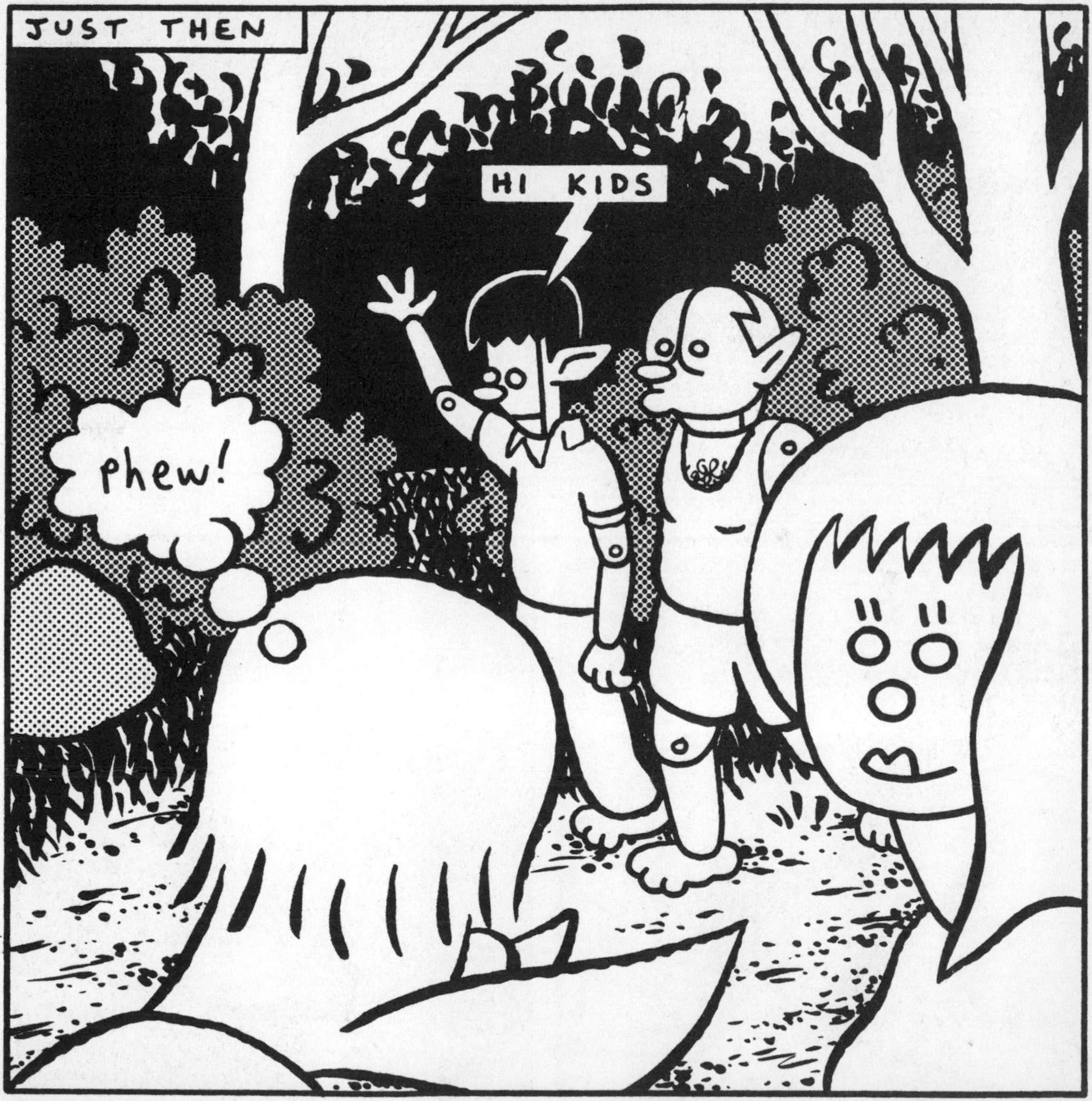
JUST THEN
HI KIDS
phew!

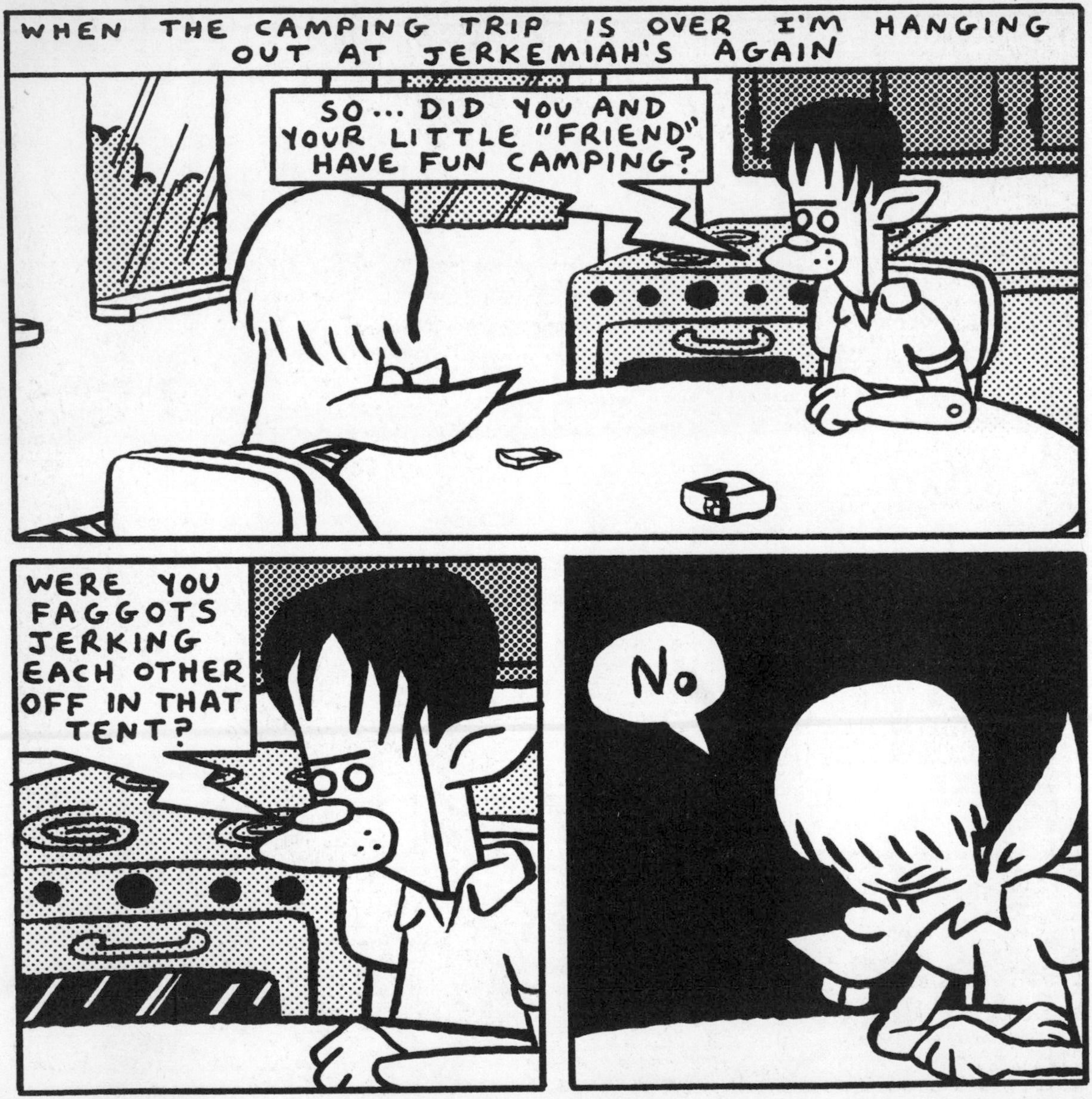
WHEN THE CAMPING TRIP IS OVER I'M HANGING OUT AT JERKEMIAH'S AGAIN
SO... DID YOU AND YOUR LITTLE "FRIEND" HAVE FUN CAMPING?
WERE YOU FAGGOTS JERKING EACH OTHER OFF IN THAT TENT?
No

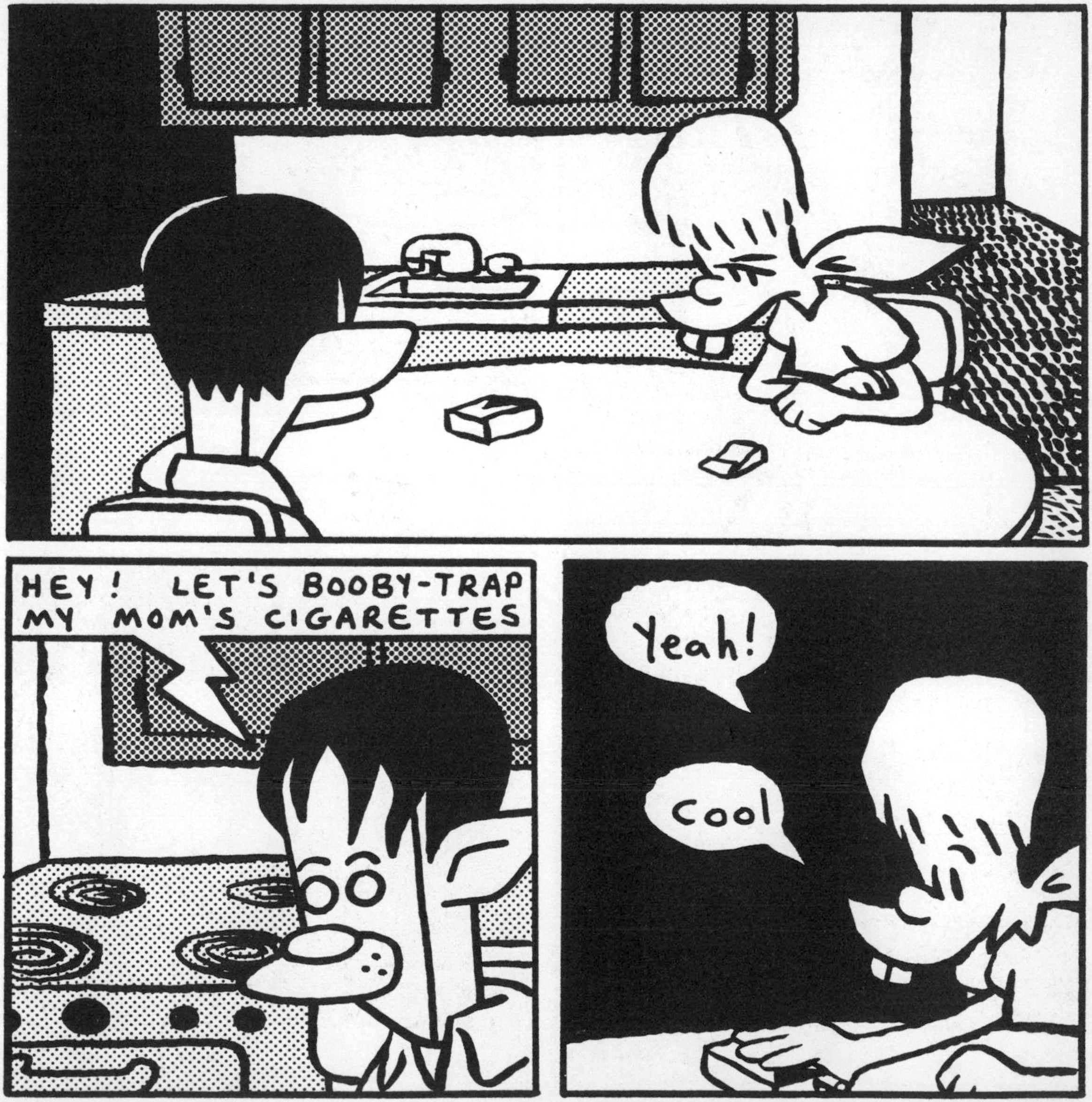
HEY! LET'S BOOBY-TRAP MY MOM'S CIGARETTES
Yeah!
Cool

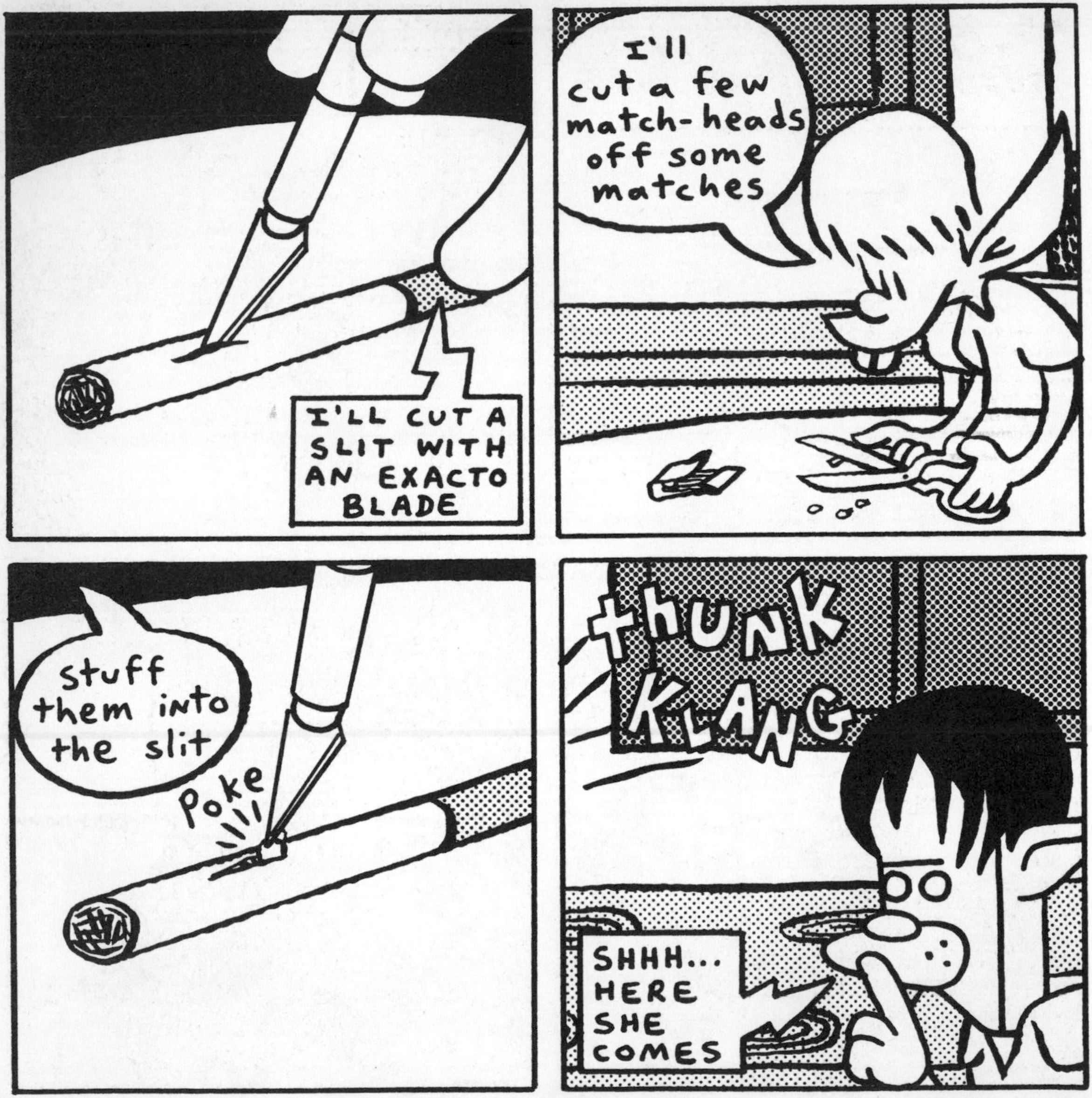
I'LL CUT A SLIT WITH AN EXACTO BLADE
I'll cut a few match-heads off some matches
stuff them into the slit
poke
thunk
KLANG
SHHH... HERE SHE COMES

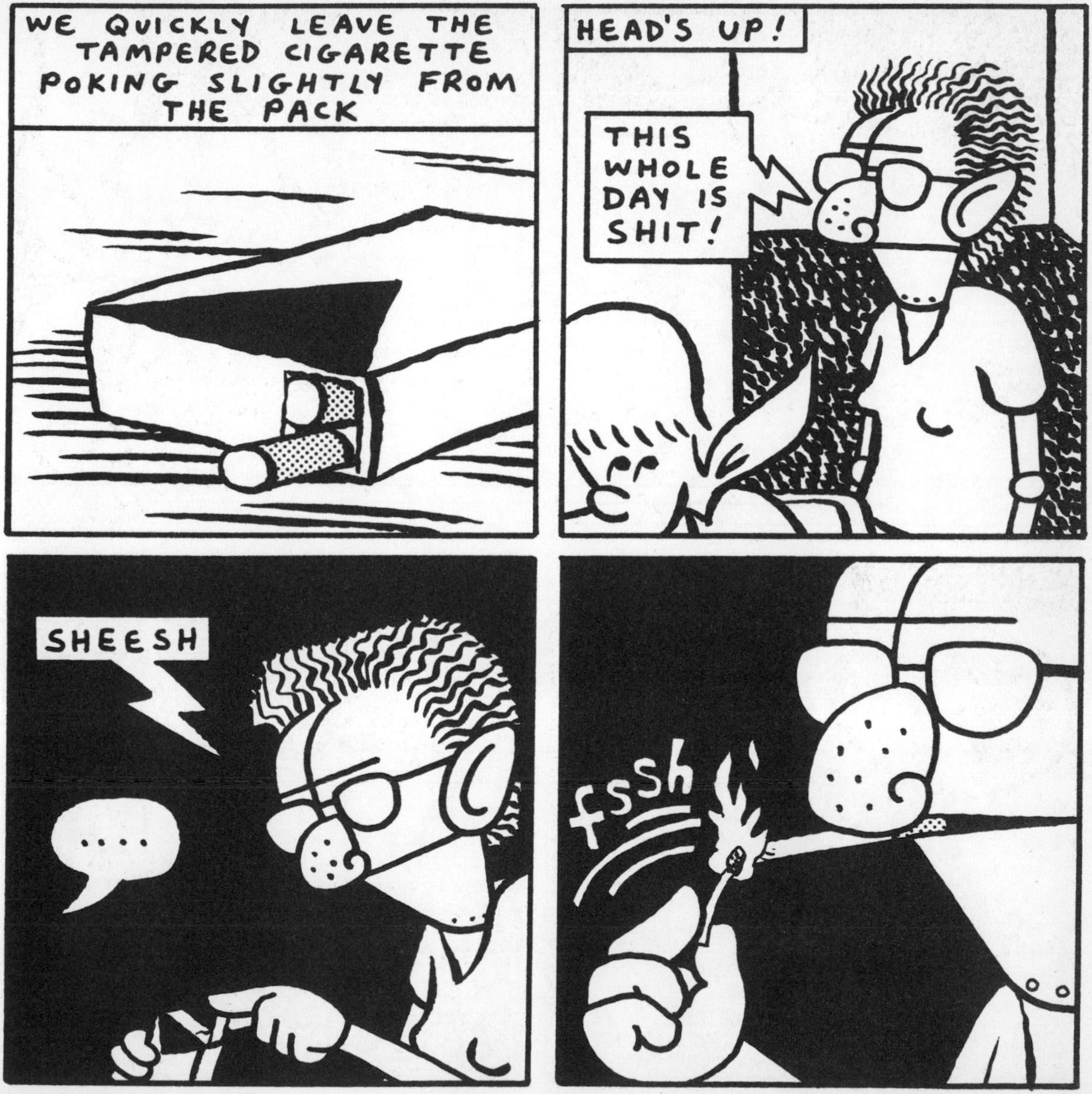
WE QUICKLY LEAVE THE TAMPERED CIGARETTE POKING SLIGHTLY FROM THE PACK
HEAD'S UP!
THIS WHOLE DAY IS SHIT!
SHEESH
....
fssh

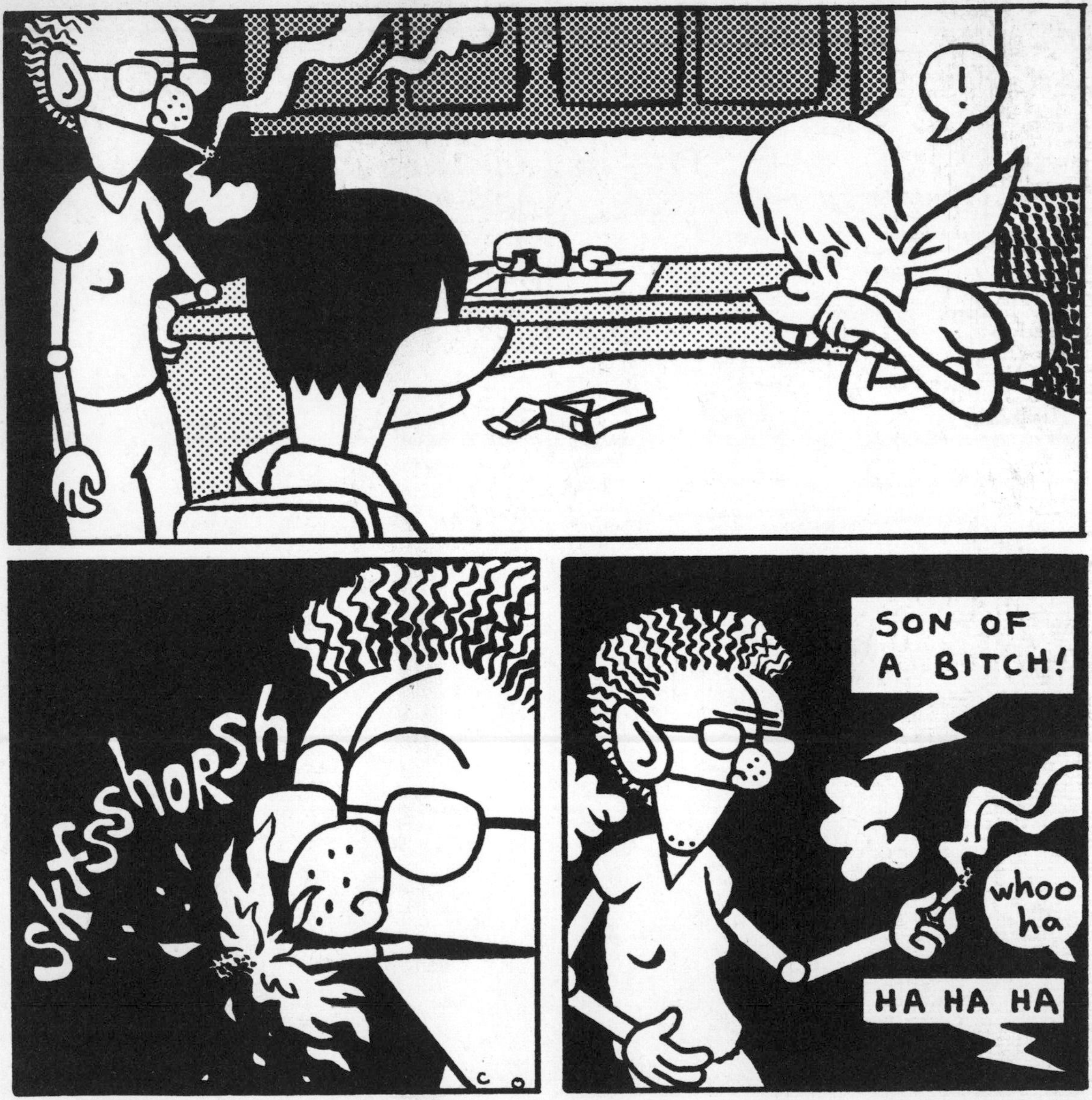
!
sktsshorsh
SON OF A BITCH!
whoo ha
HA HA HA

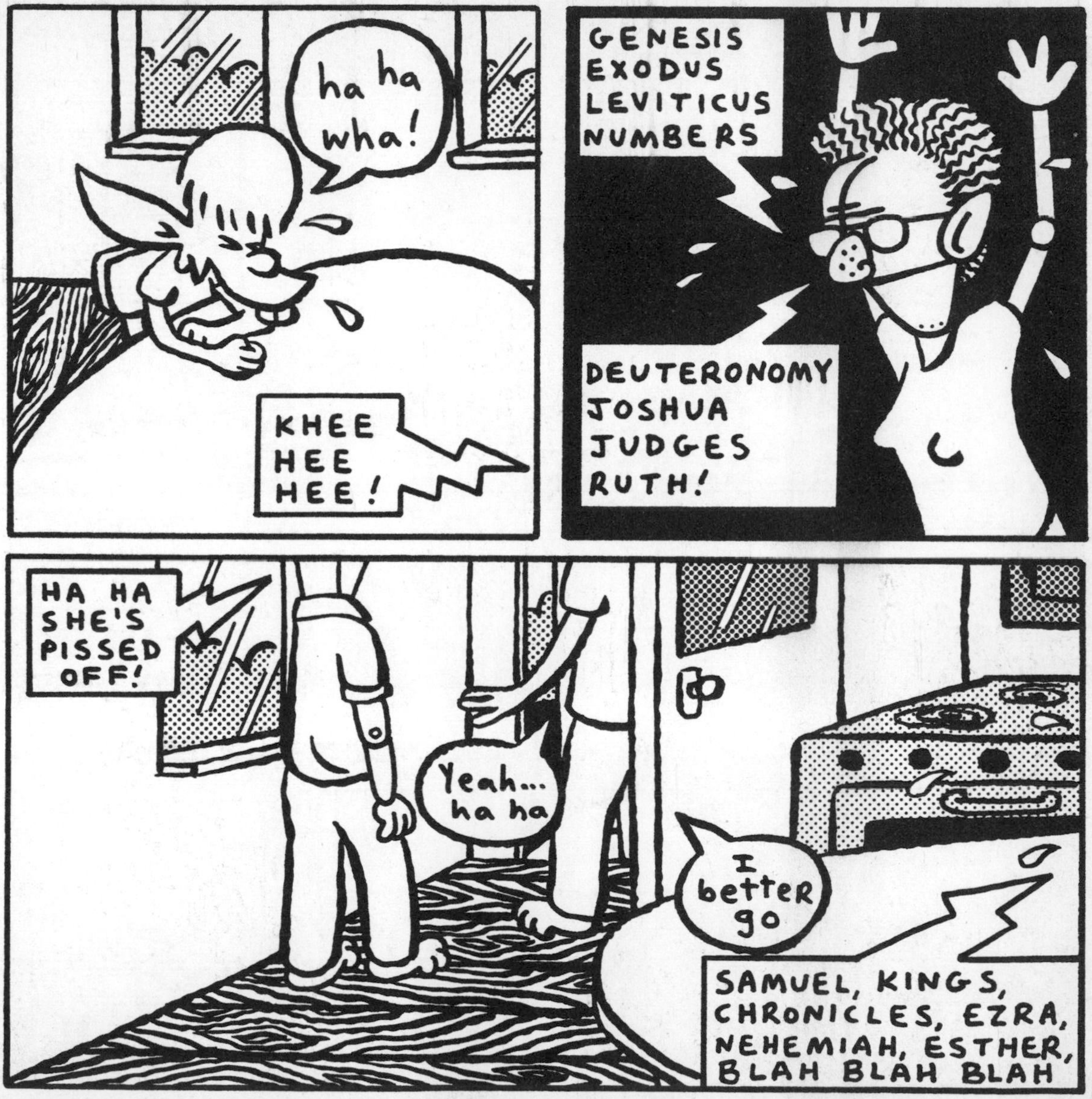
ha ha
wha!
KHEE
HEE
HEE!
GENESIS
EXODUS
LEVITICUS
NUMBERS
DEUTERONOMY
JOSHUA
JUDGES
RUTH!
HA HA
SHE'S
PISSED
OFF!
Yeah...
ha ha
I
better
go
SAMUEL, KINGS,
CHRONICLES, EZRA,
NEHEMIAH, ESTHER,
BLAH BLAH BLAH

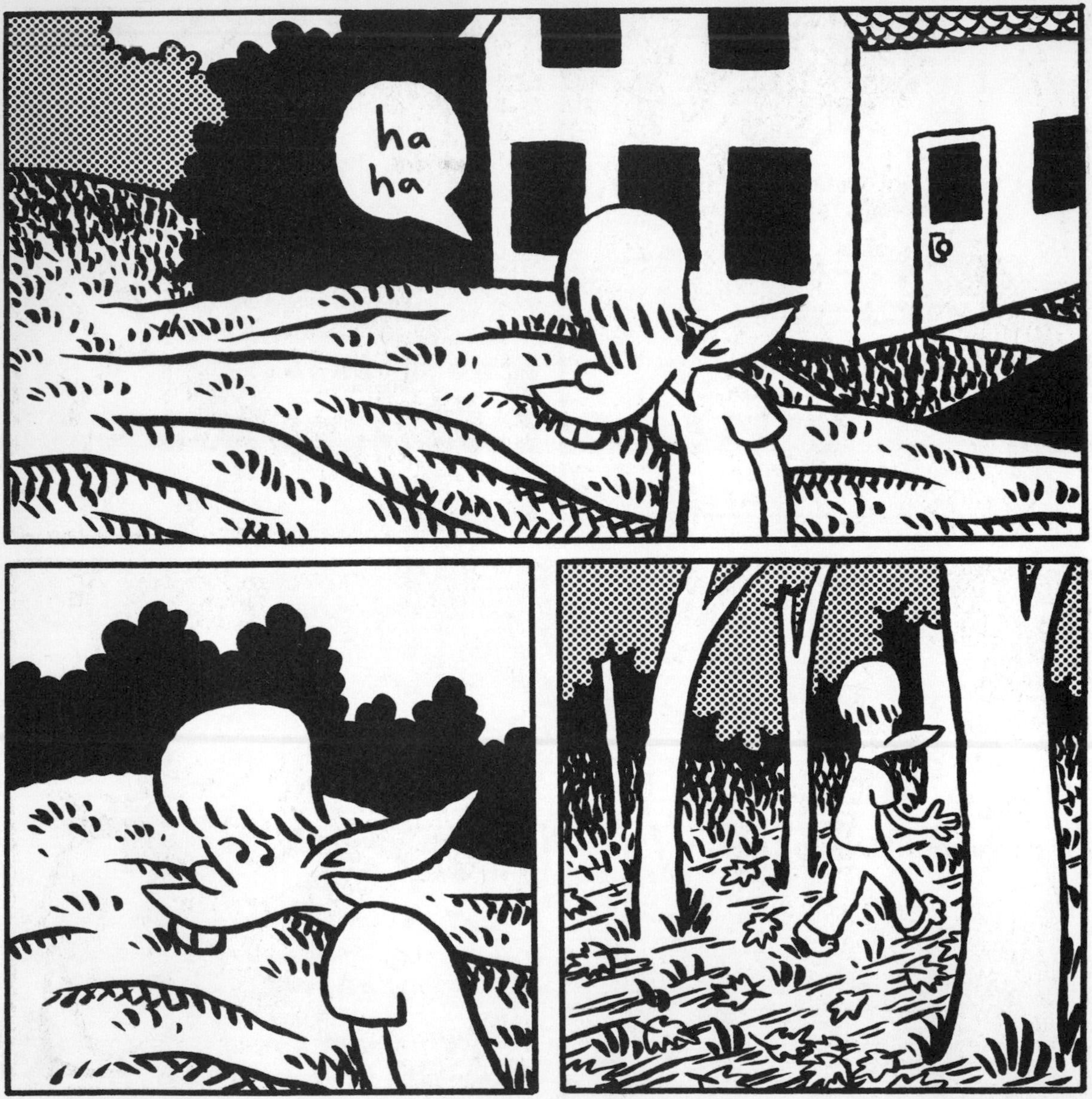
ha ha

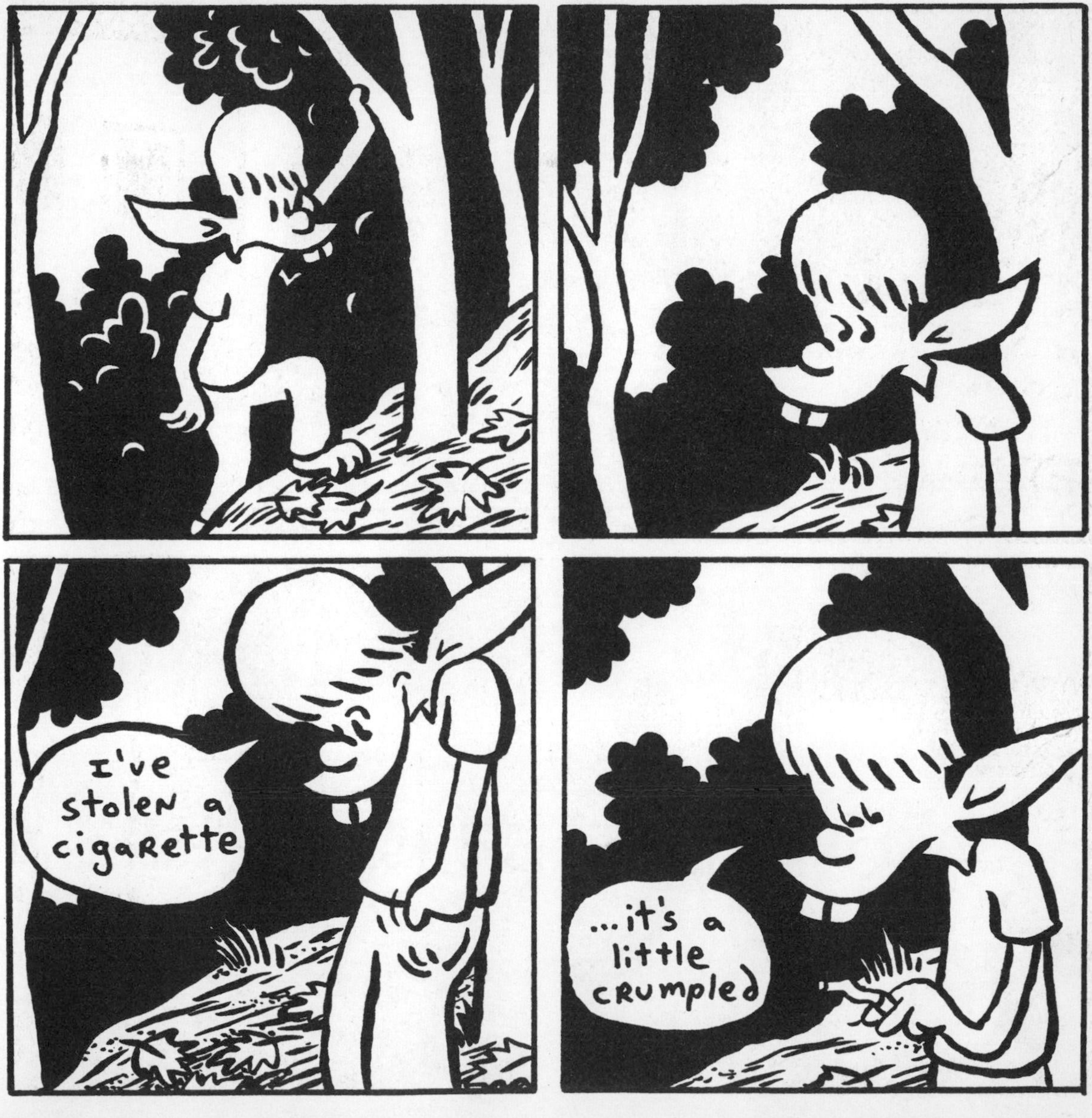
I've stolen a cigarette
...it's a little crumpled

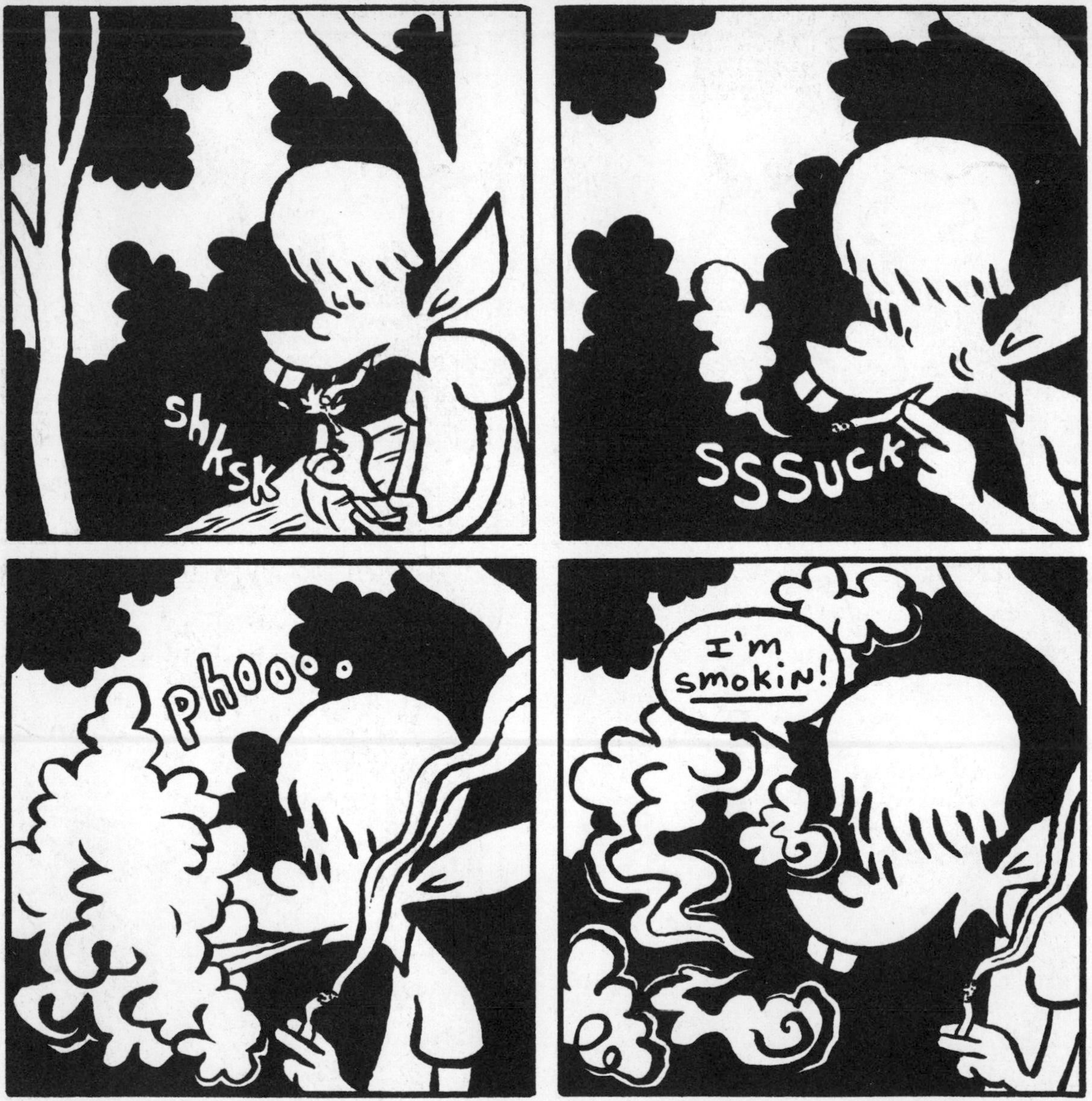
shksk
SSSUCK
phOOo o
I'm smokin!

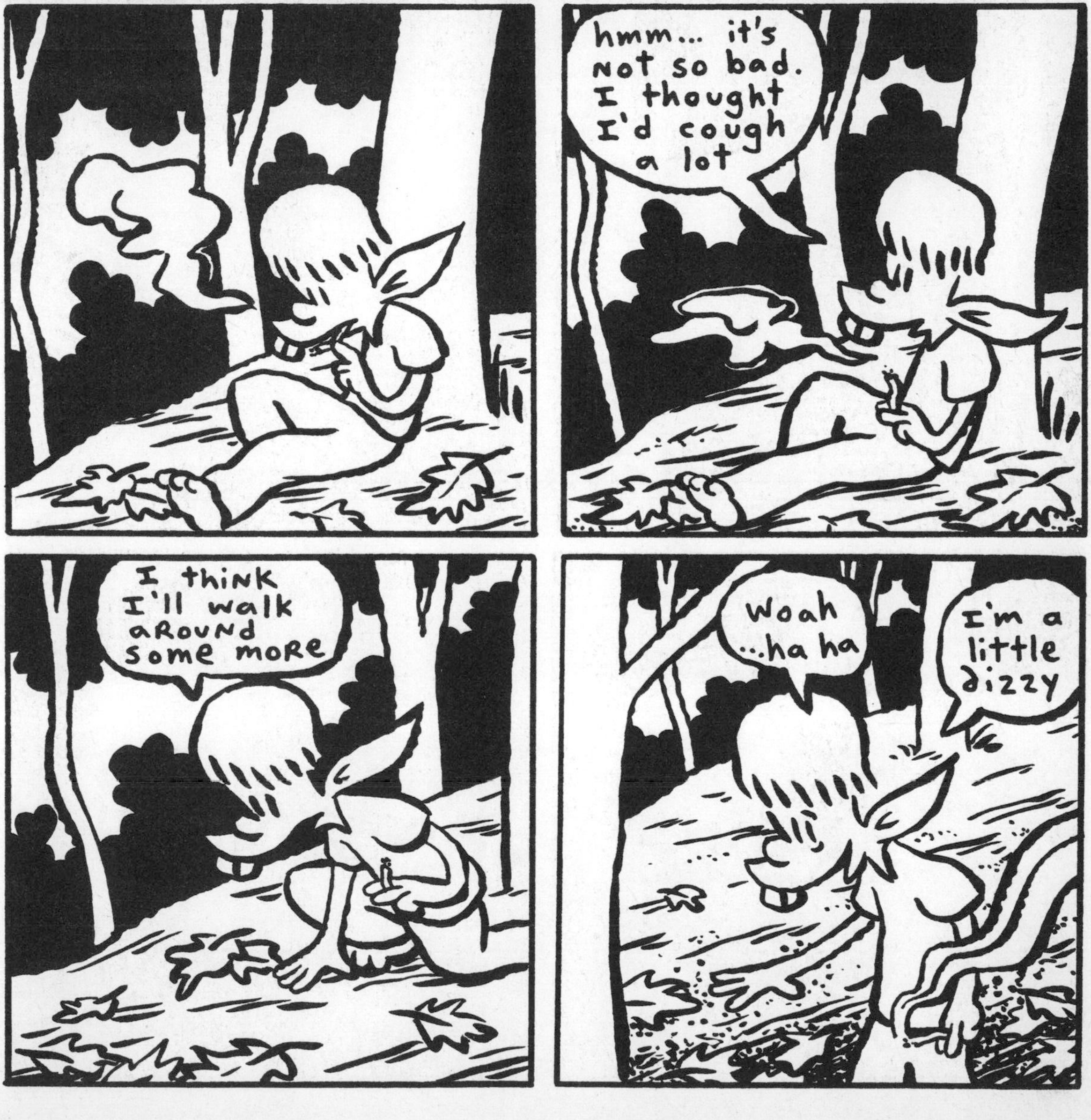
hmm... it's not so bad. I thought I'd cough a lot
I think I'll walk around some more
Woah ...ha ha
I'm a little dizzy

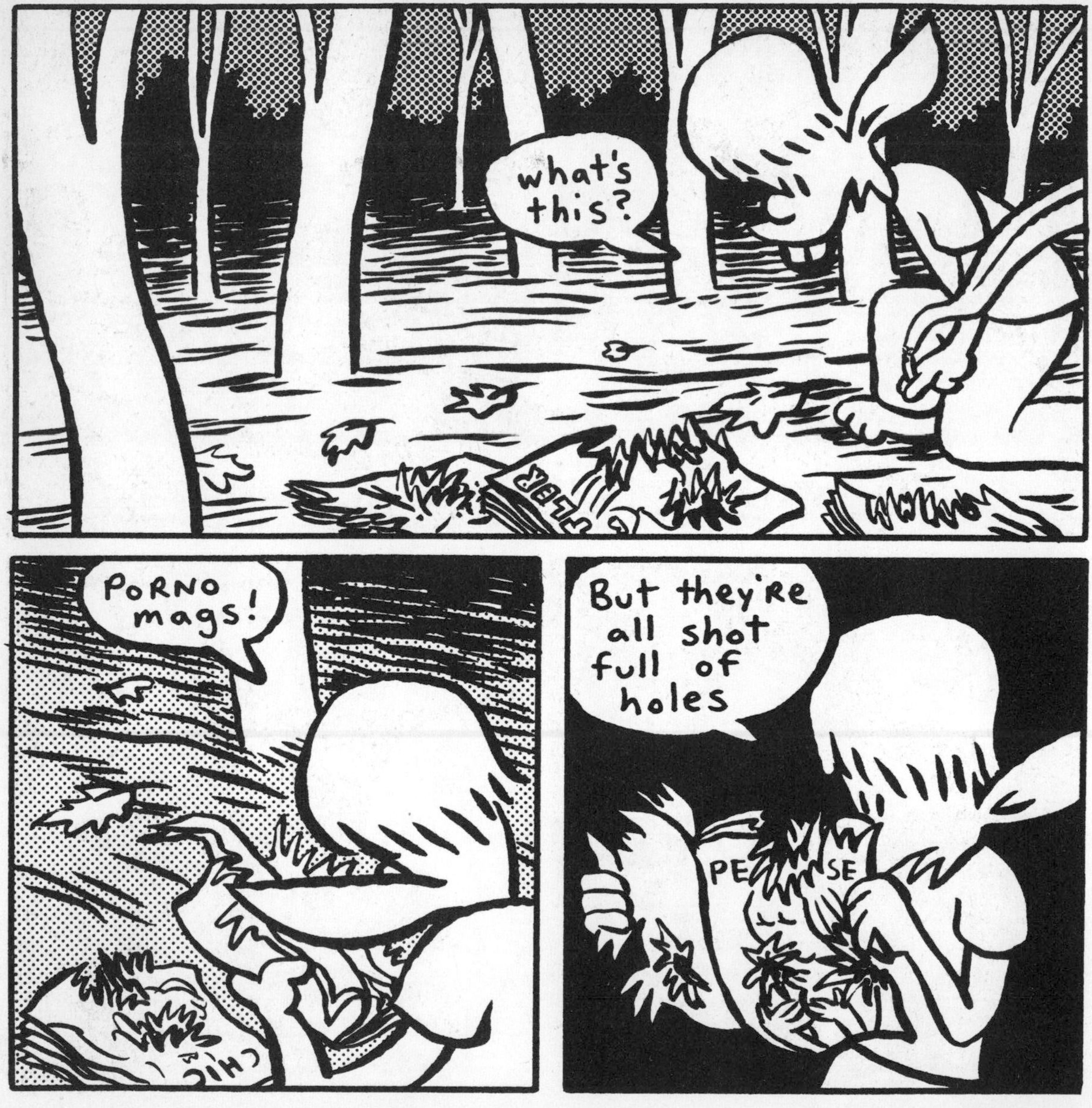
what's this?
PORNO mags!
But they're all shot full of holes

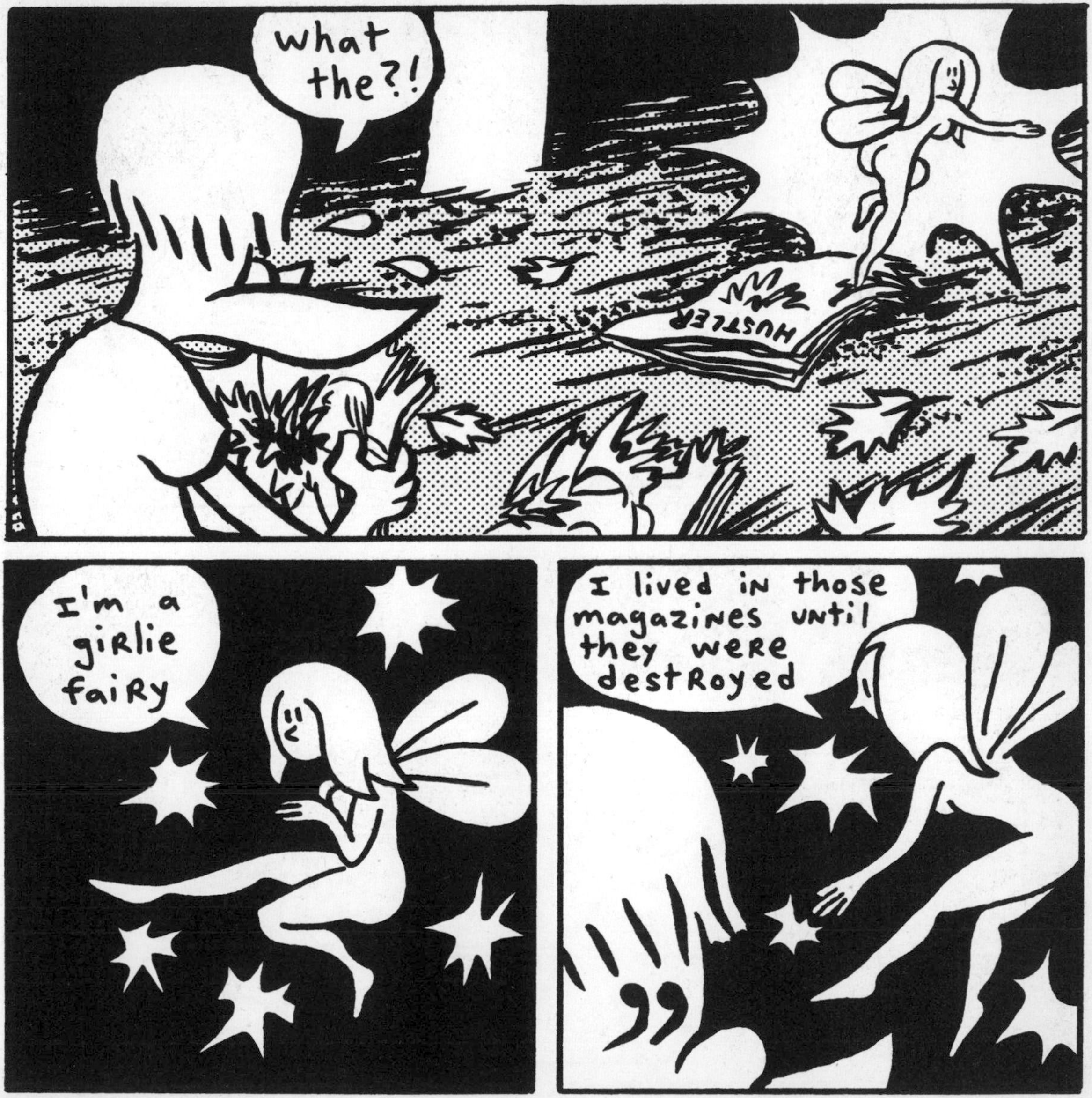
what the?!
HUSTLER
I'm a girlie fairy
I lived in those magazines until they were destroyed

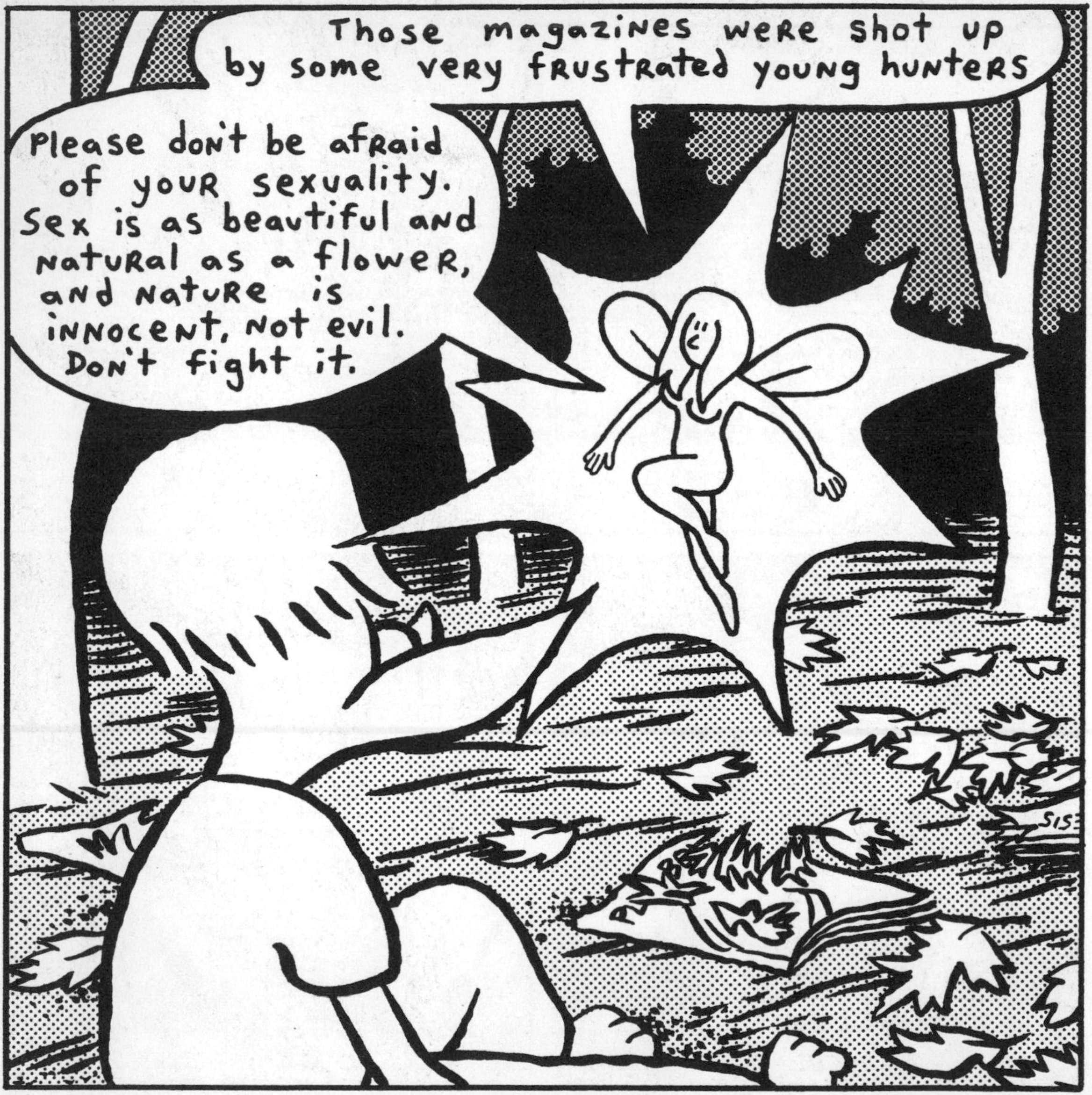
Please don't be afraid of your sexuality. Sex is as beautiful and natural as a flower, and nature is innocent, not evil. Don't fight it.
Those magazines were shot up by some very frustrated young hunters
SIS

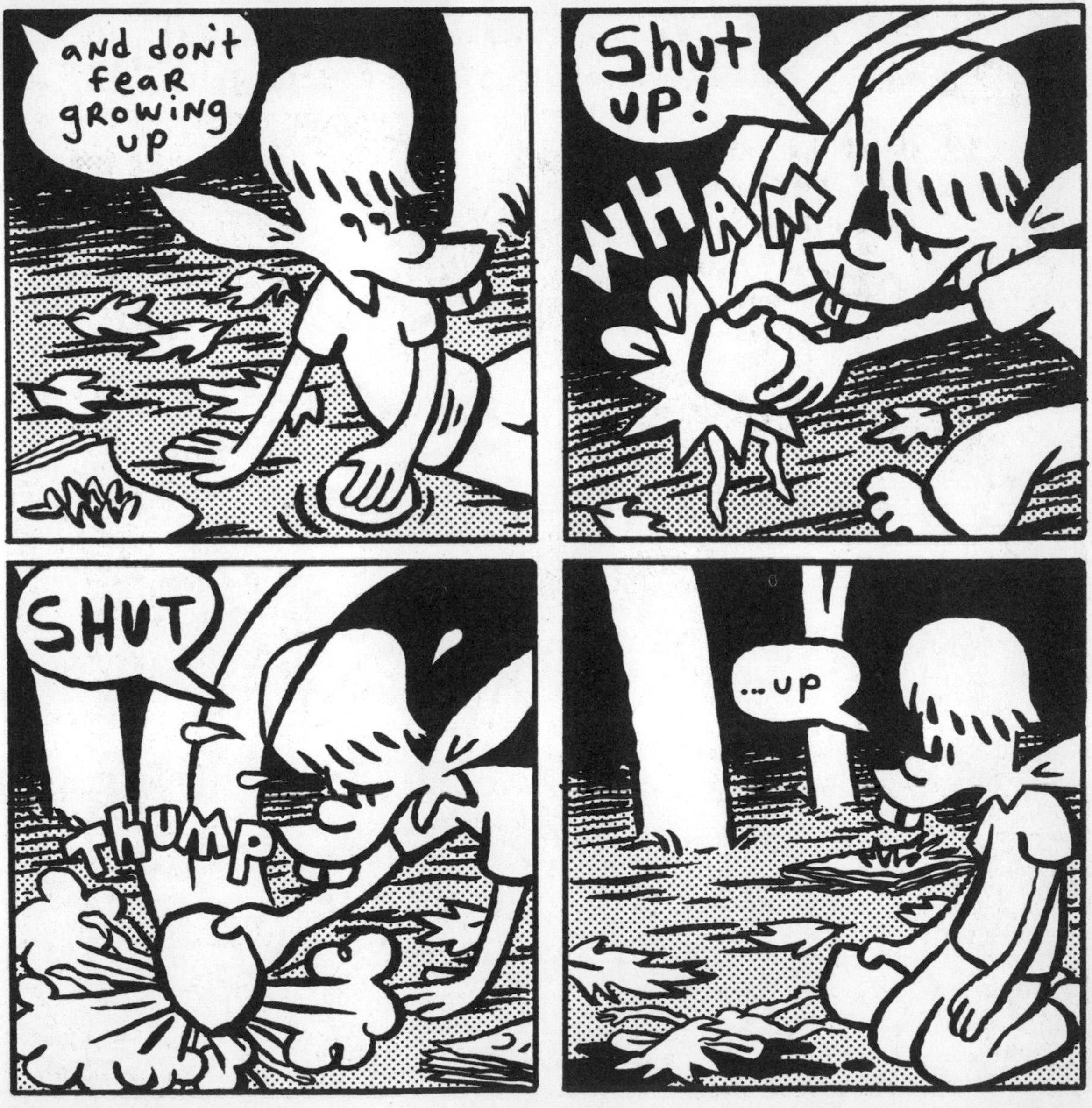
and don't fear growing up
Shut up!
WHAM
SHUT
THUMP
...up

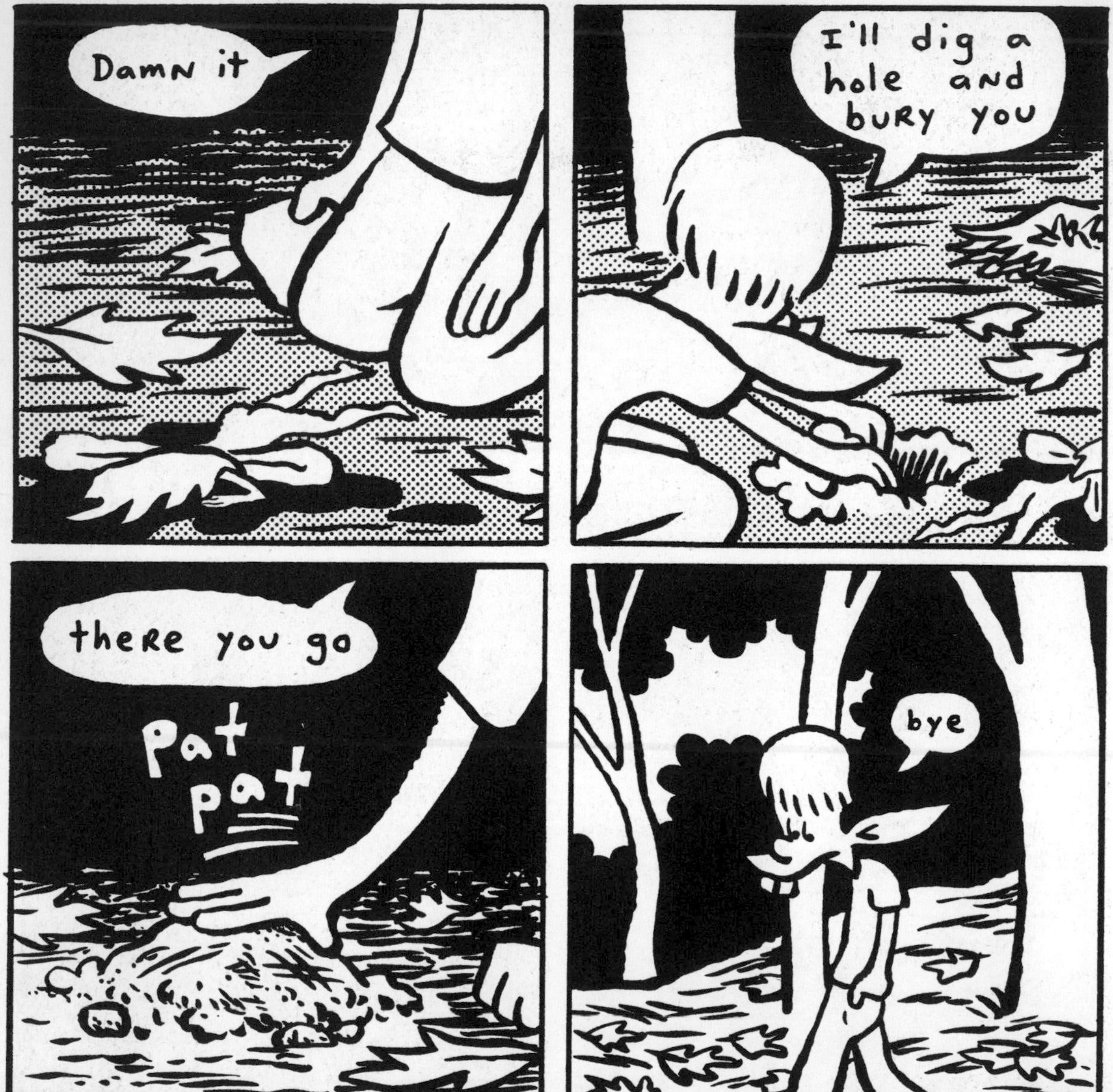
Damn it
I'll dig a hole and bury you
there you go
pat pat
bye

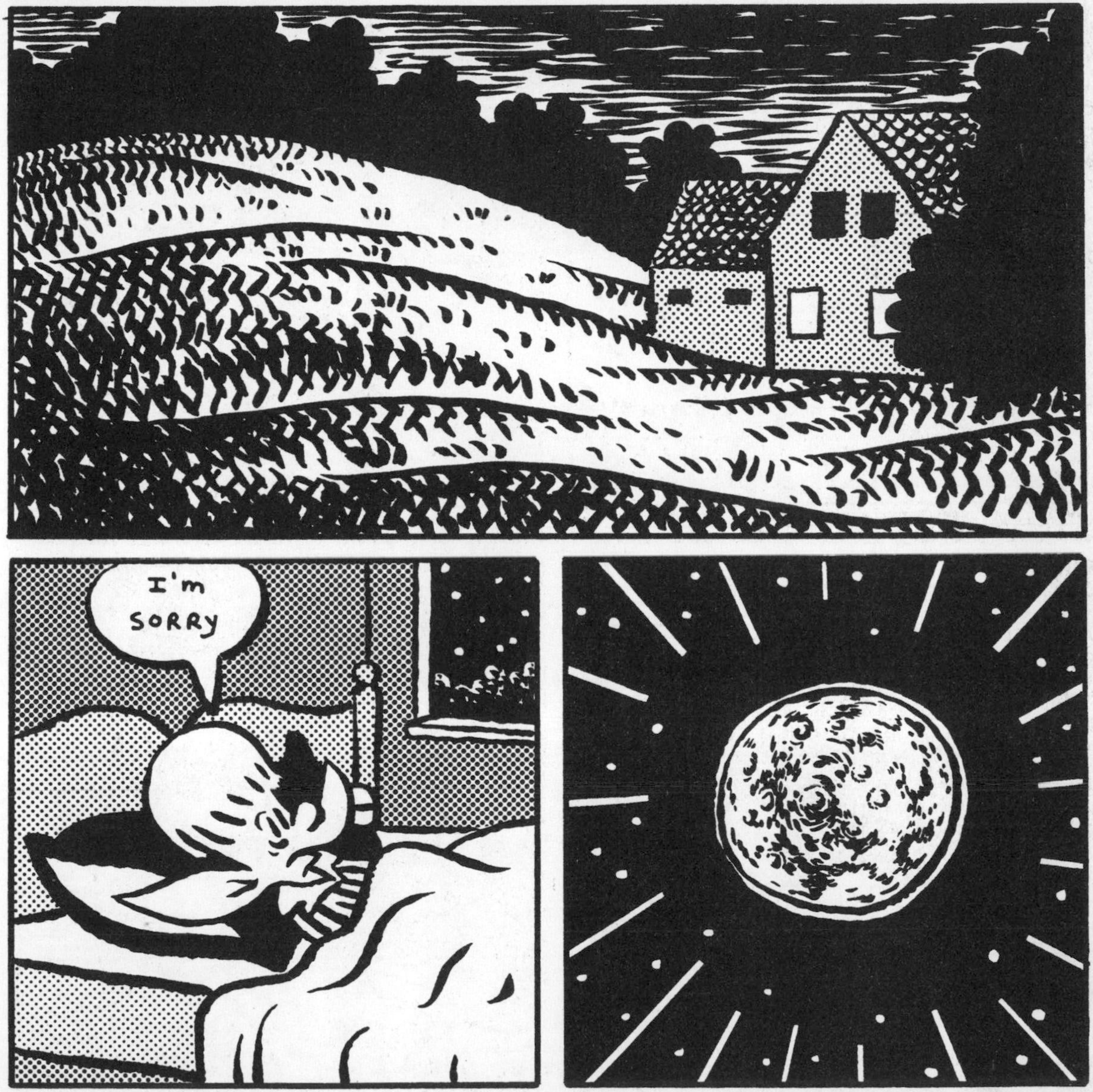
I'm SORRY

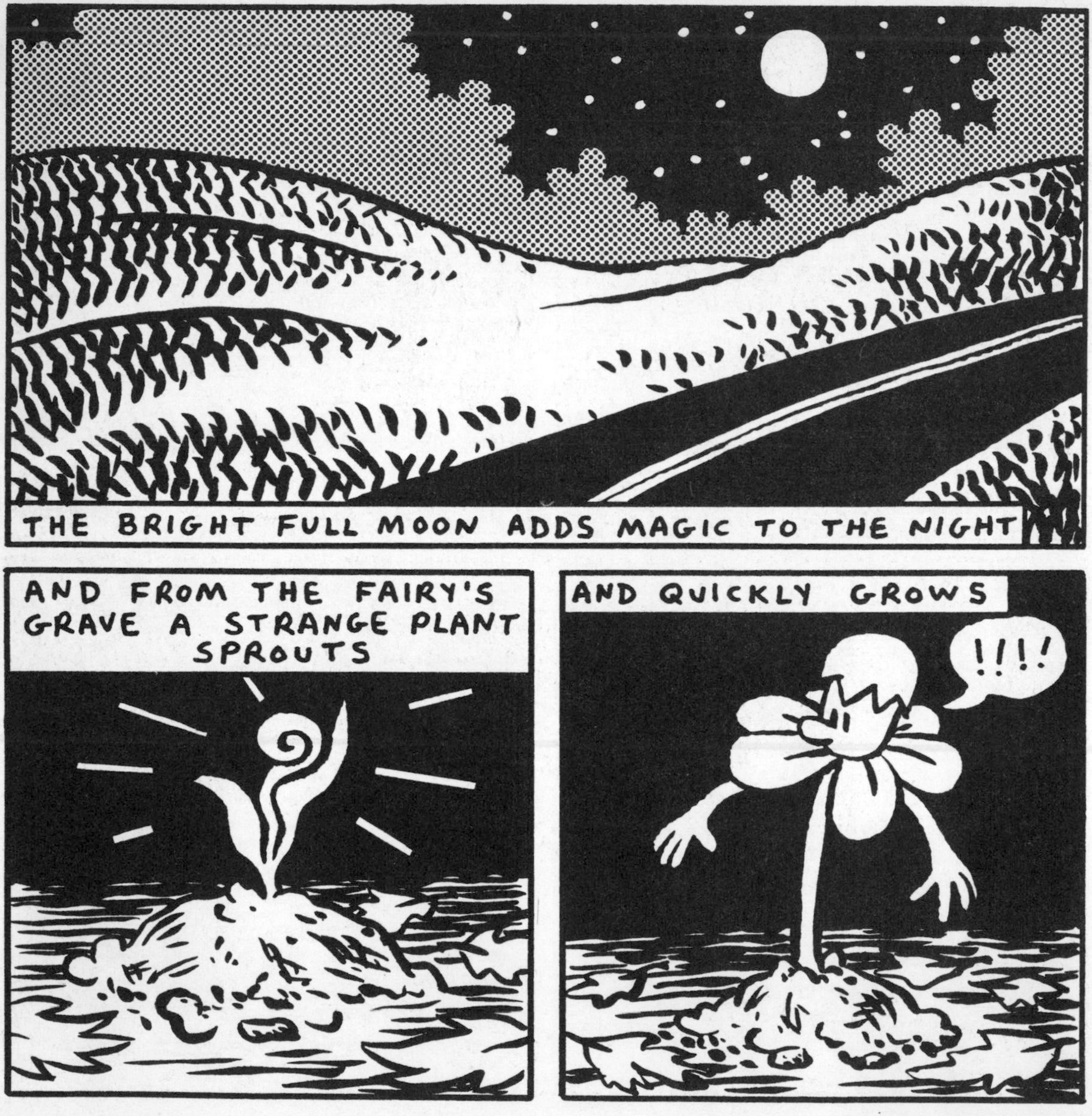
THE BRIGHT FULL MOON ADDS MAGIC TO THE NIGHT
AND FROM THE FAIRY'S GRAVE A STRANGE PLANT SPROUTS
AND QUICKLY GROWS
!!!!

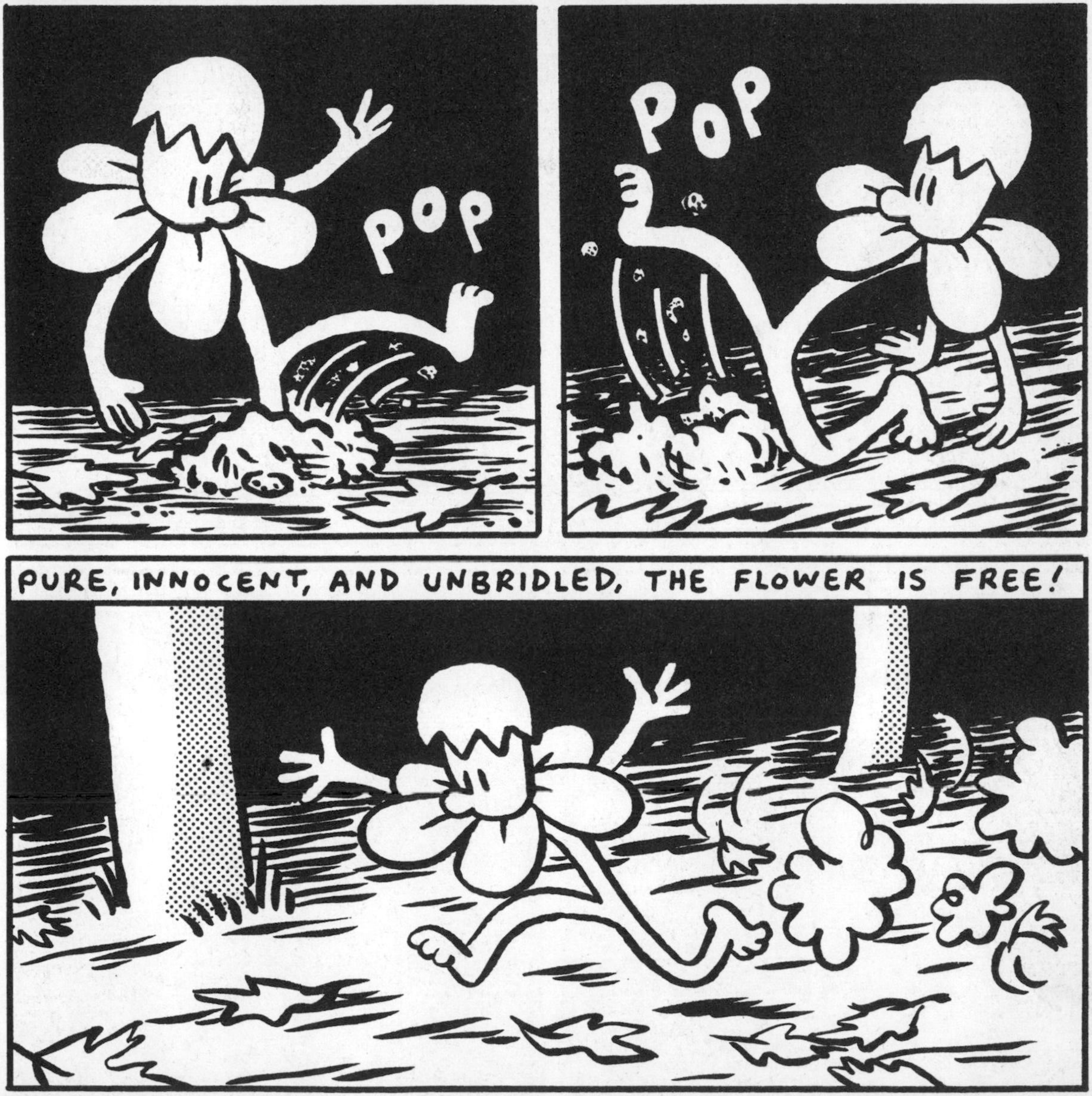
POP
POP
PURE, INNOCENT, AND UNBRIDLED, THE FLOWER IS FREE!

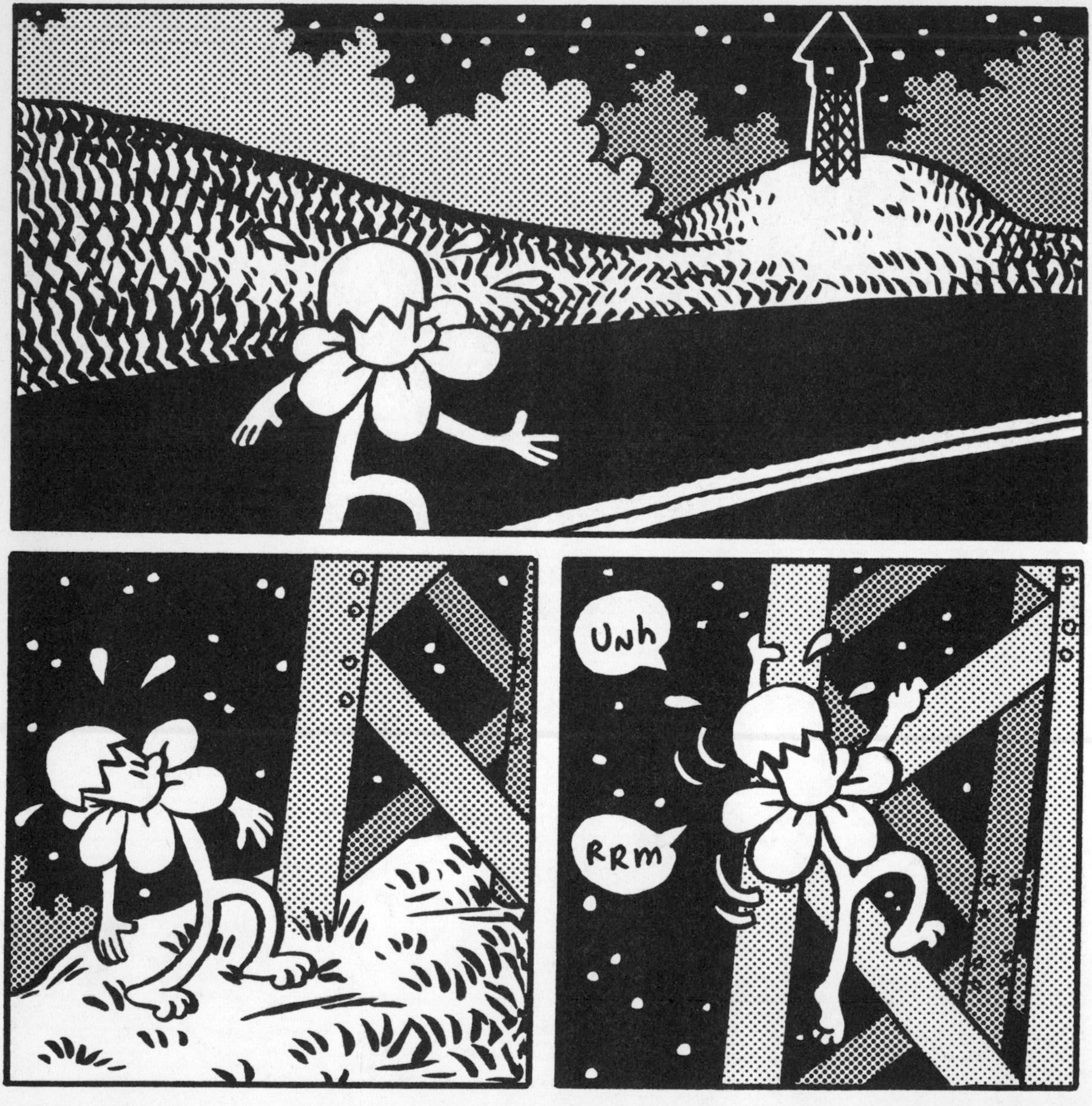
Unh
RRm

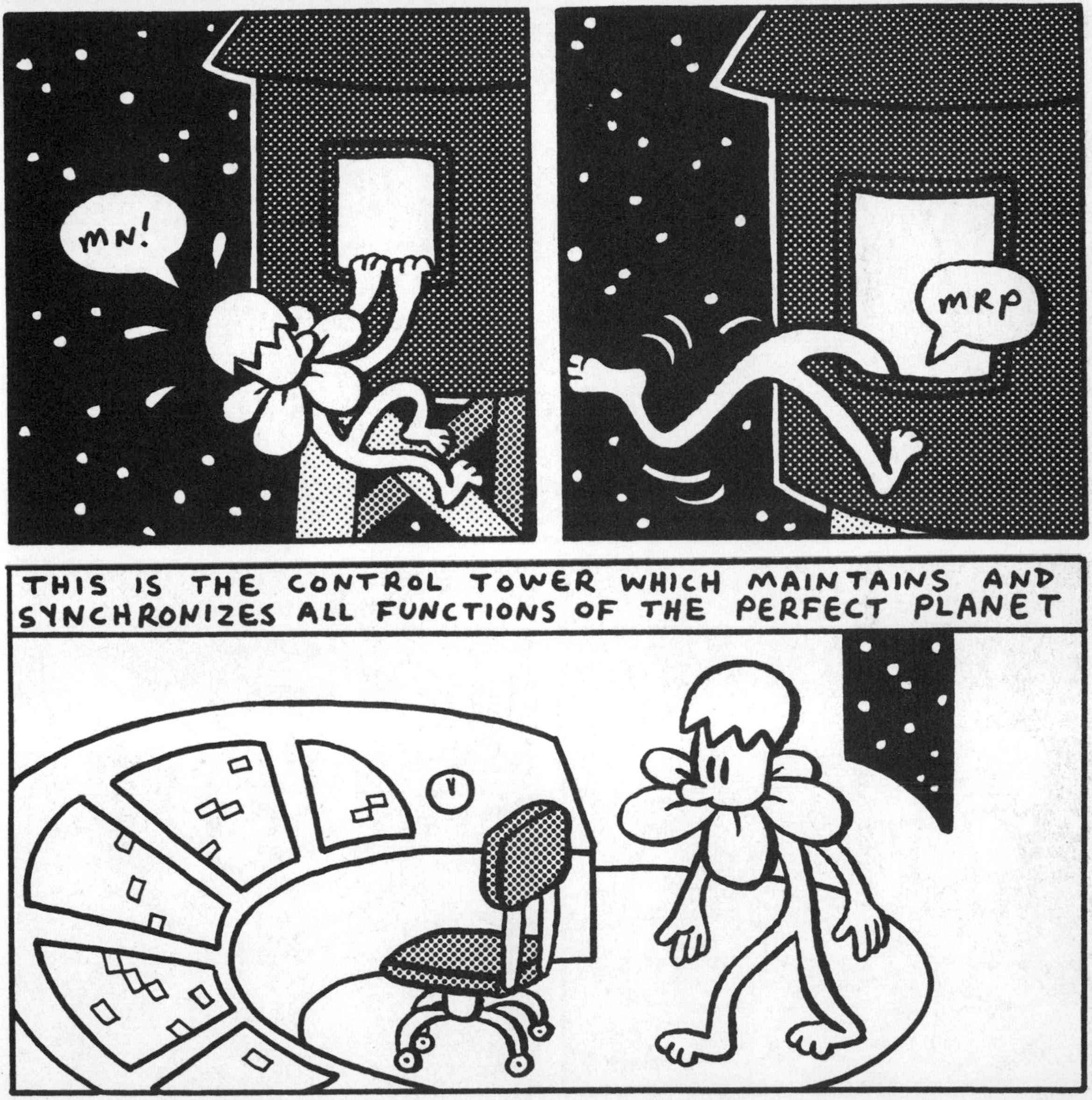
mn!
mrp
THIS IS THE CONTROL TOWER WHICH MAINTAINS AND SYNCHRONIZES ALL FUNCTIONS OF THE PERFECT PLANET

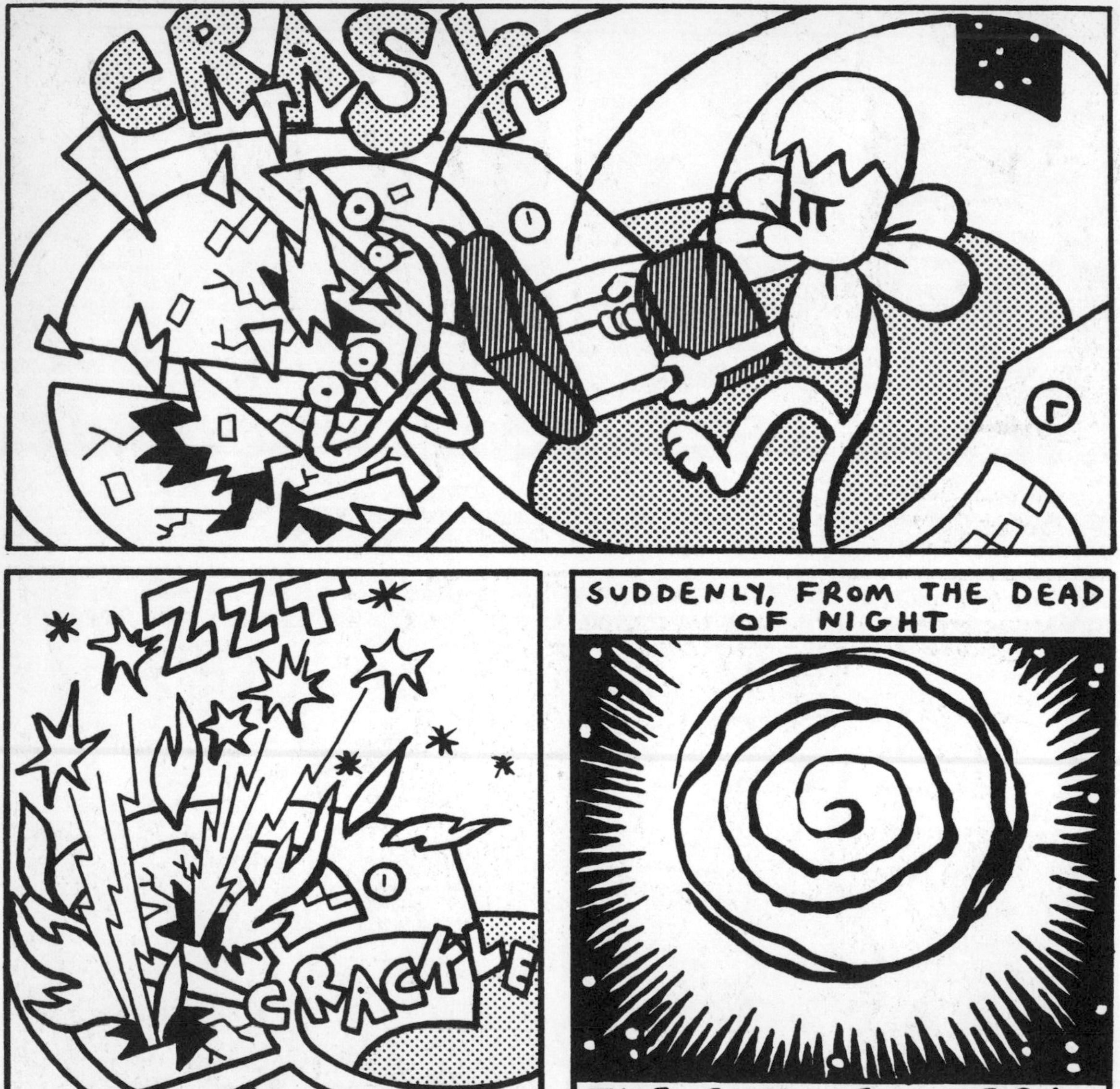
CRASH
ZZZT
CRACKLE
SUDDENLY, FROM THE DEAD OF NIGHT
THE SUN IGNITES!

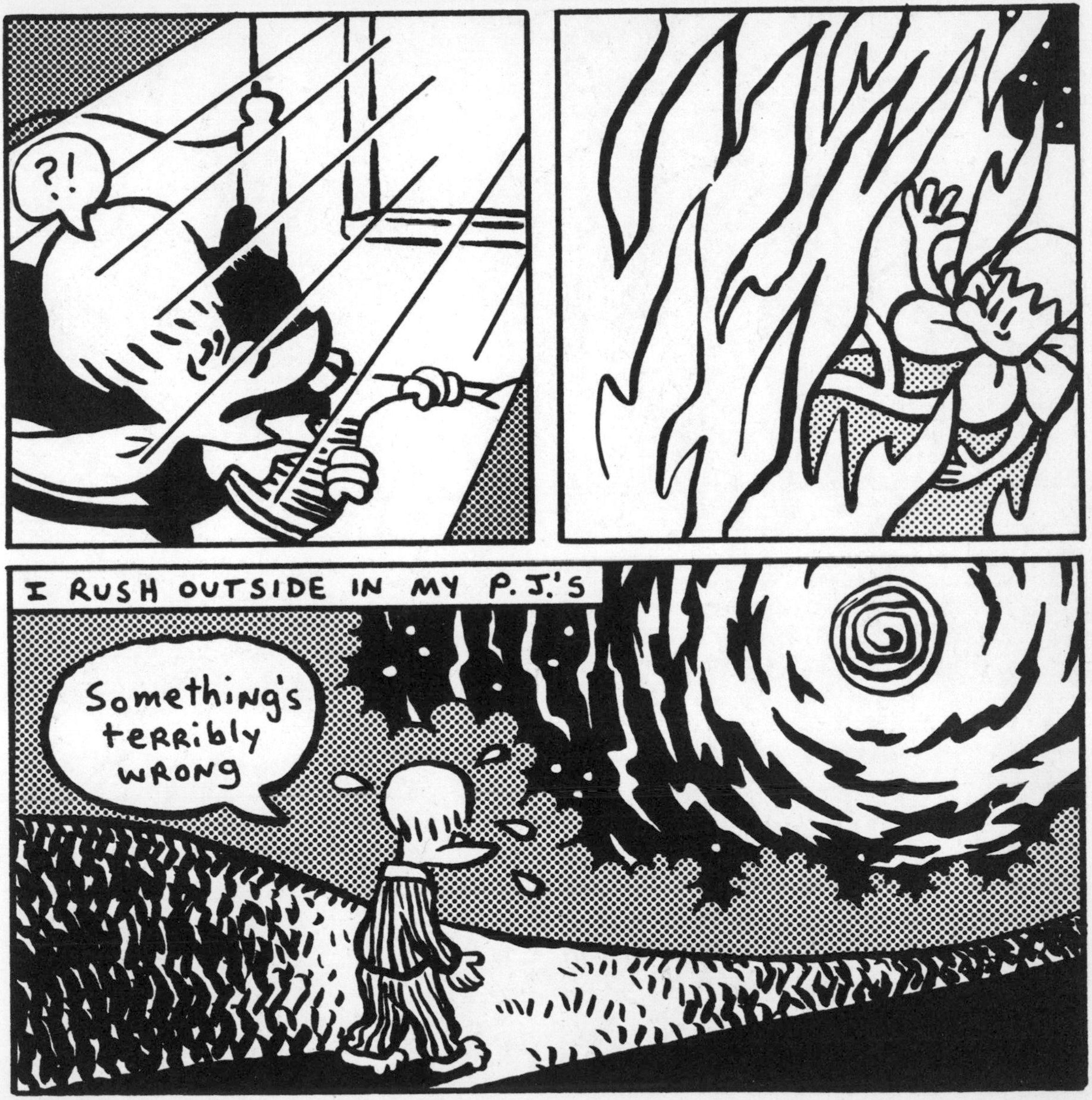
?!
I RUSH OUTSIDE IN MY P.J.'S
Something's terribly WRONG

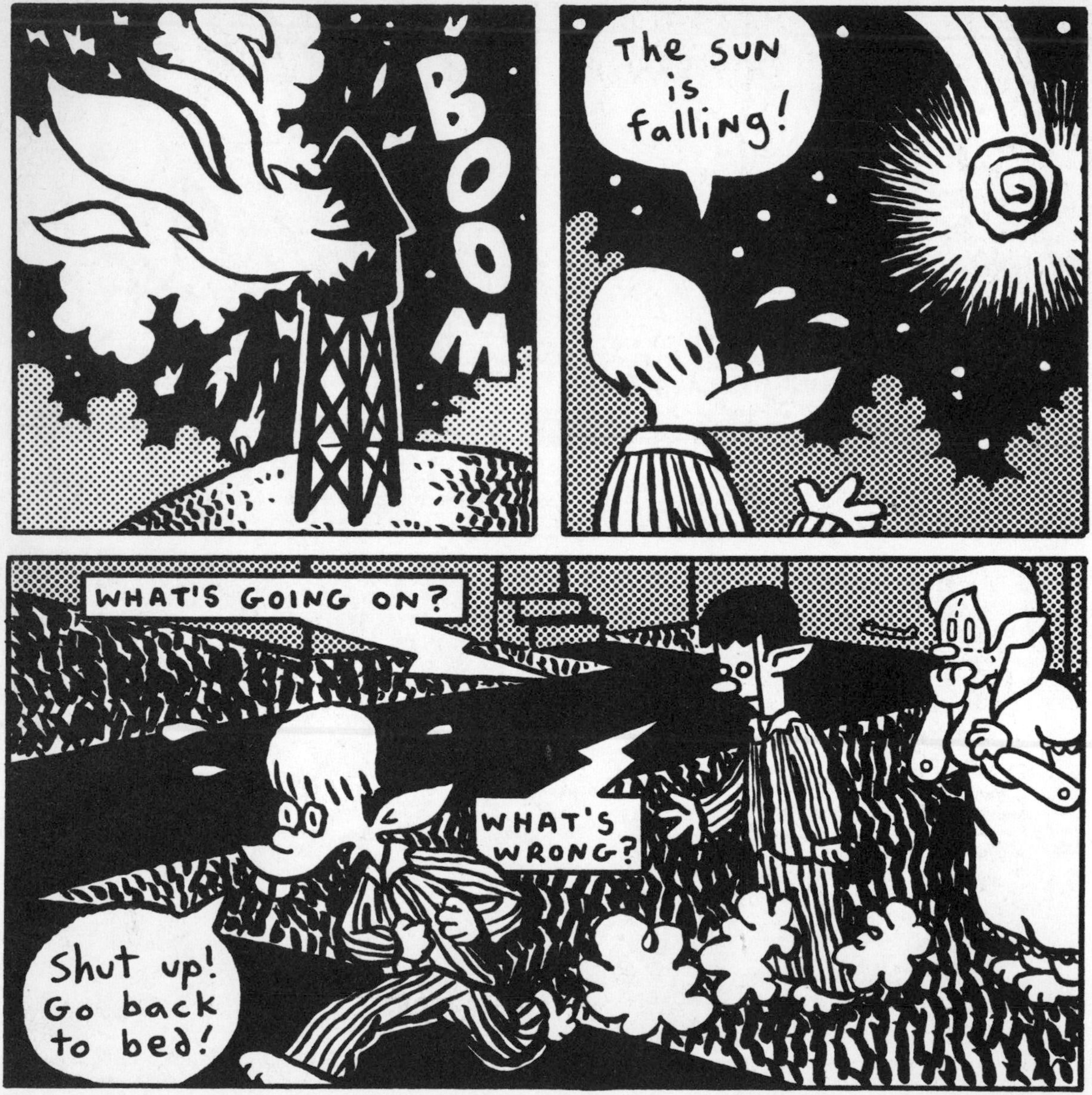
BOOM
The SUN is falling!
WHAT'S GOING ON?
WHAT'S WRONG?
Shut up! Go back to bed!

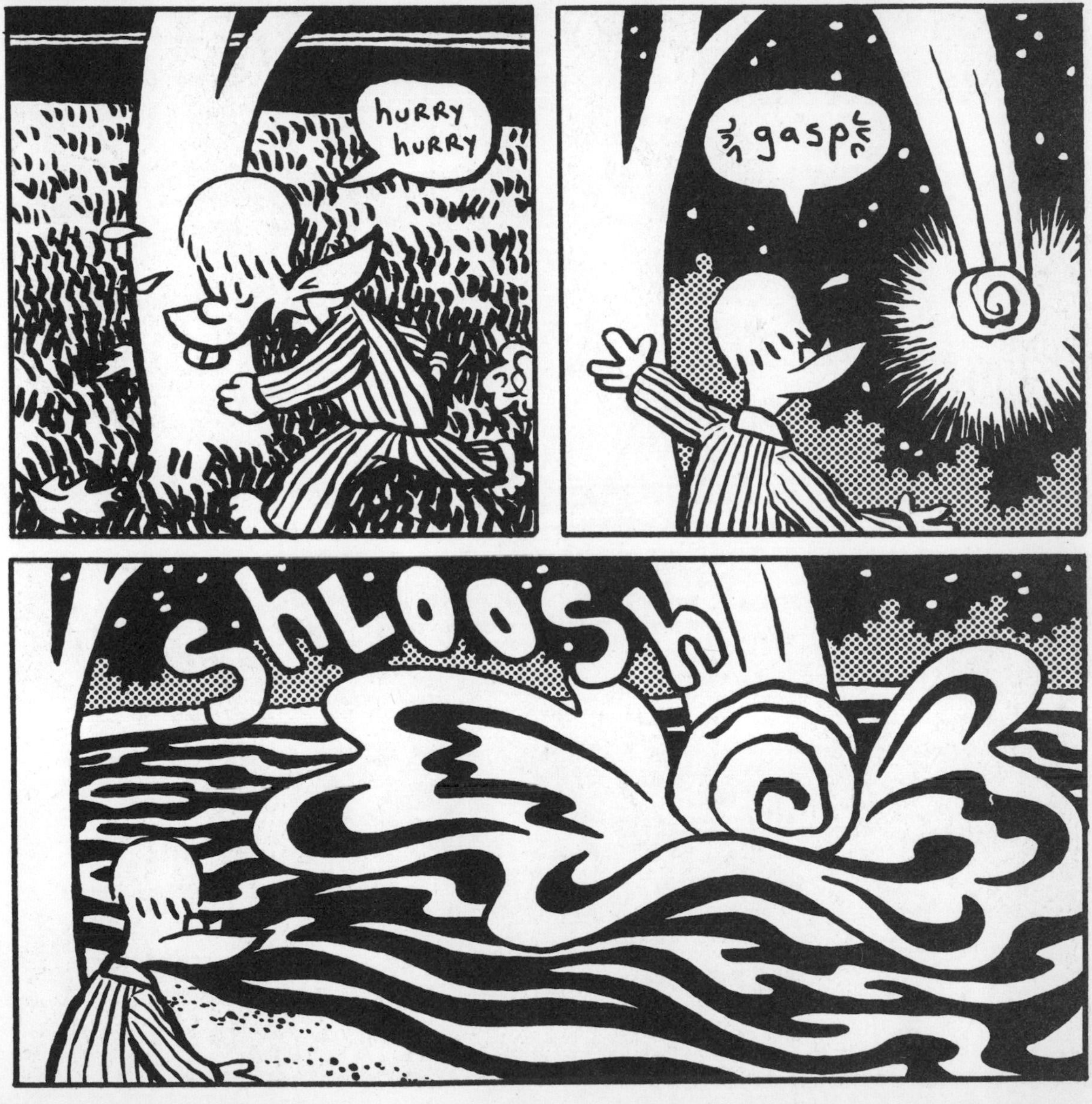
hurry hurry
gasp
SHLOOSH

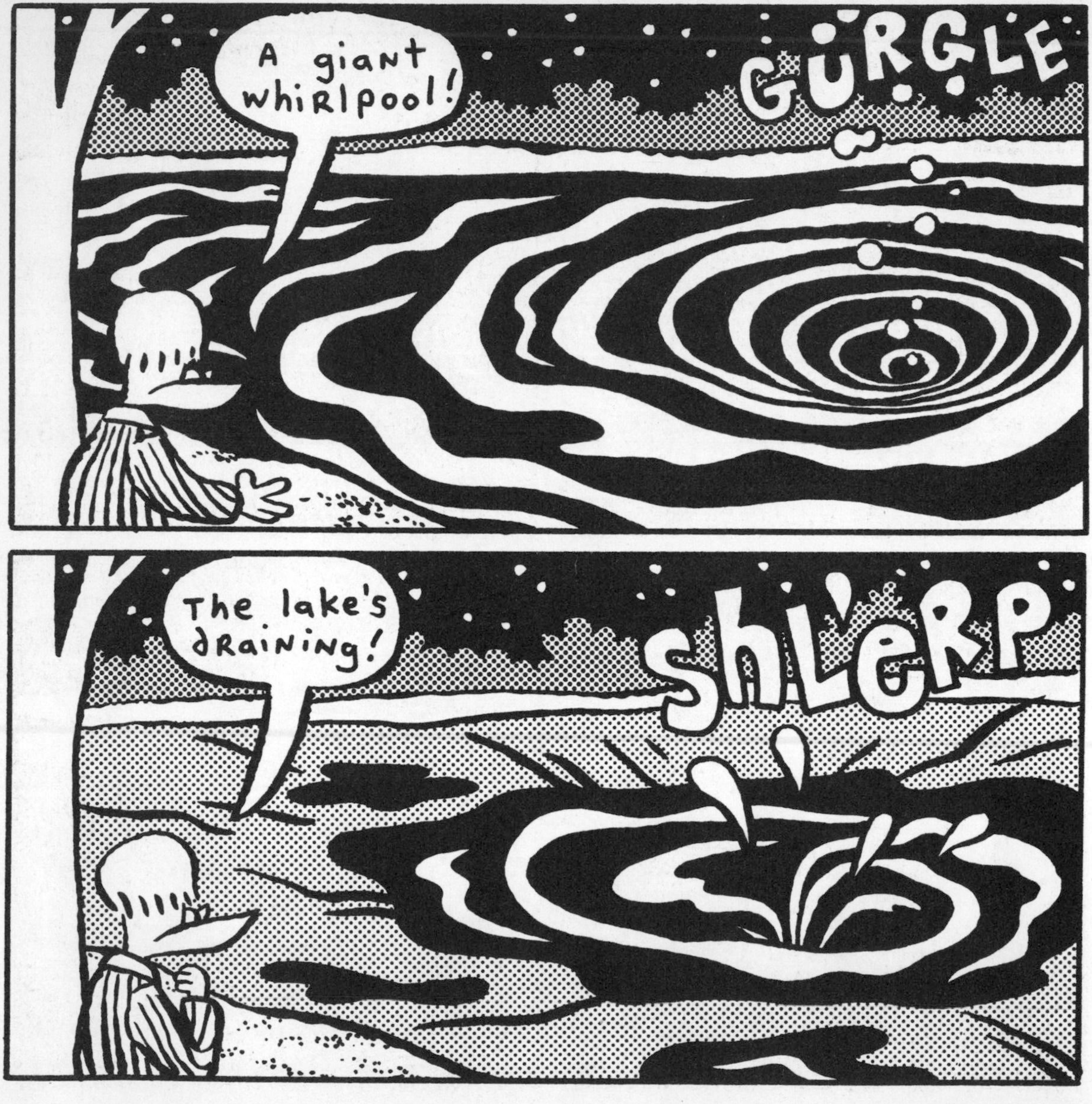
A giant whirlpool!
GURGLE
The lake's draining!
SHLERP

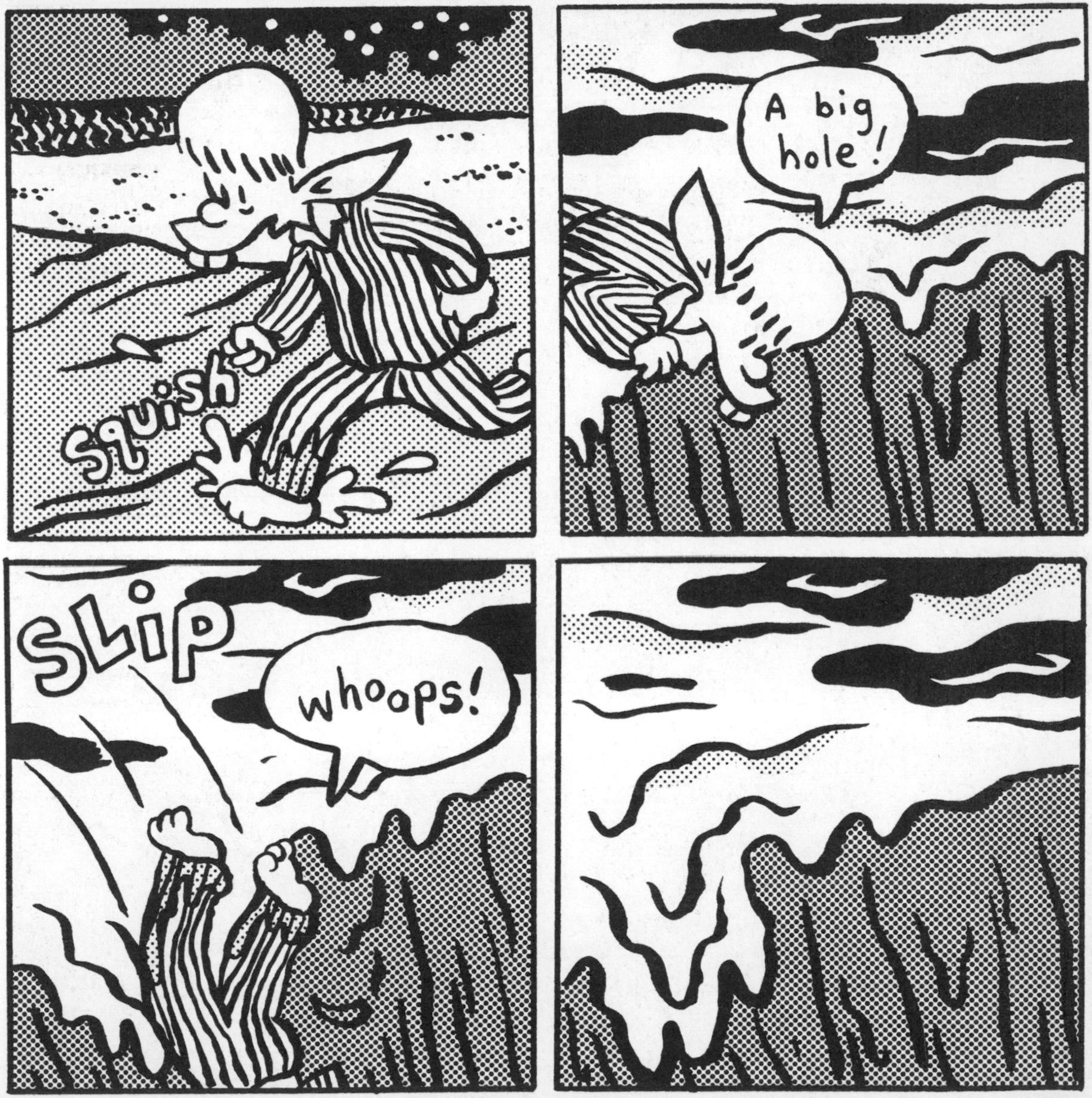
squish
A big hole!
SLIP
whoops!

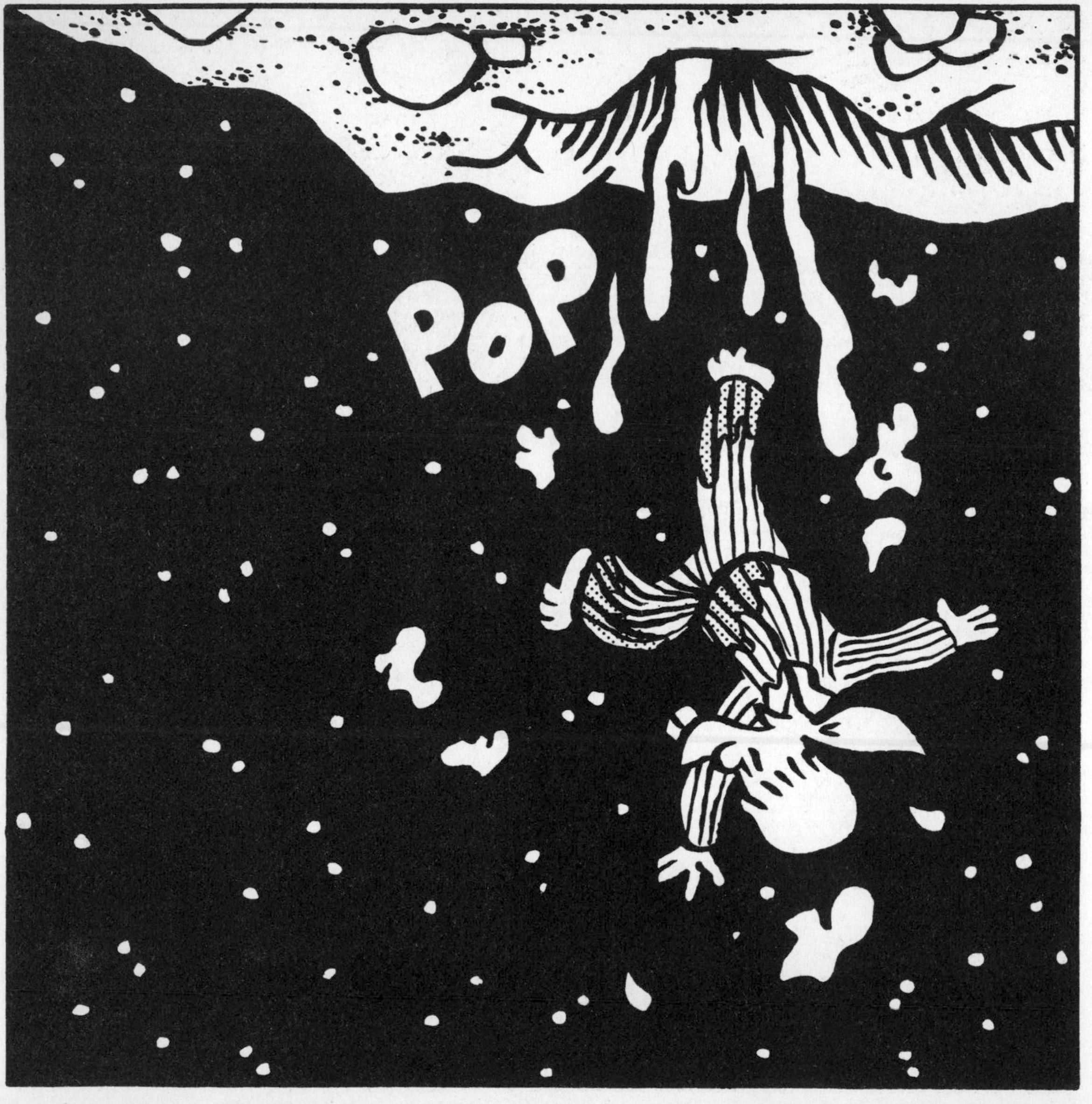
POP

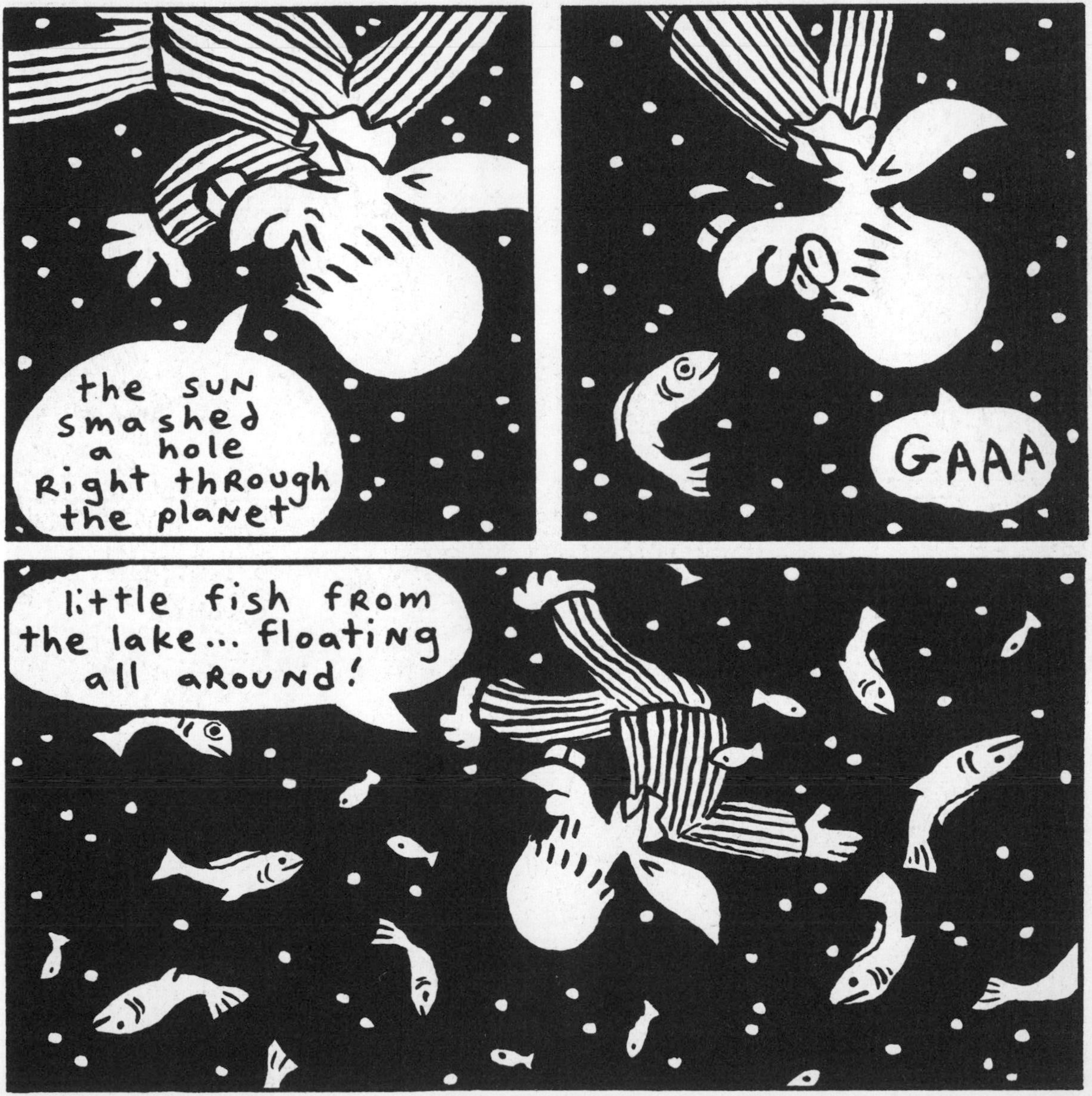
the SUN smashed a hole Right through the planet
GAAA
little fish FROM the lake... floating all aROUNd!

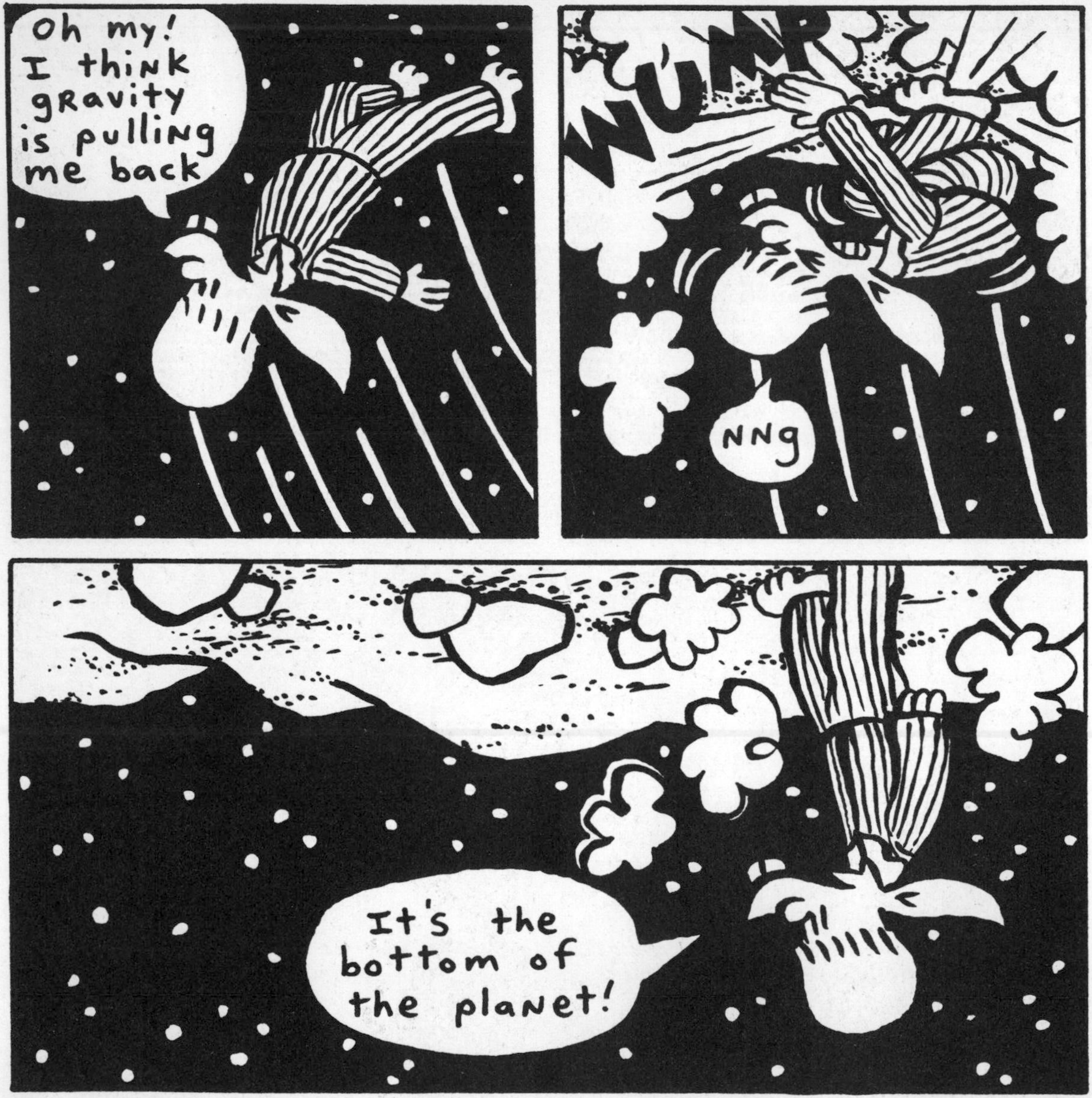
Oh my! I think gravity is pulling me back
WUMP
NNG
It's the bottom of the planet!

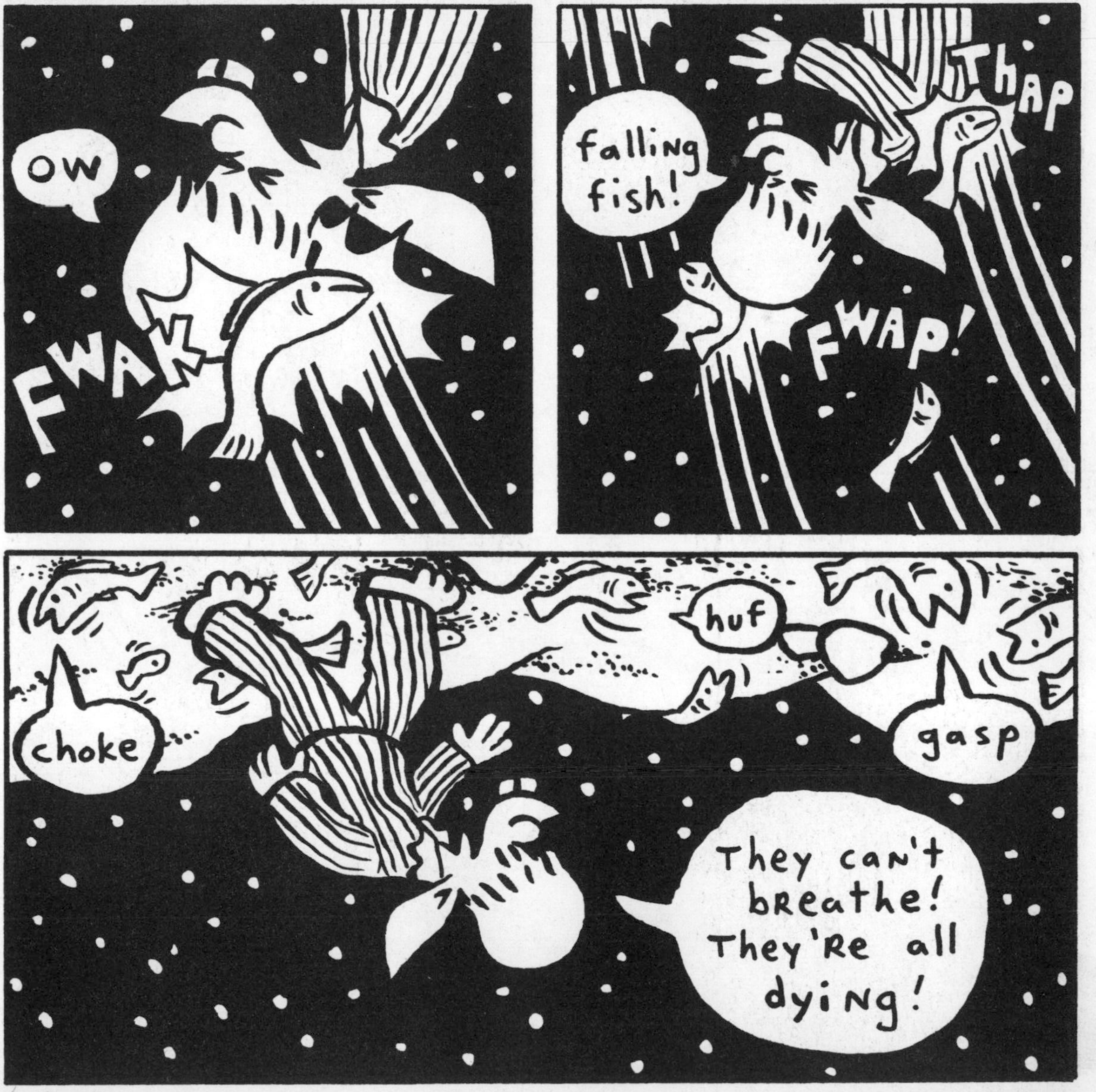
OW
FWAK
falling fish!
THAP
FWAP!
choke
huf
gasp
They can't breathe! They're all dying!

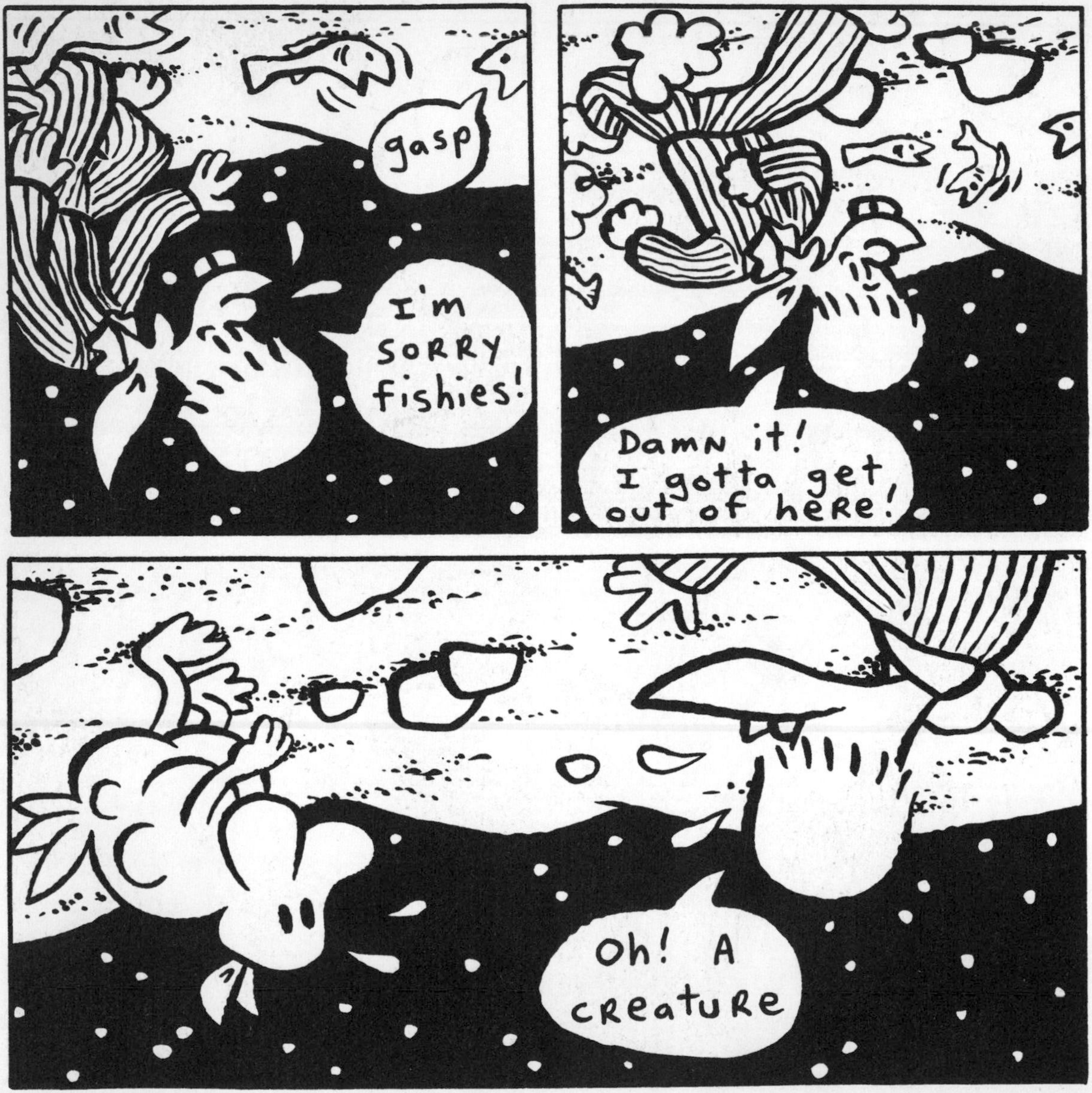
gasp
I'm SORRY fishies!
Damn it! I gotta get out of here!
Oh! A creature

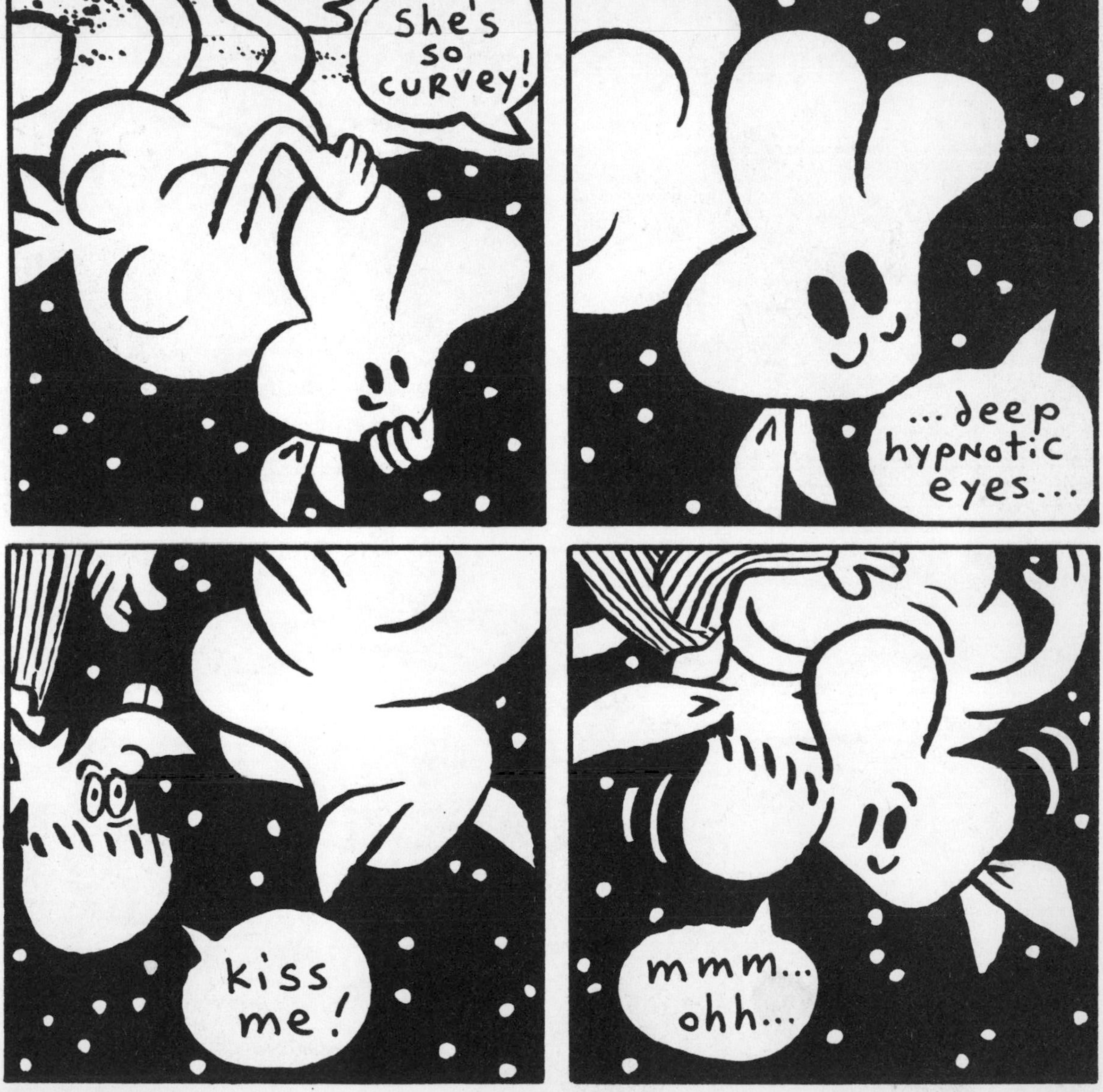
She's so curvey!
...deep hypnotic eyes...
kiss me!
mmm... ohh...

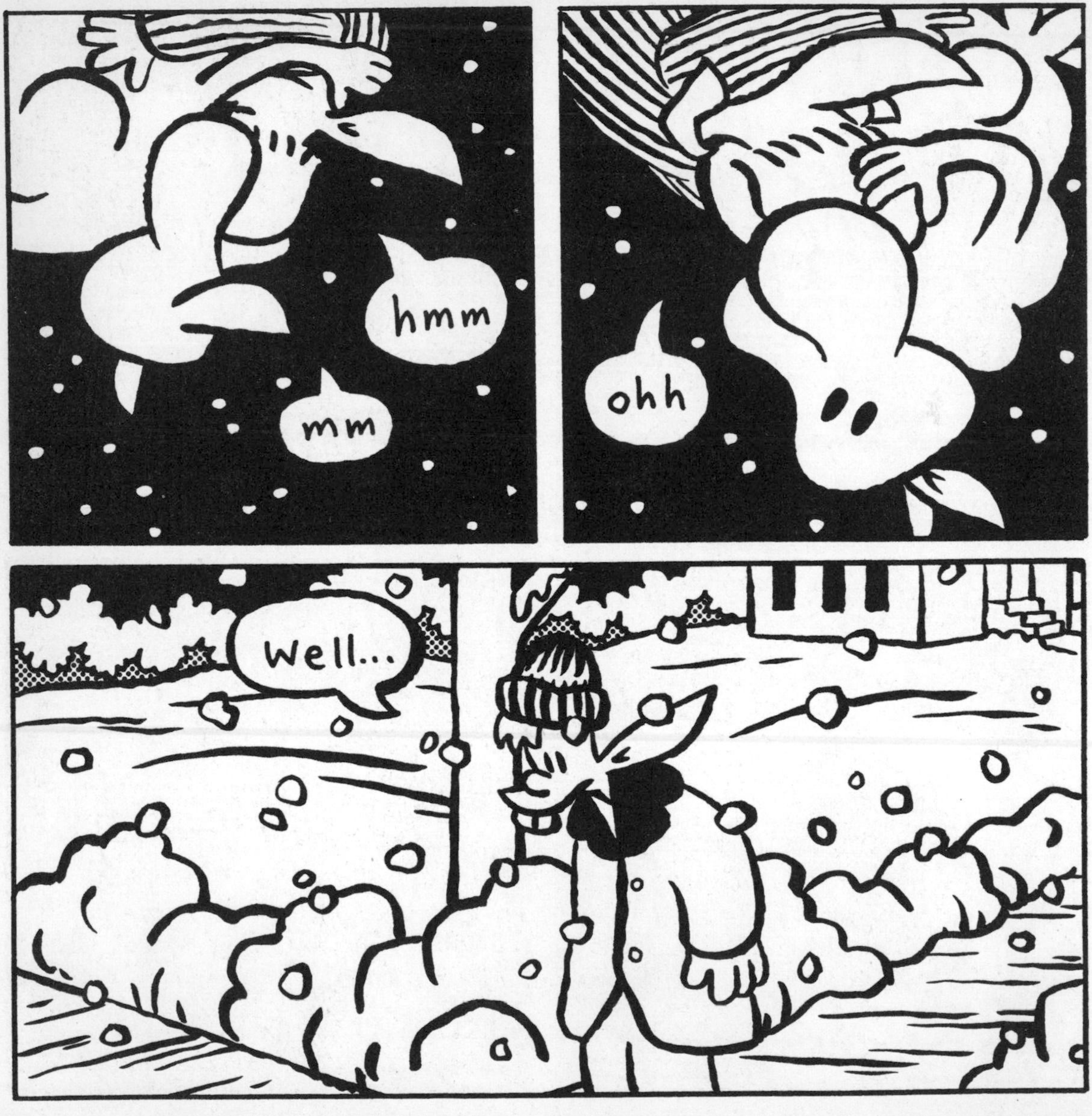
hmm
mm
ohh
Well...

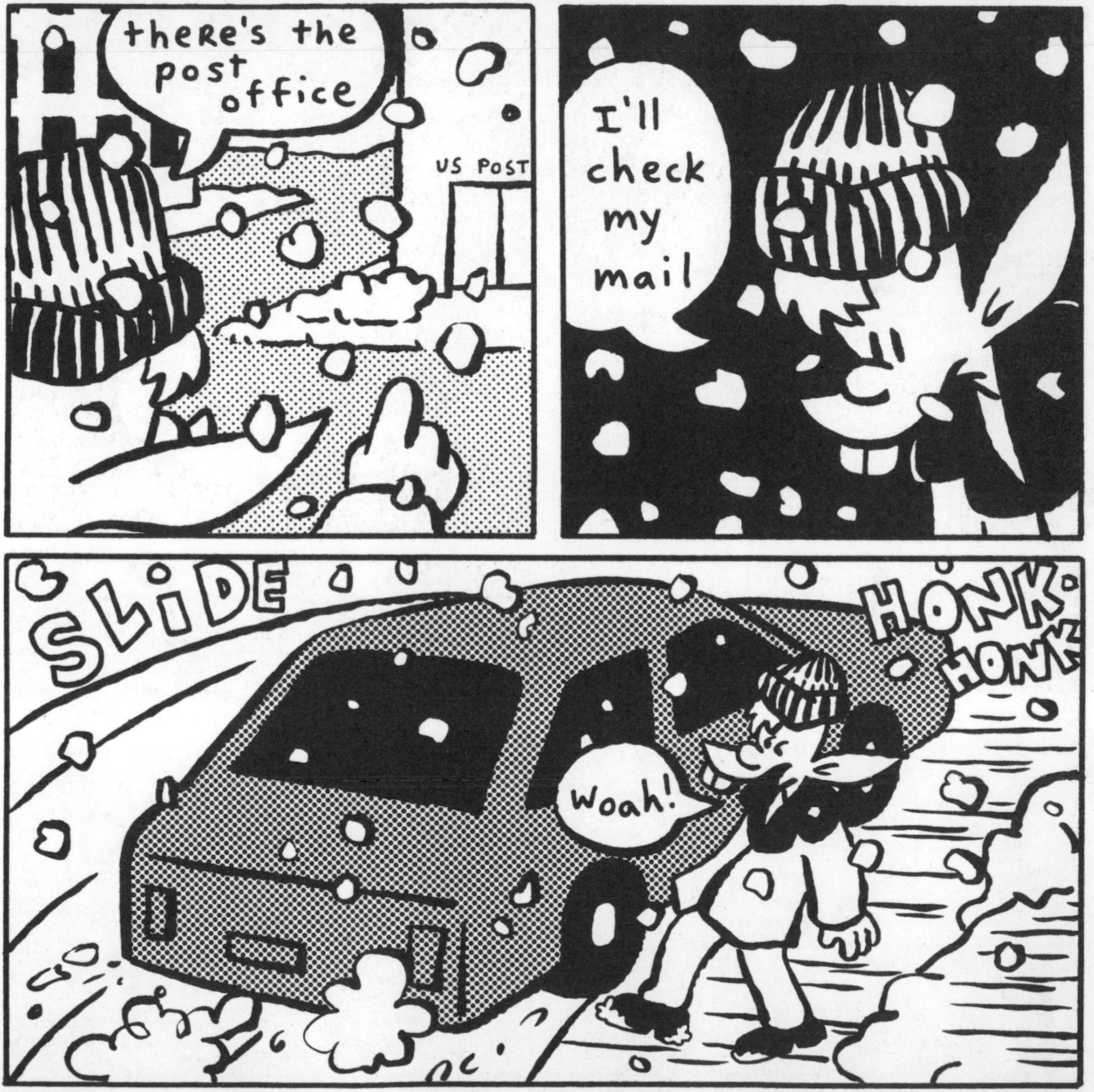
there's the post office
US POST
I'll check my mail
SLIDE
HONK
HONK
Woah!

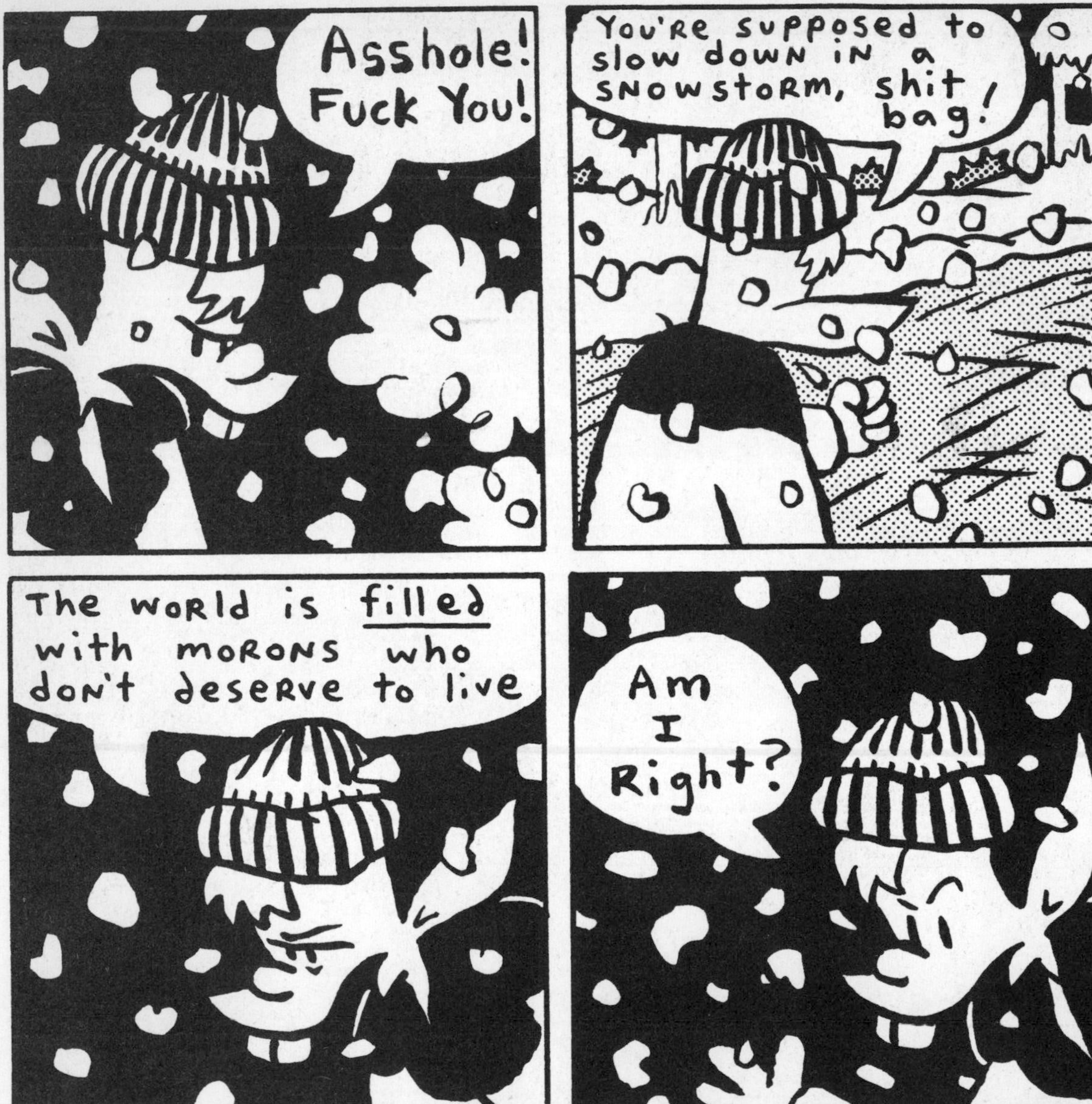
Asshole! Fuck You!
You're supposed to slow down in a snowstorm, shit bag!
The world is filled with morons who don't deserve to live
Am I Right?

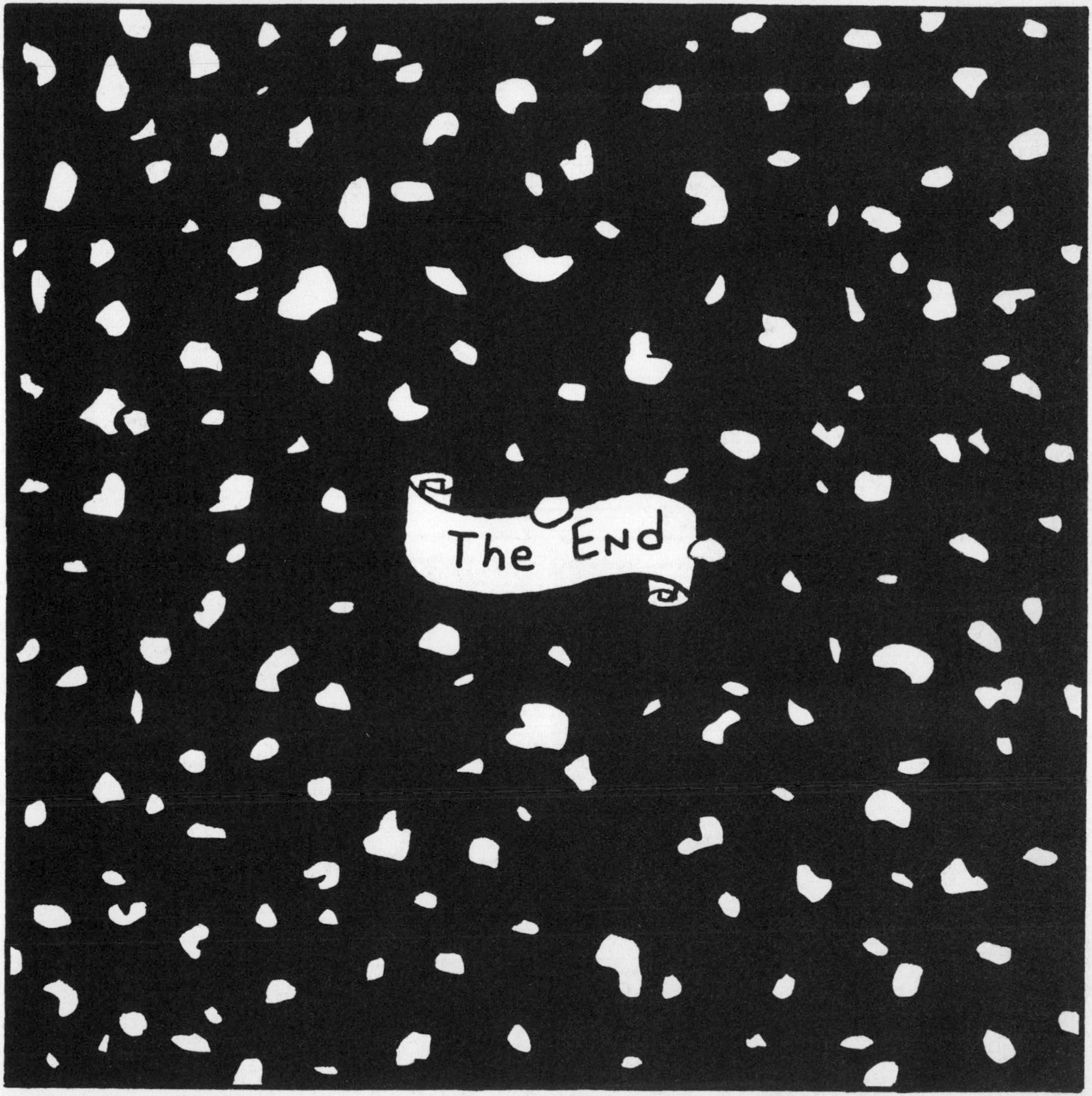
The End

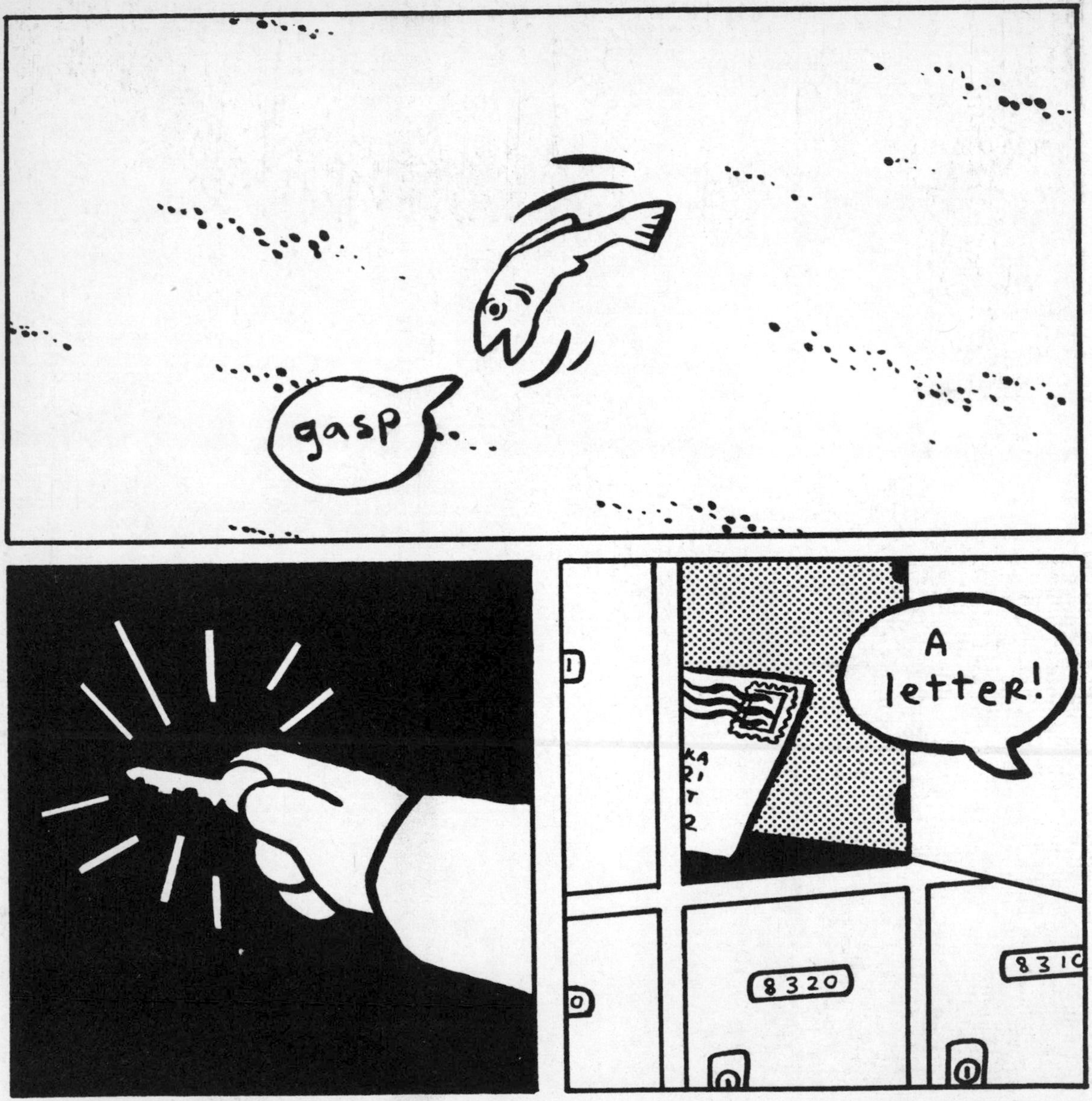
gasp
A letter!
8320

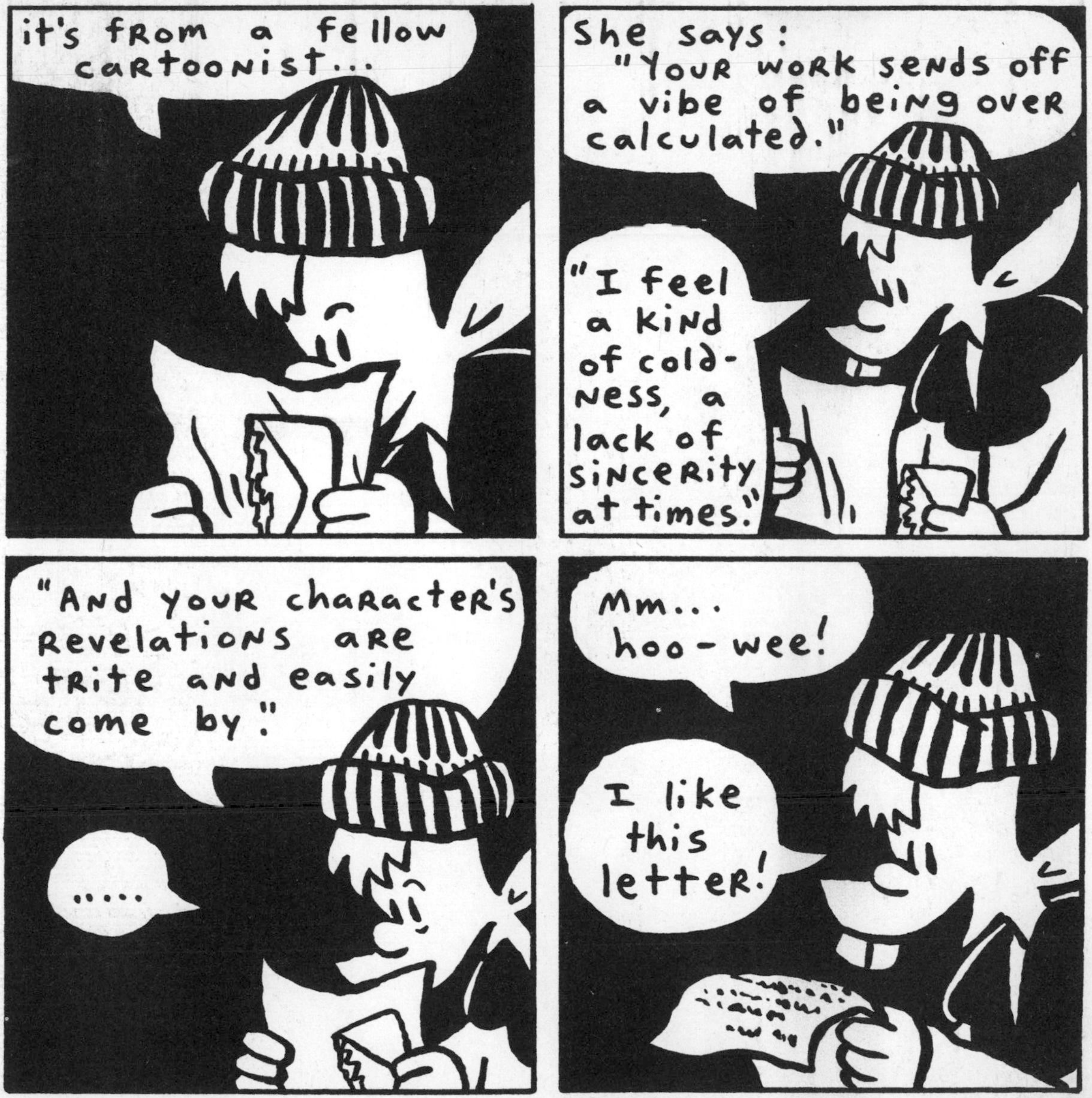
it's from a fellow cartoonist...
She says: "Your work sends off a vibe of being over calculated."
"I feel a kind of coldness, a lack of sincerity at times."
"And your character's revelations are trite and easily come by."
.....
Mm... hoo-wee!
I like this letter!

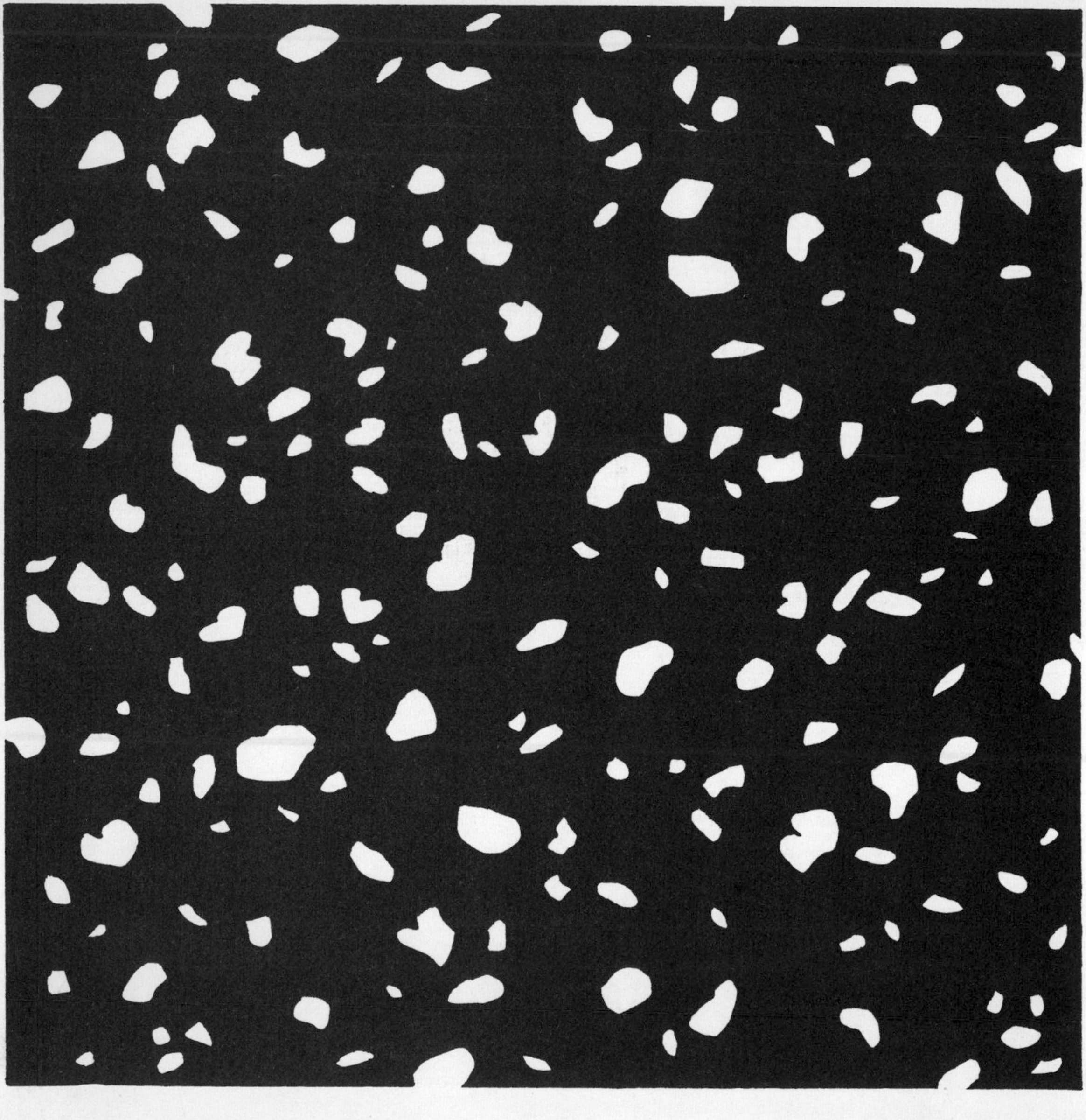

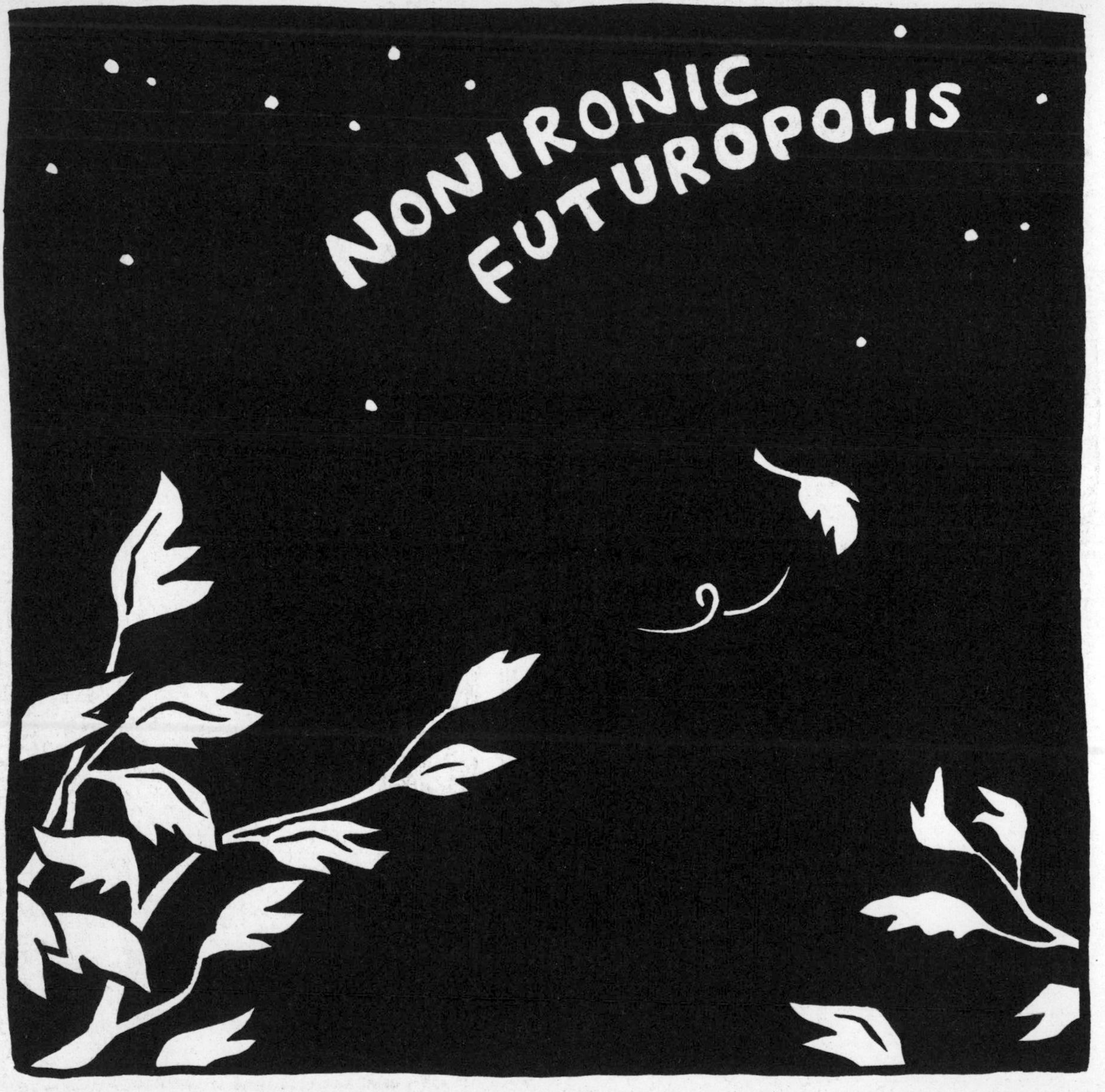
NONIRONIC
FUTUROPOLIS

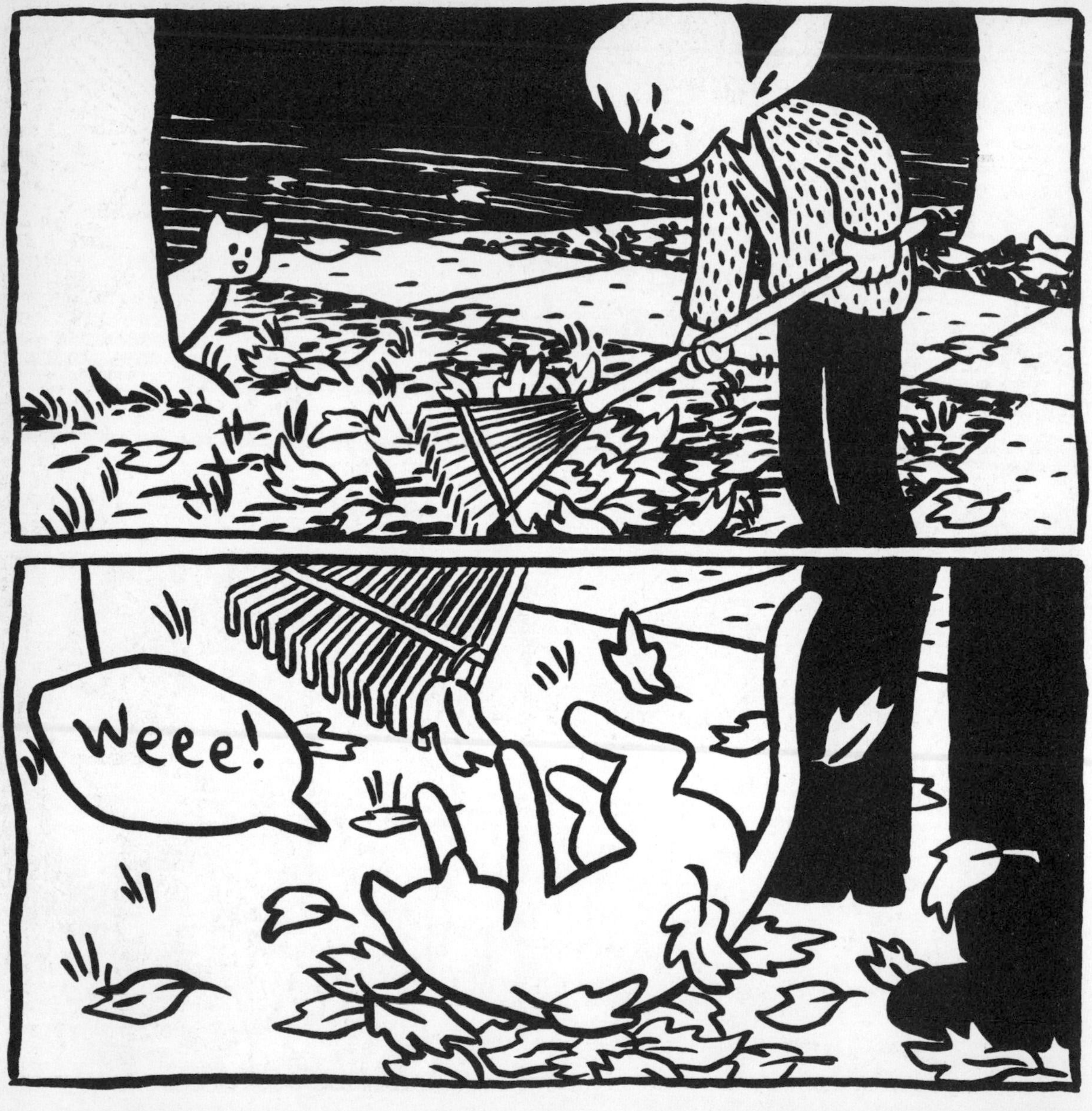
weee!

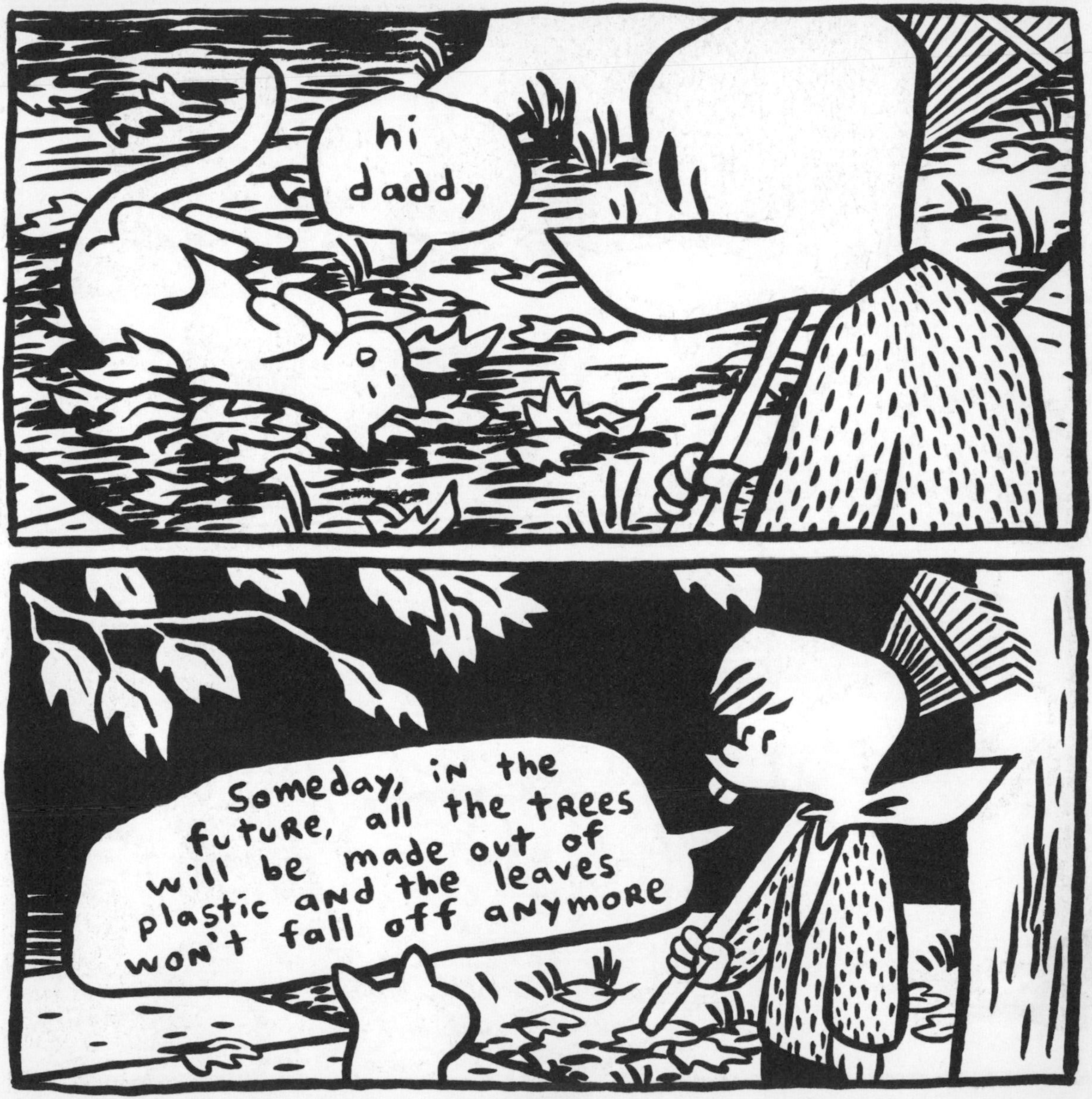
hi daddy
Someday, in the future, all the trees will be made out of plastic and the leaves won't fall off anymore

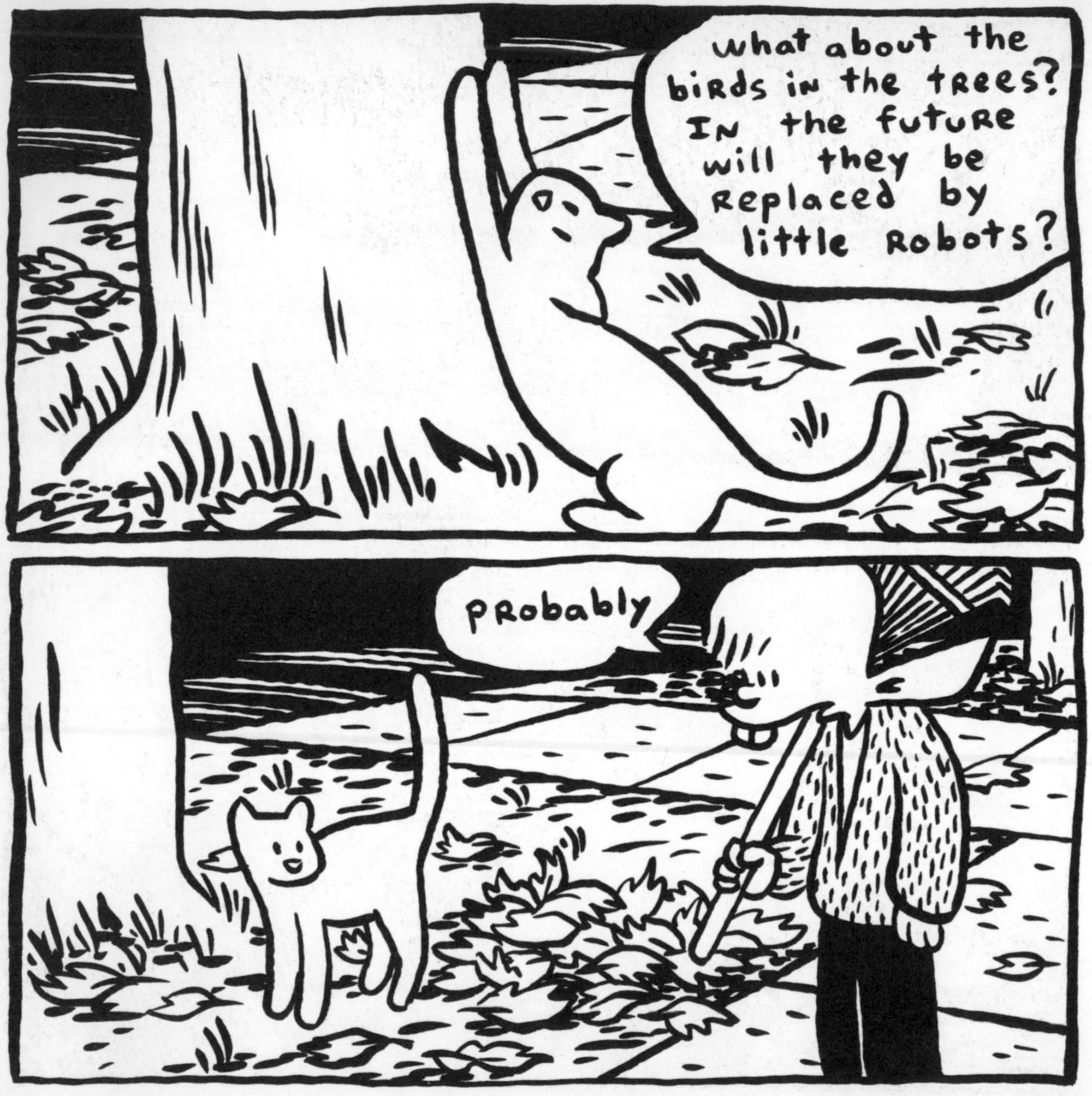
what about the birds in the trees? In the future will they be replaced by little Robots?
probably

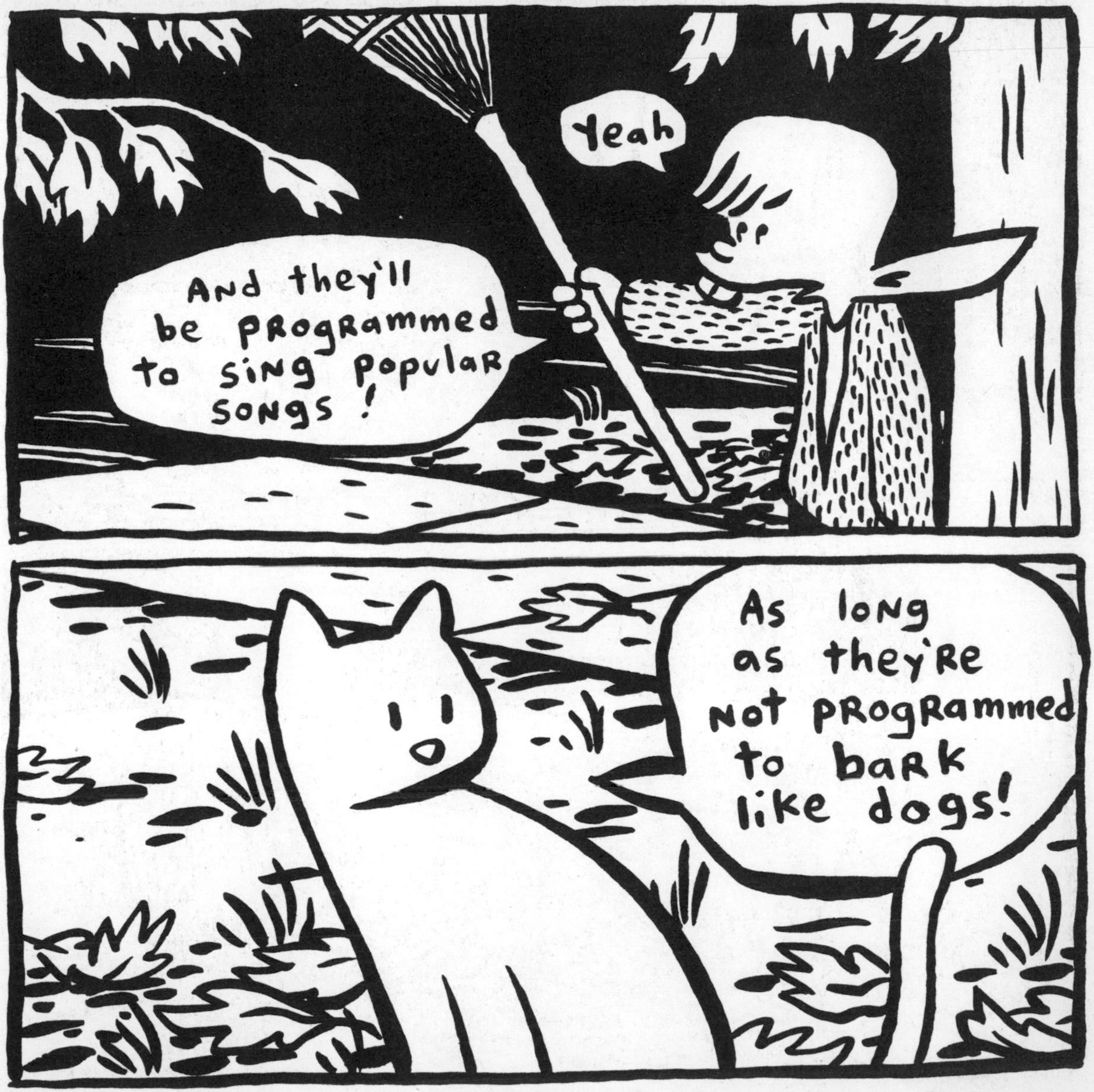
Yeah
And they'll be programmed to sing popular songs!
As long as they're not programmed to bark like dogs!

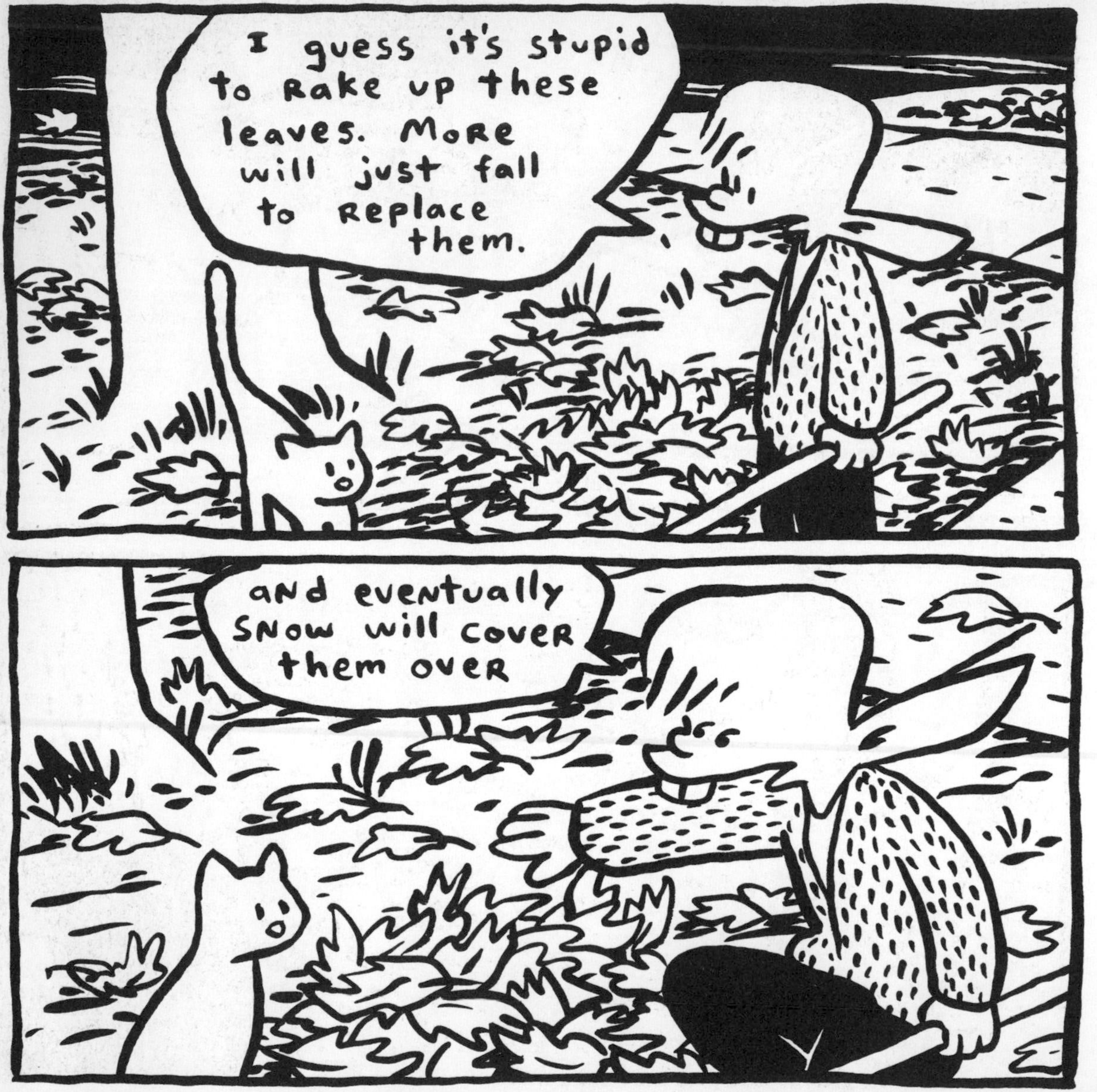
I guess it's stupid to rake up these leaves. More will just fall to replace them.
and eventually snow will cover them over

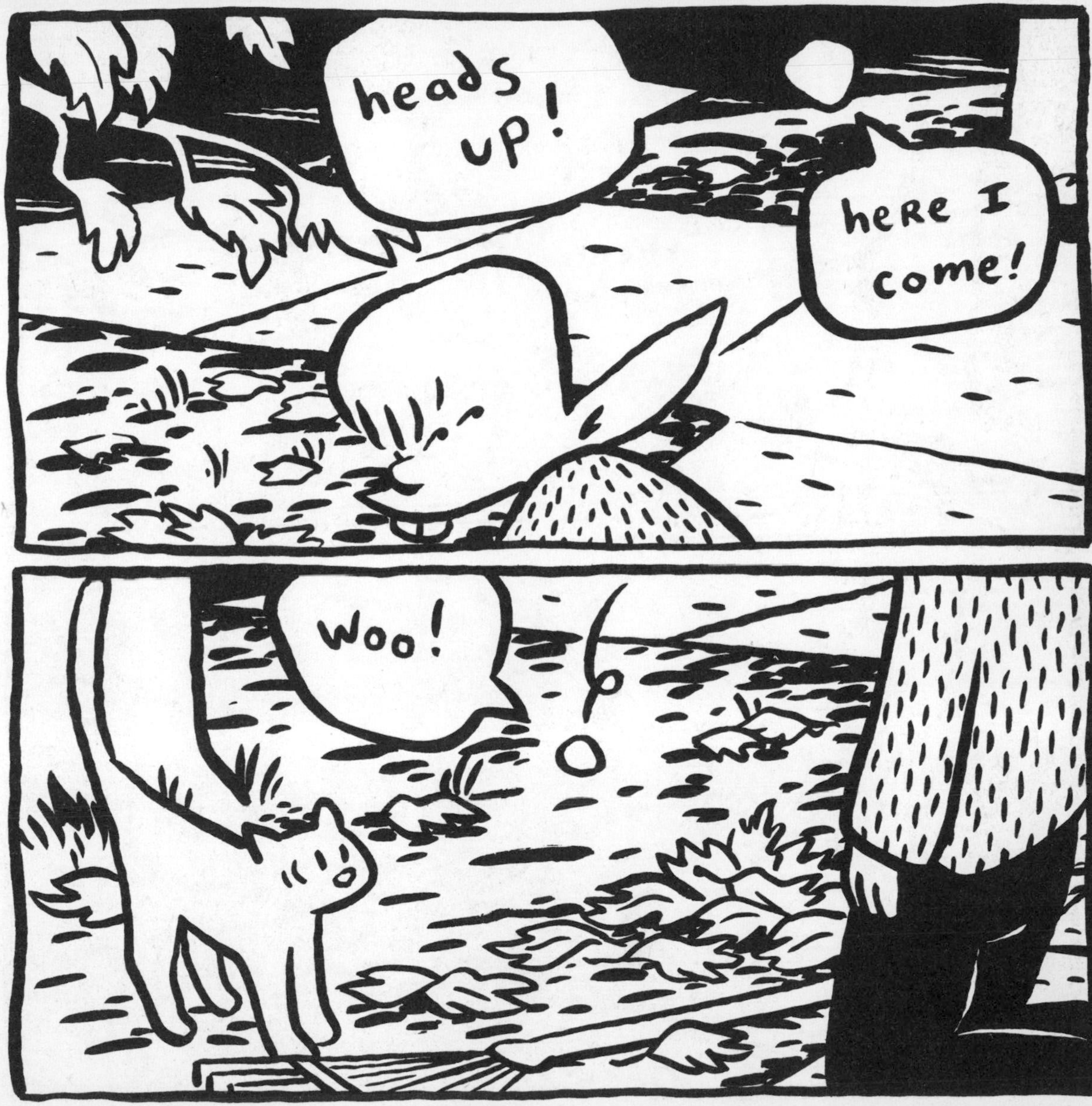
heads up!
here I come!
woo!

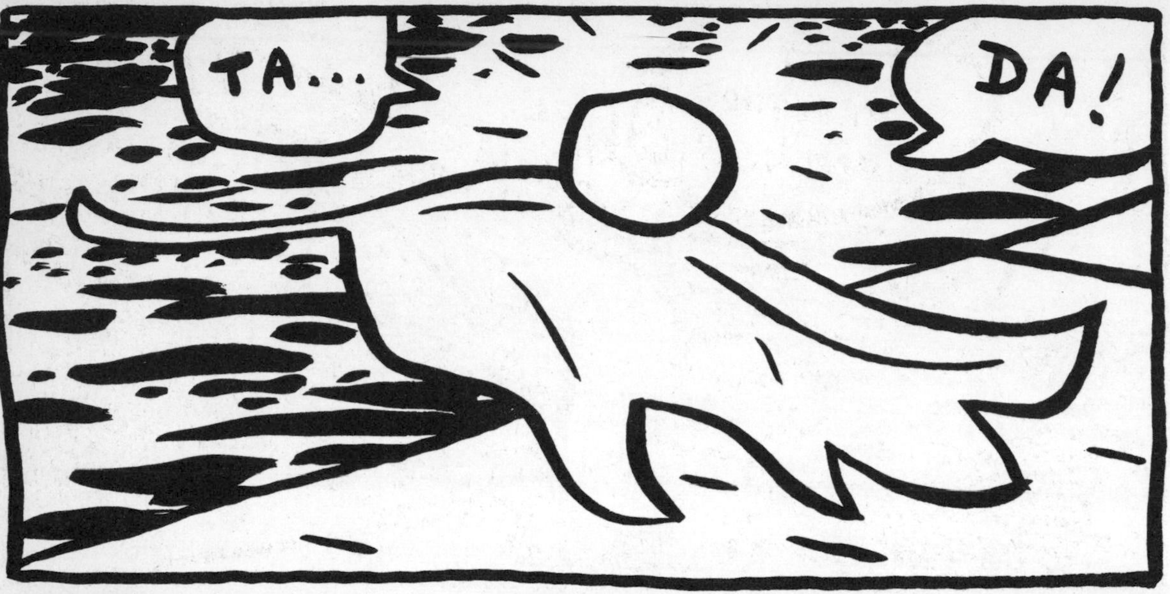
TA...
DA!

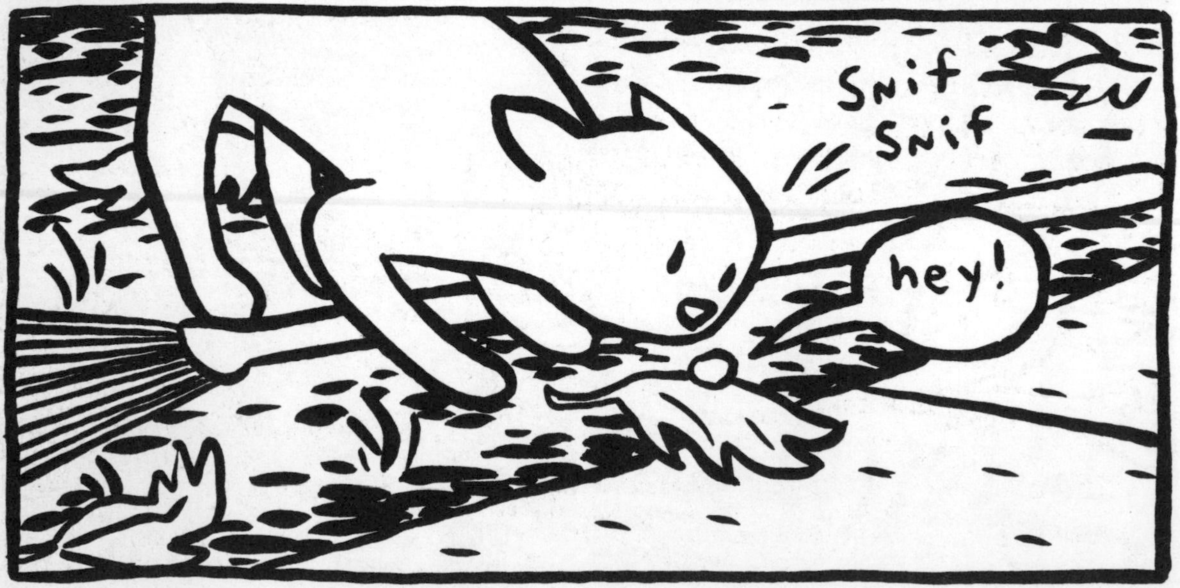
SNIF
SNIF
hey!

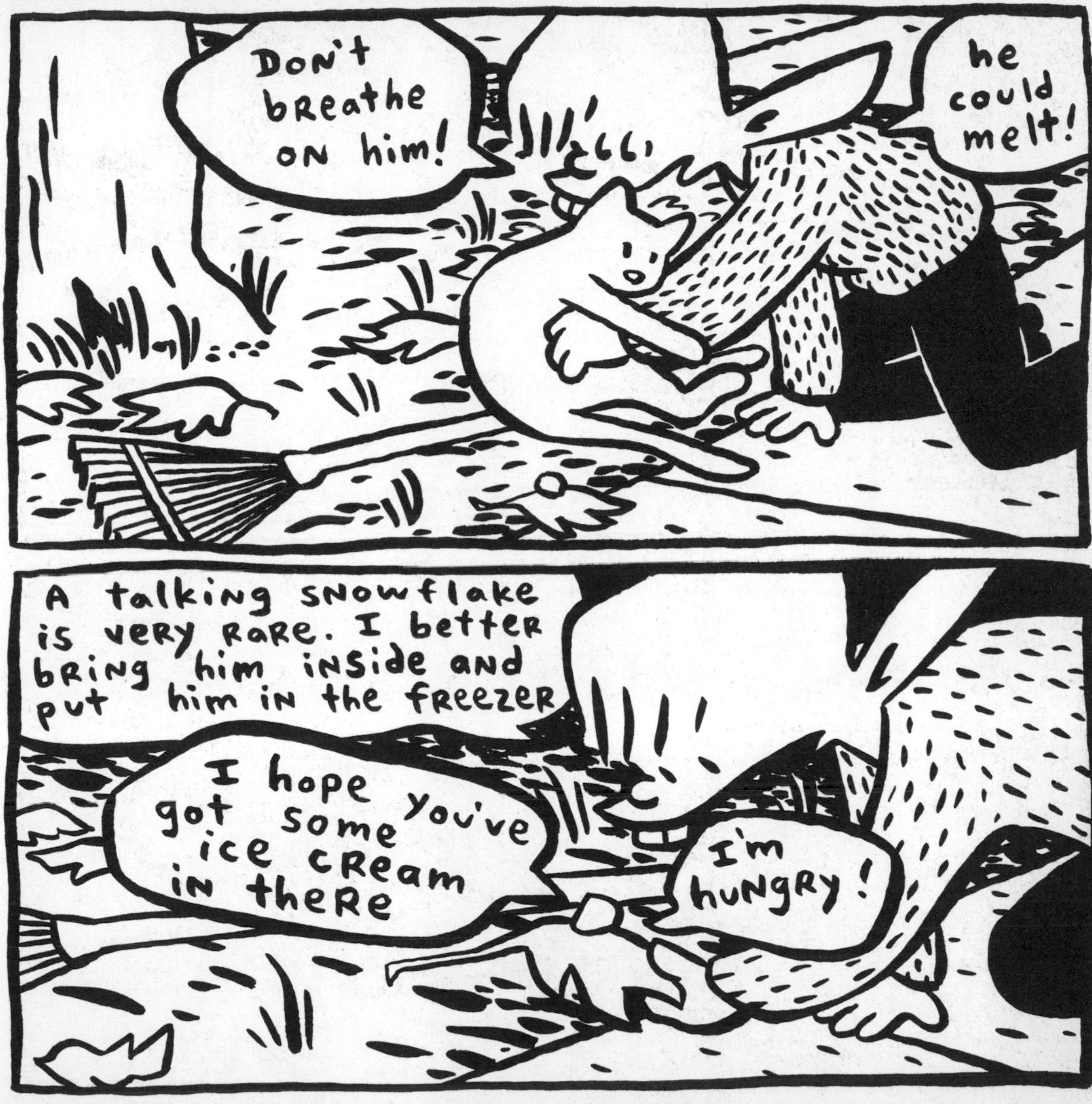
Don't breathe on him!
he could melt!
A talking snowflake is very rare. I better bring him inside and put him in the freezer
I hope you've got some ice cream in there
I'm hungry!

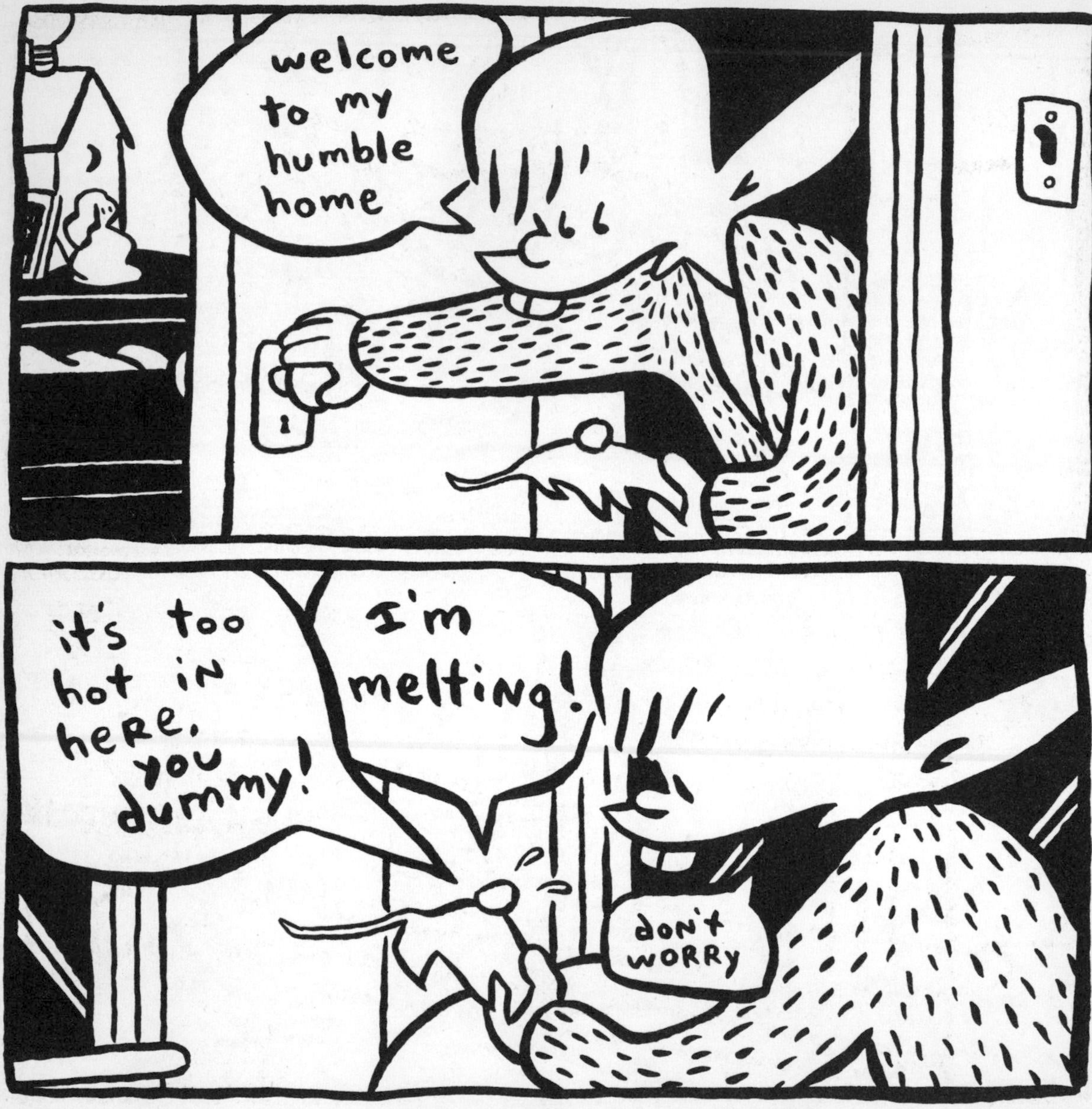
welcome to my humble home
it's too hot in here, you dummy!
I'm melting!
don't worry

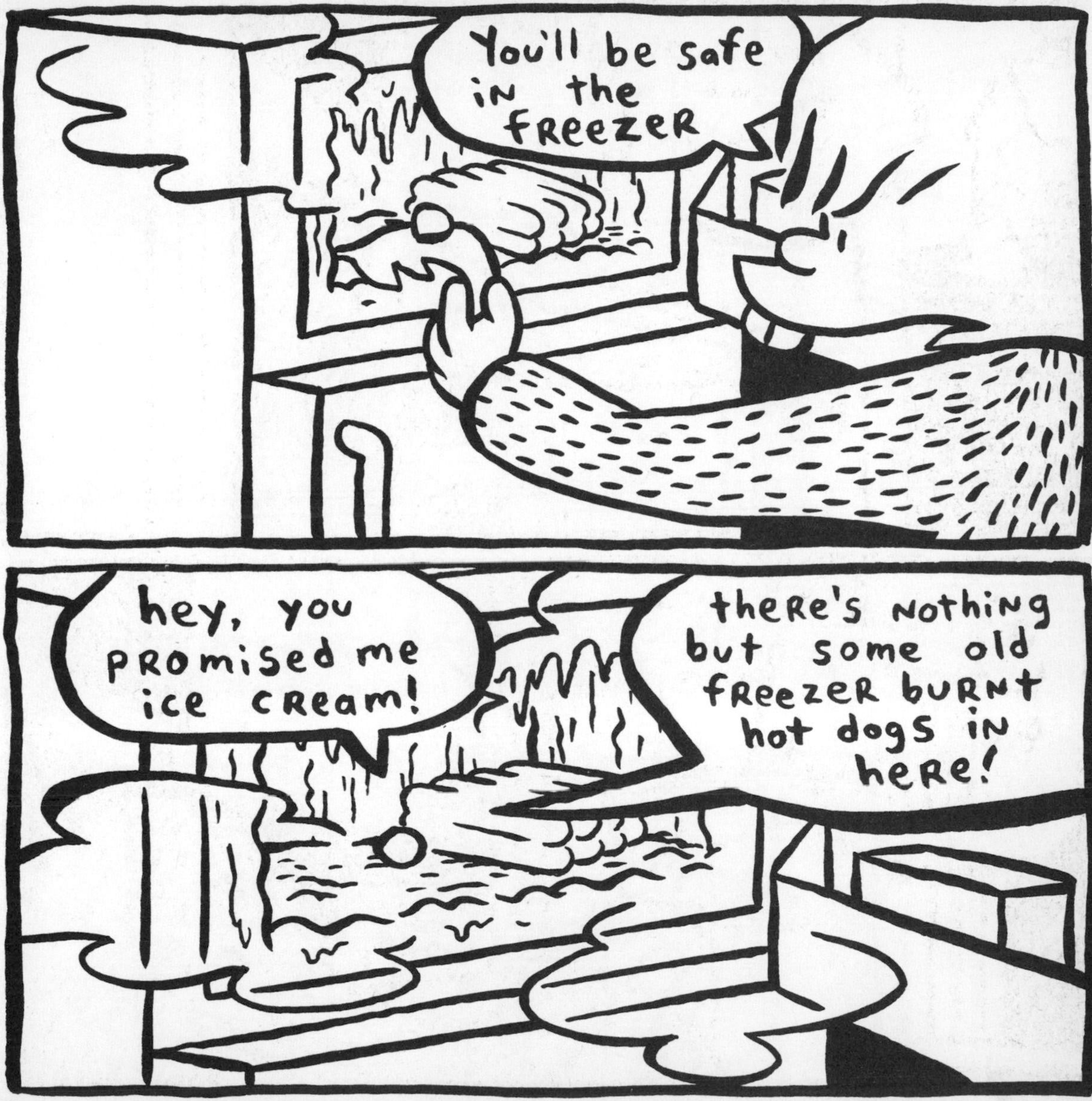
You'll be safe in the freezer
hey, you promised me ice cream!
there's nothing but some old freezer burnt hot dogs in here!

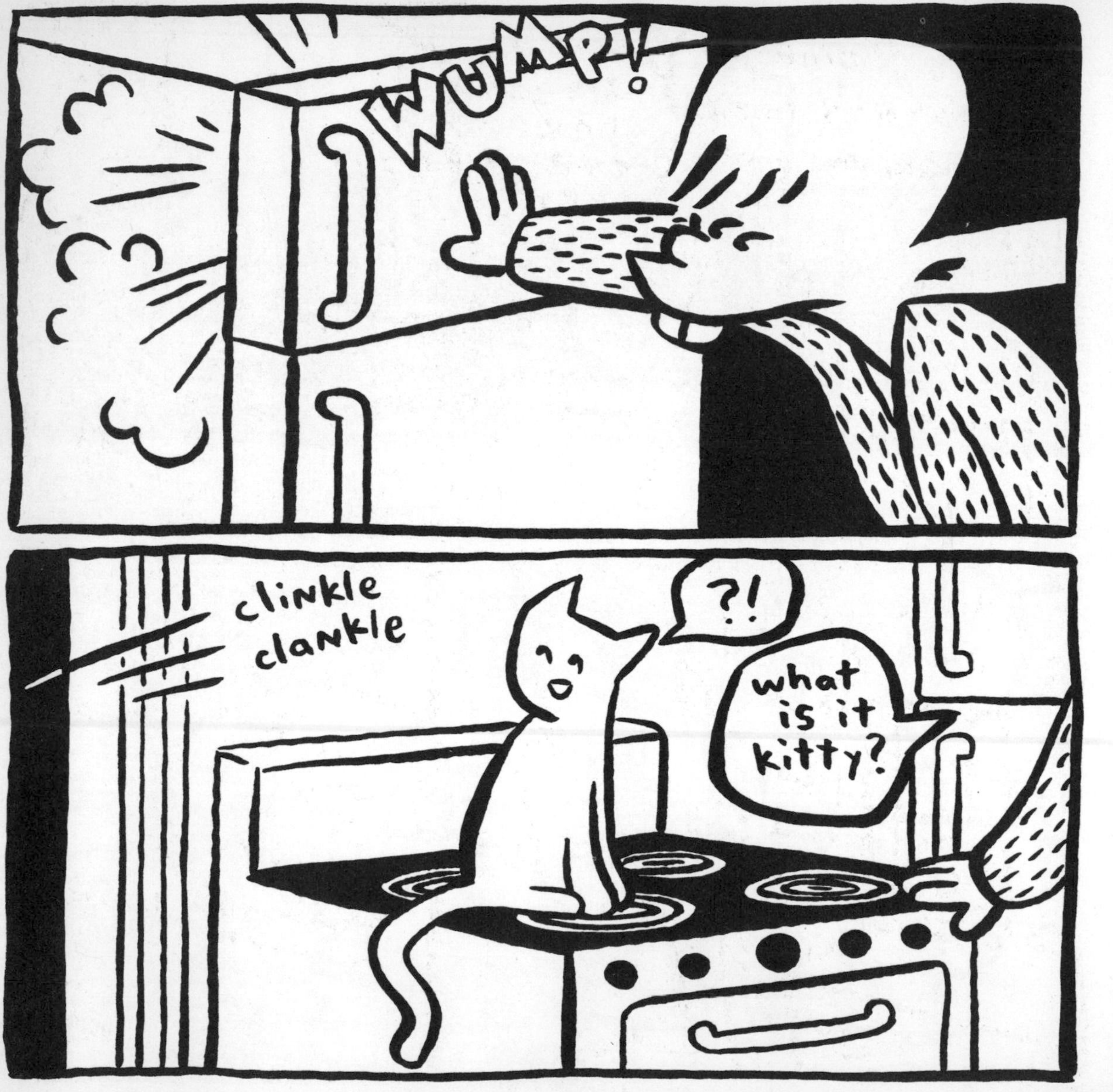
WUMP!
clinkle clankle
?!
what is it kitty?

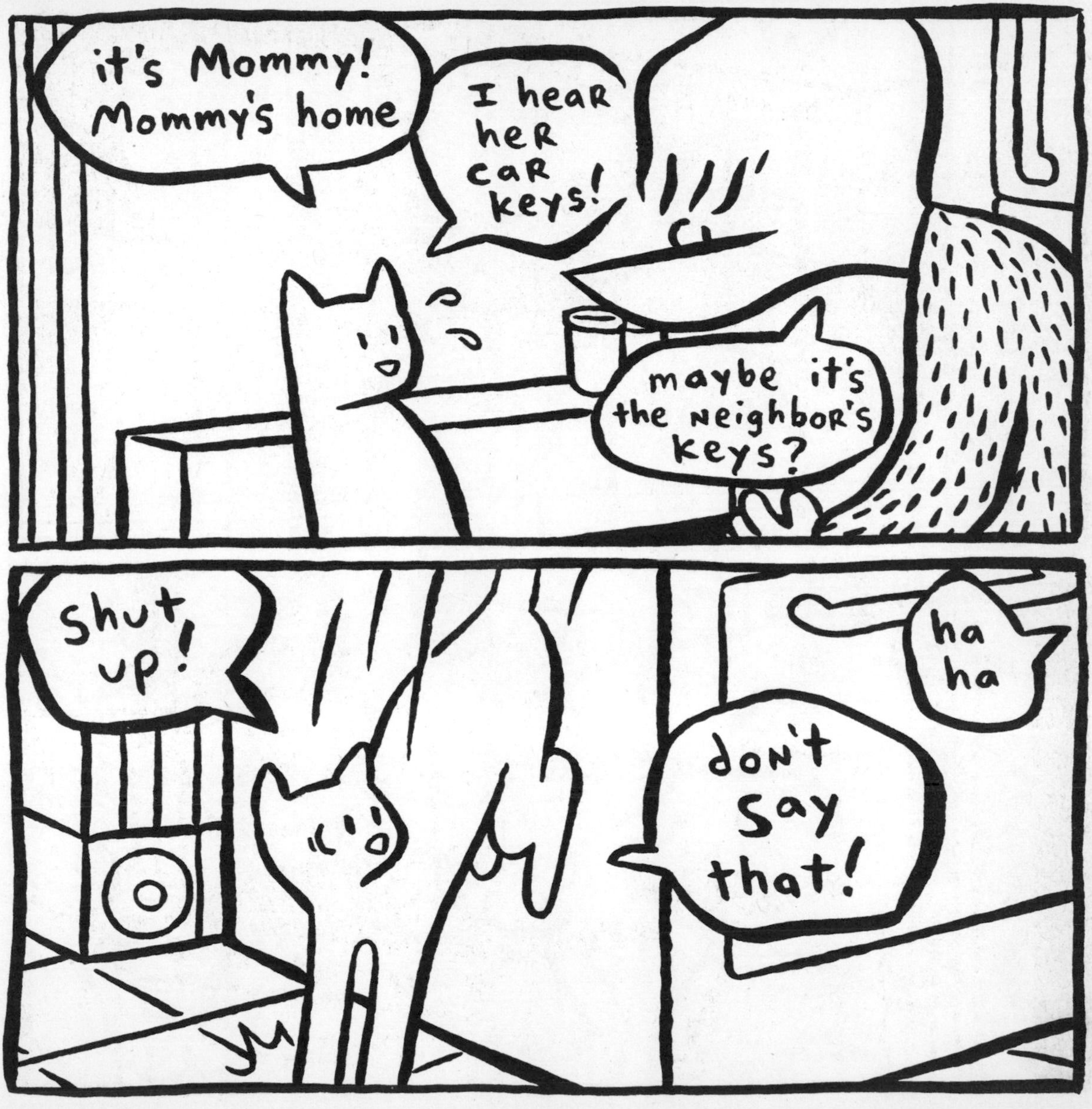
it's Mommy! Mommy's home
I hear her car keys!
maybe it's the neighbor's keys?
Shut up!
ha ha
don't say that!

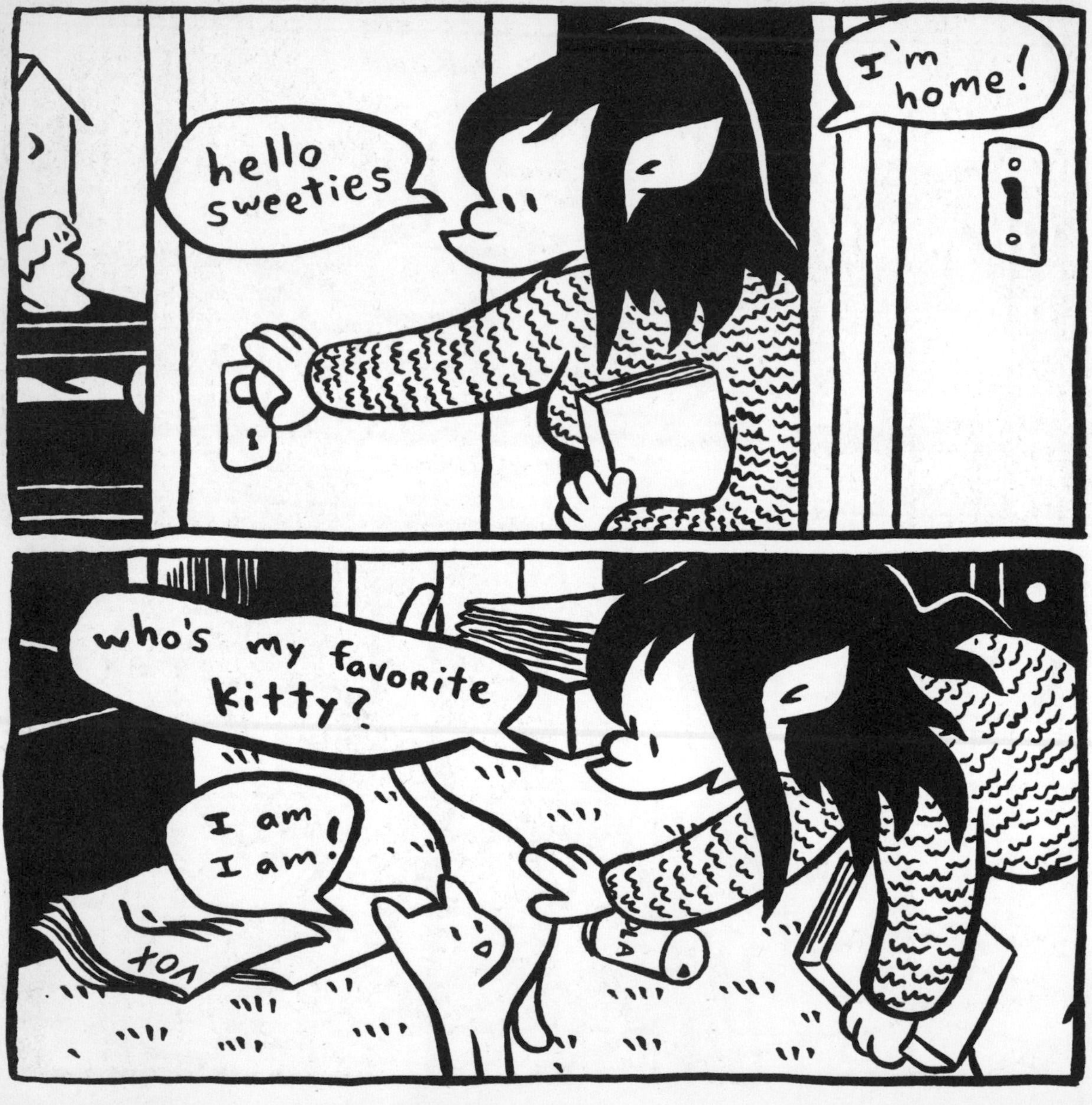
I'm home!
hello sweeties
who's my favorite kitty?
I am I am!
VOX

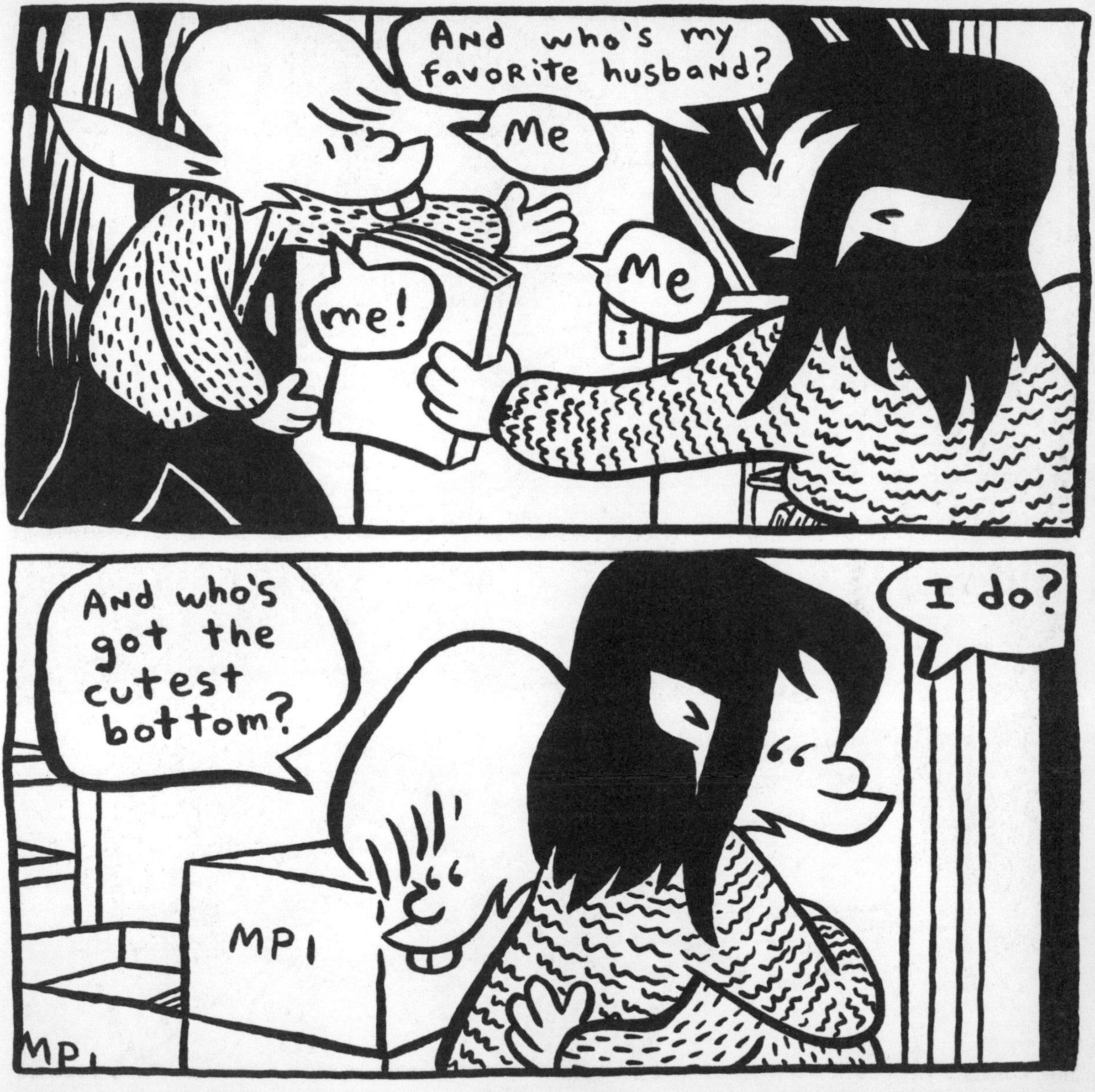
AND who's my favoRite husbaND?
Me
me!
Me
AND who's got the cutest bottom?
I do?
MP1
MP1

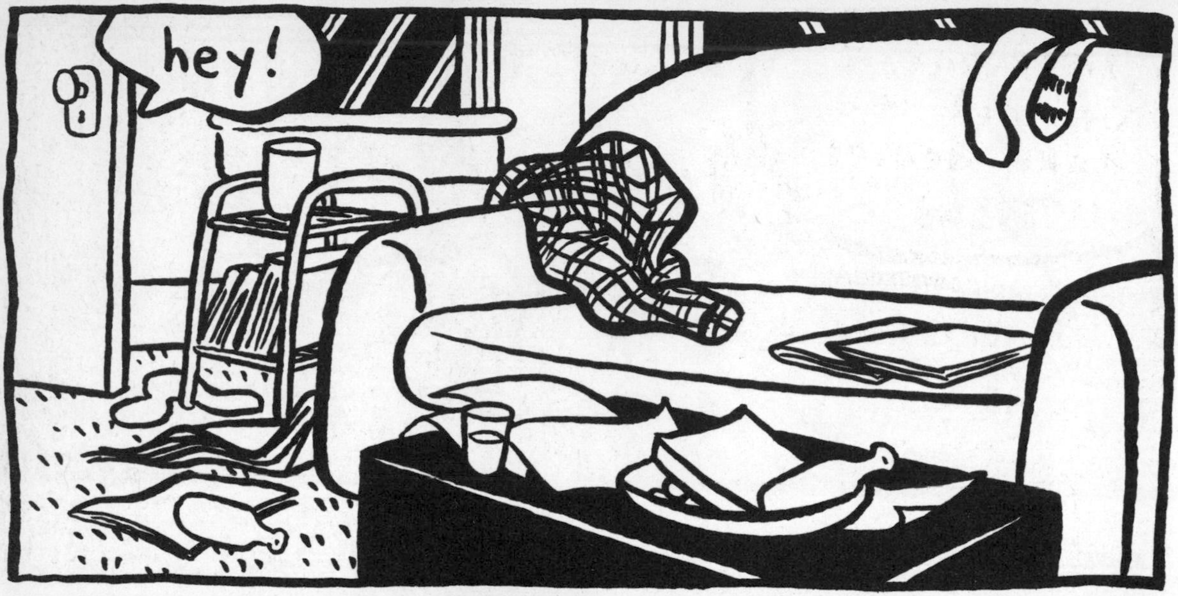
hey!

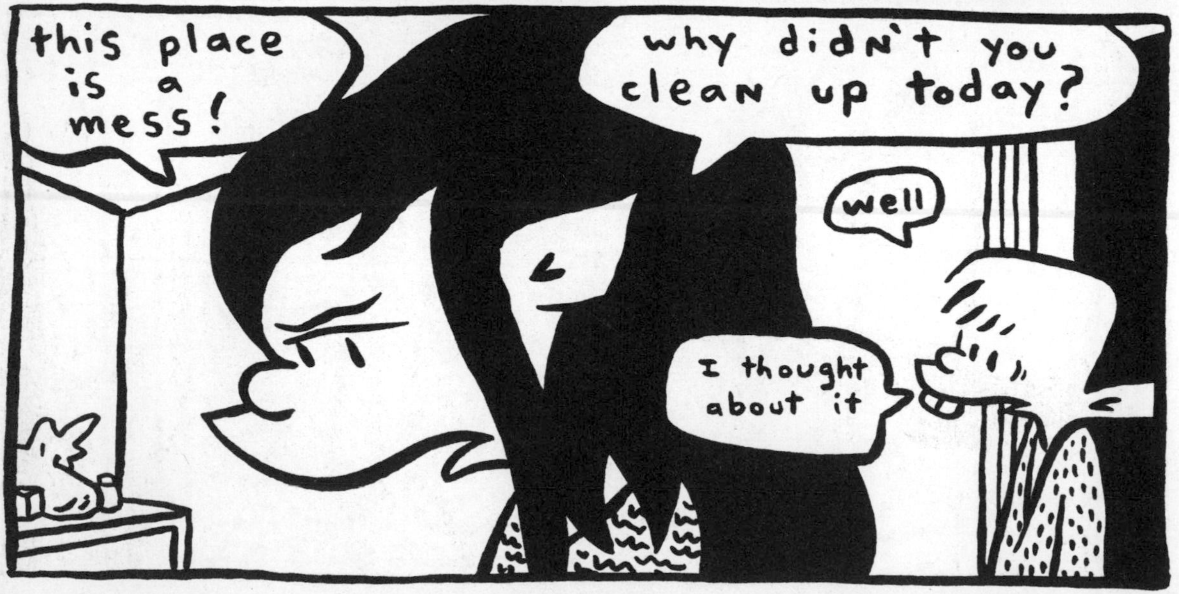
this place is a mess!
why didn't you clean up today?
well
I thought about it

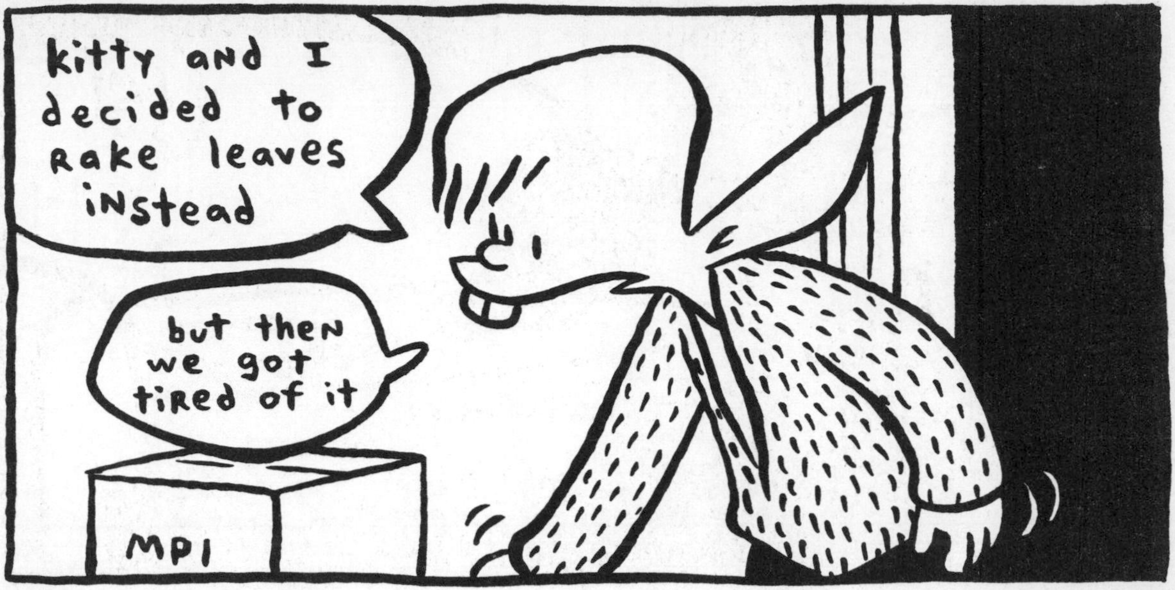
kitty and I decided to rake leaves instead
but then we got tired of it
MPI

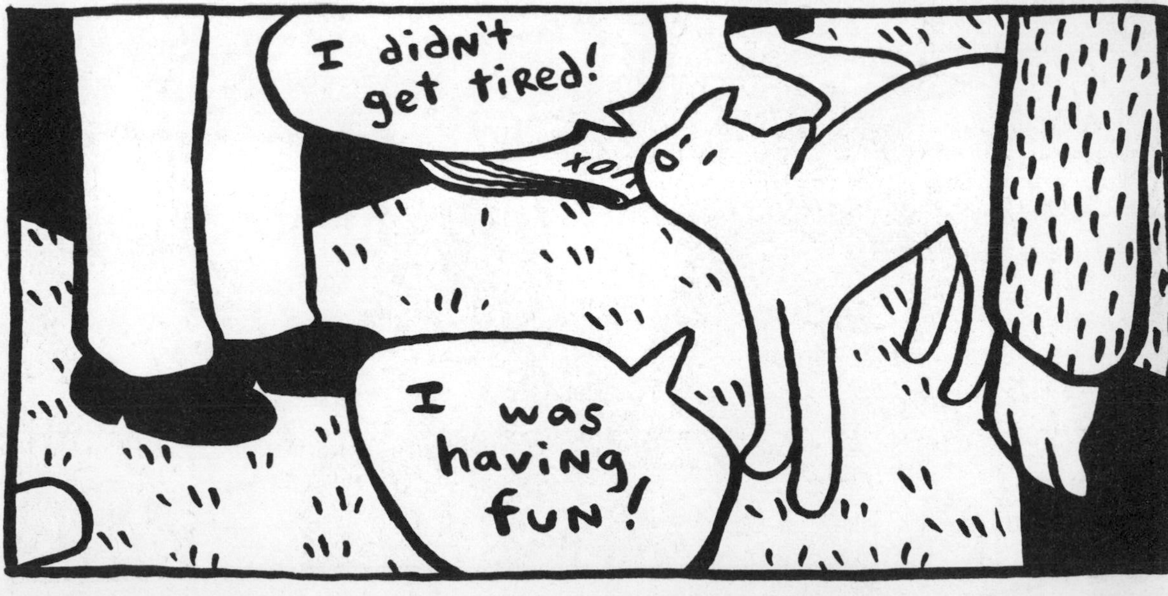
I didn't get tired!
I was having fun!

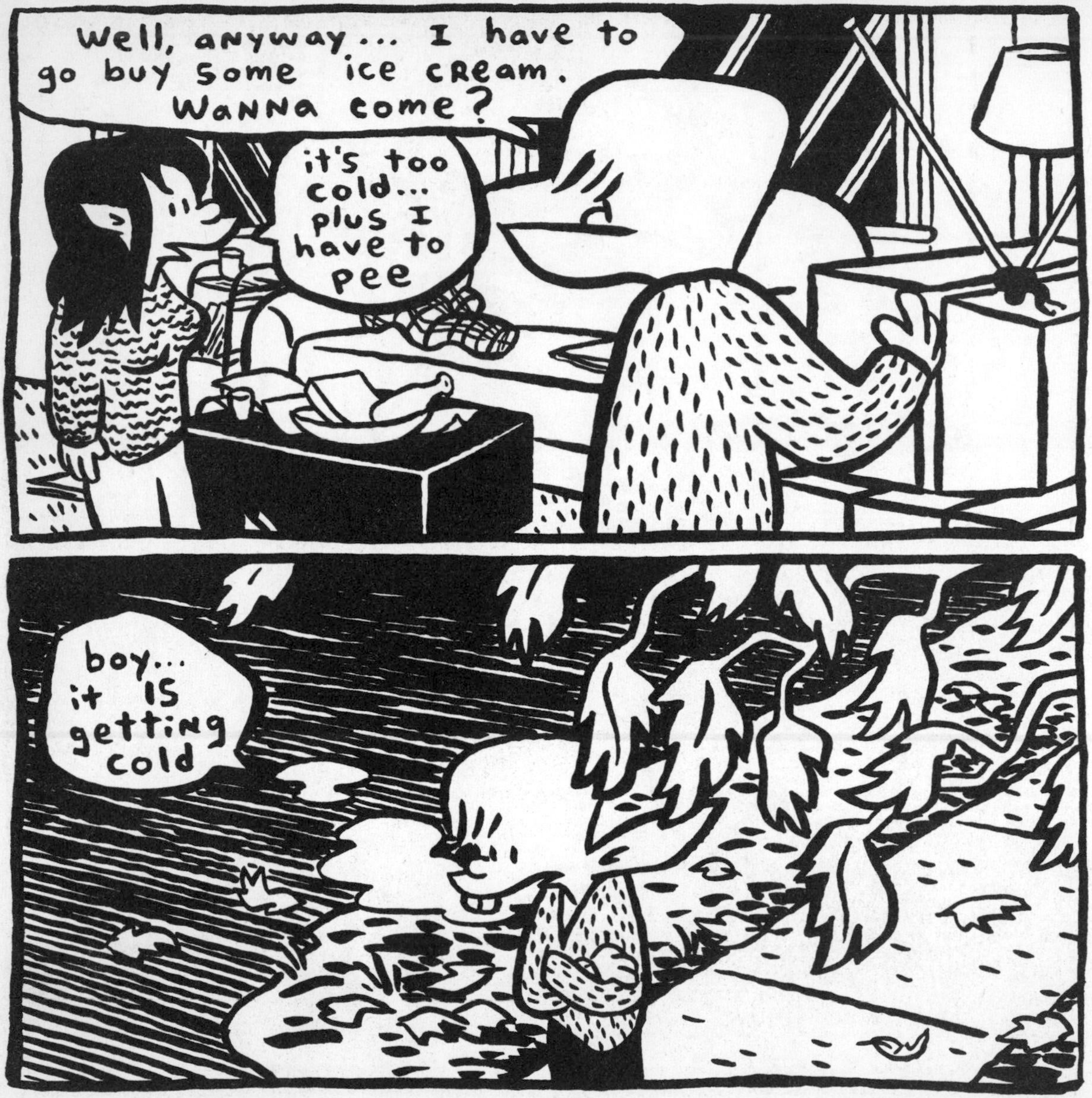
Well, anyway... I have to go buy some ice cream. Wanna come?
it's too cold... plus I have to pee
boy... it IS getting cold

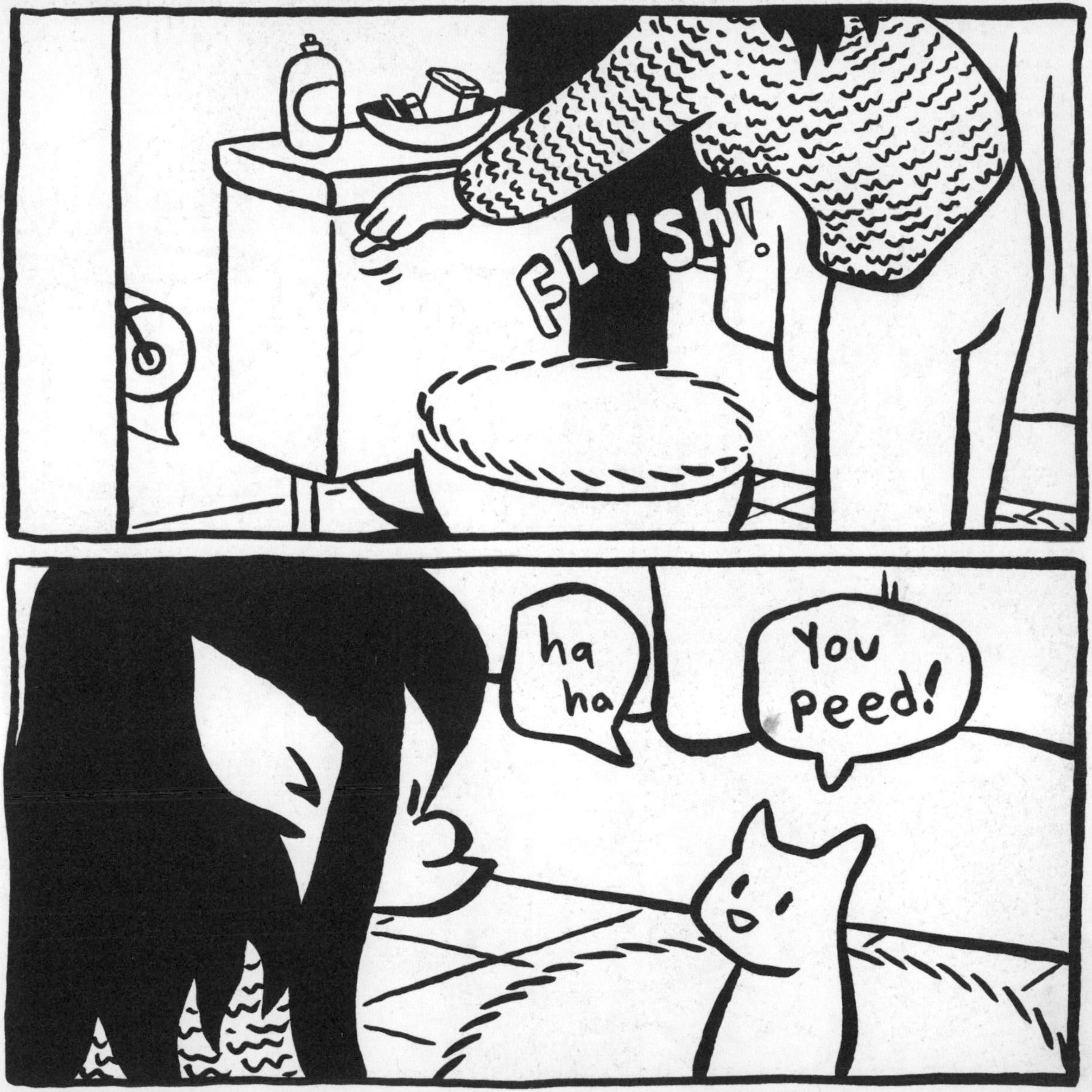
FLUSH!
ha ha
You peed!

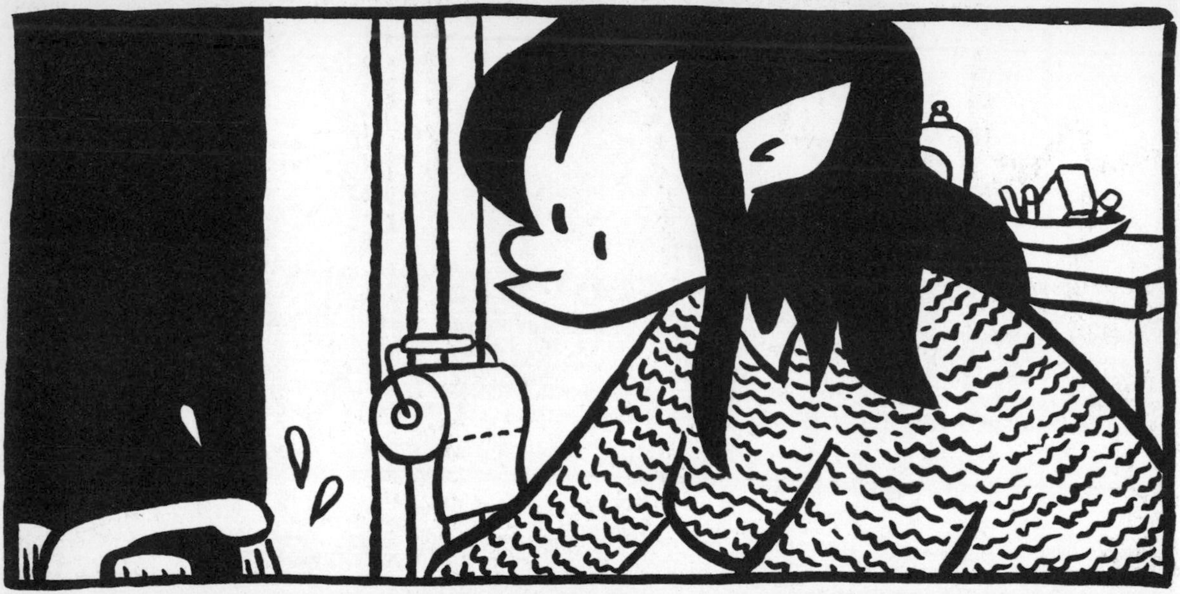
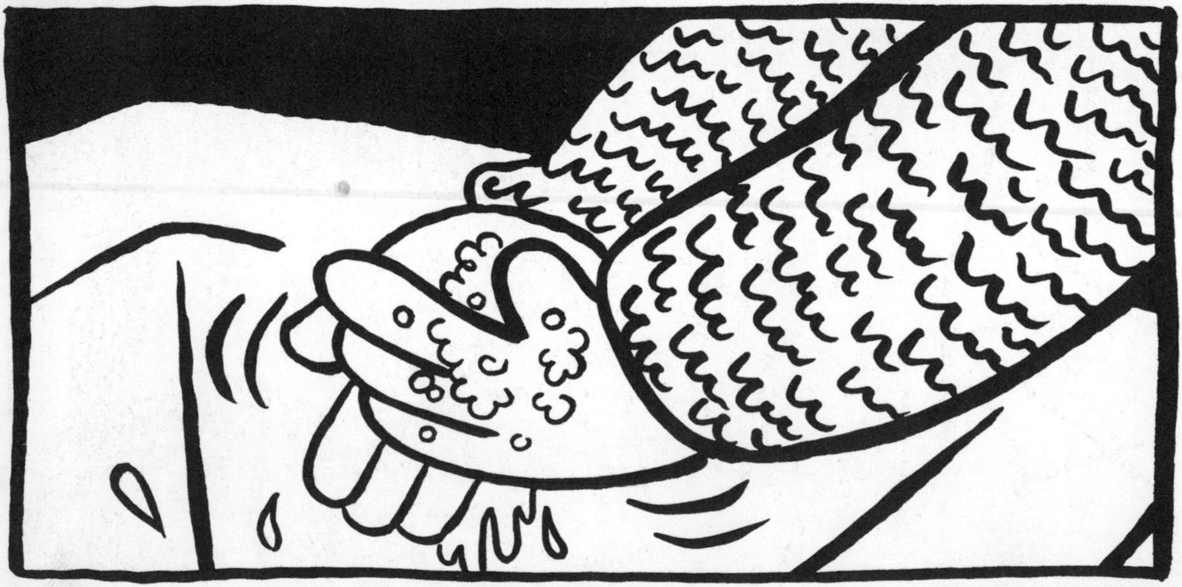

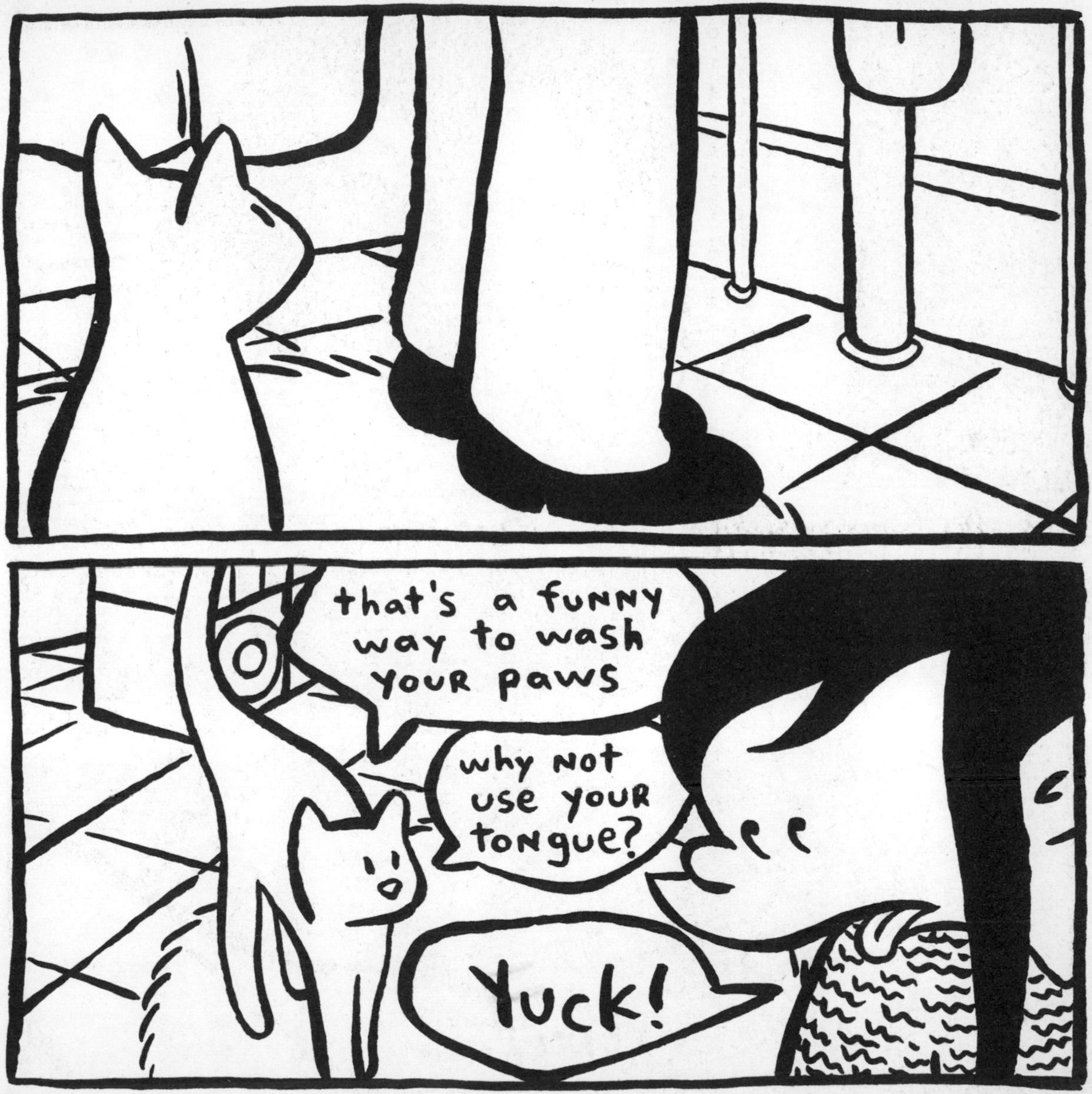
that's a funny way to wash your paws
why not use your tongue?
Yuck!

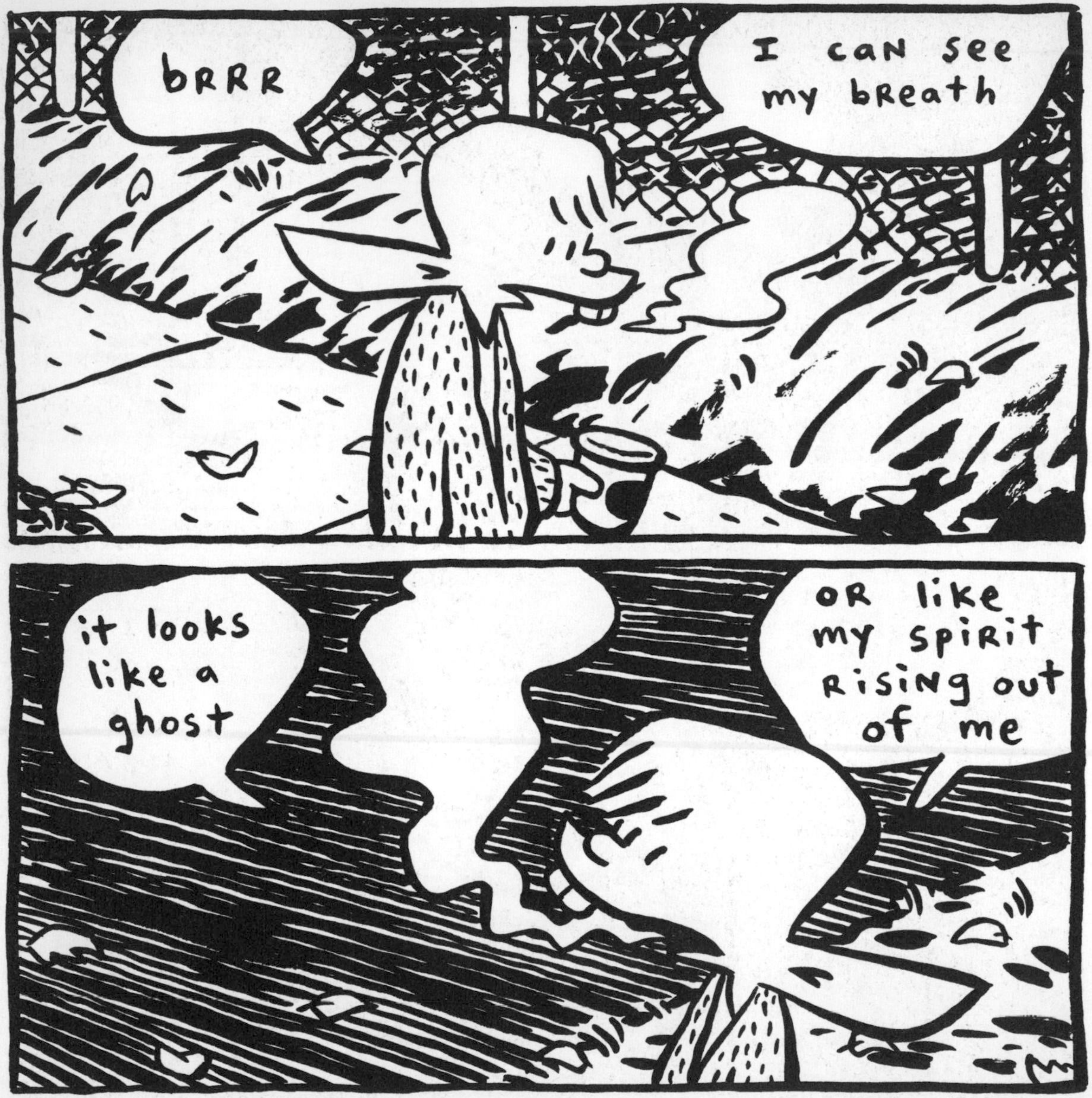
bRRR
I can see my bReath
it looks like a ghost
OR like my spiRit Rising out of me

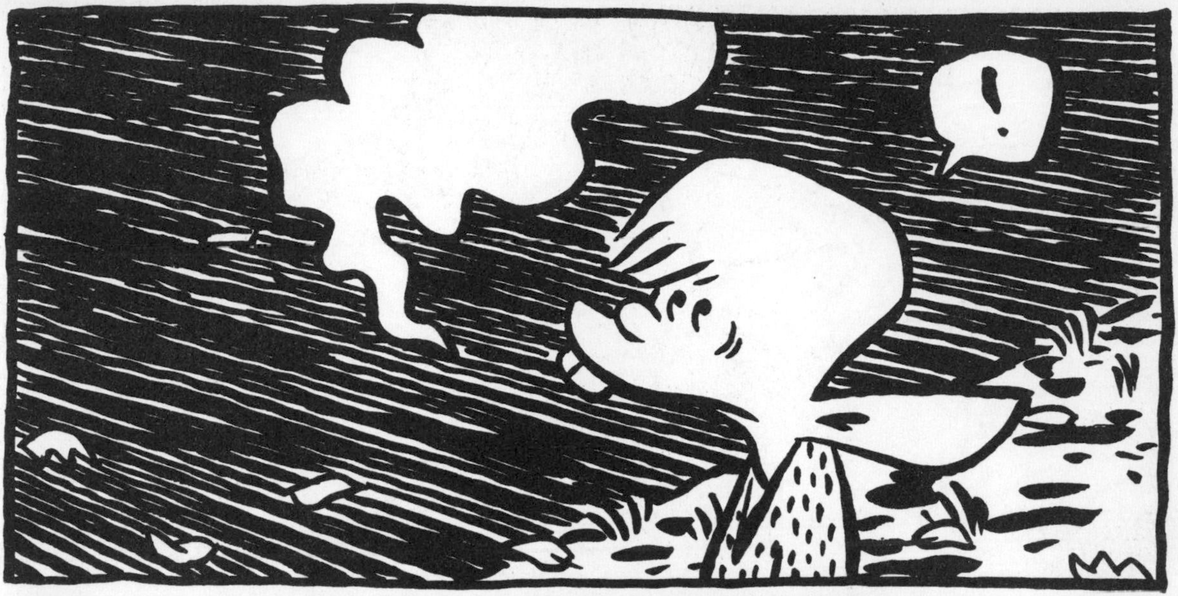
!

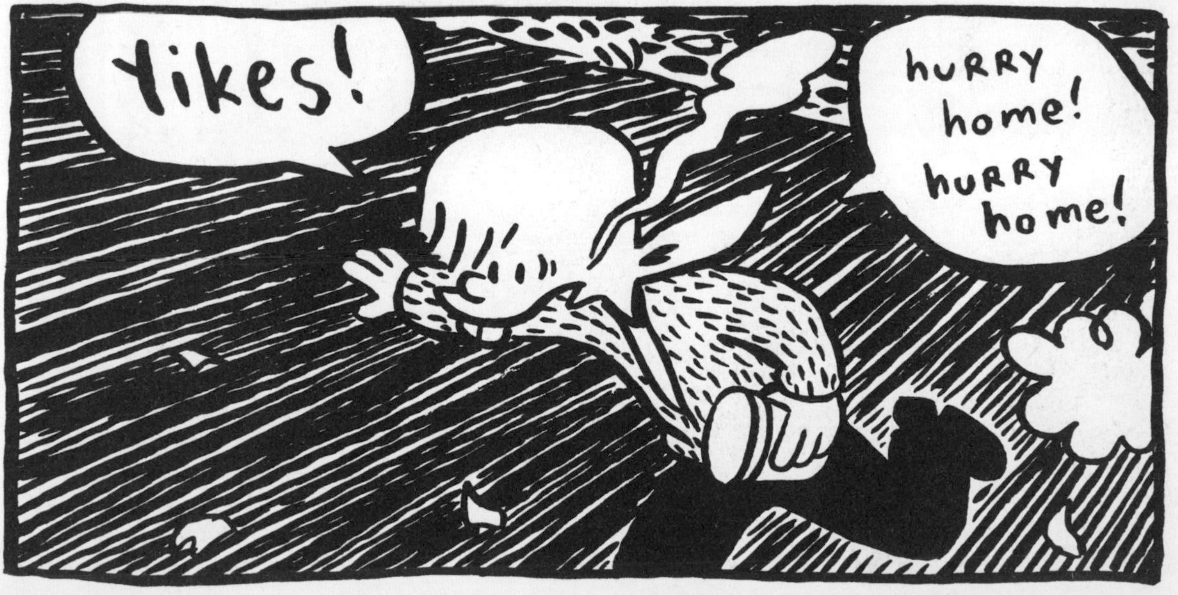
Yikes!
hURRY home! hURRY home!

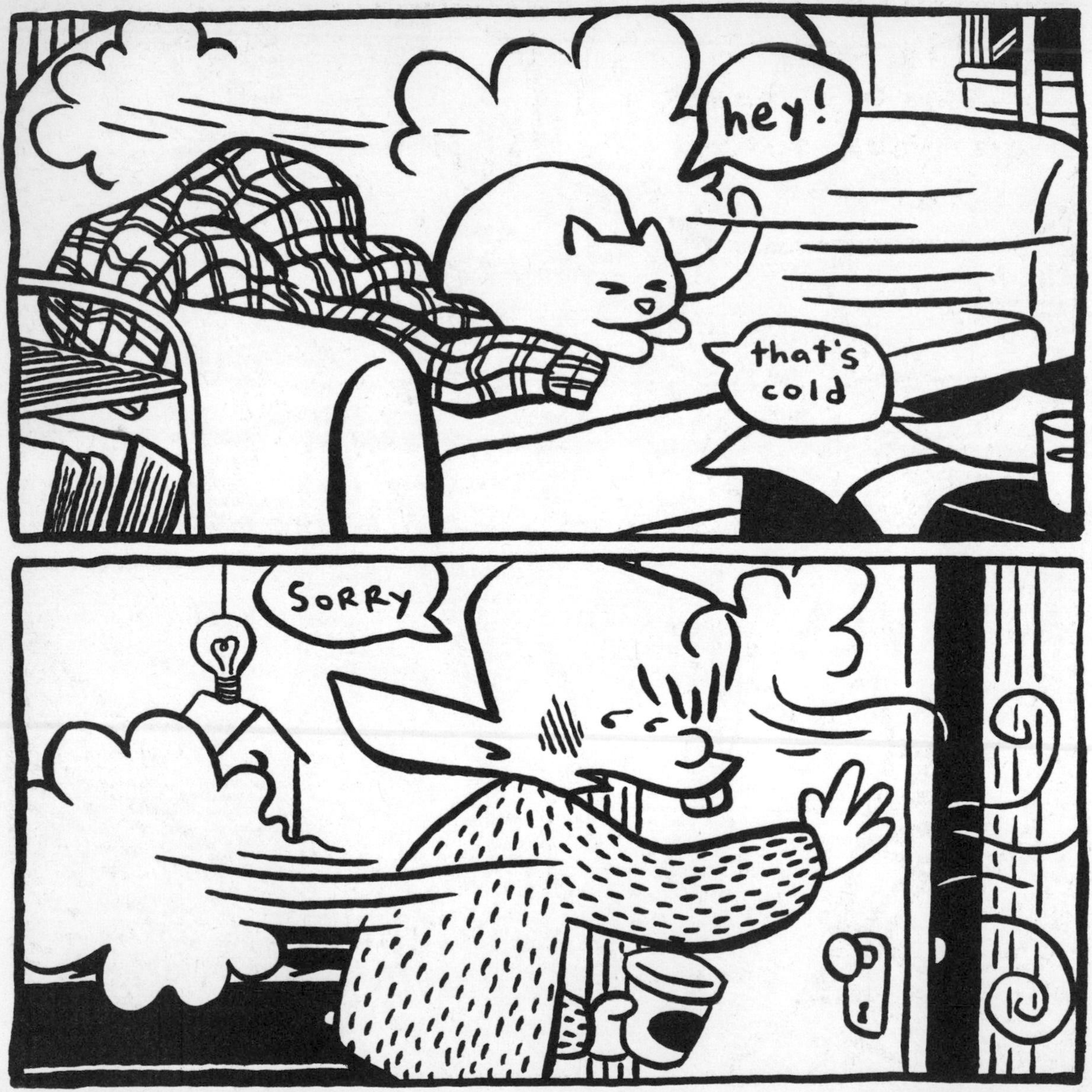
hey!
that's cold
SORRY

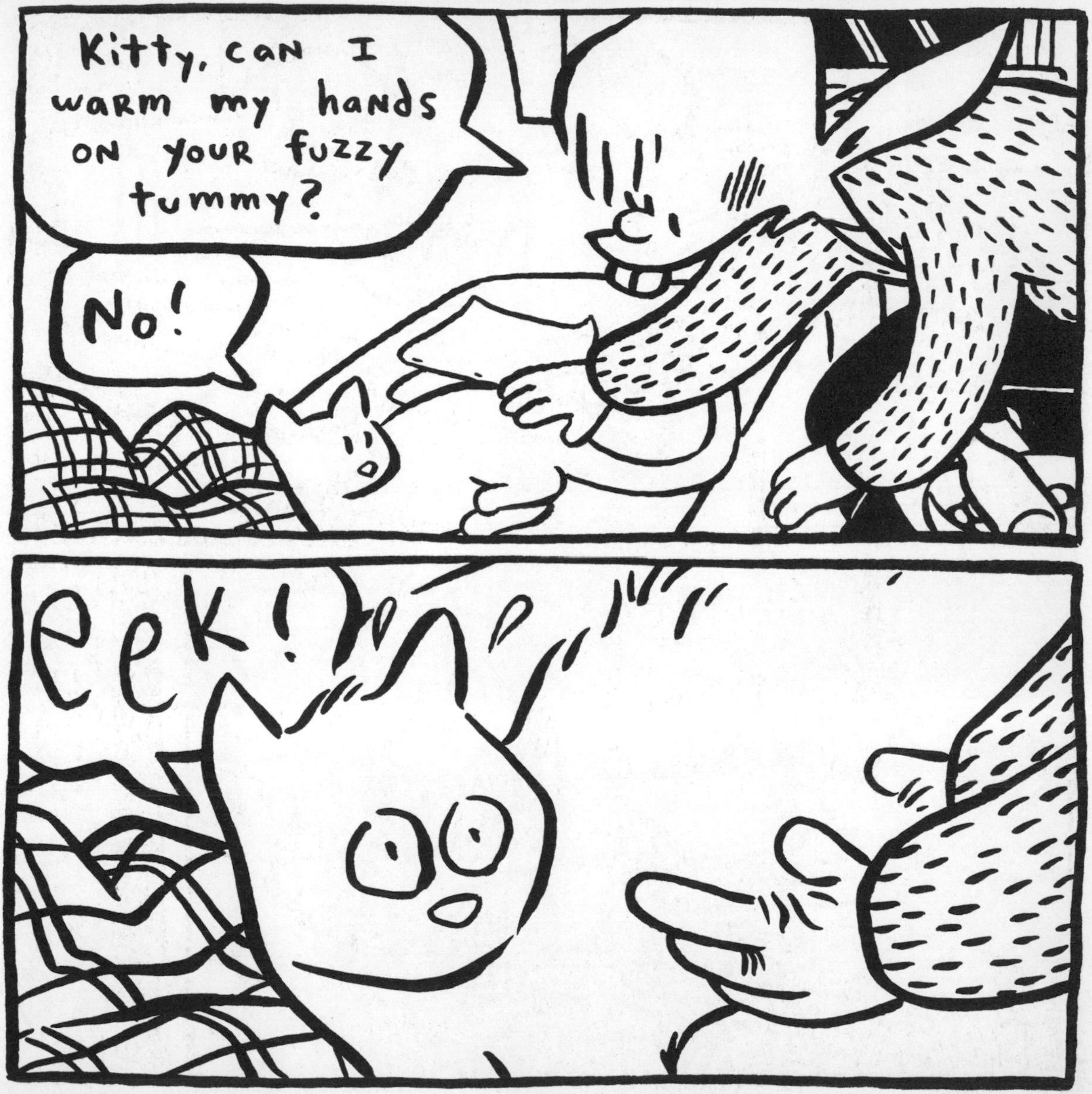
Kitty, can I warm my hands on your fuzzy tummy?
No!
eek!

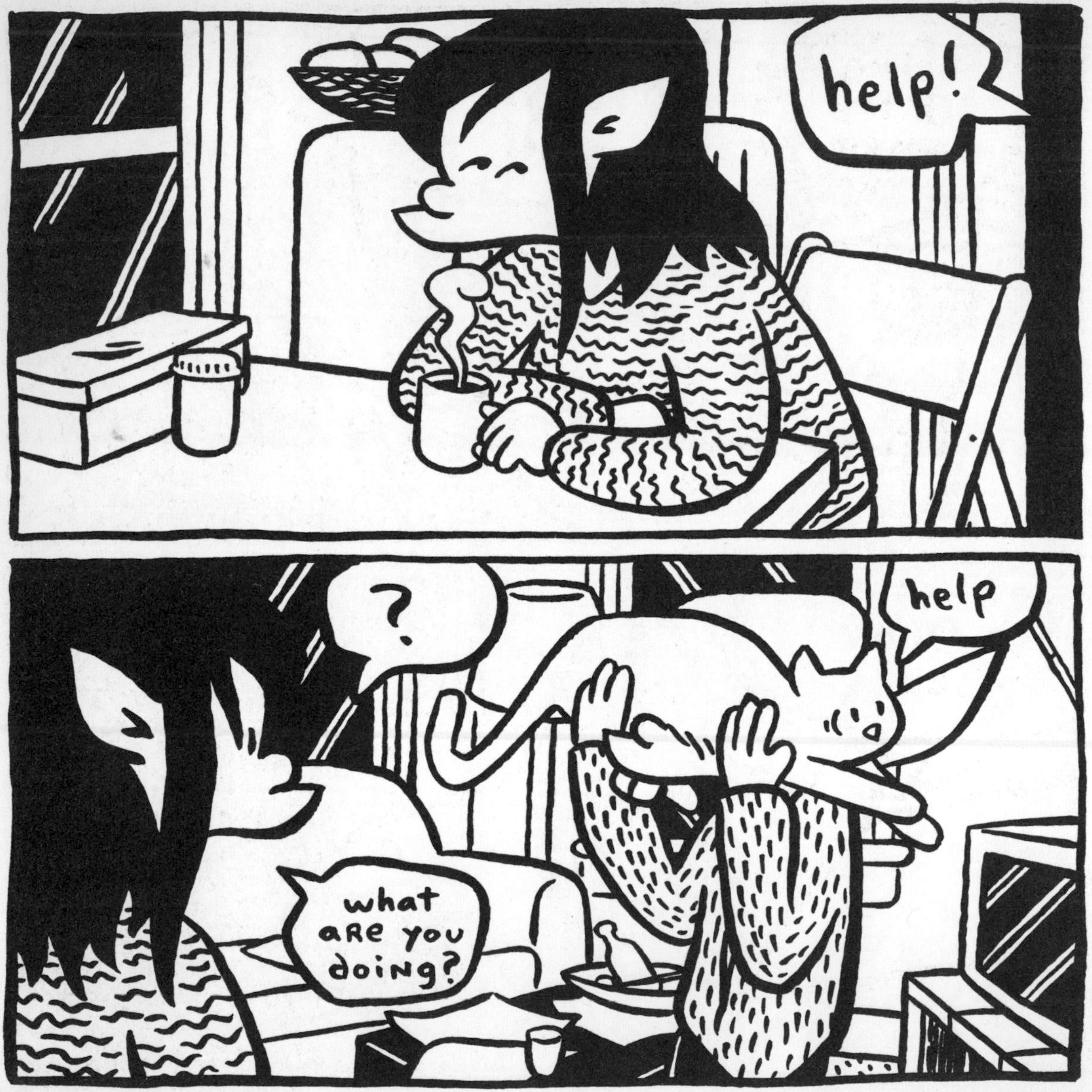
help!
?
help
what are you doing?

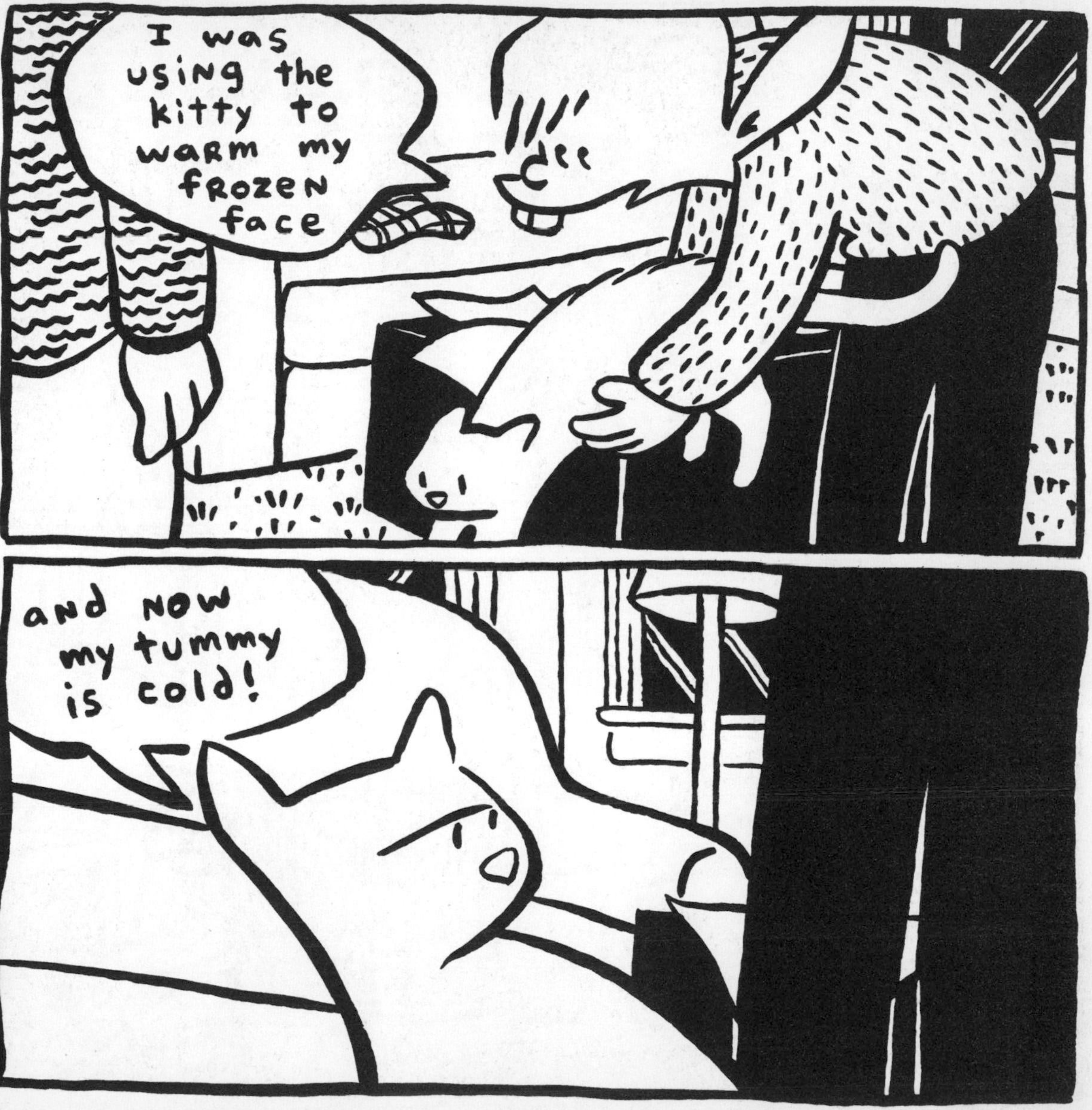
I was using the kitty to warm my frozen face
and now my tummy is cold!

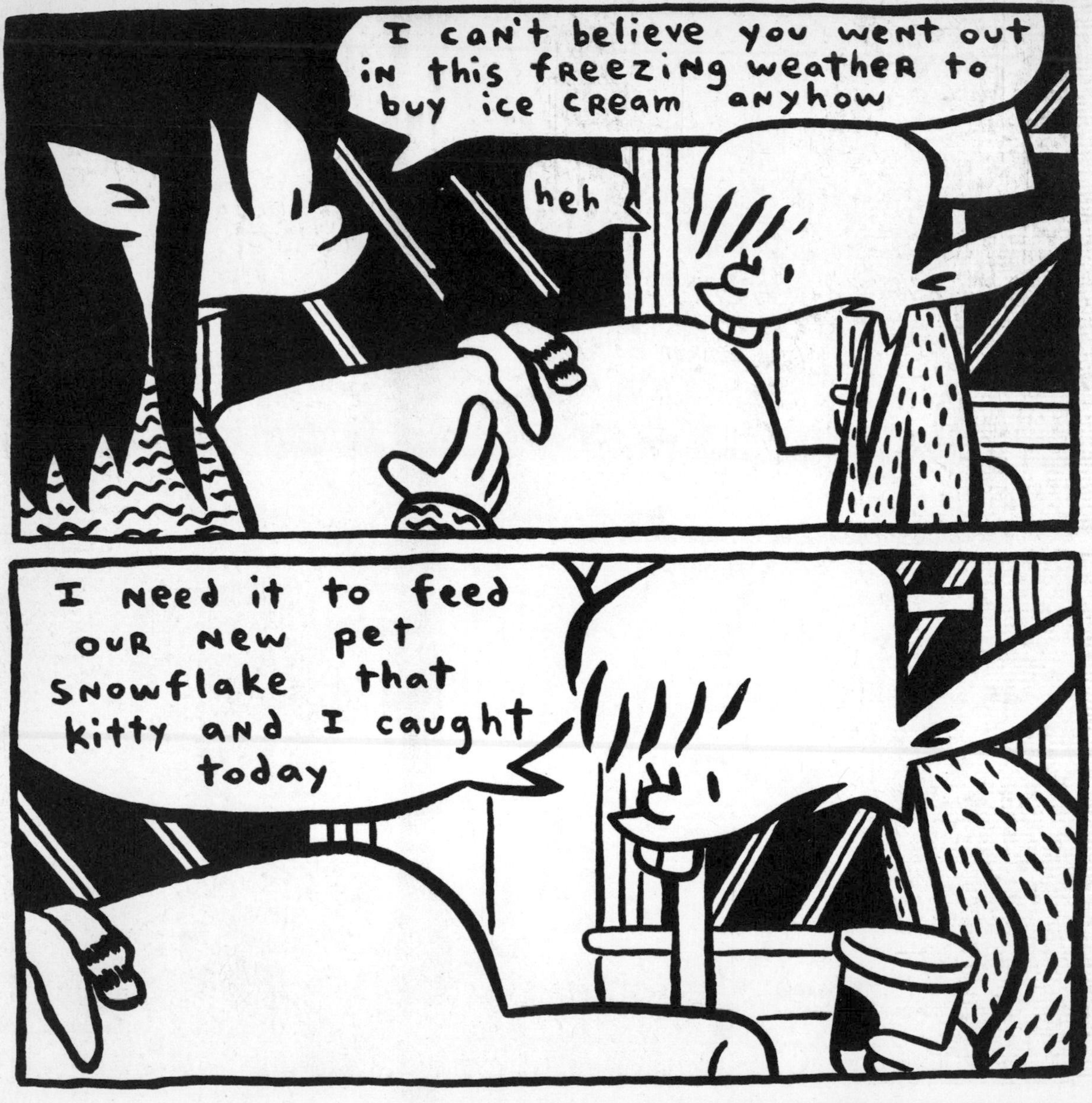
I can't believe you went out in this freezing weather to buy ice cream anyhow
heh
I need it to feed our new pet snowflake that kitty and I caught today

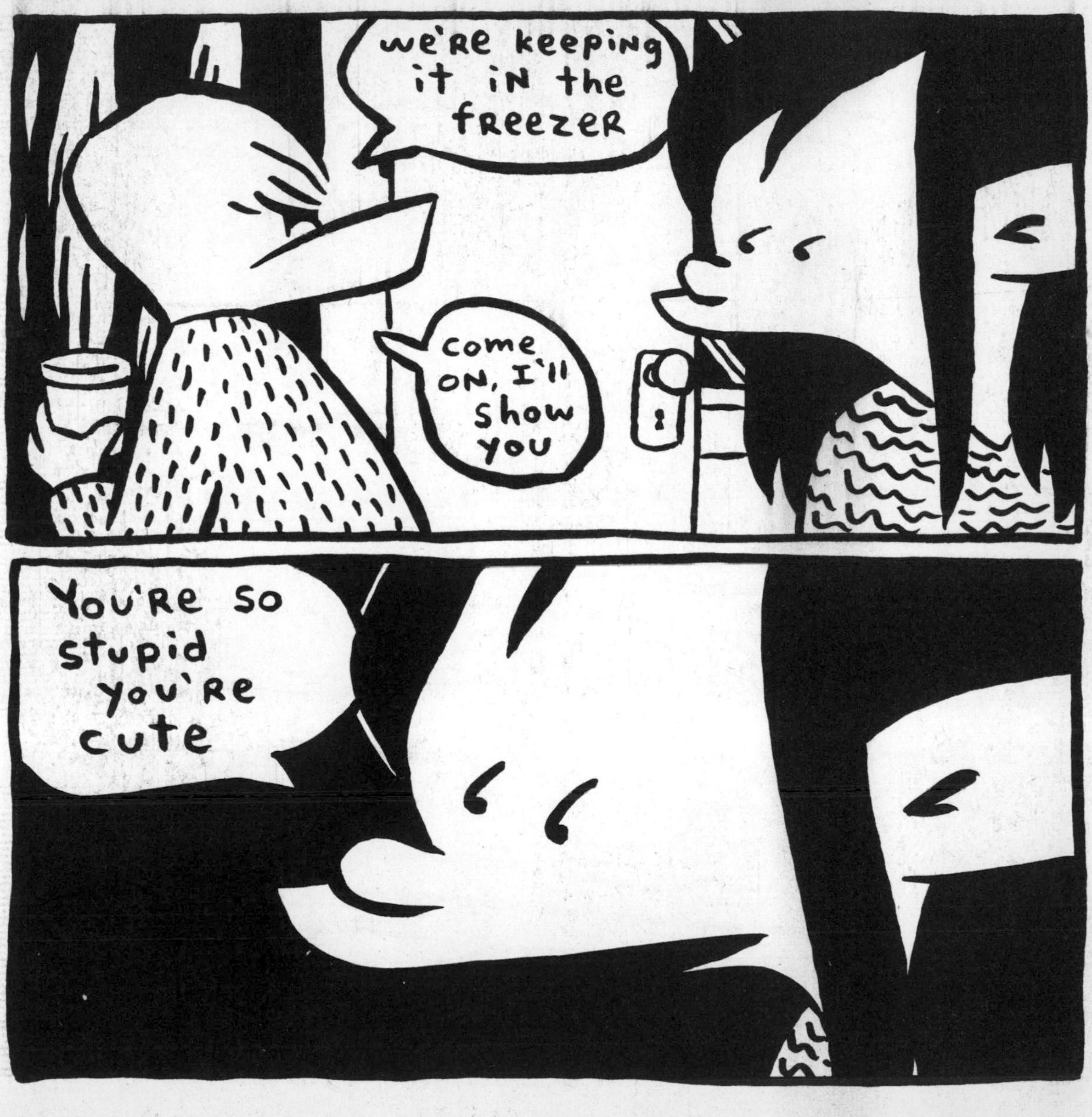
we're keeping it in the freezer
come on, I'll show you
You're so stupid you're cute

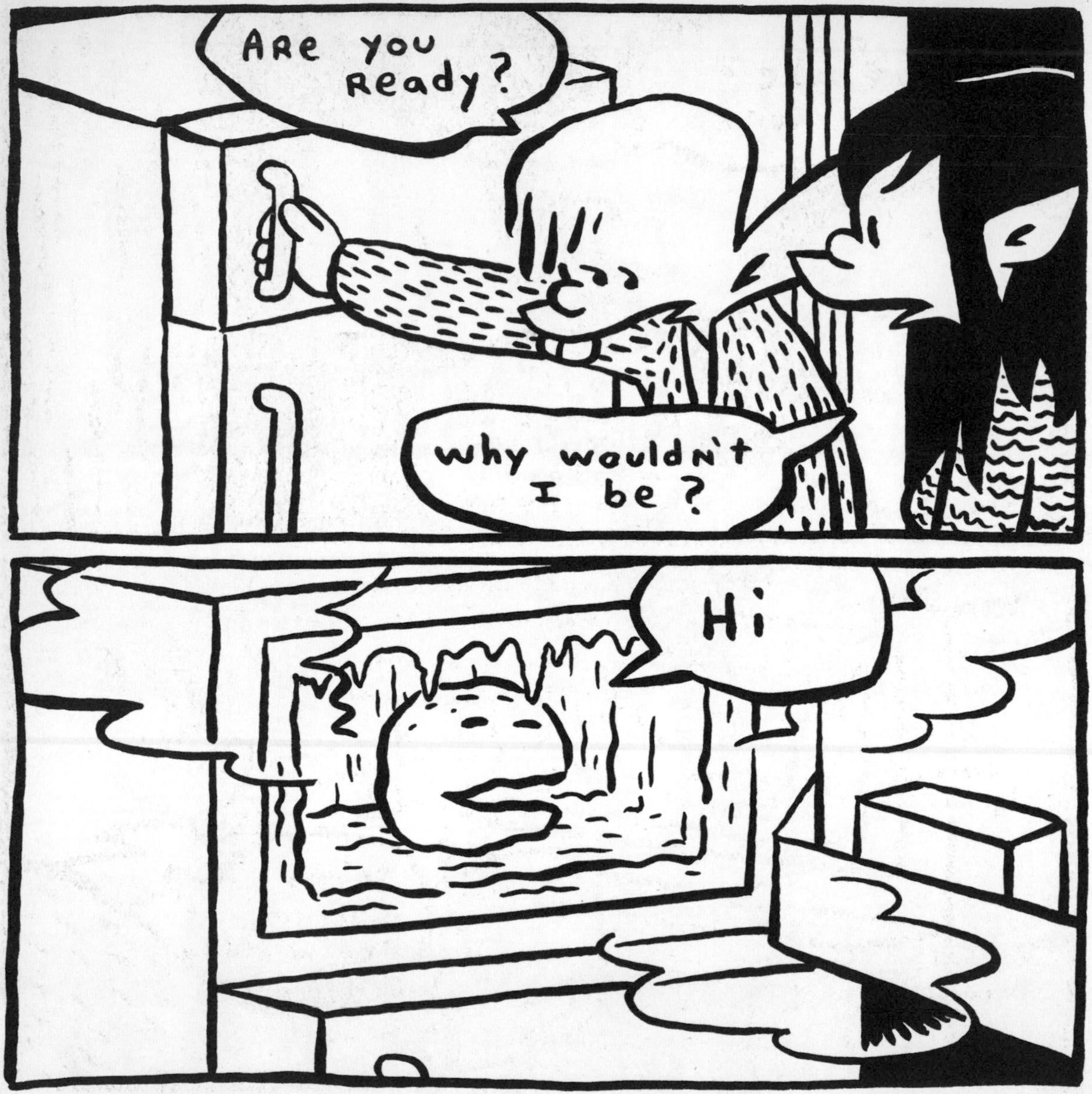
Are you Ready?
why wouldn't I be?
Hi

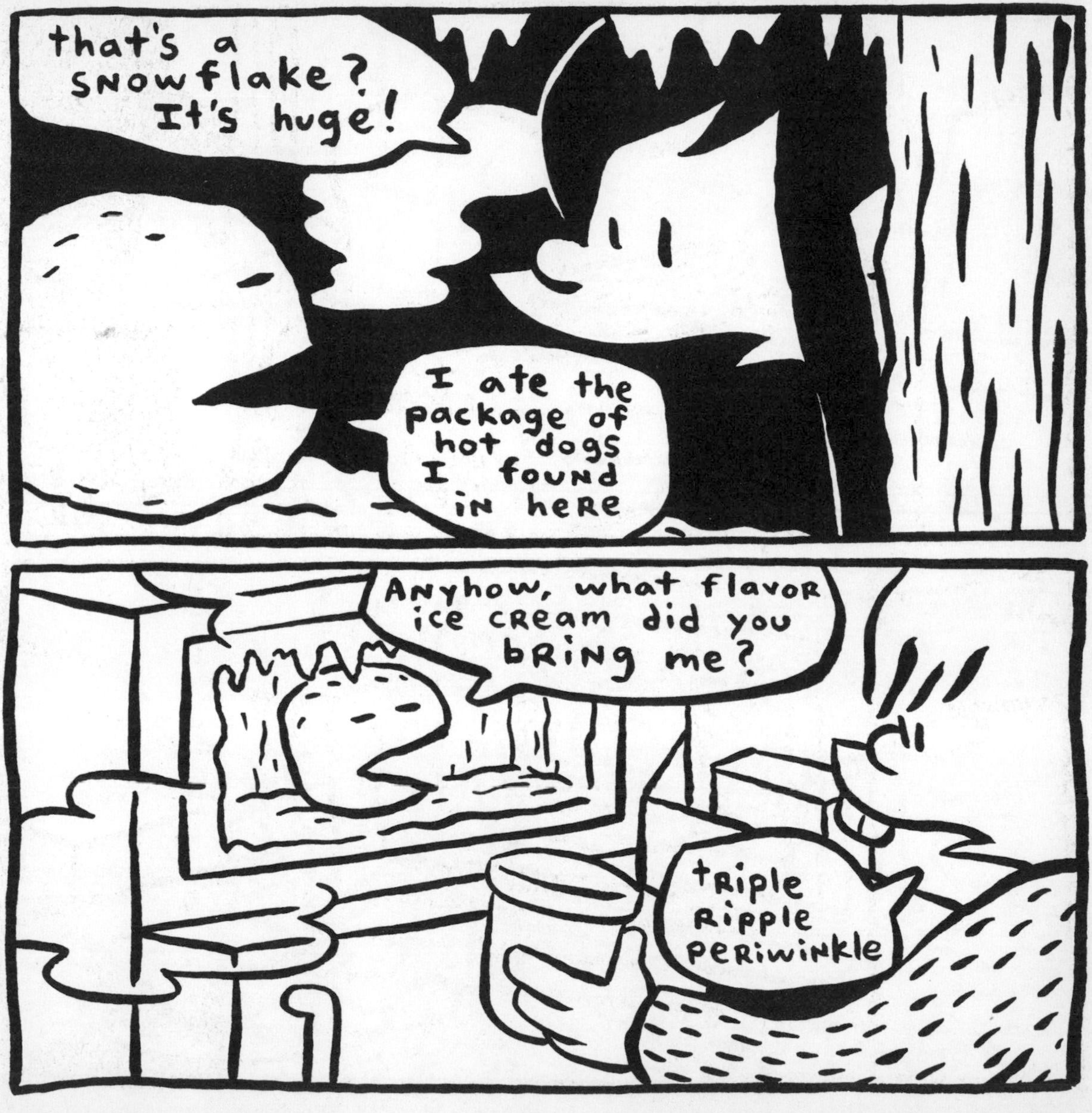
that's a snowflake? It's huge!
I ate the package of hot dogs I found in here
Anyhow, what flavor ice cream did you bring me?
triple ripple periwinkle

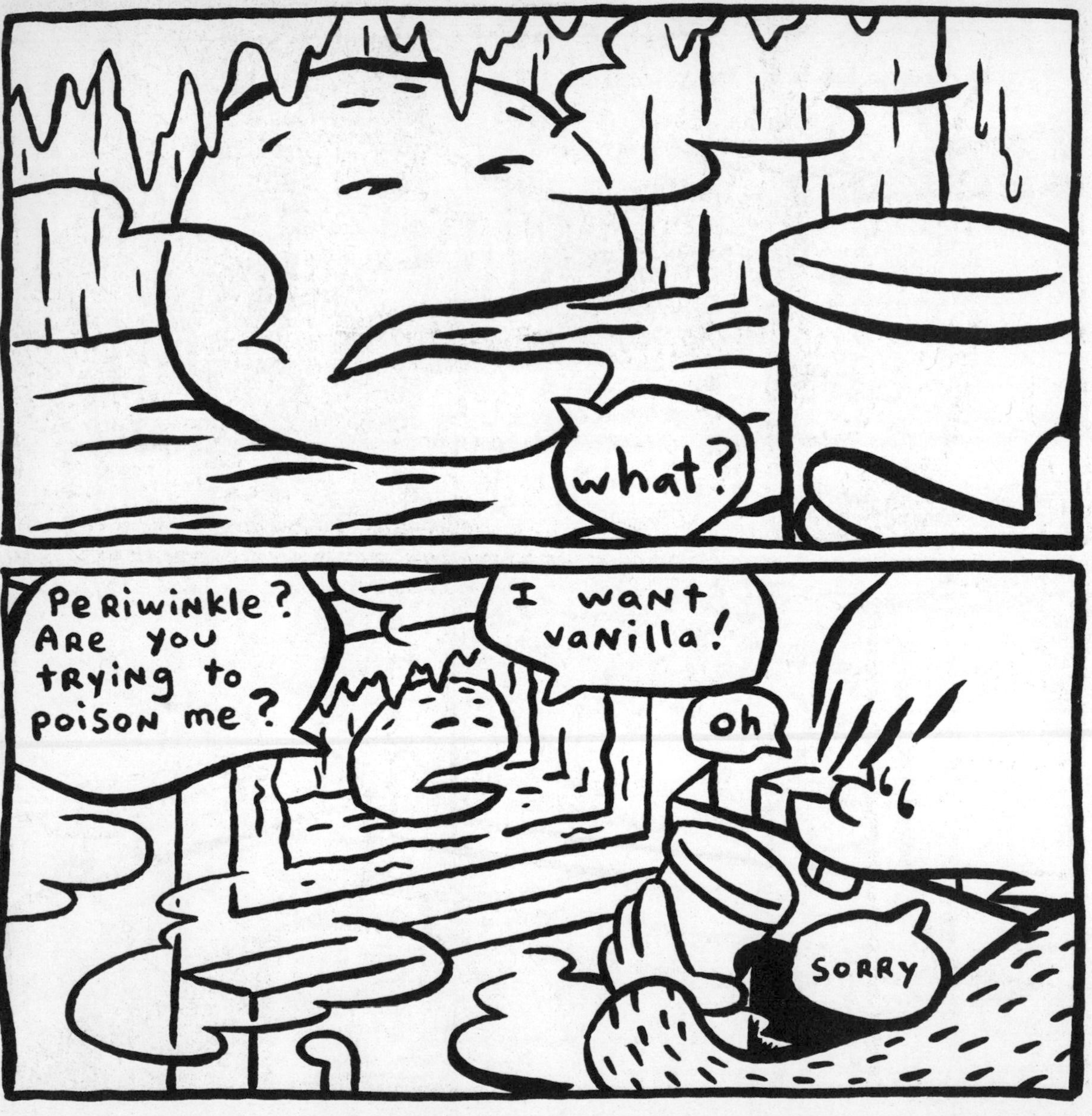
what?
Periwinkle? Are you trying to poison me?
I want vanilla!
oh
SORRY

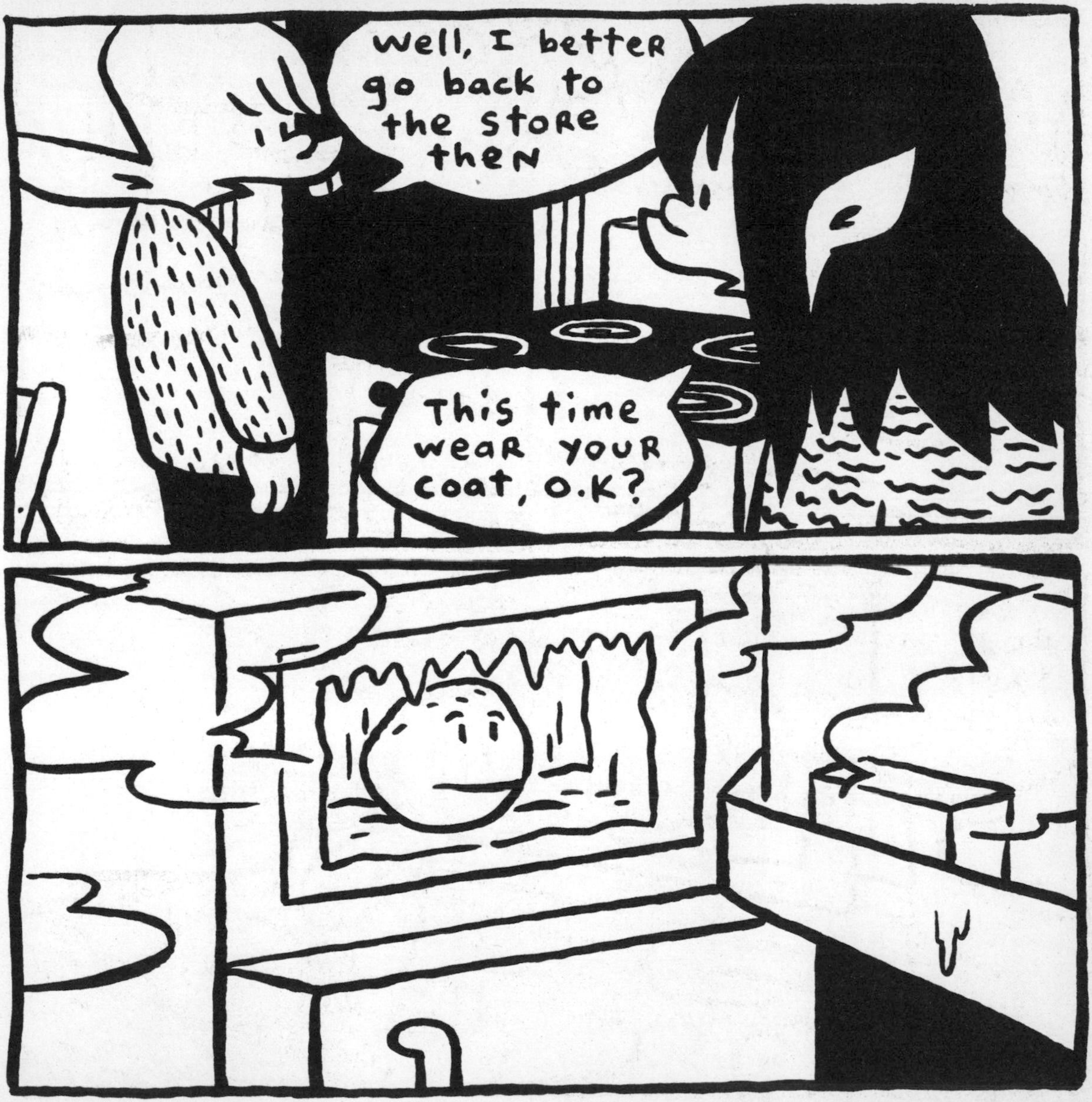
Well, I better go back to the store then
This time wear your coat, O.K?

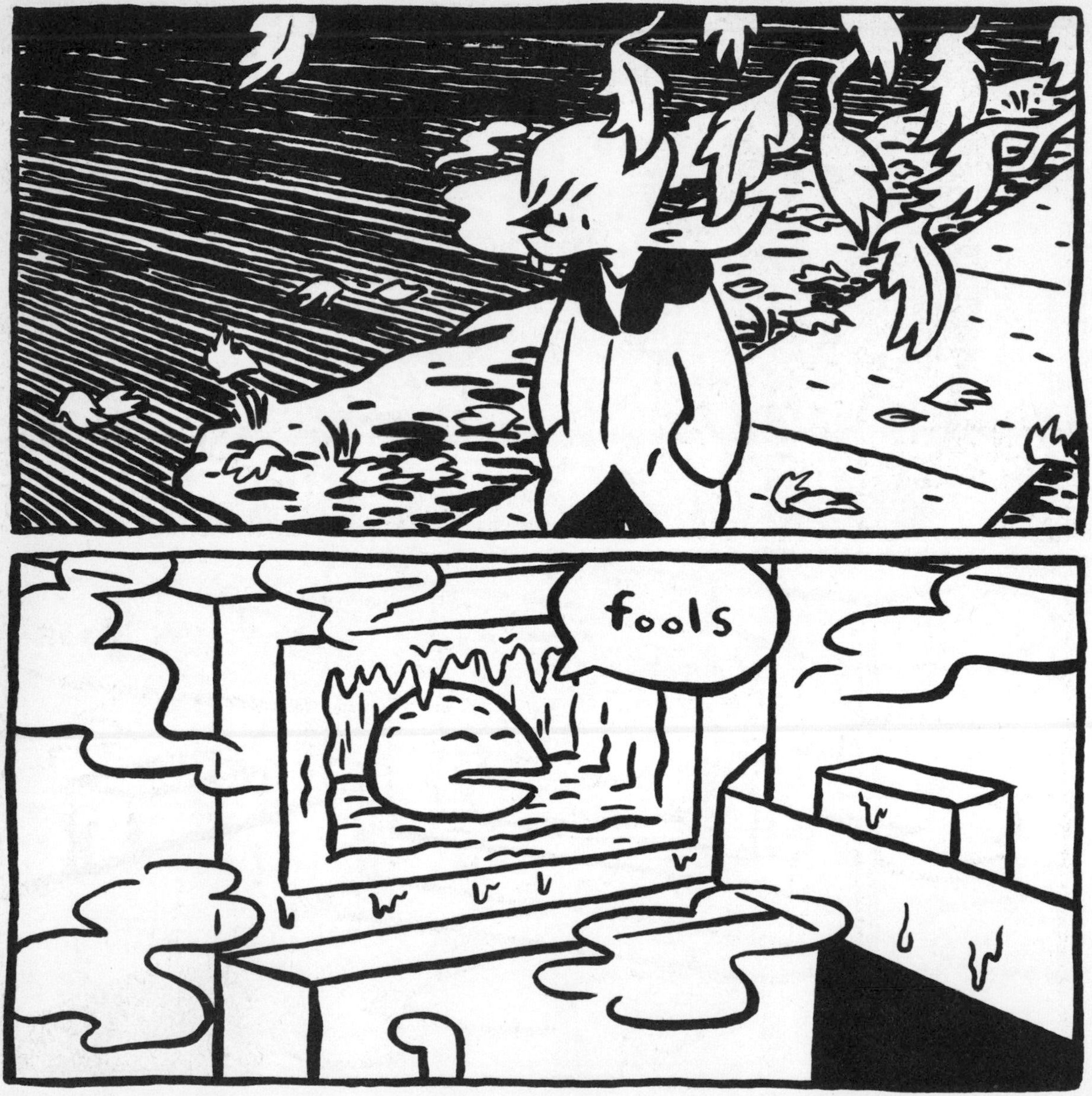
fools

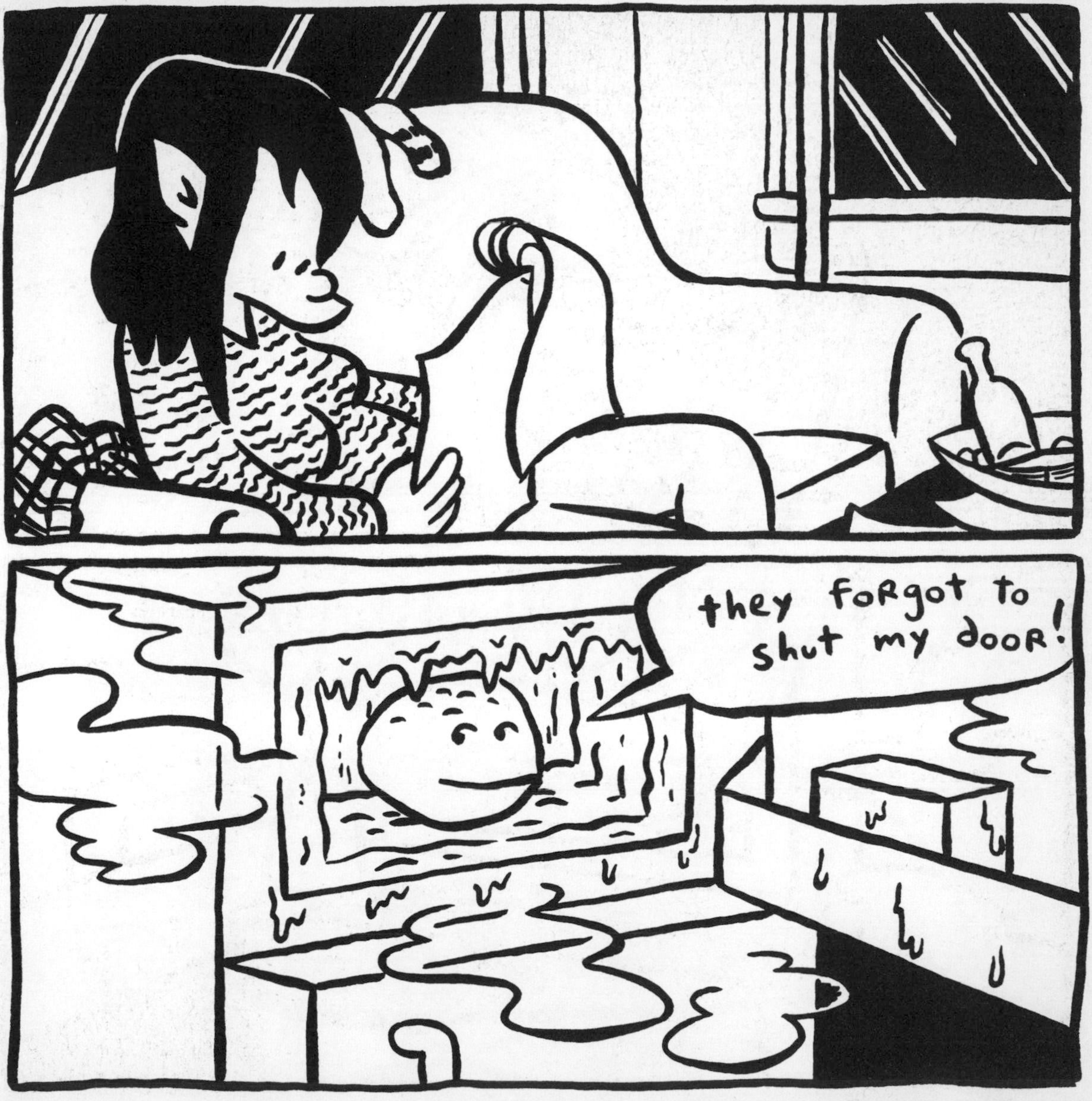
they forgot to shut my door!

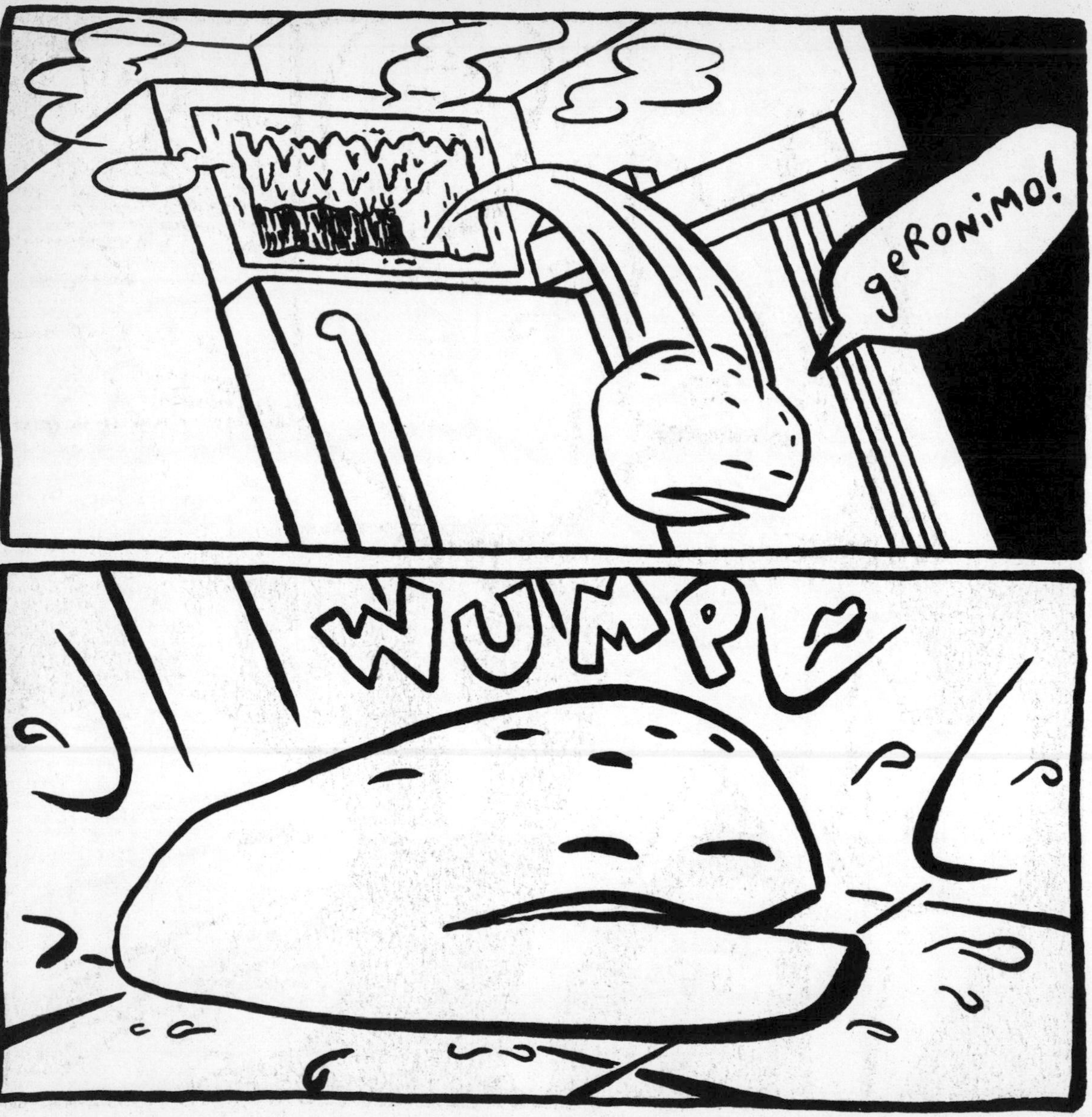
geRONIMO!
WUMP

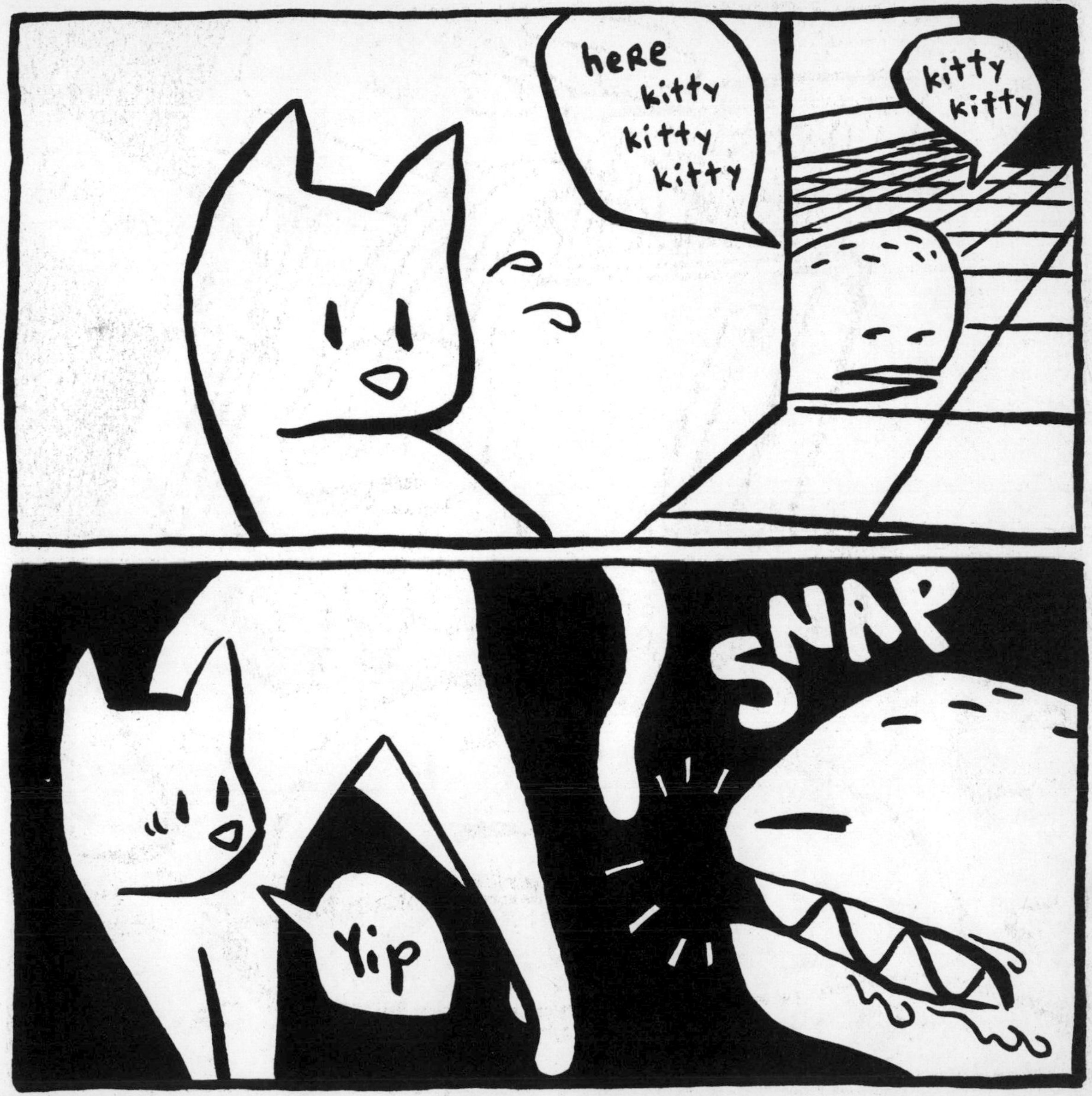
here kitty kitty kitty
kitty kitty
SNAP
Yip

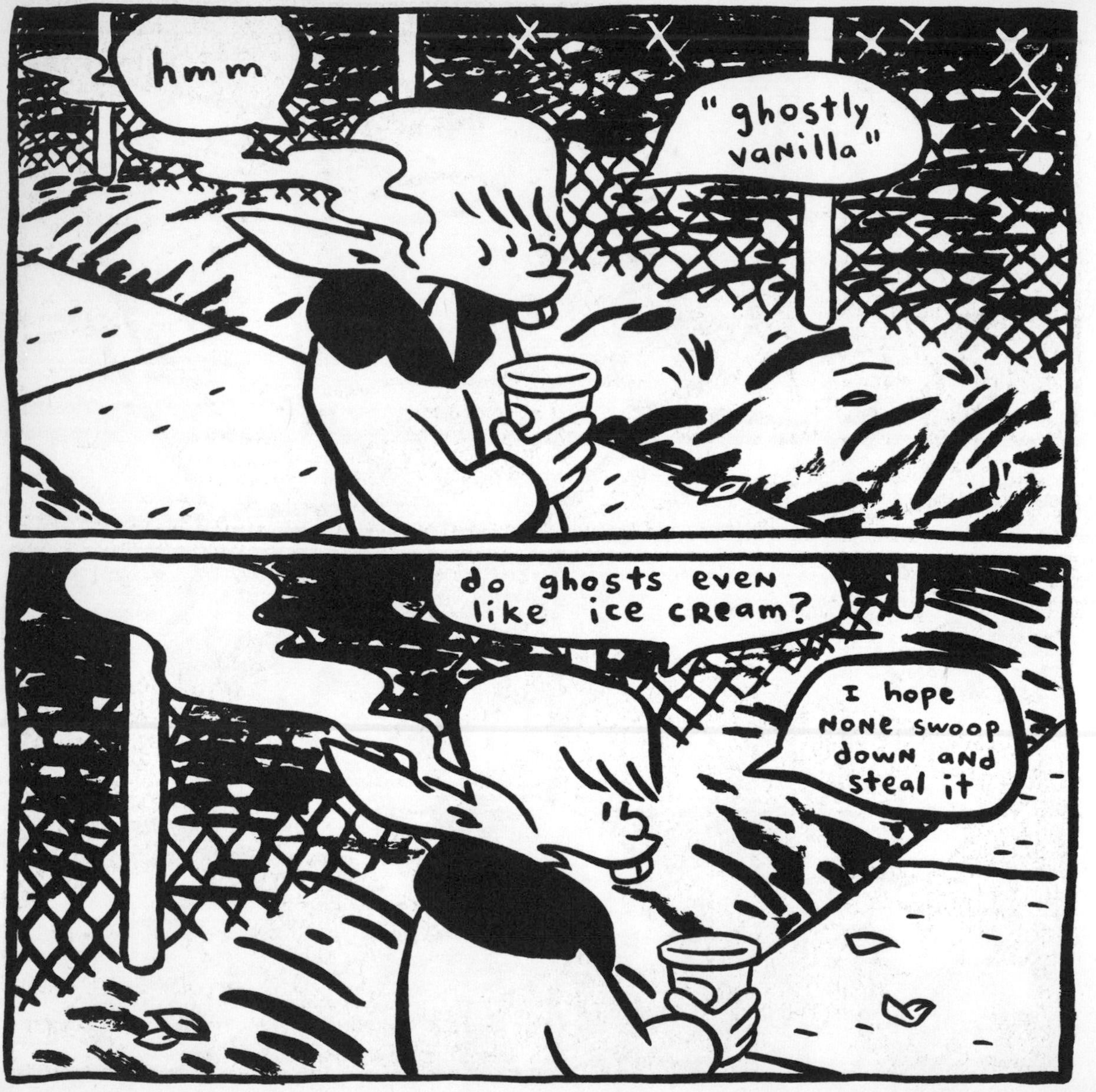

hmm
"ghostly vanilla"
do ghosts even like ice cream?
I hope NONE swoop down AND steal it

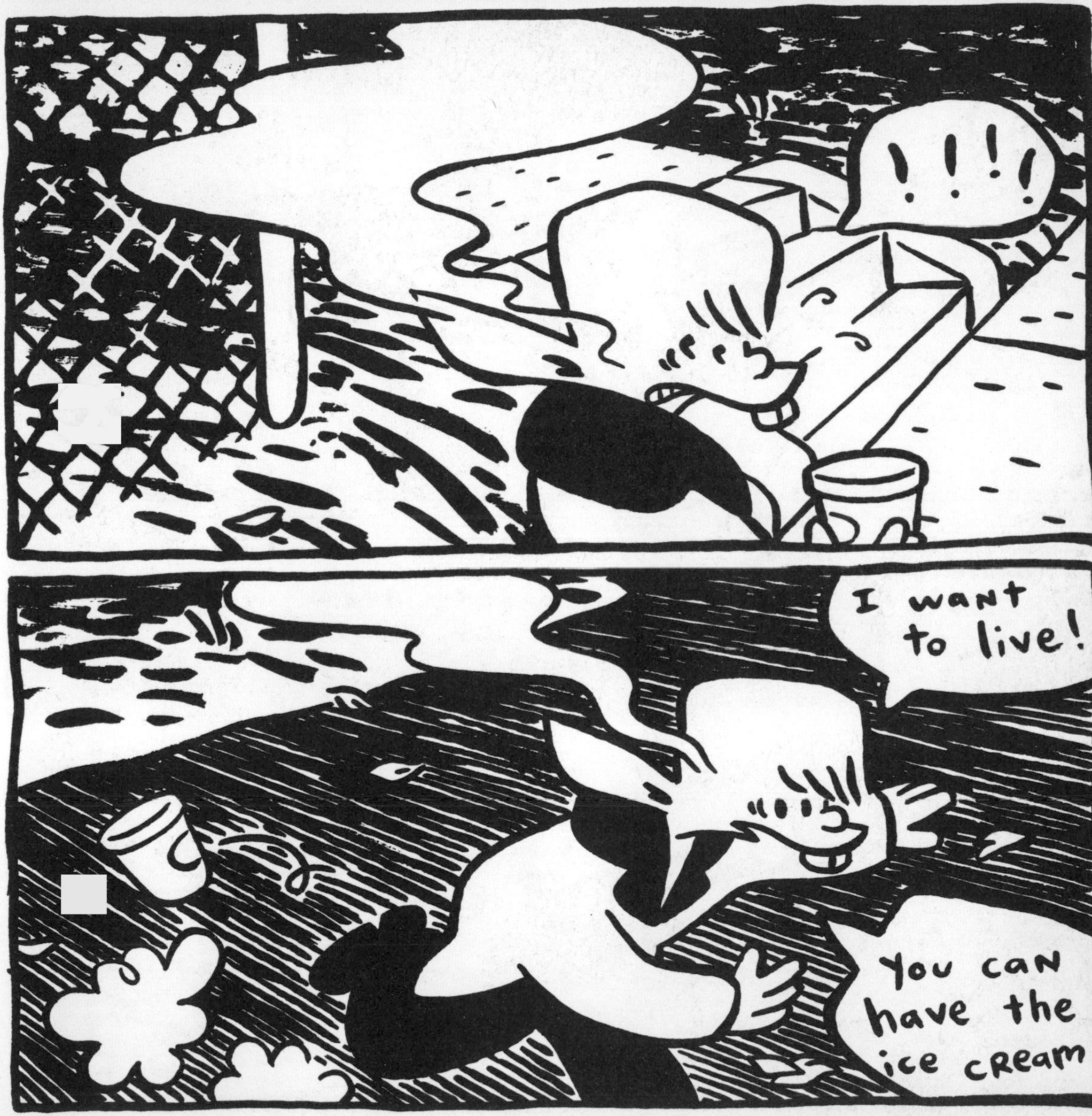
!!!!
I want to live!
You can have the ice cream

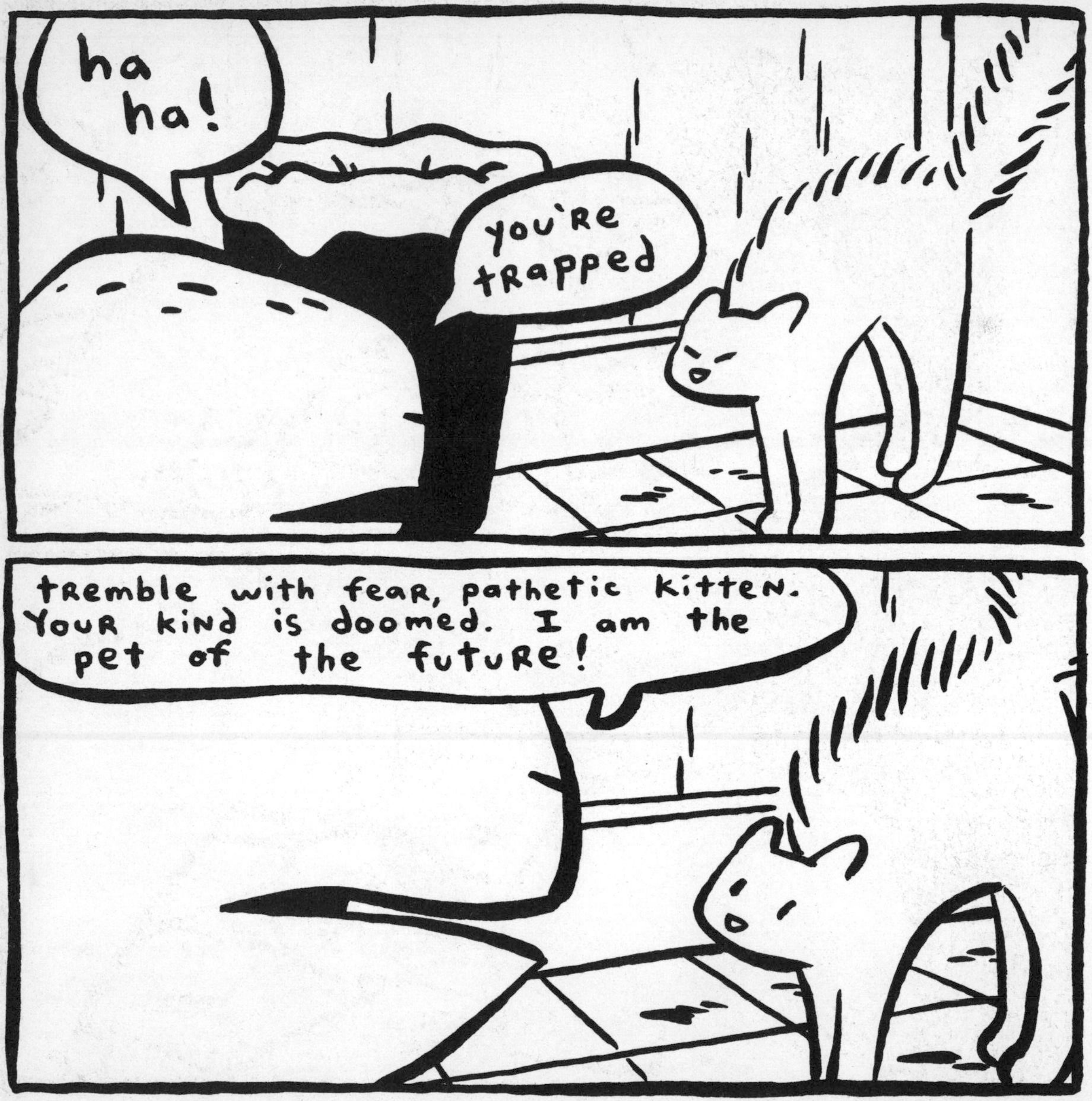
ha ha!
you're trapped
tremble with fear, pathetic kitten. Your kind is doomed. I am the pet of the future!

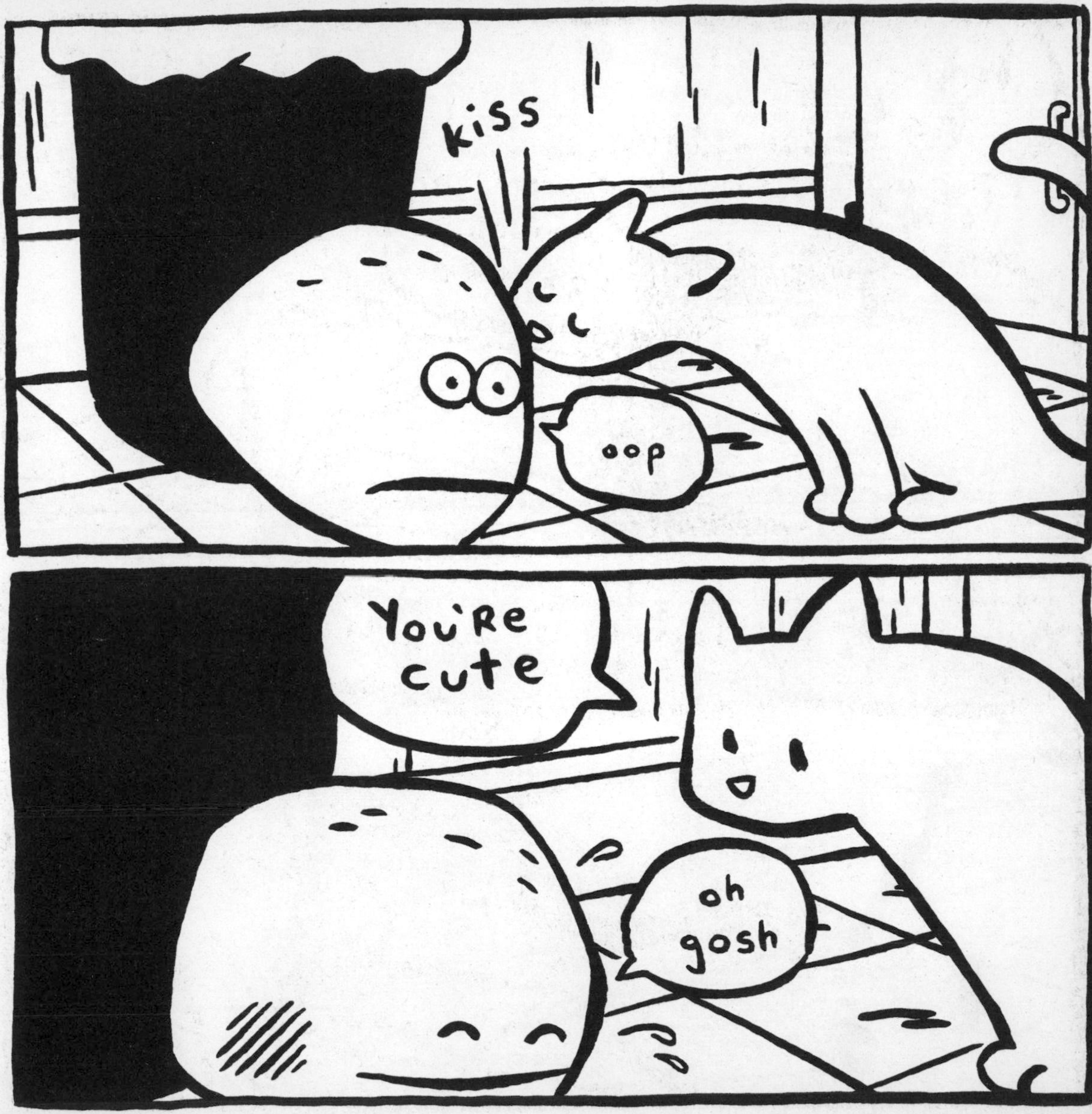
KiSS
oop
You're cute
oh gosh

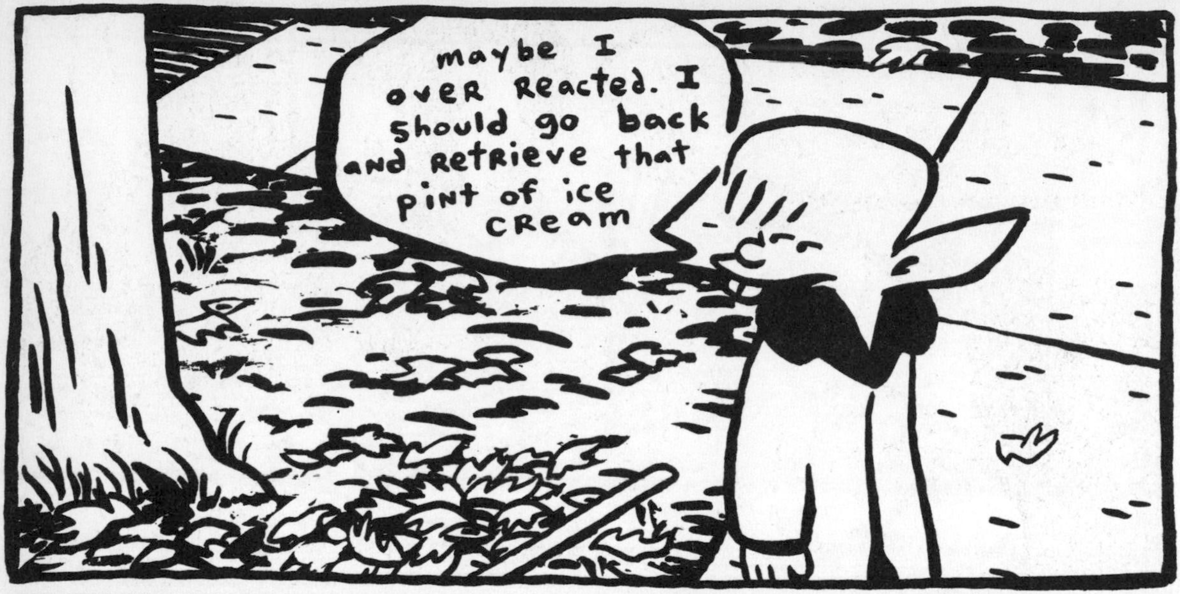
maybe I over Reacted. I should go back and Retrieve that pint of ice cream

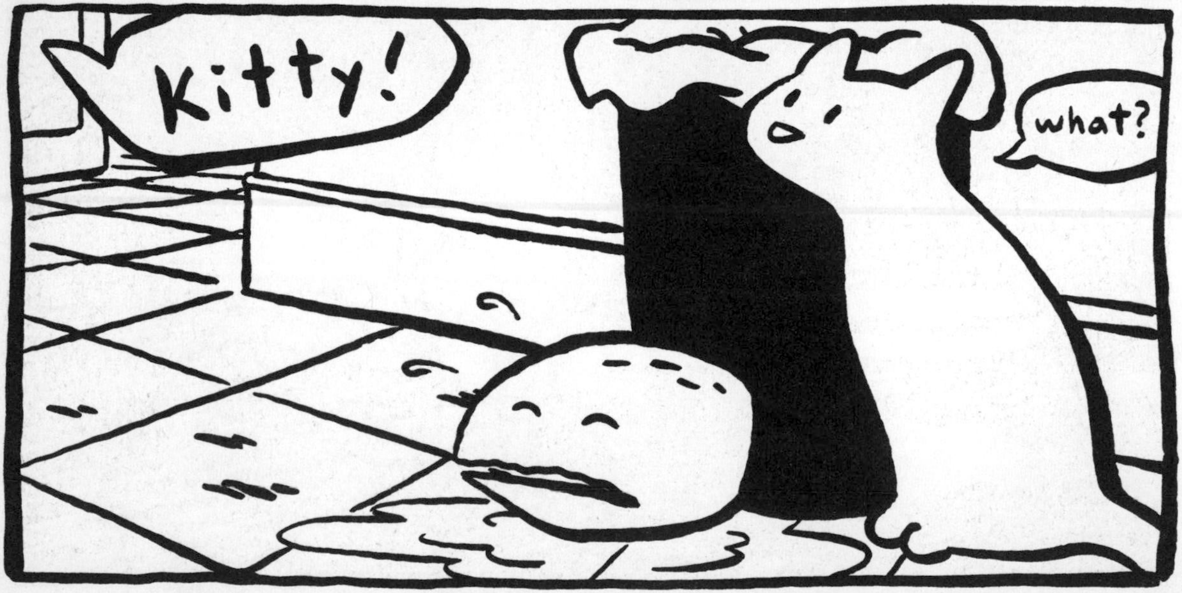
Kitty!
what?

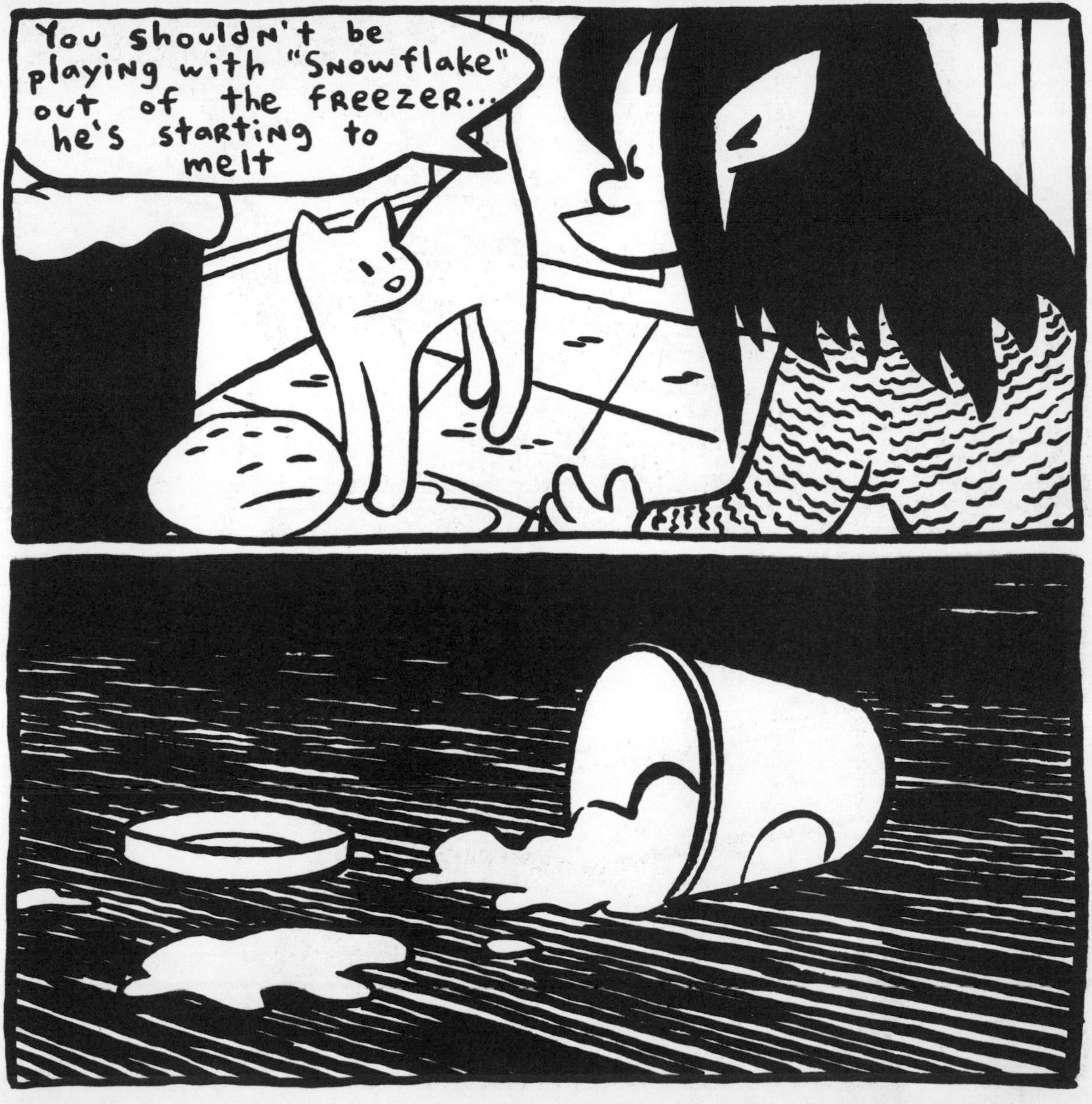
You shouldn't be playing with "Snowflake" out of the freezer... he's starting to melt

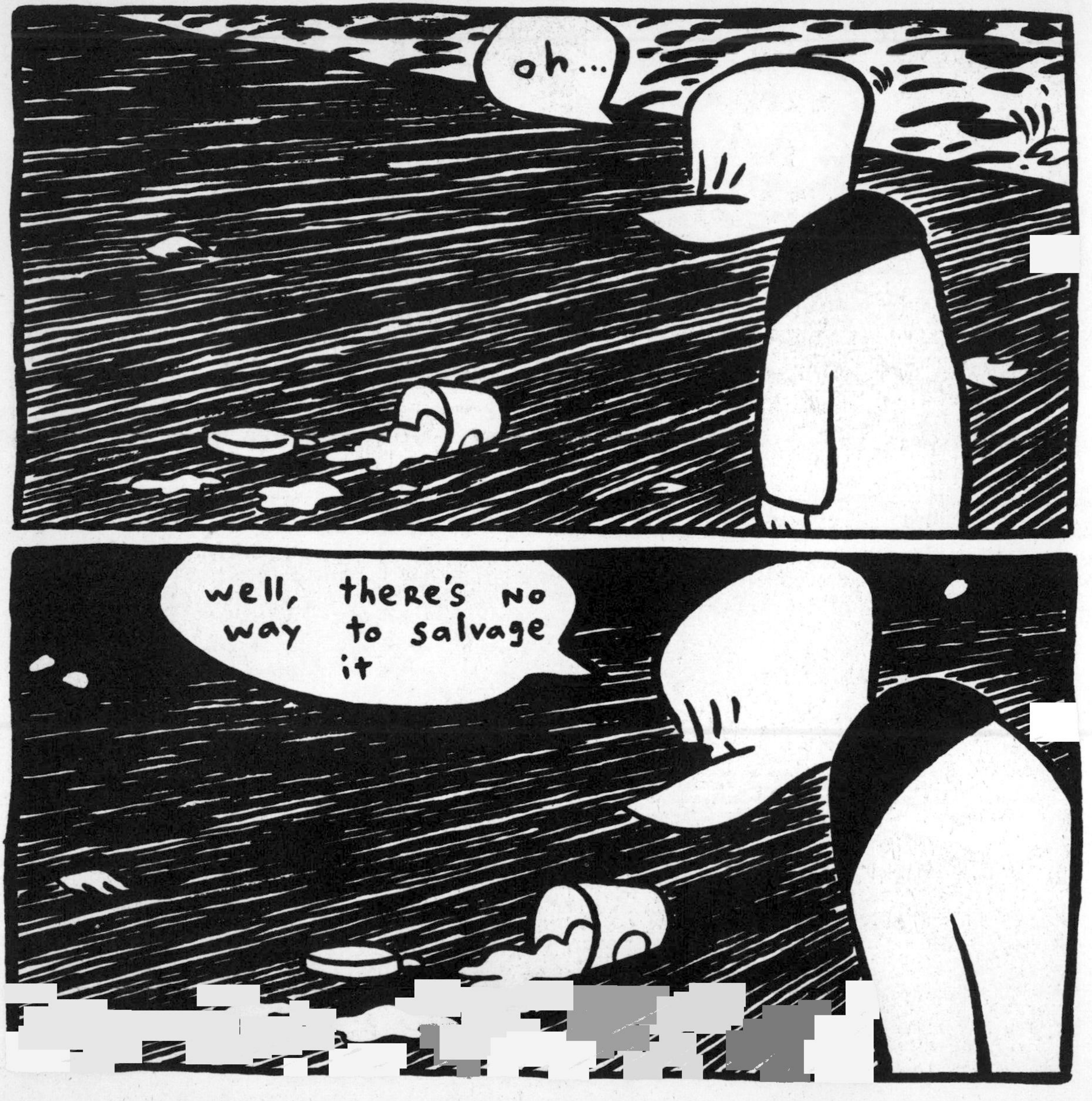
oh...
well, there's no way to salvage it

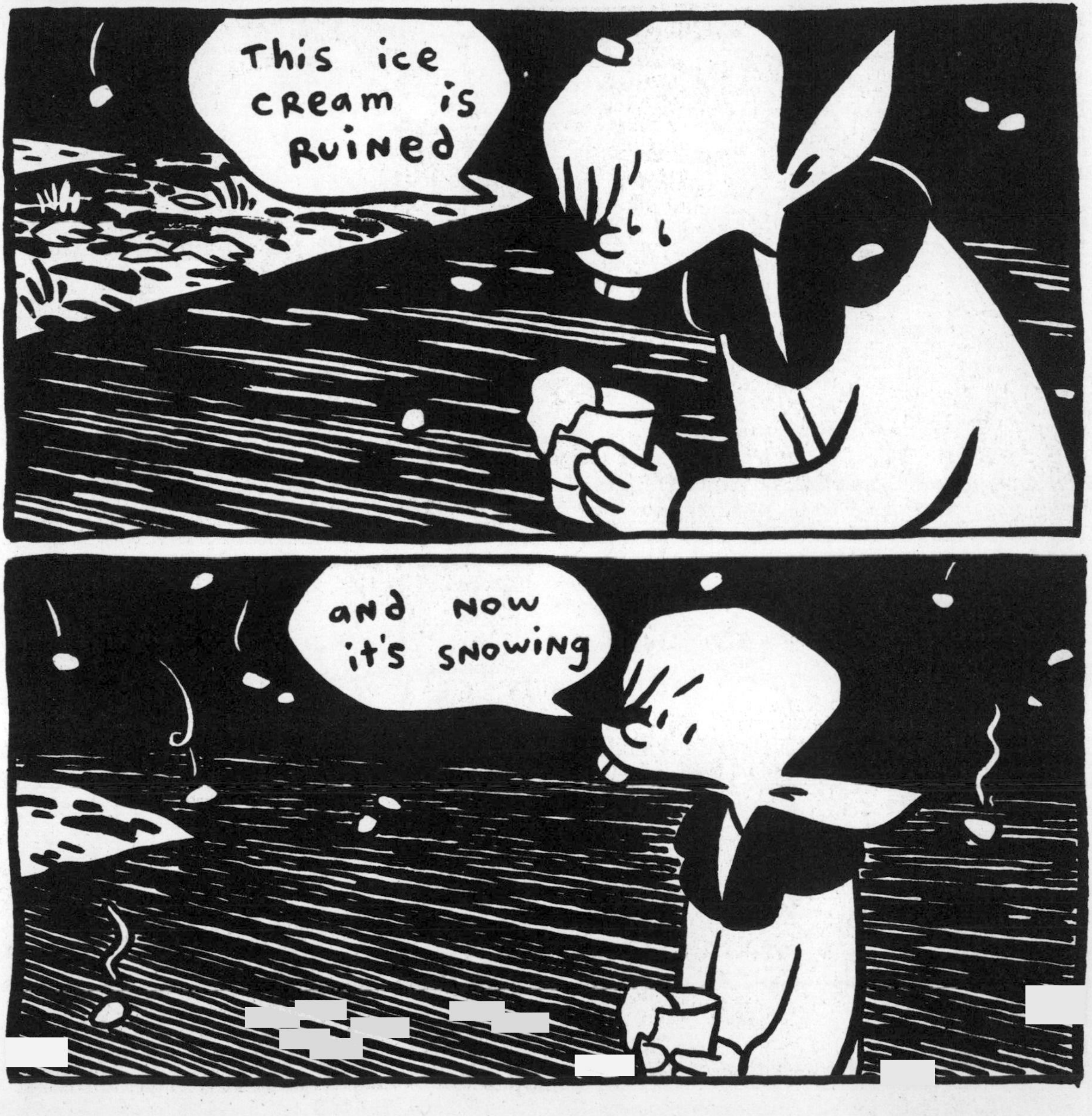
This ice cream is ruined
and now it's snowing

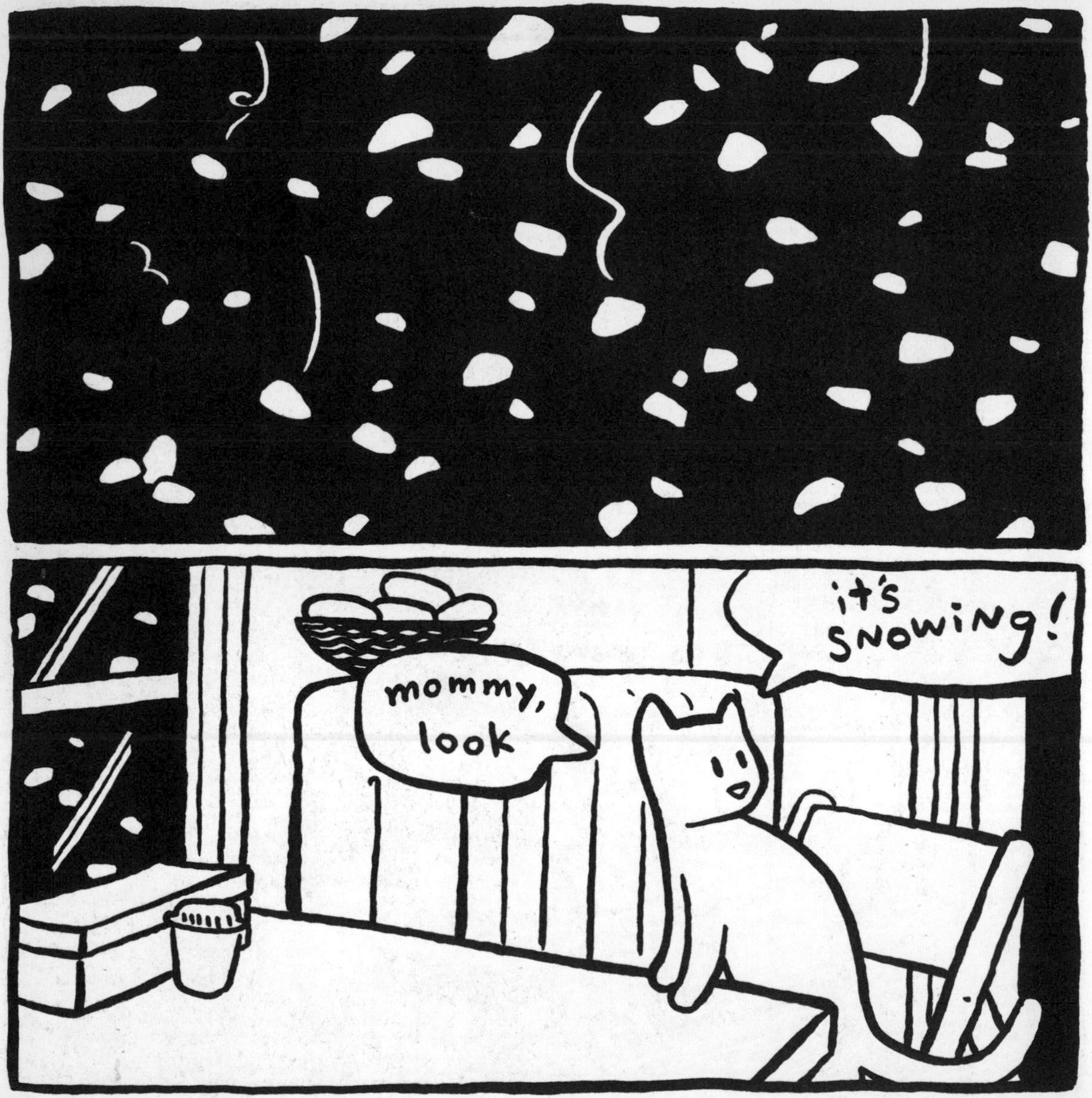
mommy,
look
it's
SNOWING!

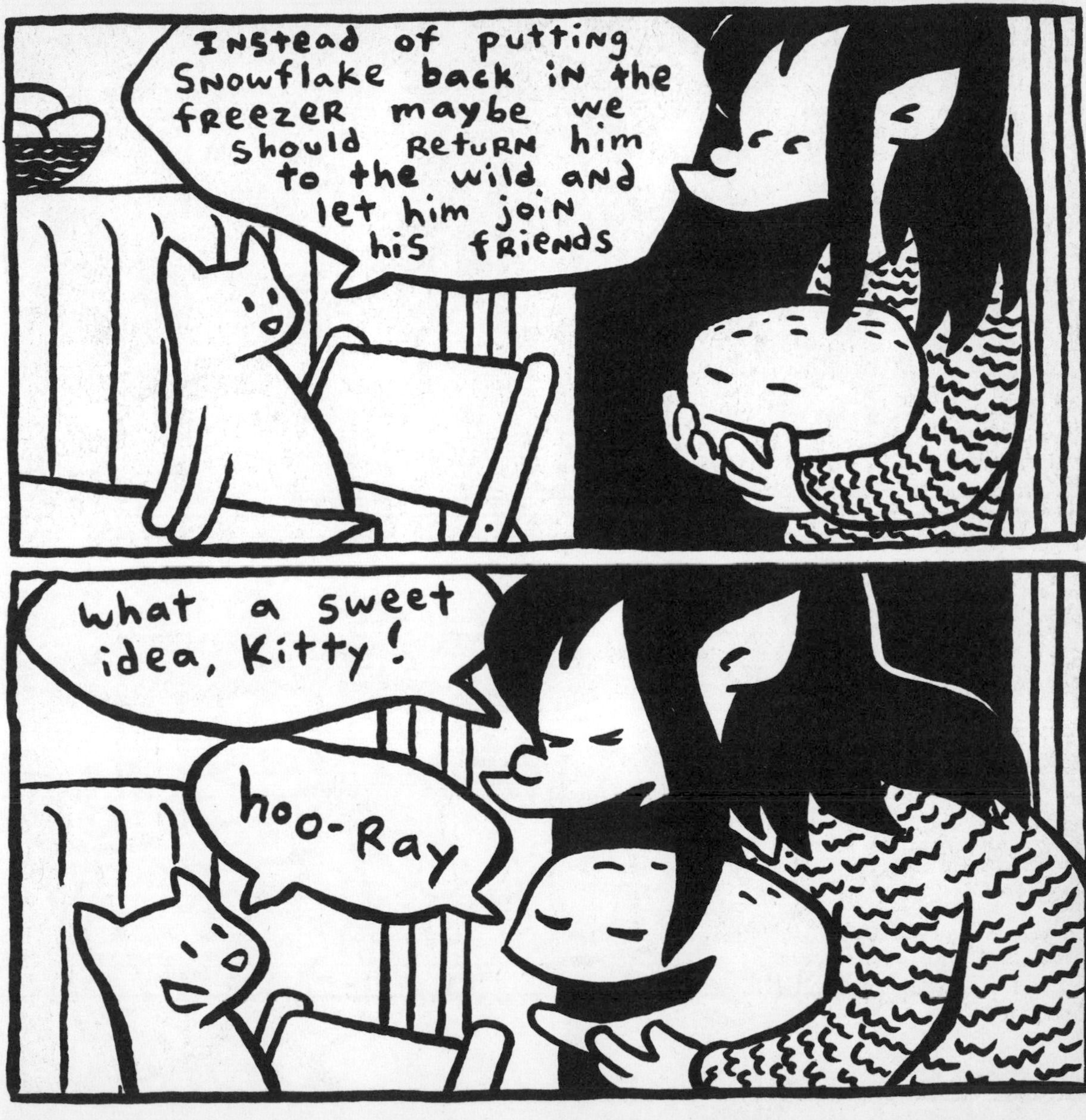
Instead of putting Snowflake back in the freezer maybe we should return him to the wild and let him join his friends
what a sweet idea, Kitty!
hoo-Ray

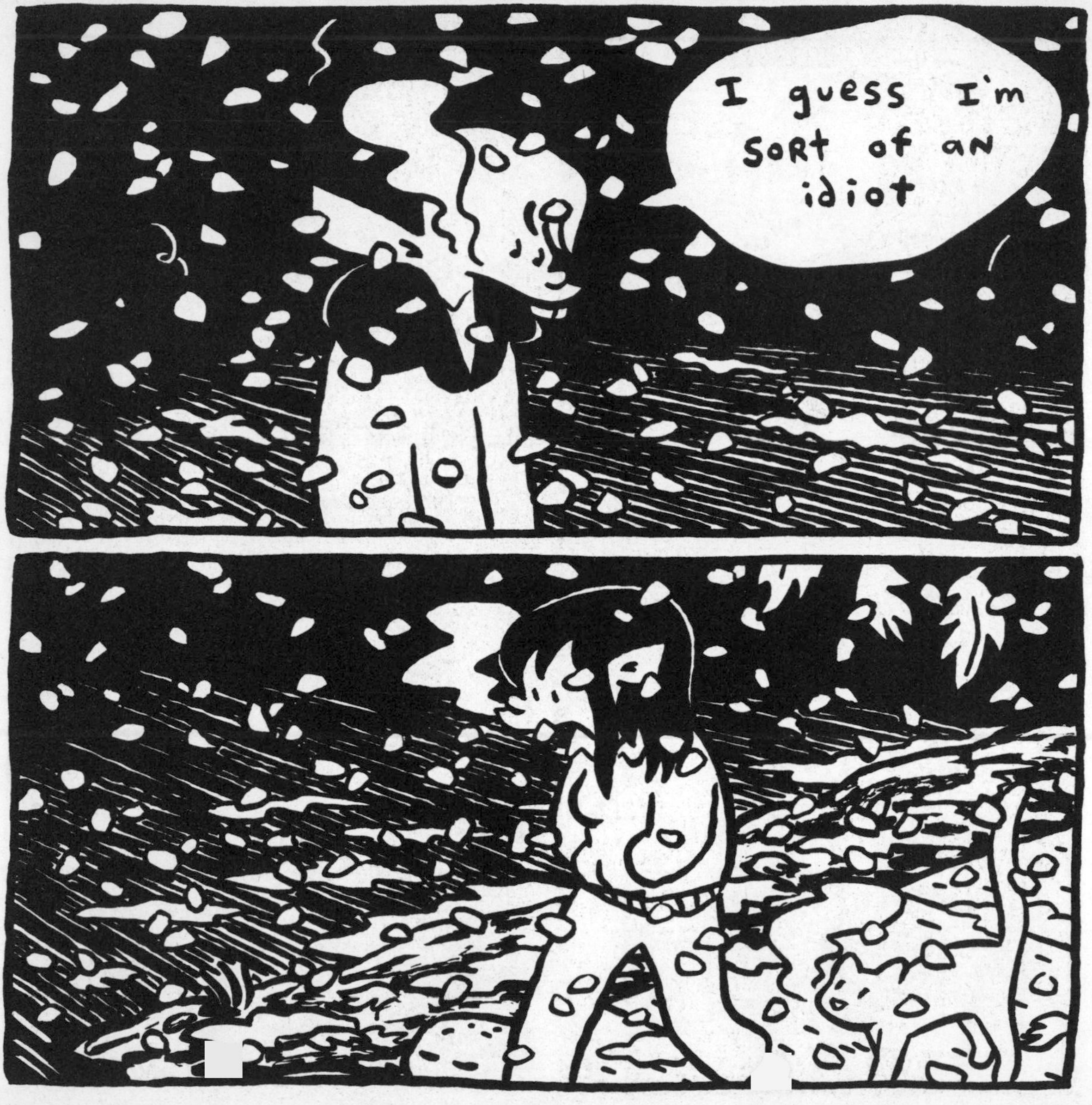
I guess I'm sort of an idiot

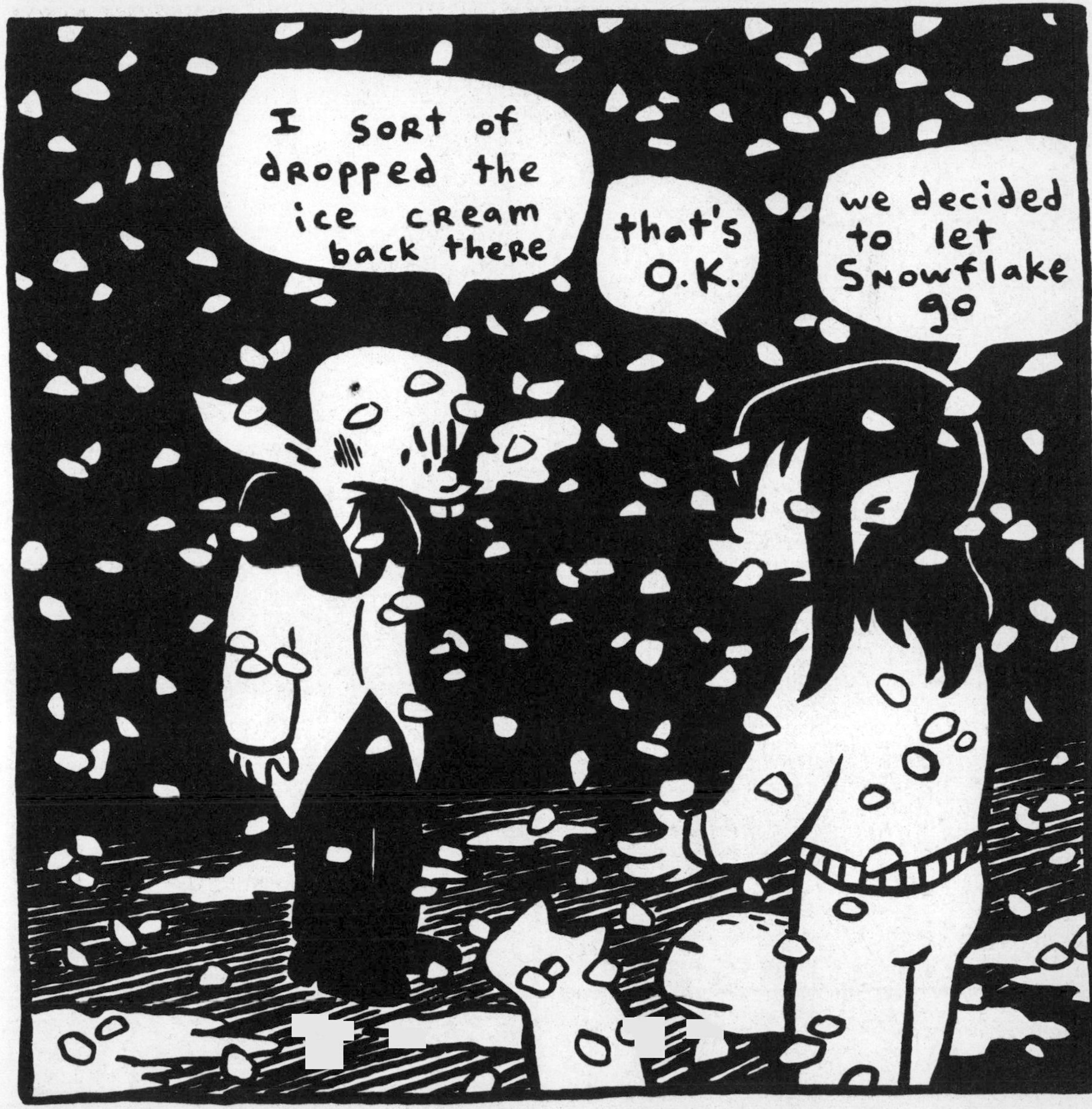
I sort of dropped the ice cream back there
that's O.K.
we decided to let Snowflake go

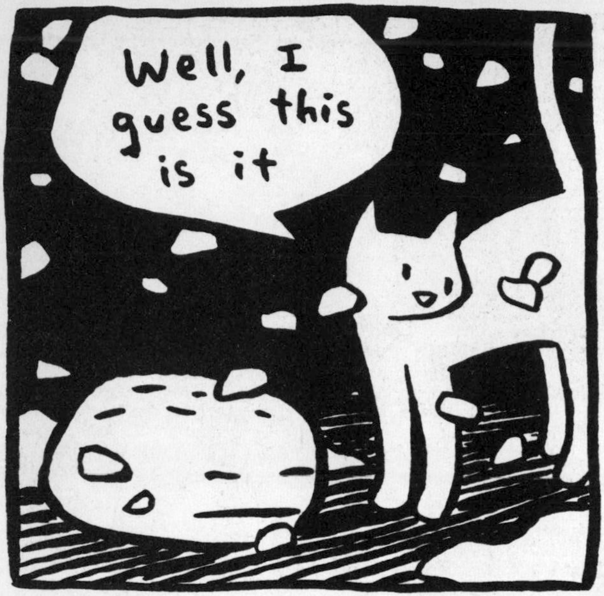
Well, I guess this is it

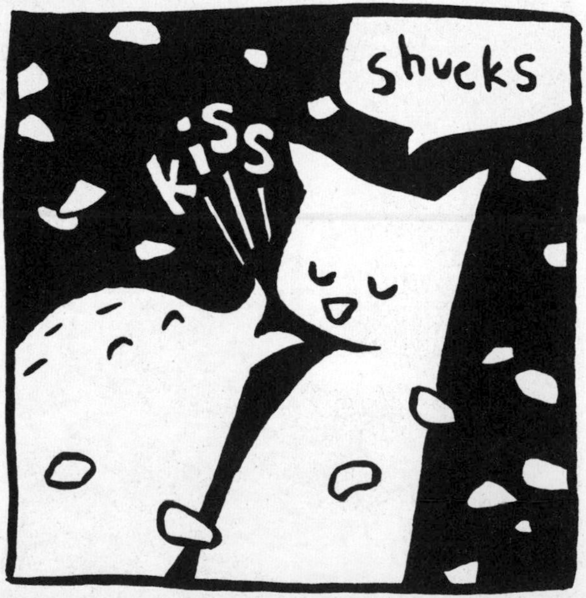
shucks
KiSS

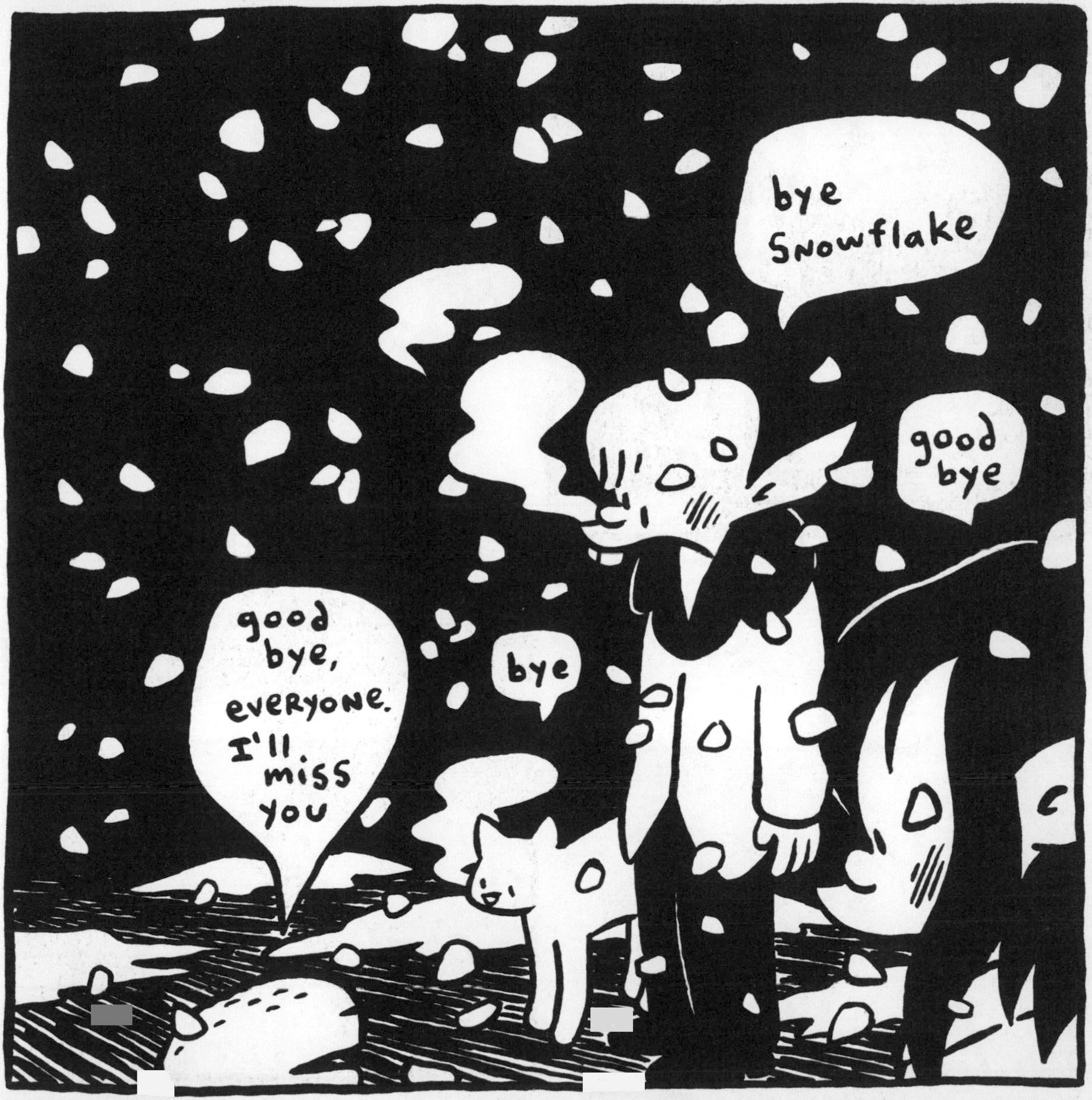
bye Snowflake
good bye
good bye, everyone. I'll miss you
bye

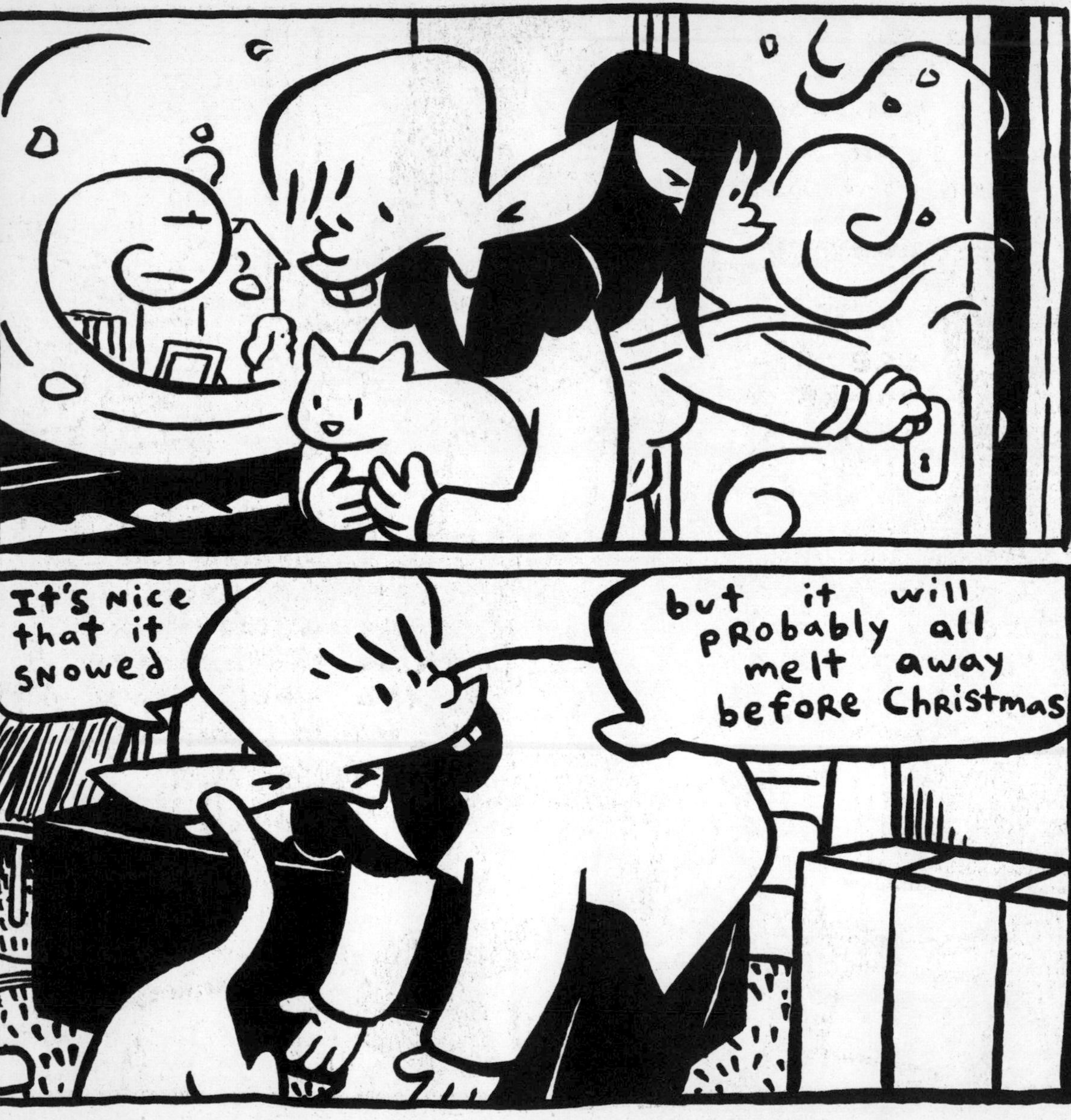
It's nice that it snowed
but it will probably all melt away before Christmas

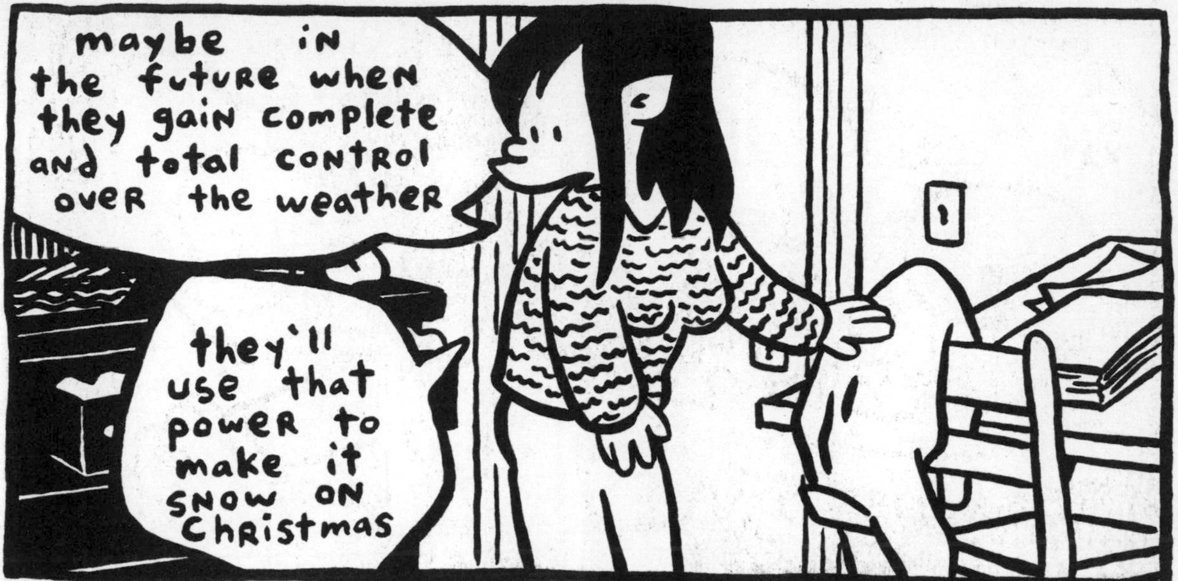
maybe in the future when they gain complete and total control over the weather
they'll use that power to make it snow on Christmas

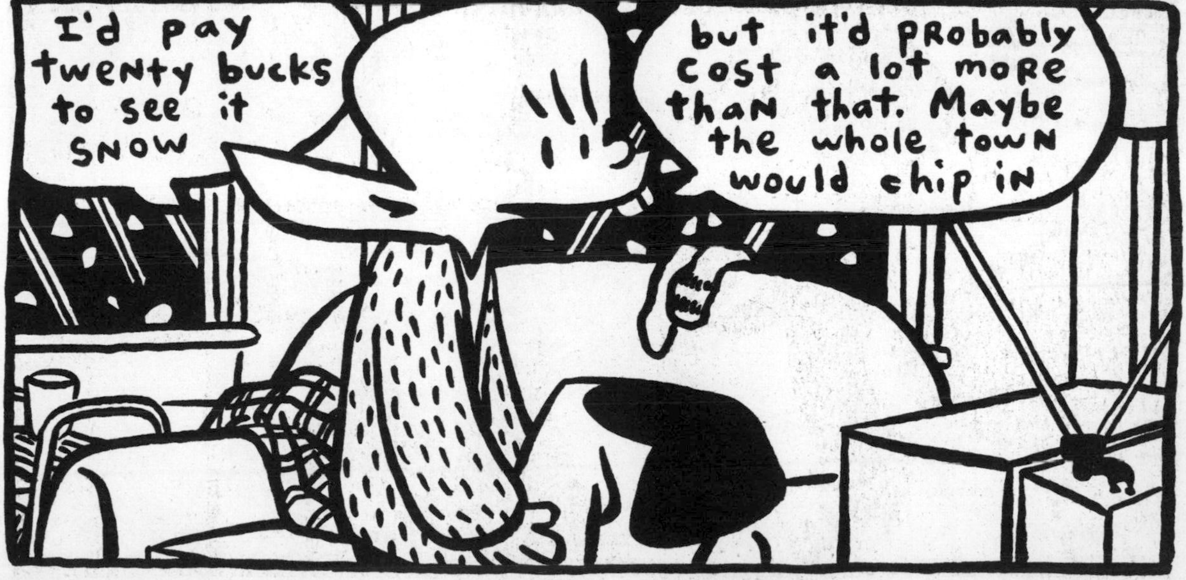
I'd pay twenty bucks to see it snow
but it'd probably cost a lot more than that. Maybe the whole town would chip in

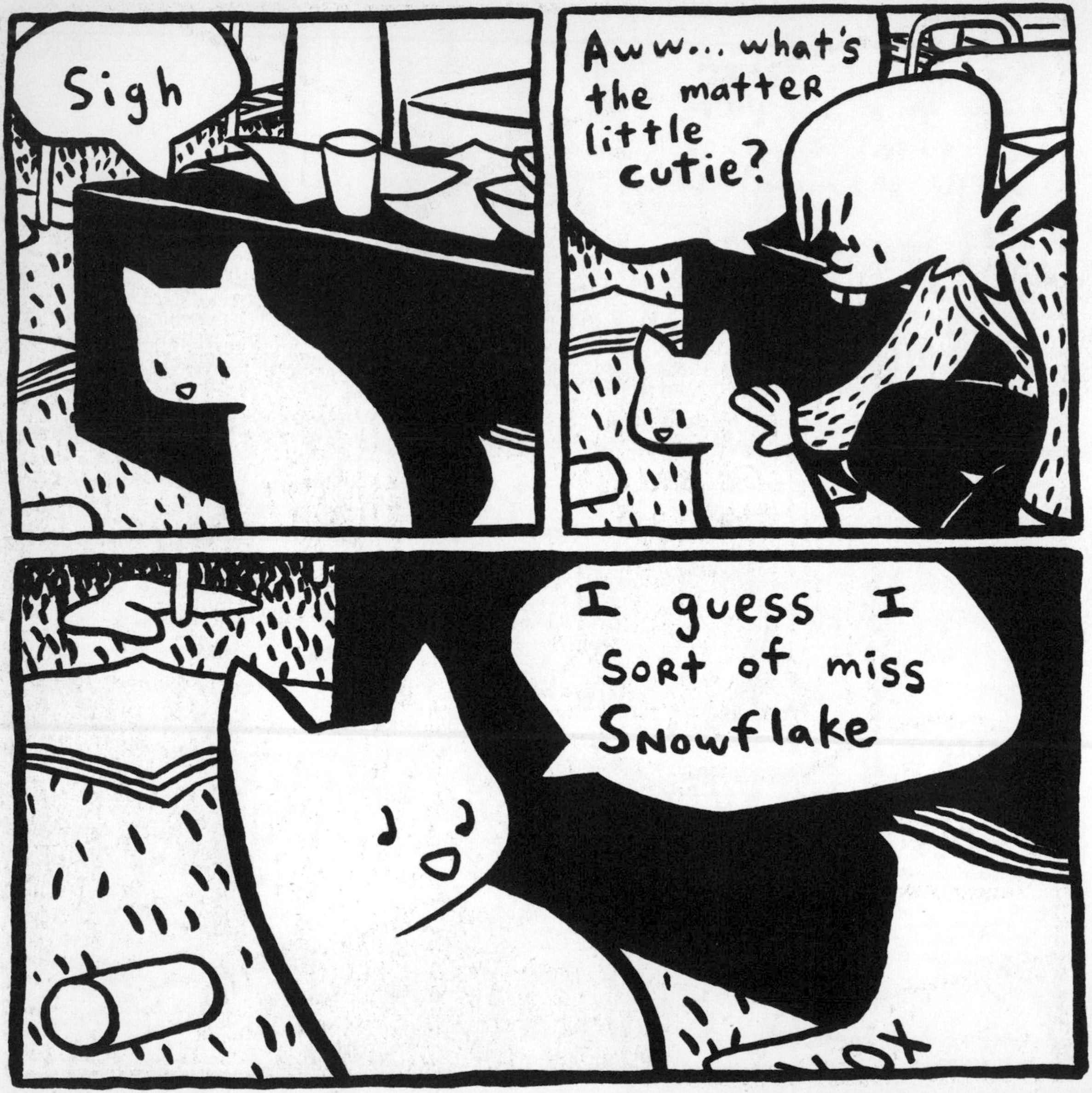
Sigh
Aww... what's the matter little cutie?
I guess I sort of miss Snowflake

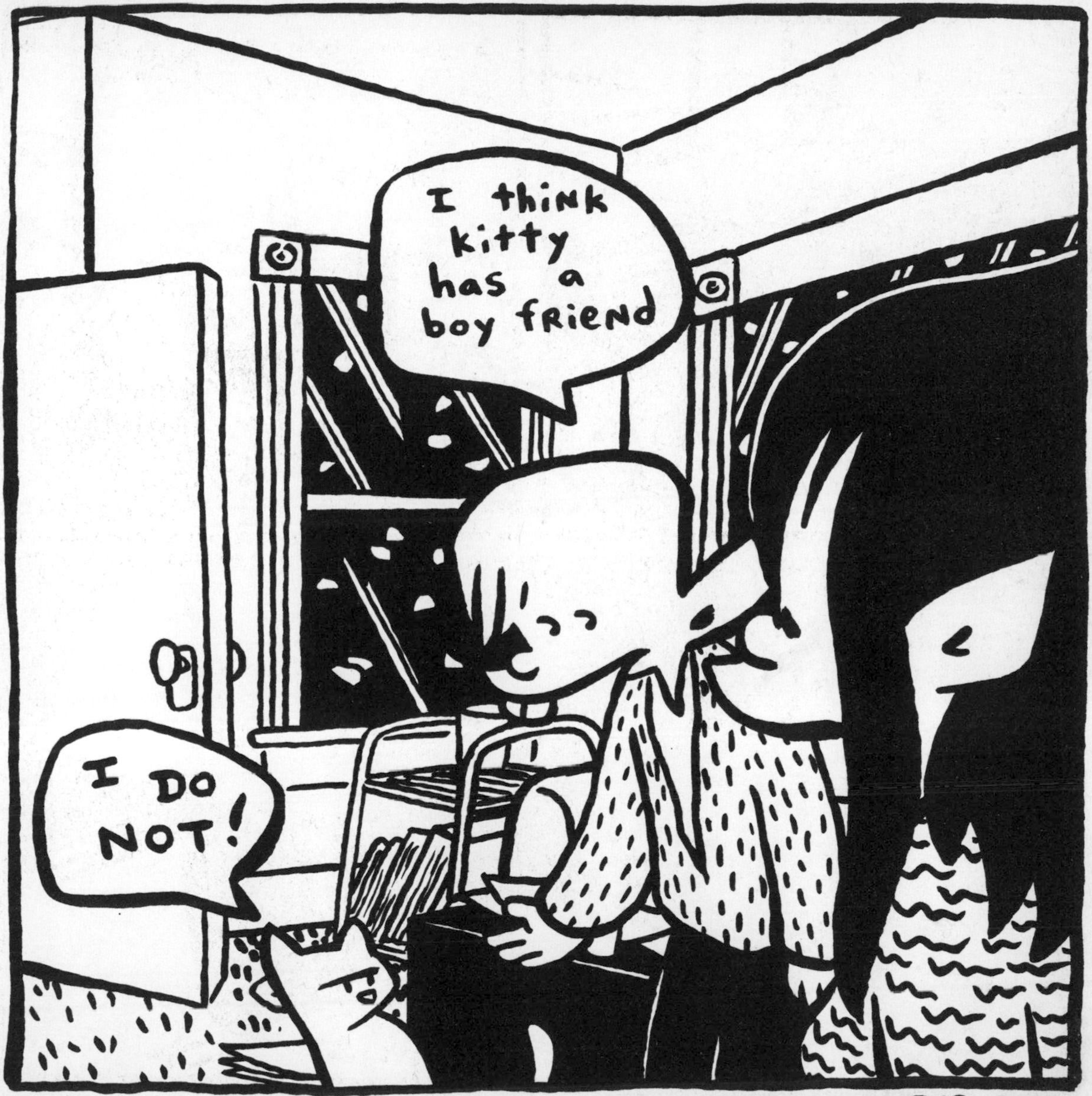
I think kitty has a boy friend
I DO NOT!

THE END

FROG & FLY

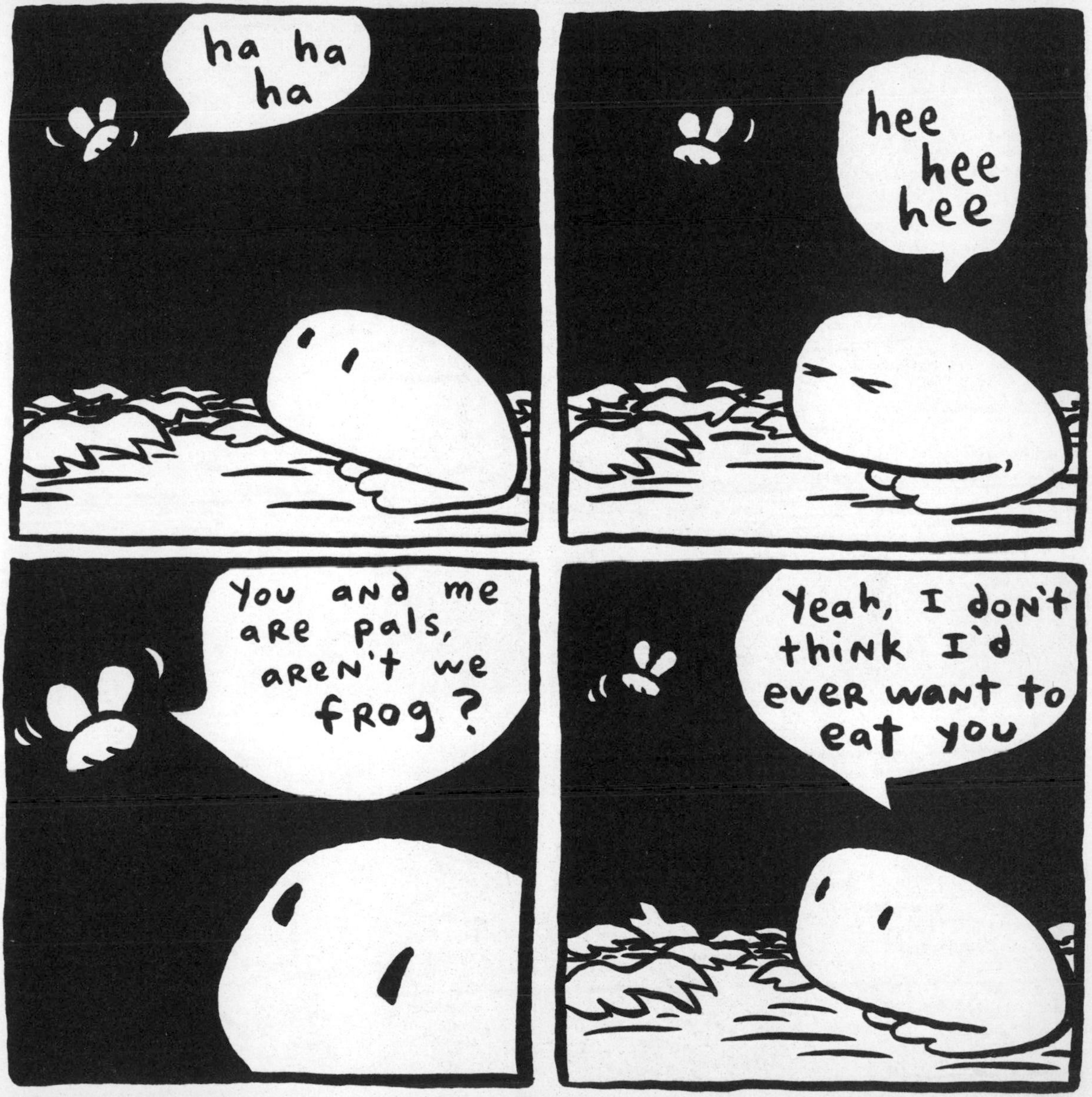

ha ha ha
hee hee hee
You and me are pals, aren't we frog?
Yeah, I don't think I'd ever want to eat you

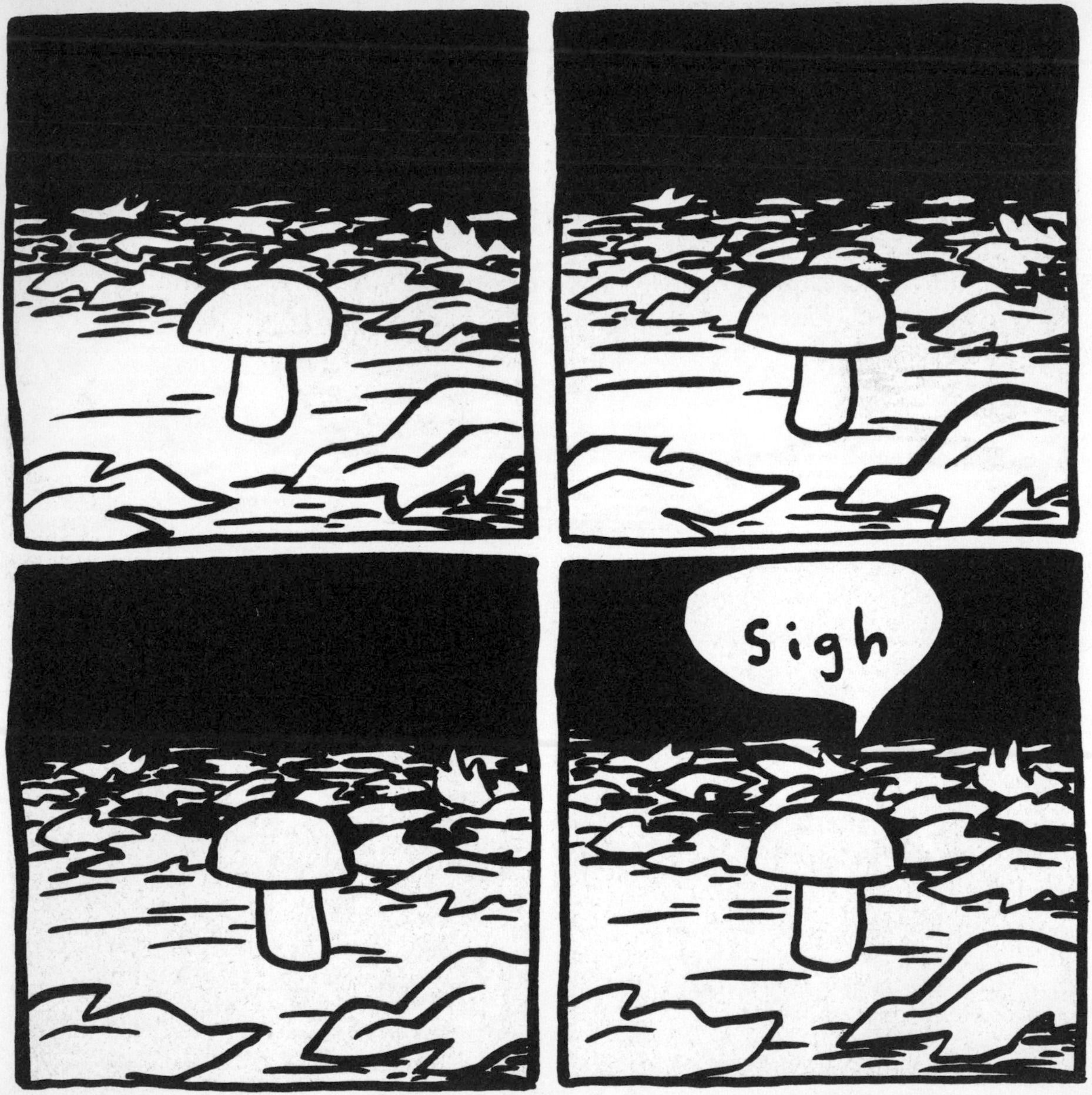
Sigh

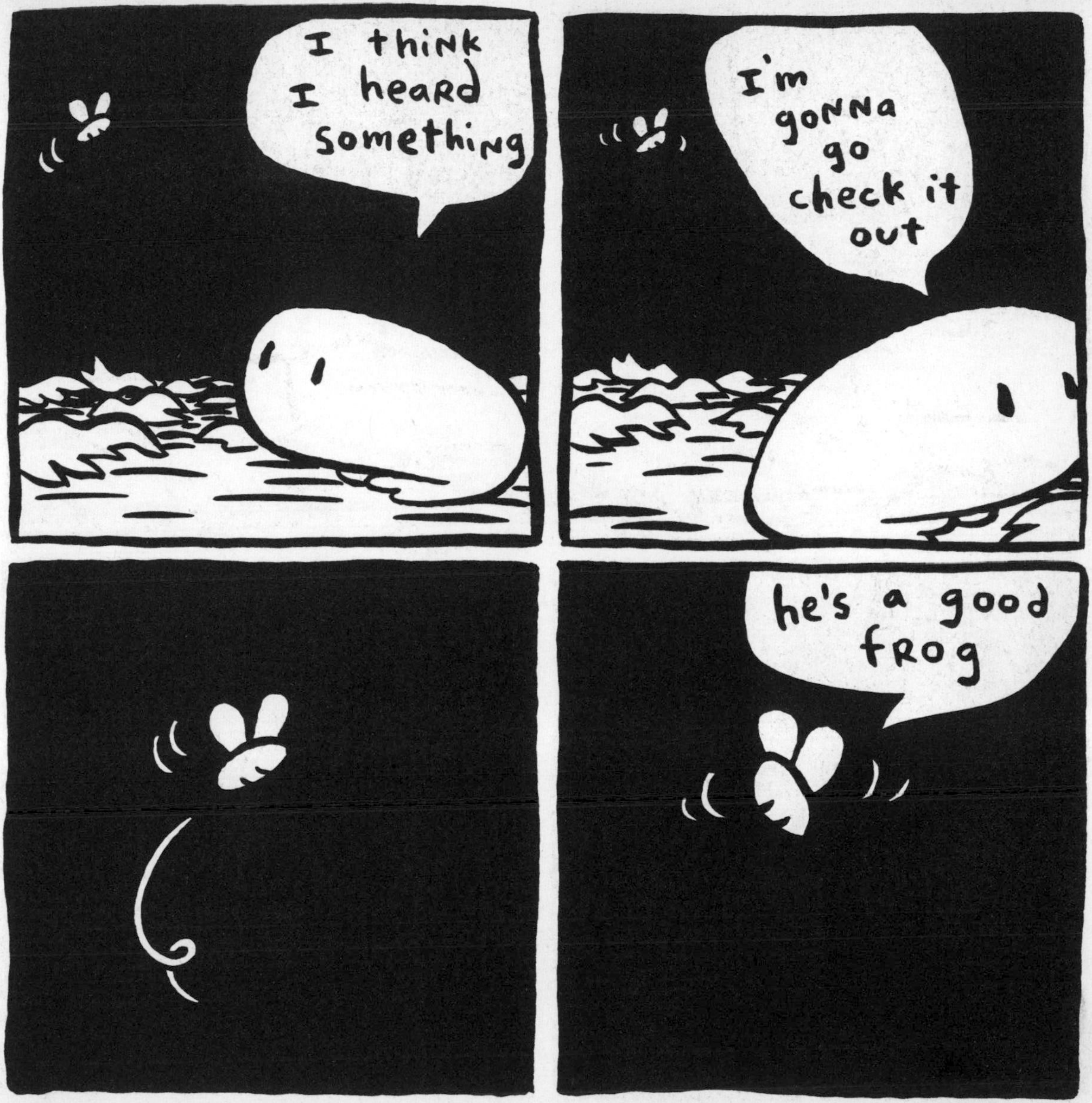
I think I heard something
I'm gonna go check it out
he's a good frog

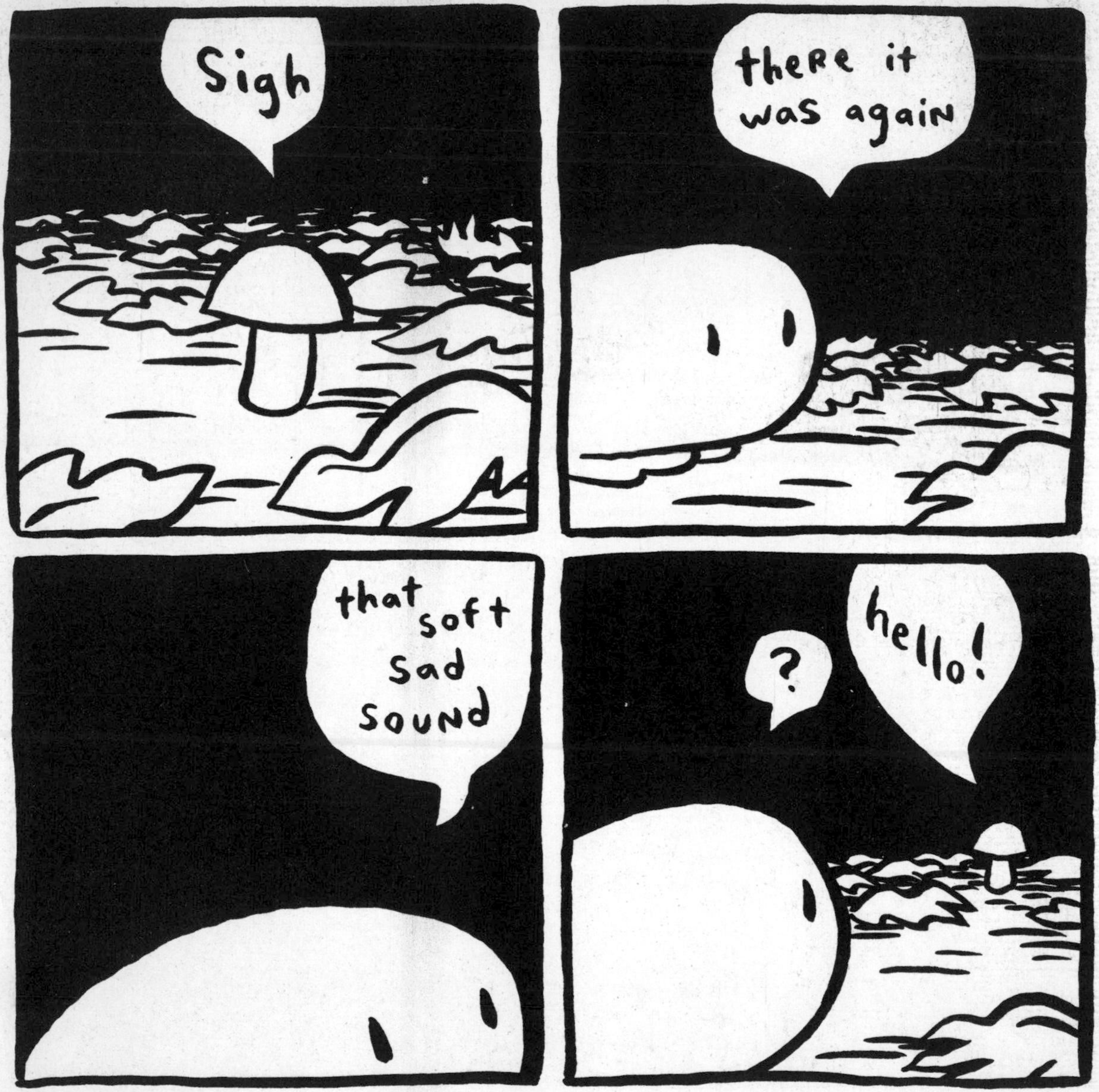
Sigh
there it was again
that soft sad sound
?
hello!

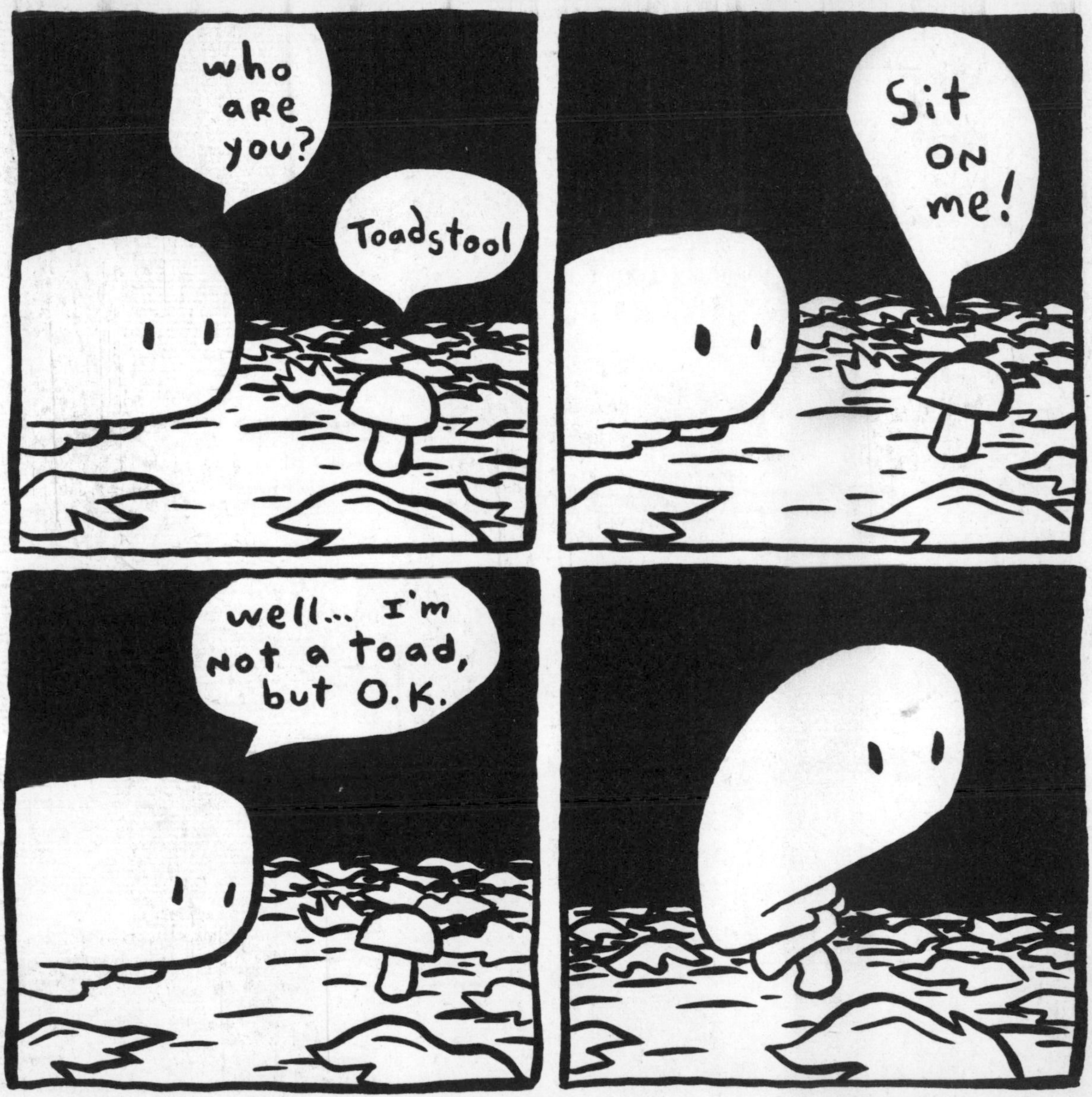
who are you?
Toadstool
Sit on me!
well... I'm not a toad, but O.K.

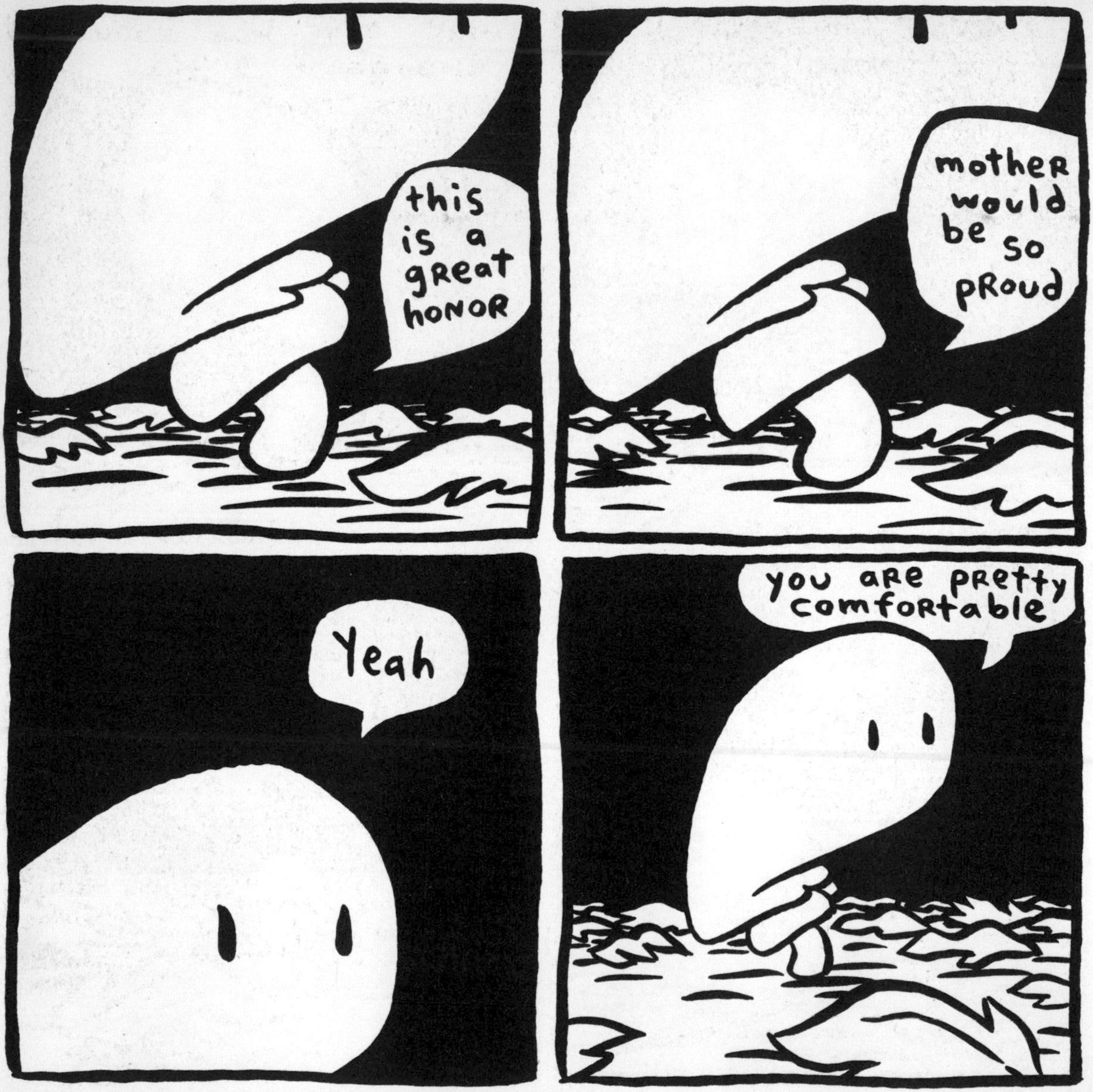
this is a great honor
mother would be so proud
Yeah
you are pretty comfortable

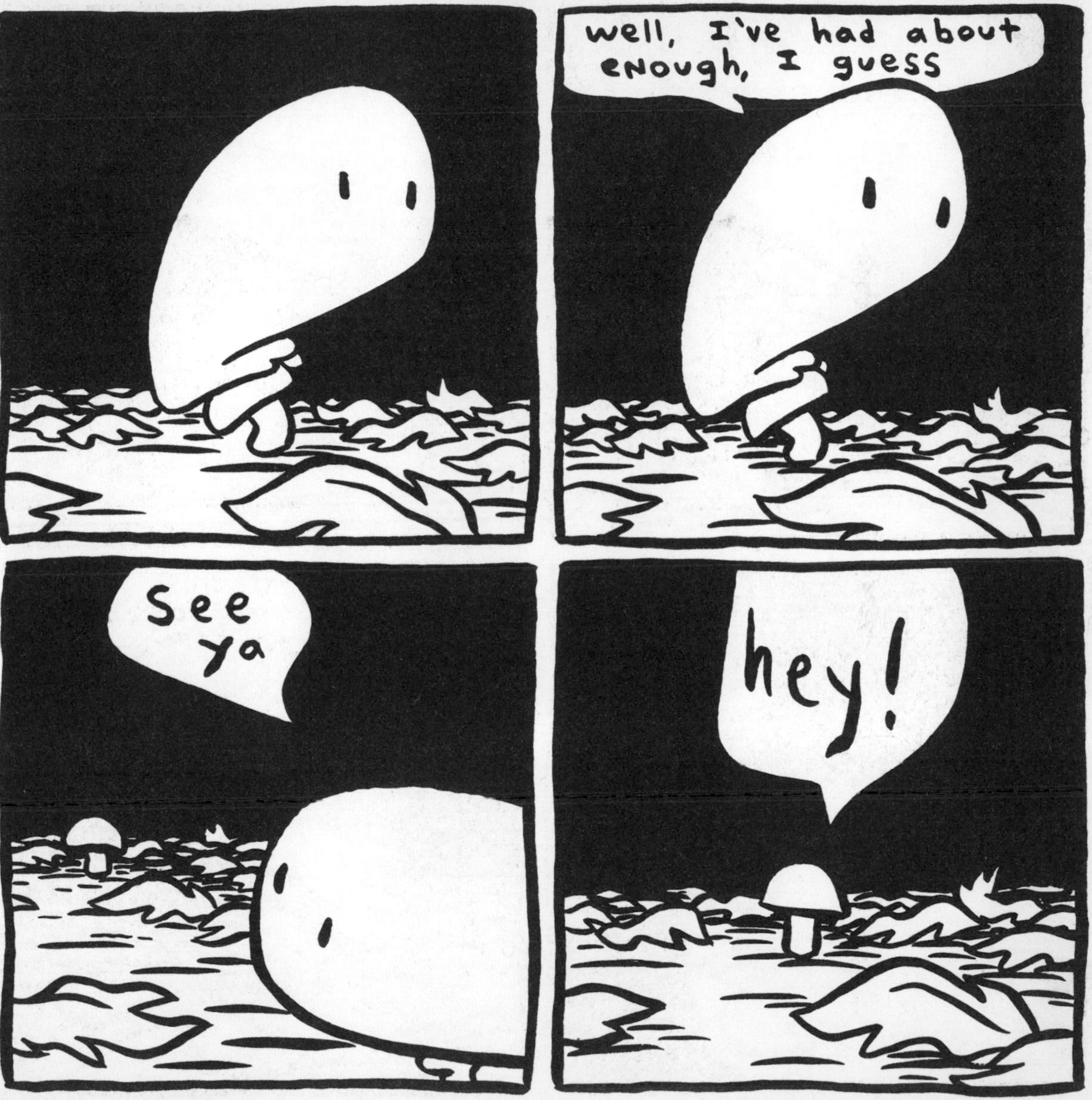
well, I've had about enough, I guess
see ya
hey!

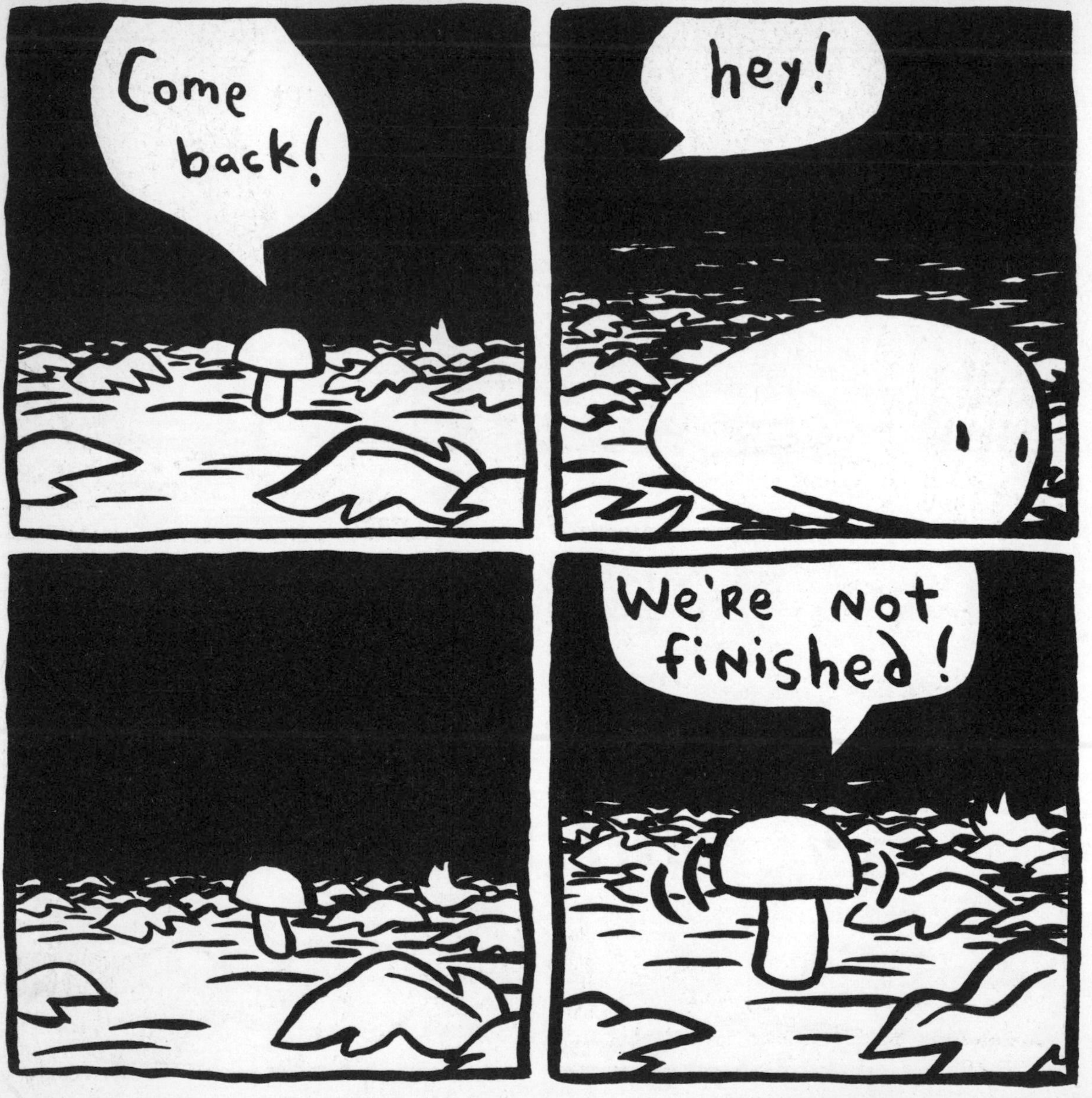
Come back!
hey!
We're not finished!

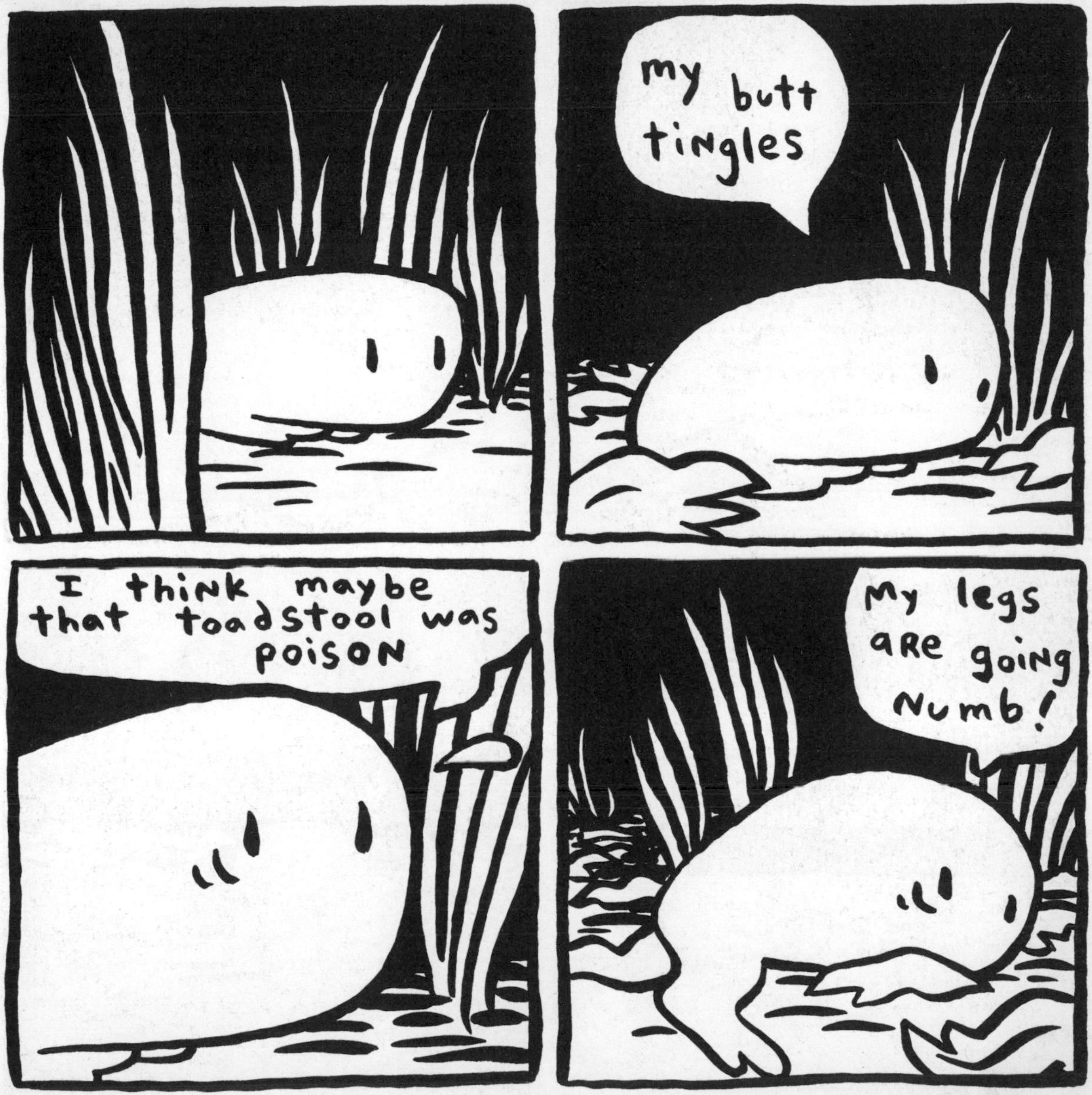
my butt tingles
I think maybe that toadstool was poison
My legs are going numb!

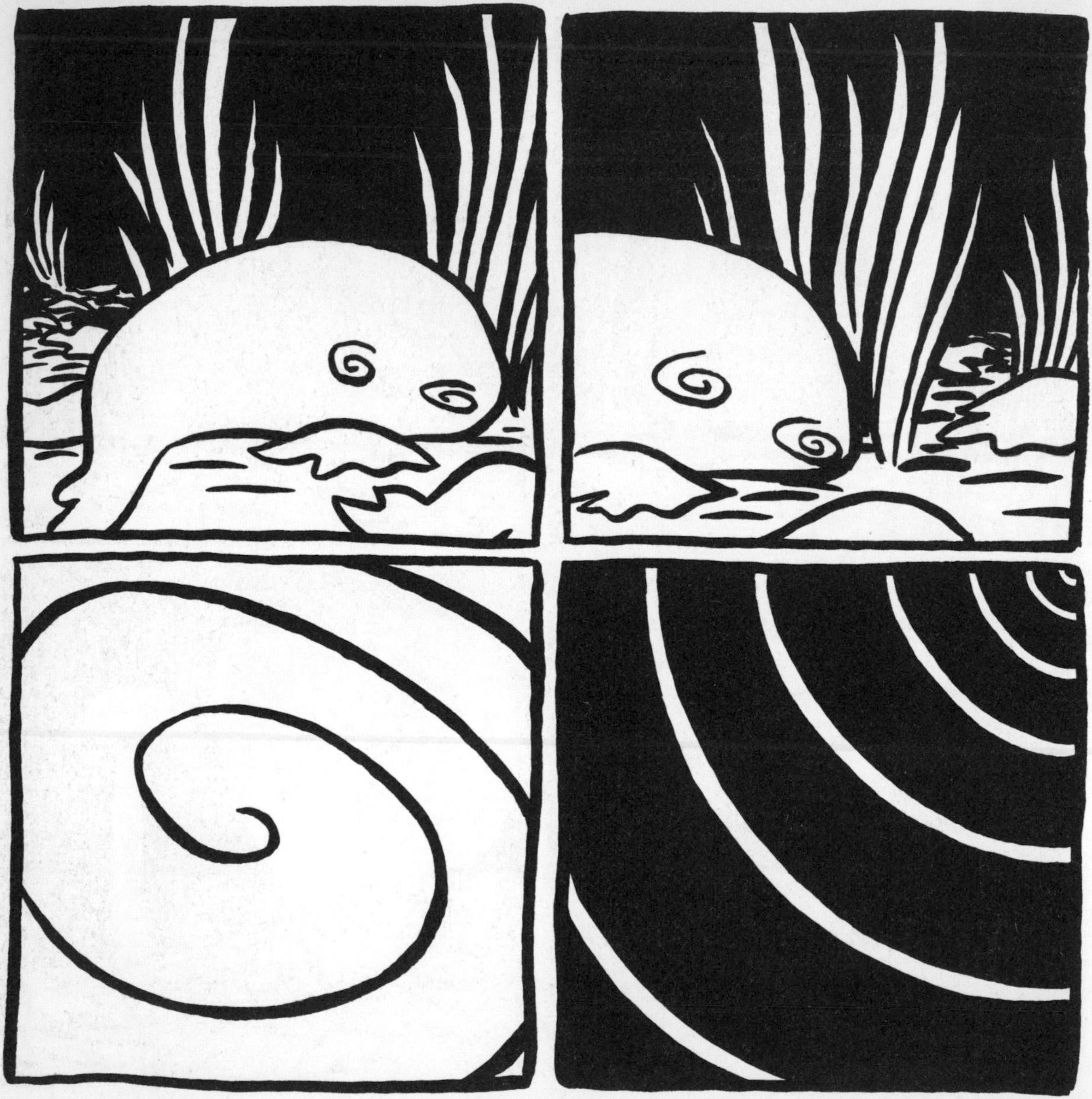

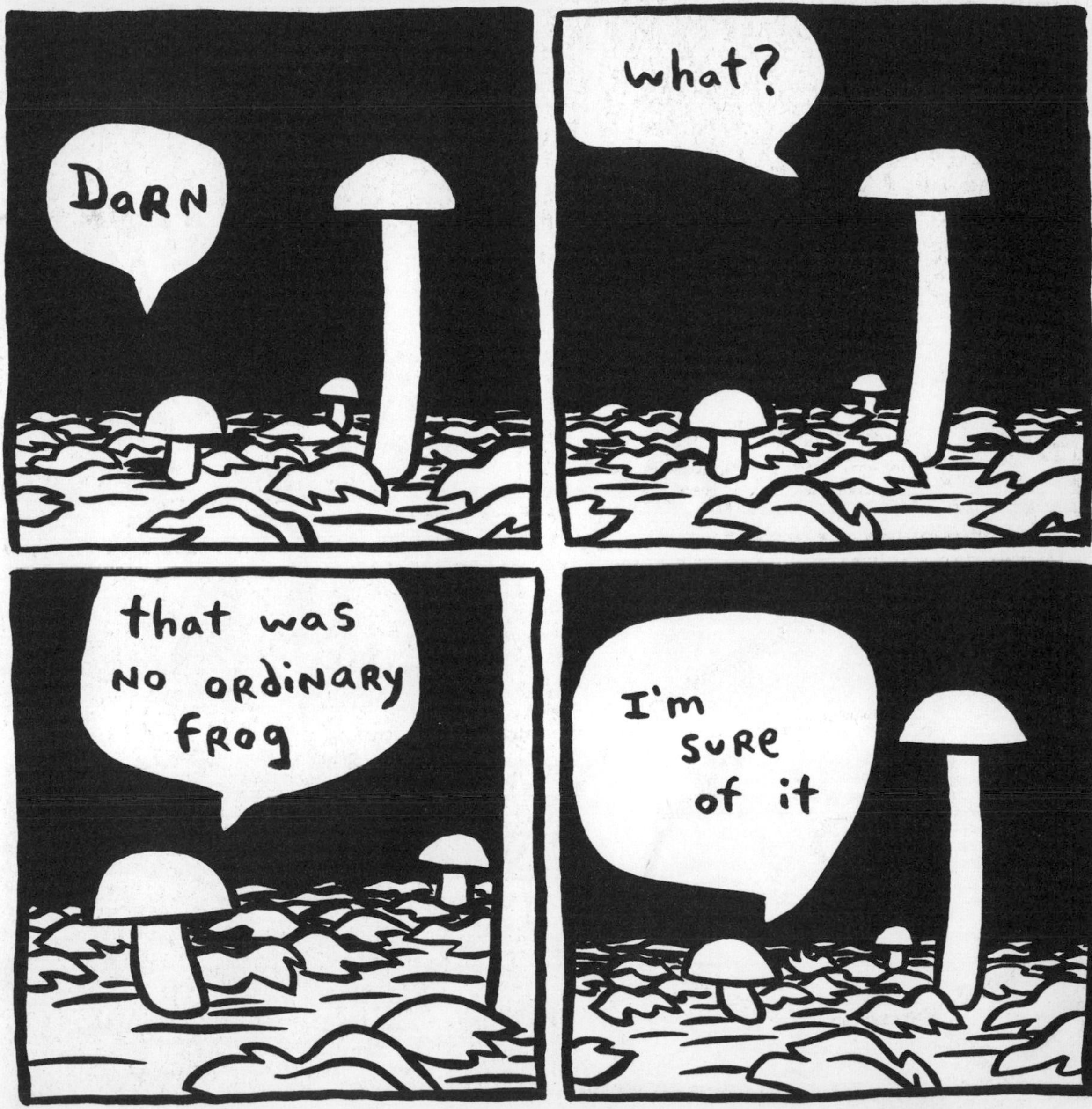
DaRN
what?
that was NO ORdiNaRy fRog
I'm suRe of it

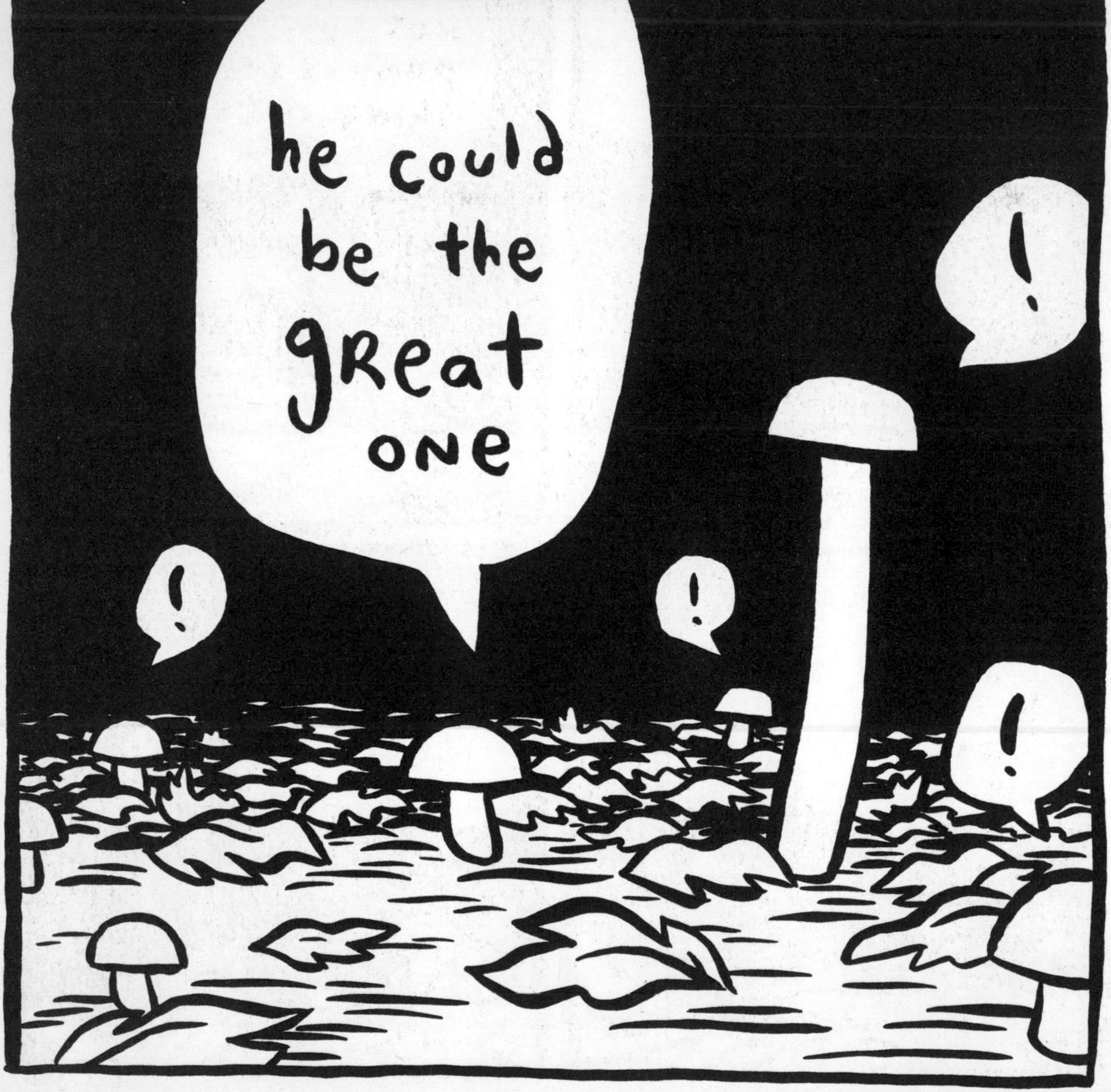

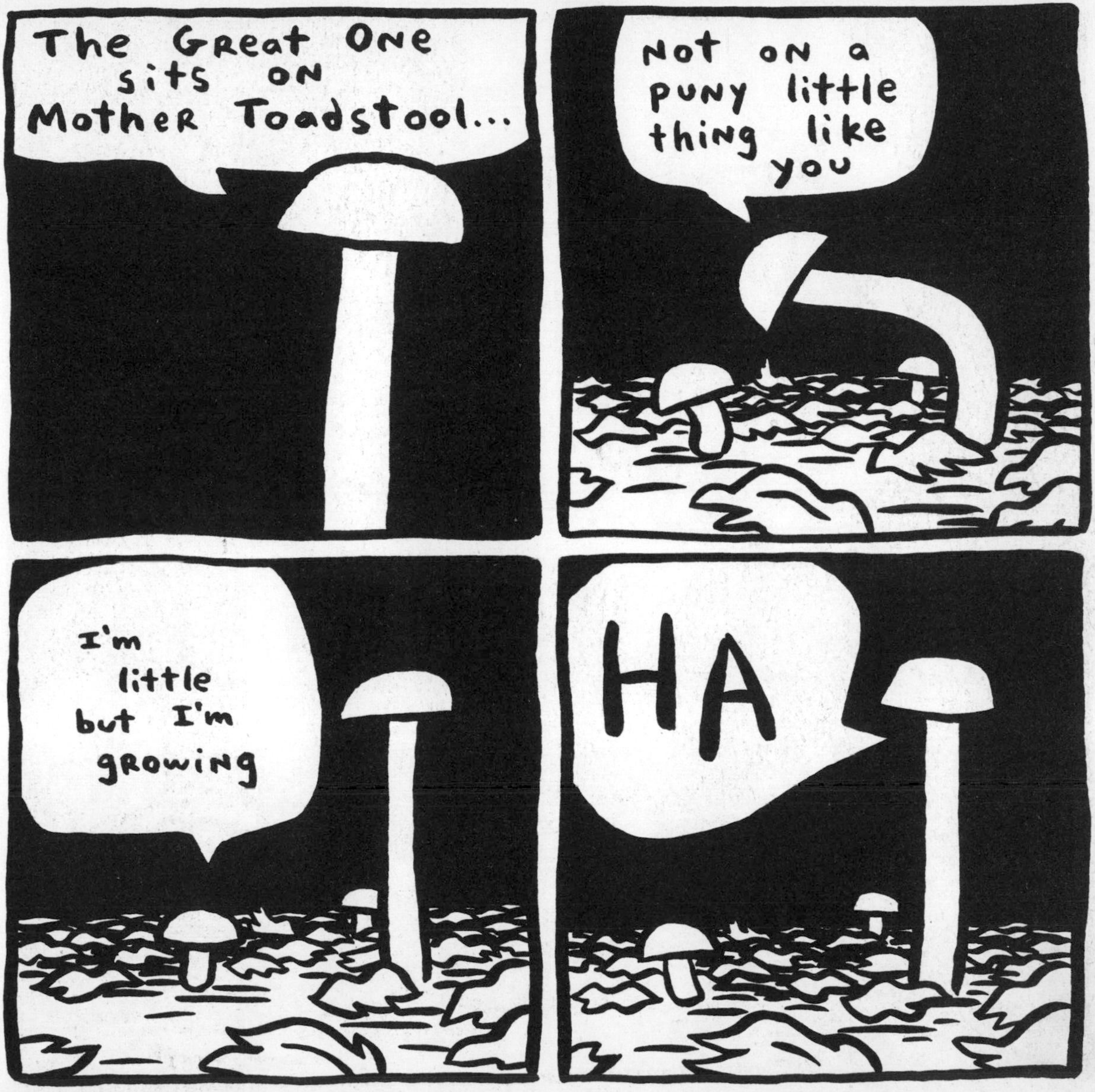
The Great One sits on Mother Toadstool...
Not on a puny little thing like you
I'm little but I'm growing
HA

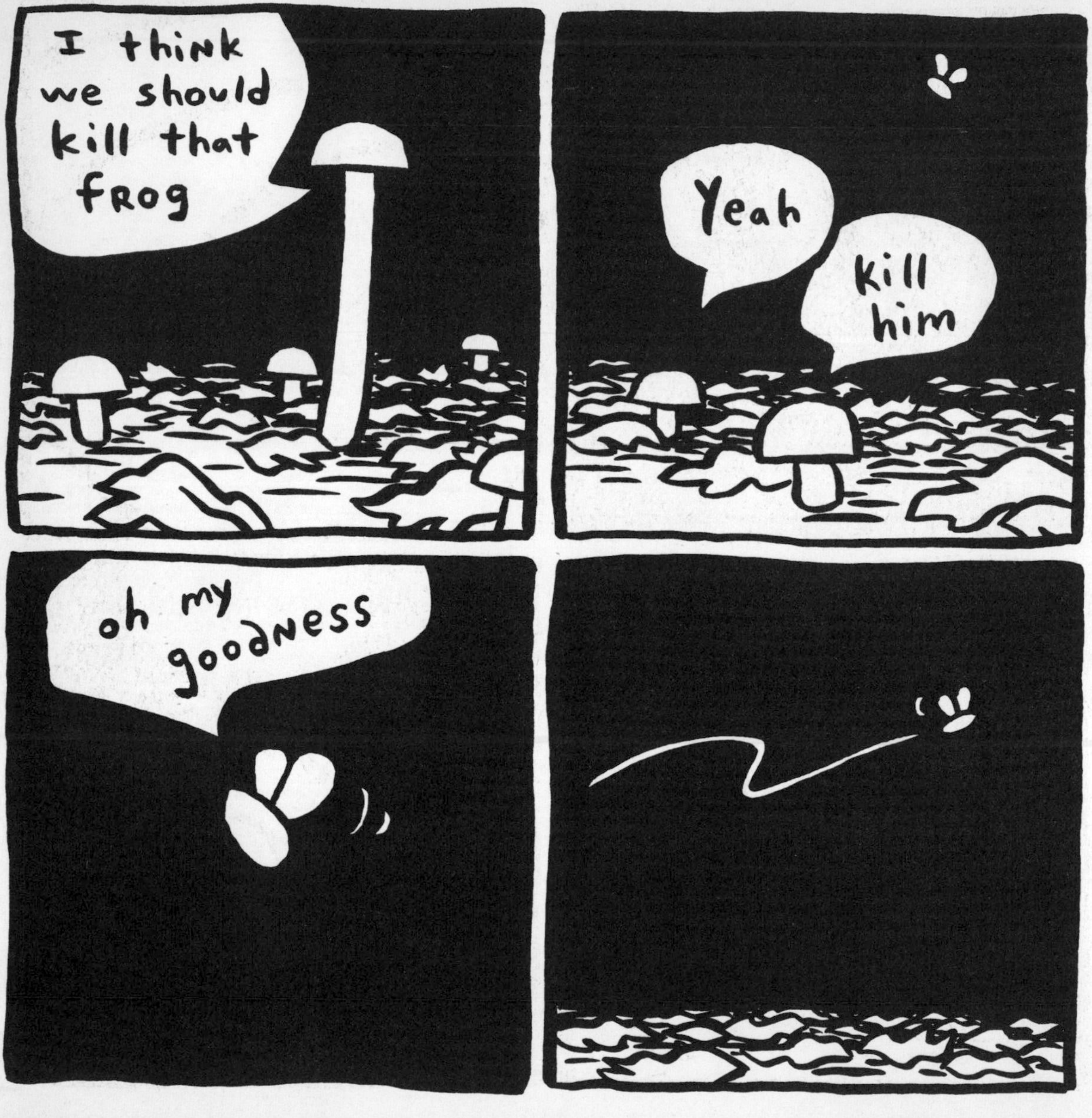
I think we should kill that frog
Yeah
kill him
oh my goodness

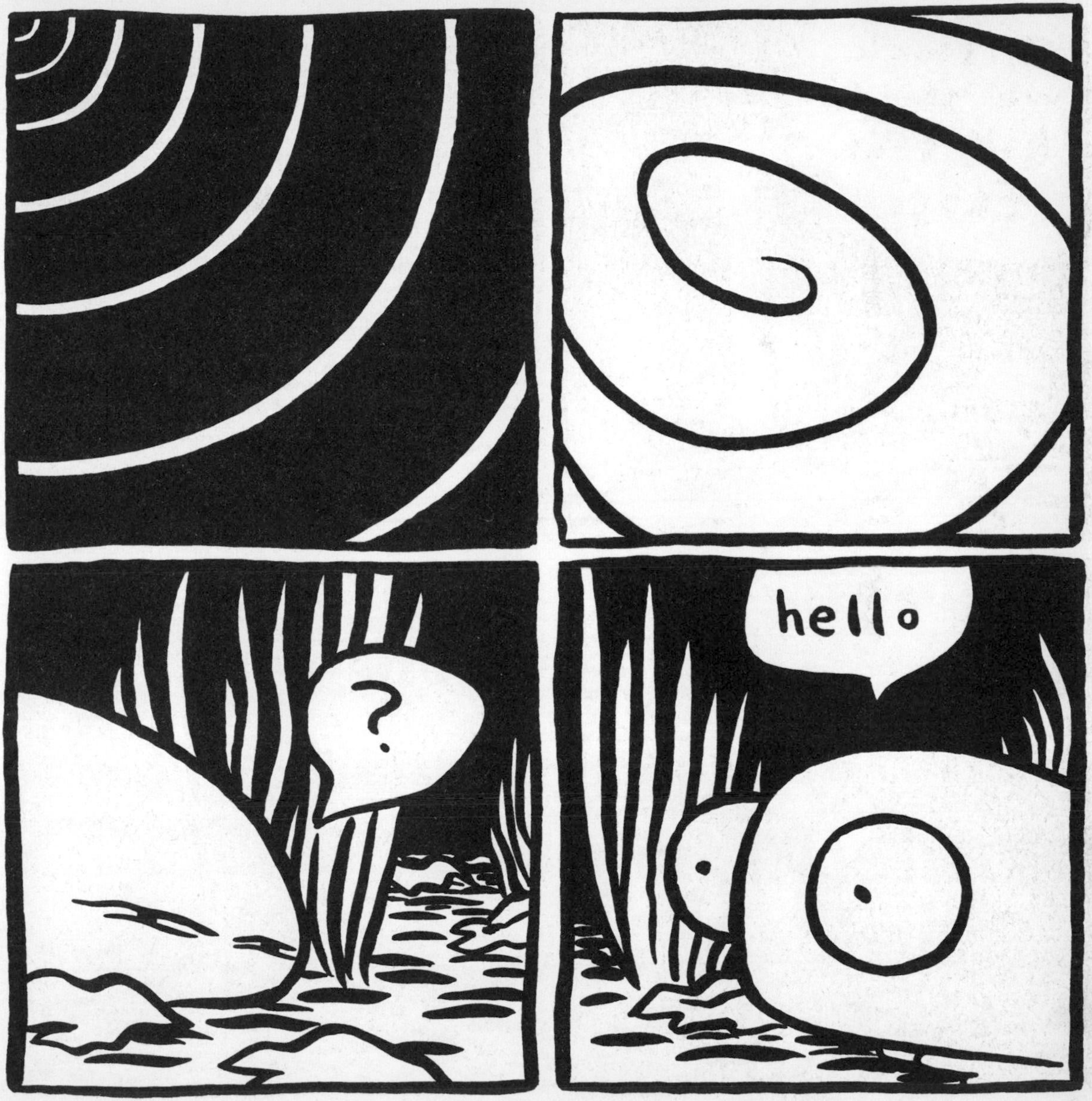
?
hello

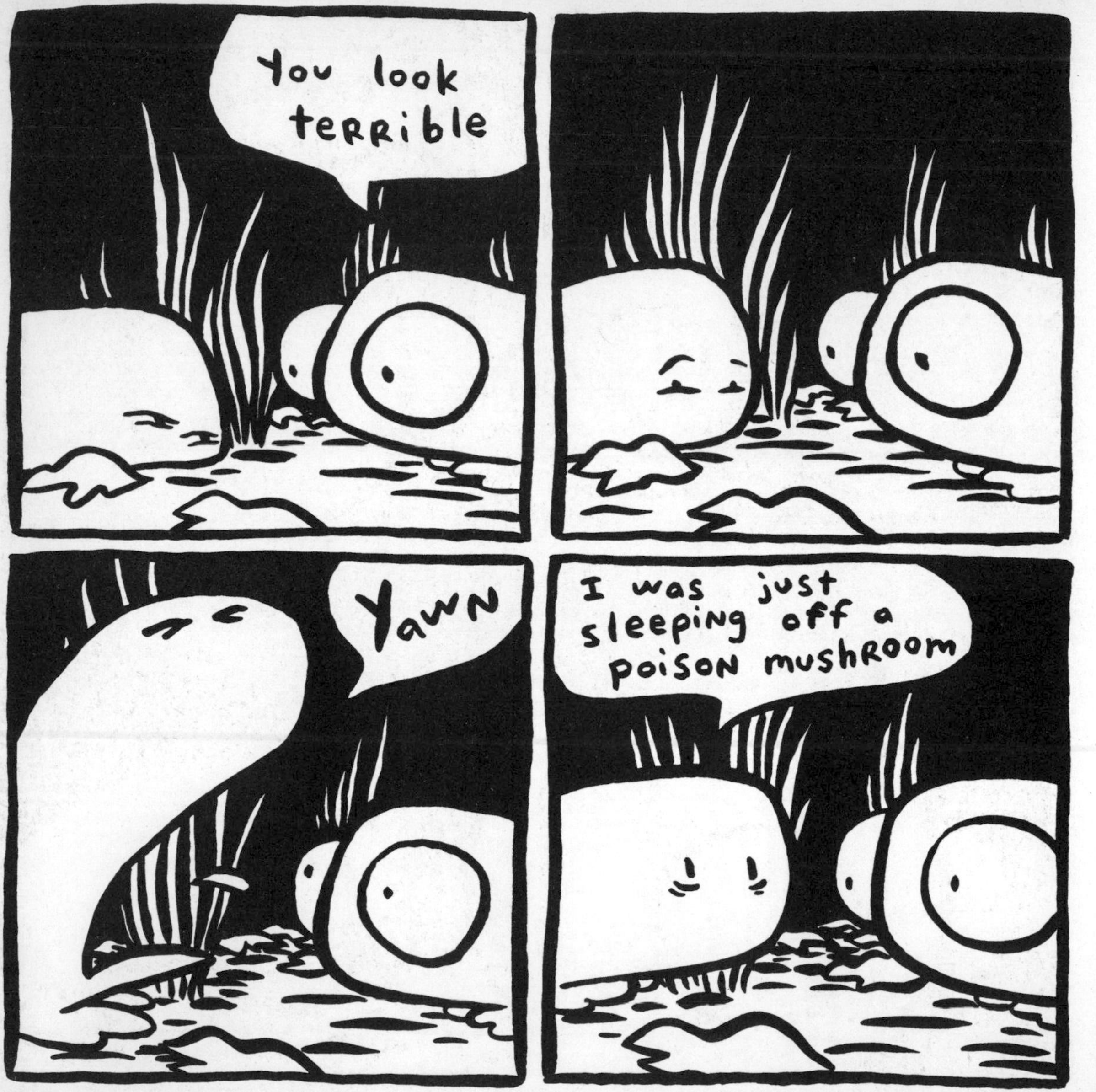
You look terrible
Yawn
I was just sleeping off a poison mushroom

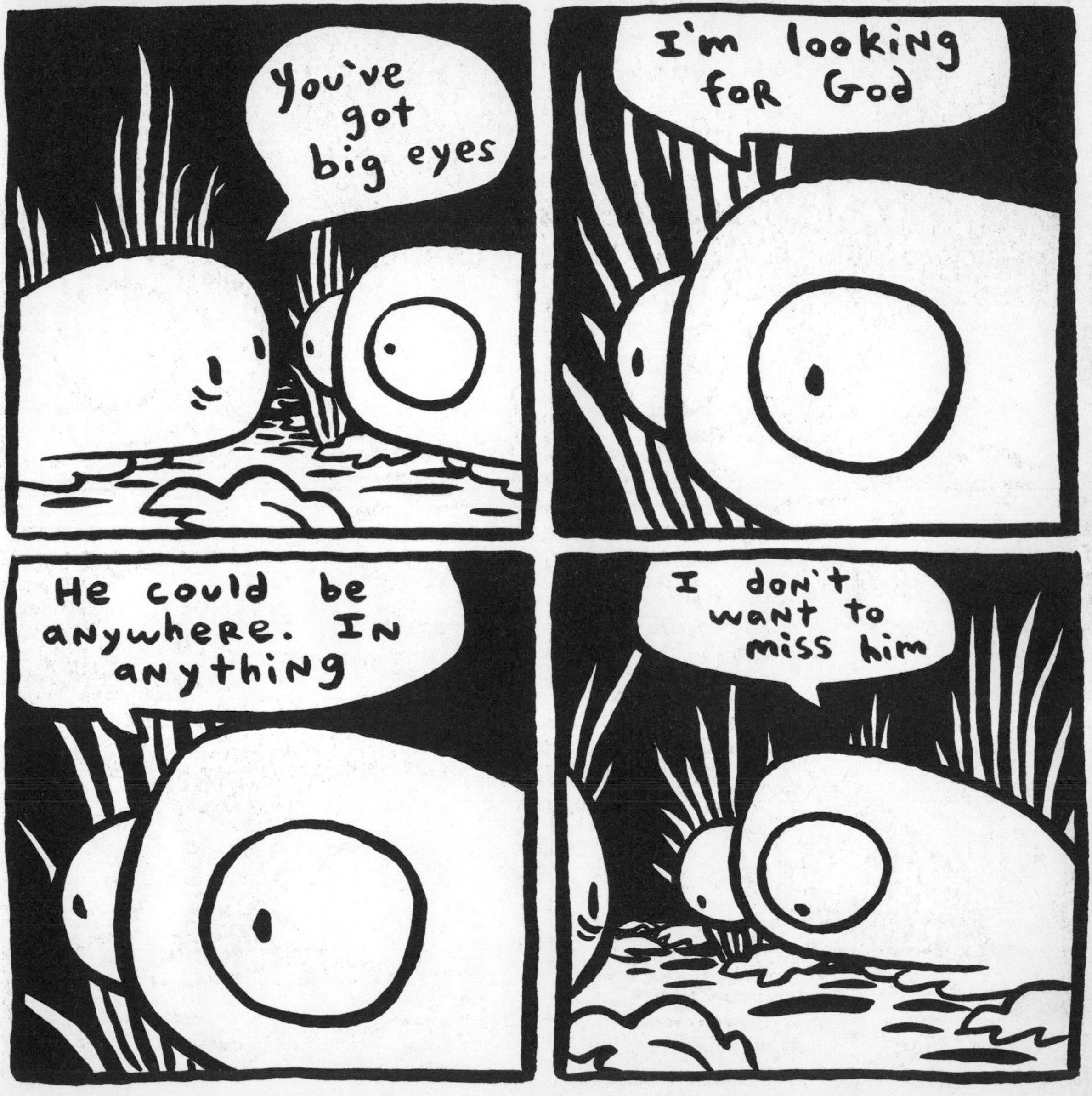
You've got big eyes
I'm looking for God
He could be anywhere. In anything
I don't want to miss him

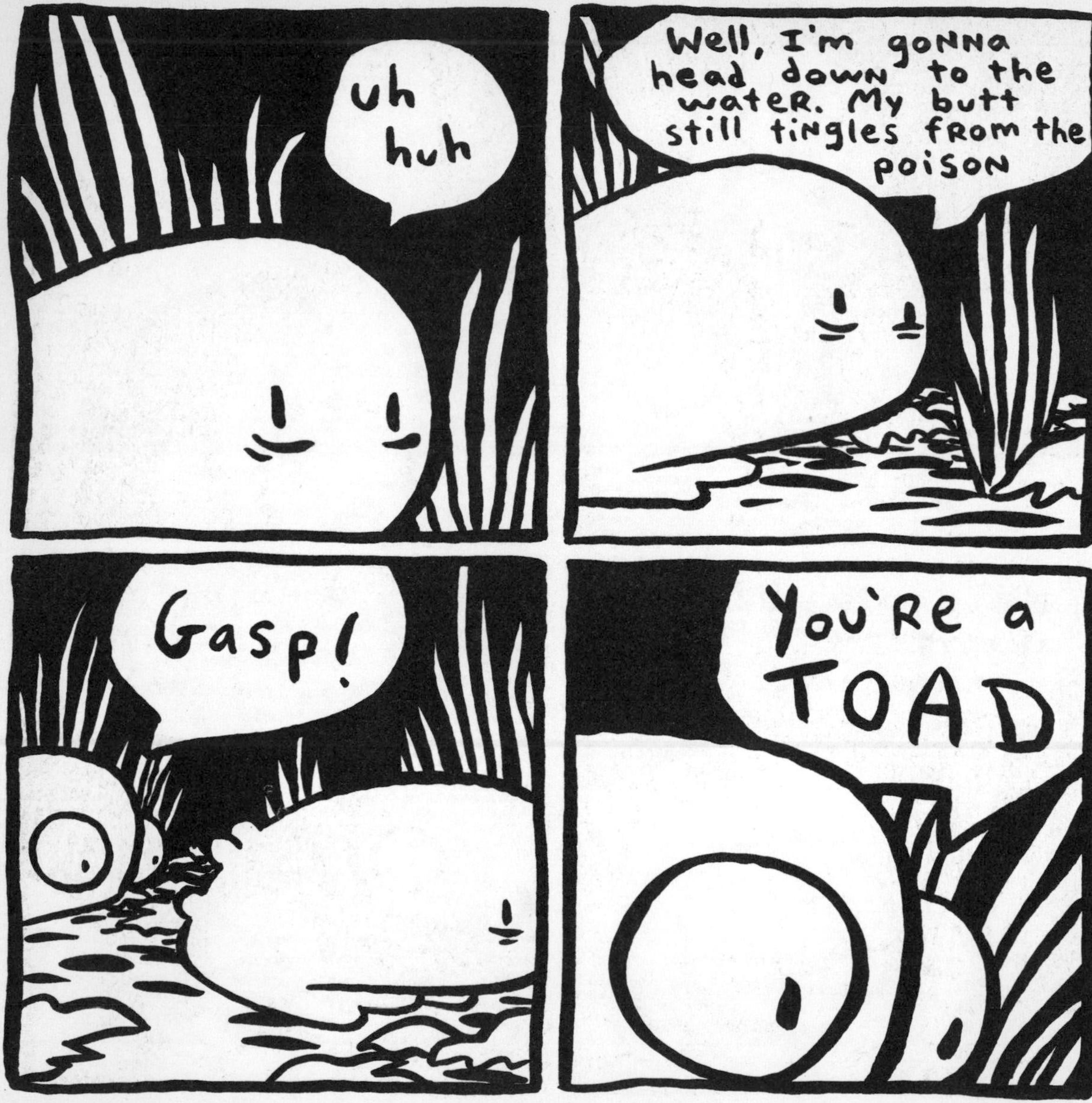
uh huh
Well, I'm gonna head down to the water. My butt still tingles from the poison
Gasp!
You're a TOAD

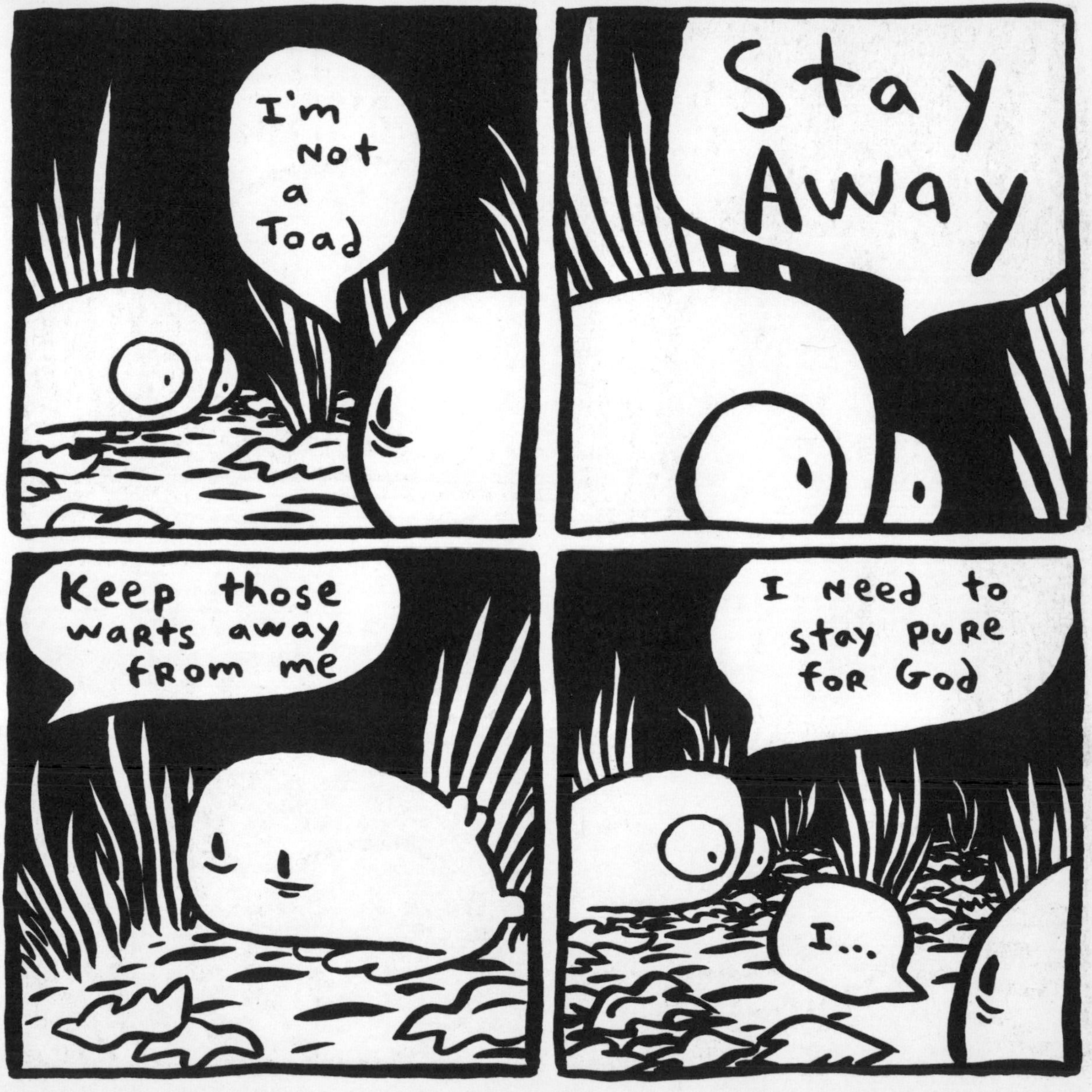

I'm Not a Toad
Stay Away
Keep those warts away from me
I need to stay pure for God
I...

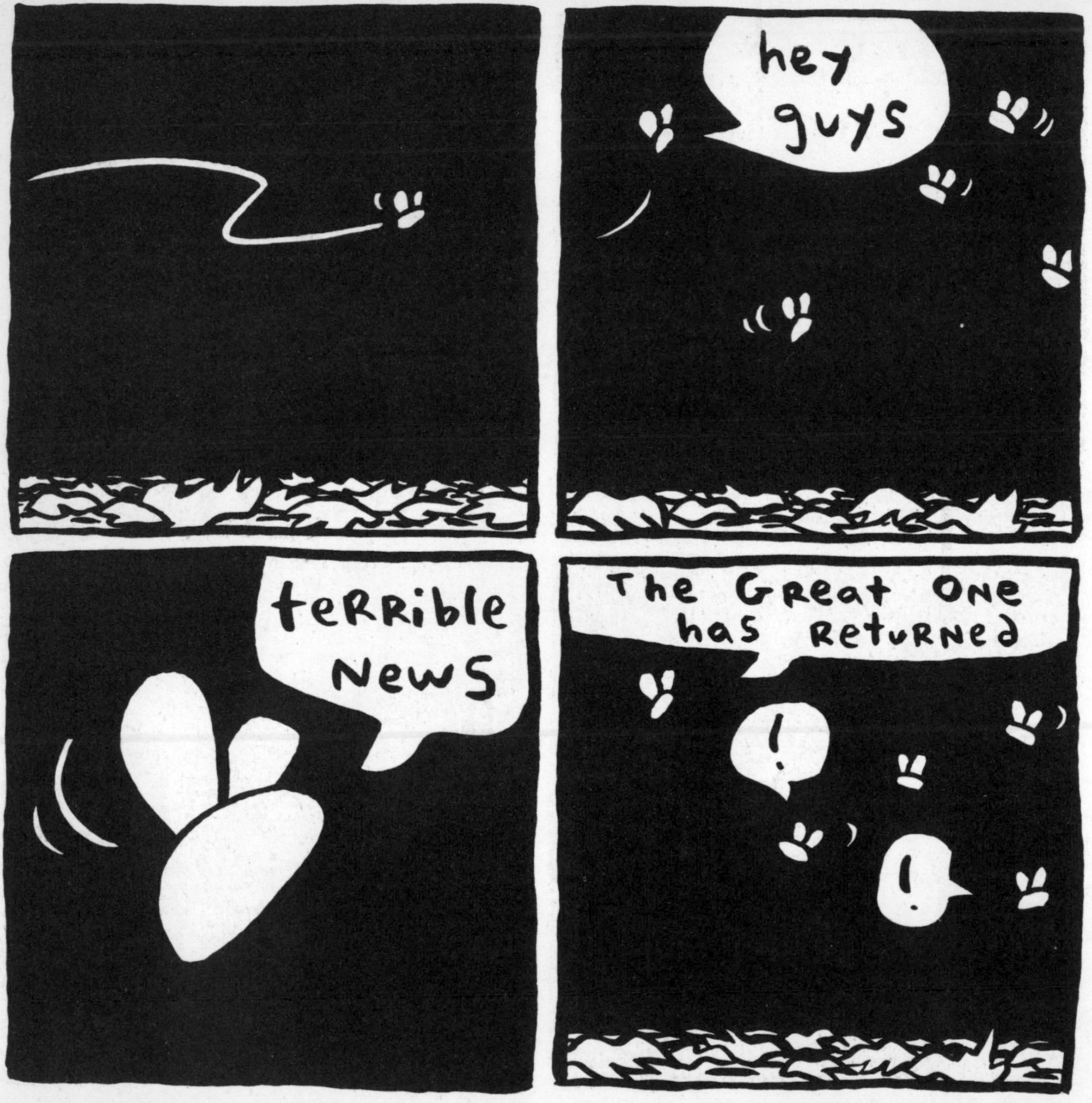
hey guys
terrible News
The Great One has returned
!
!

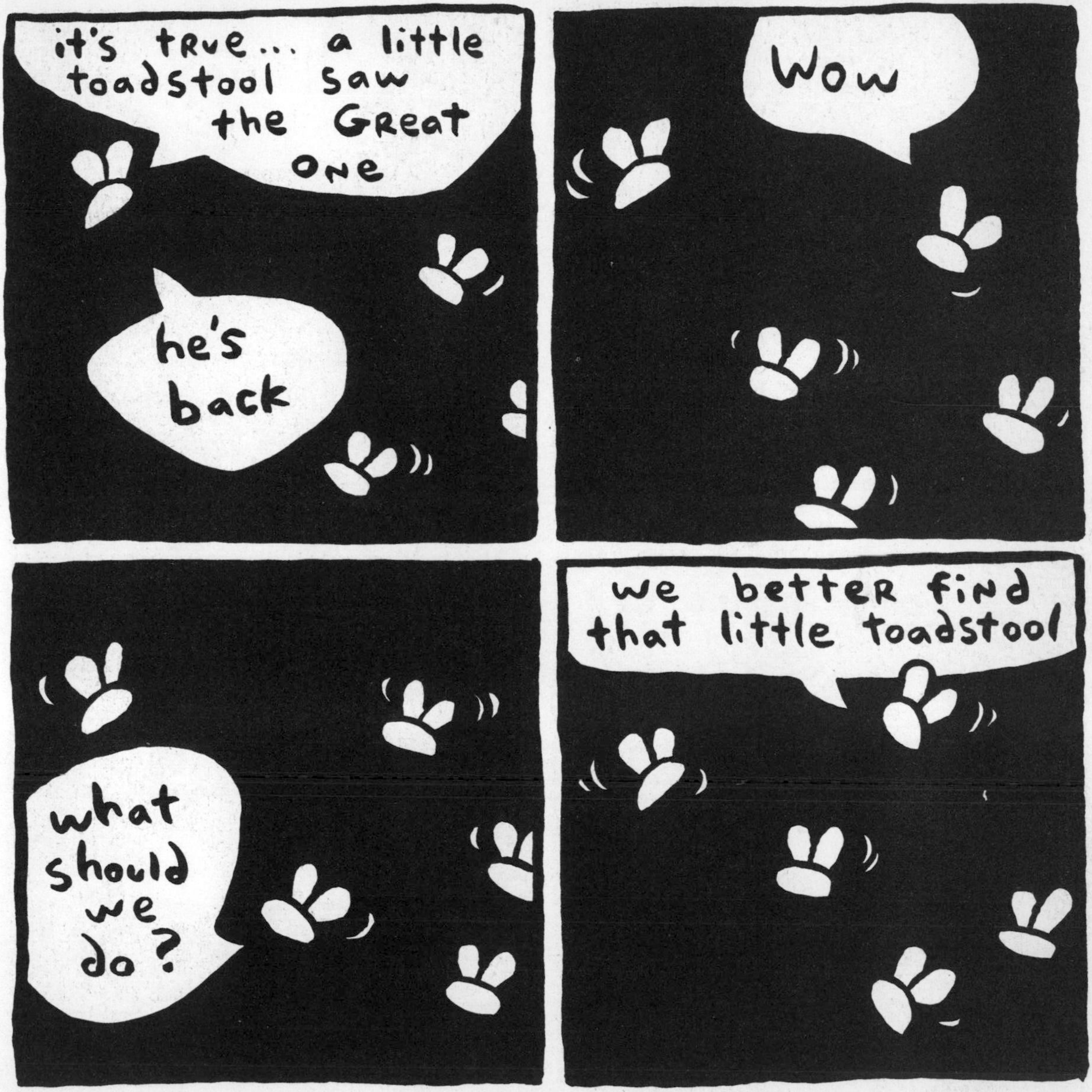
it's true... a little toadstool saw the Great one
he's back
wow
what should we do?
we better find that little toadstool

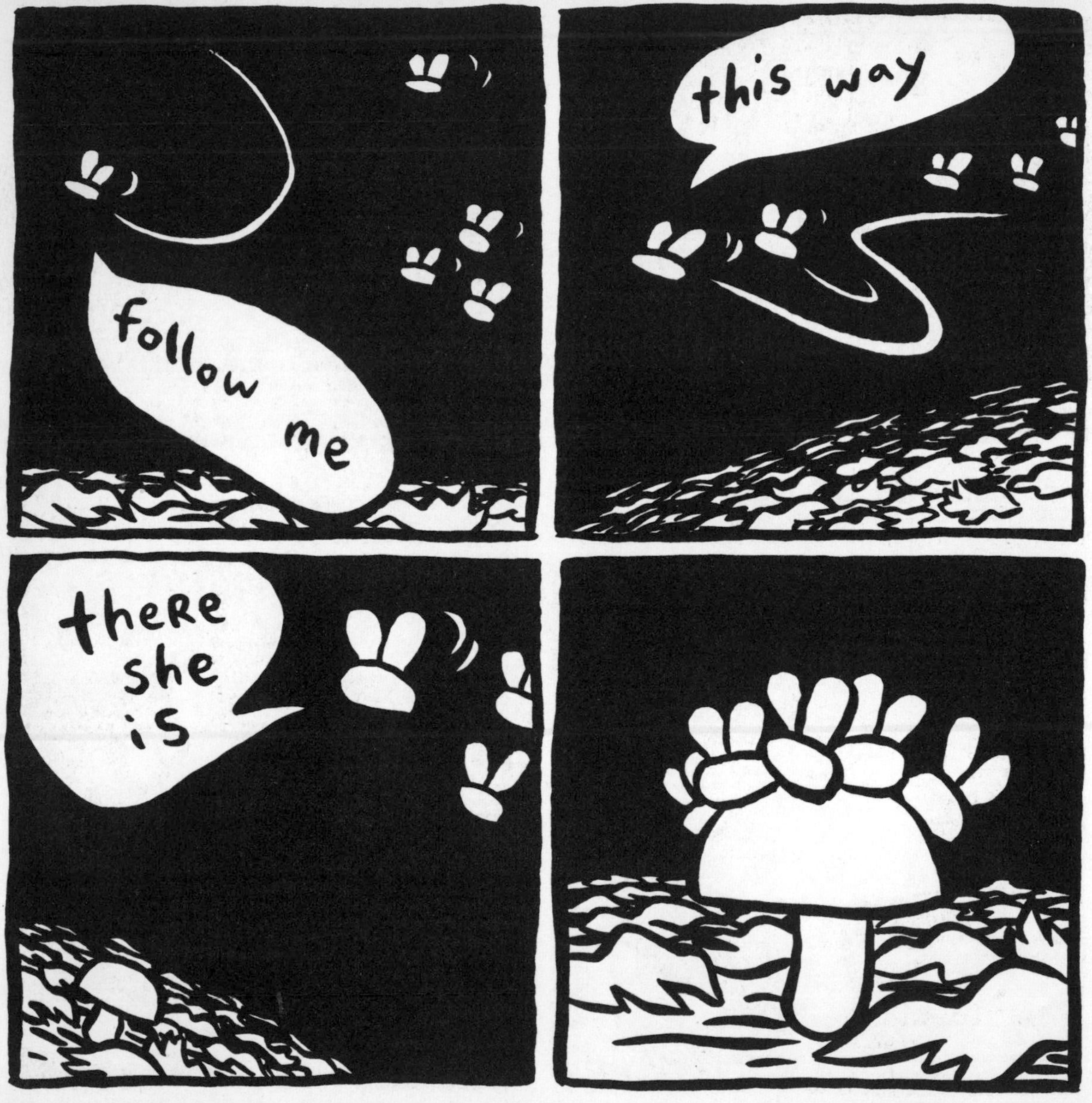
follow me
this way
there she is

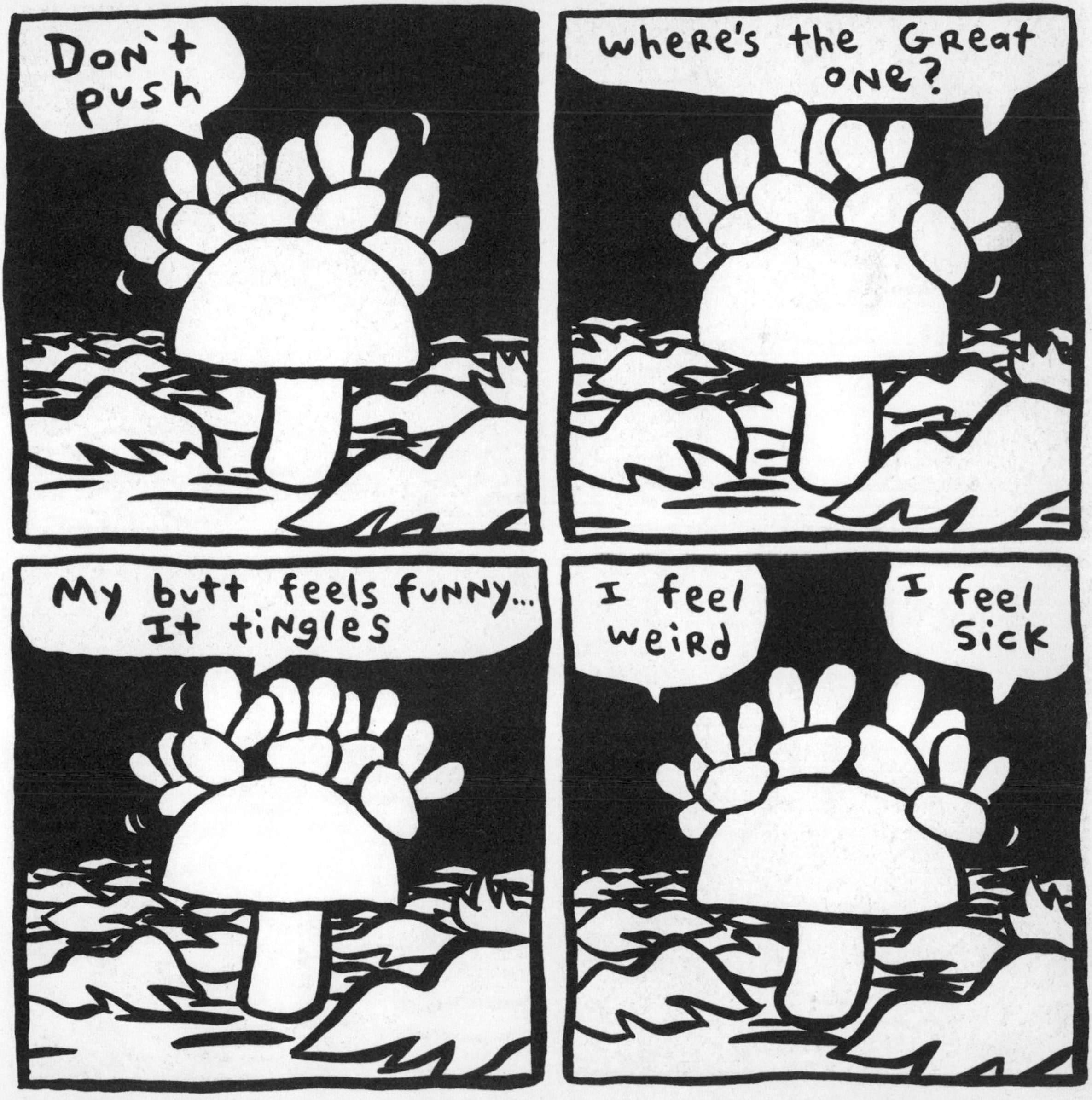
Don't push
where's the Great one?
My butt feels funny... It tingles
I feel weird
I feel sick

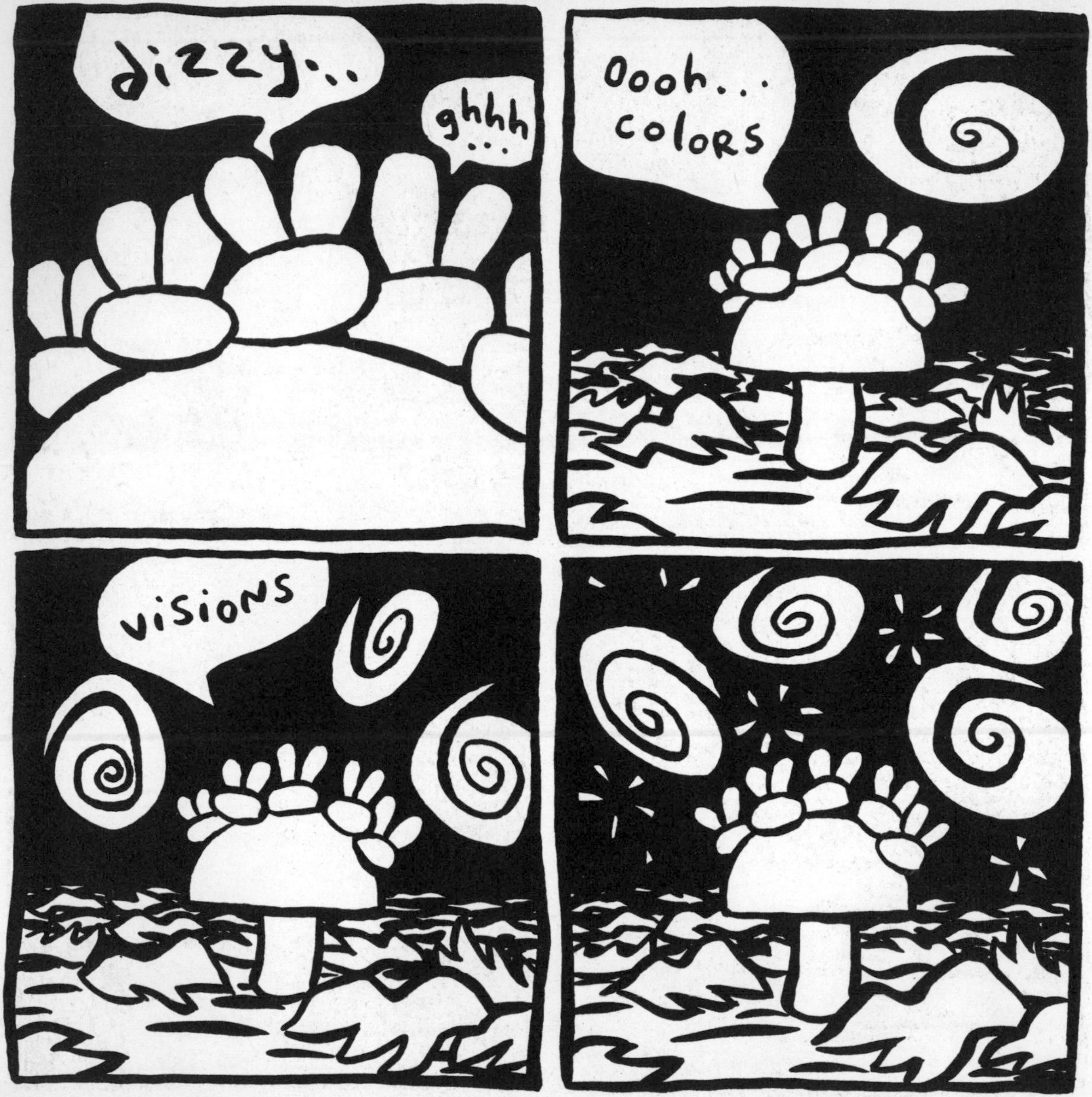
dizzy...
ghhh...
Oooh... colors
visions

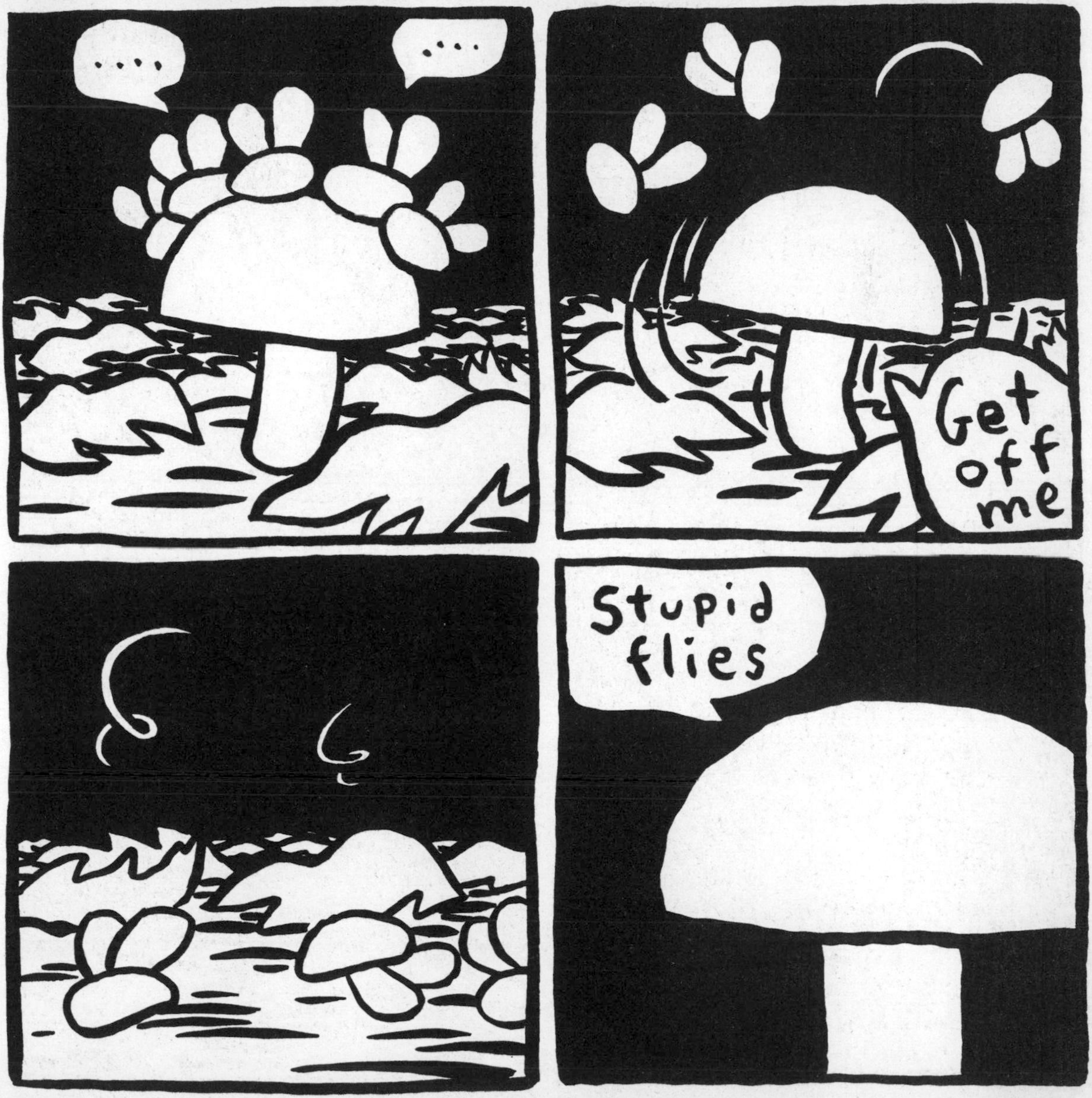
....
....
Get off me
Stupid flies

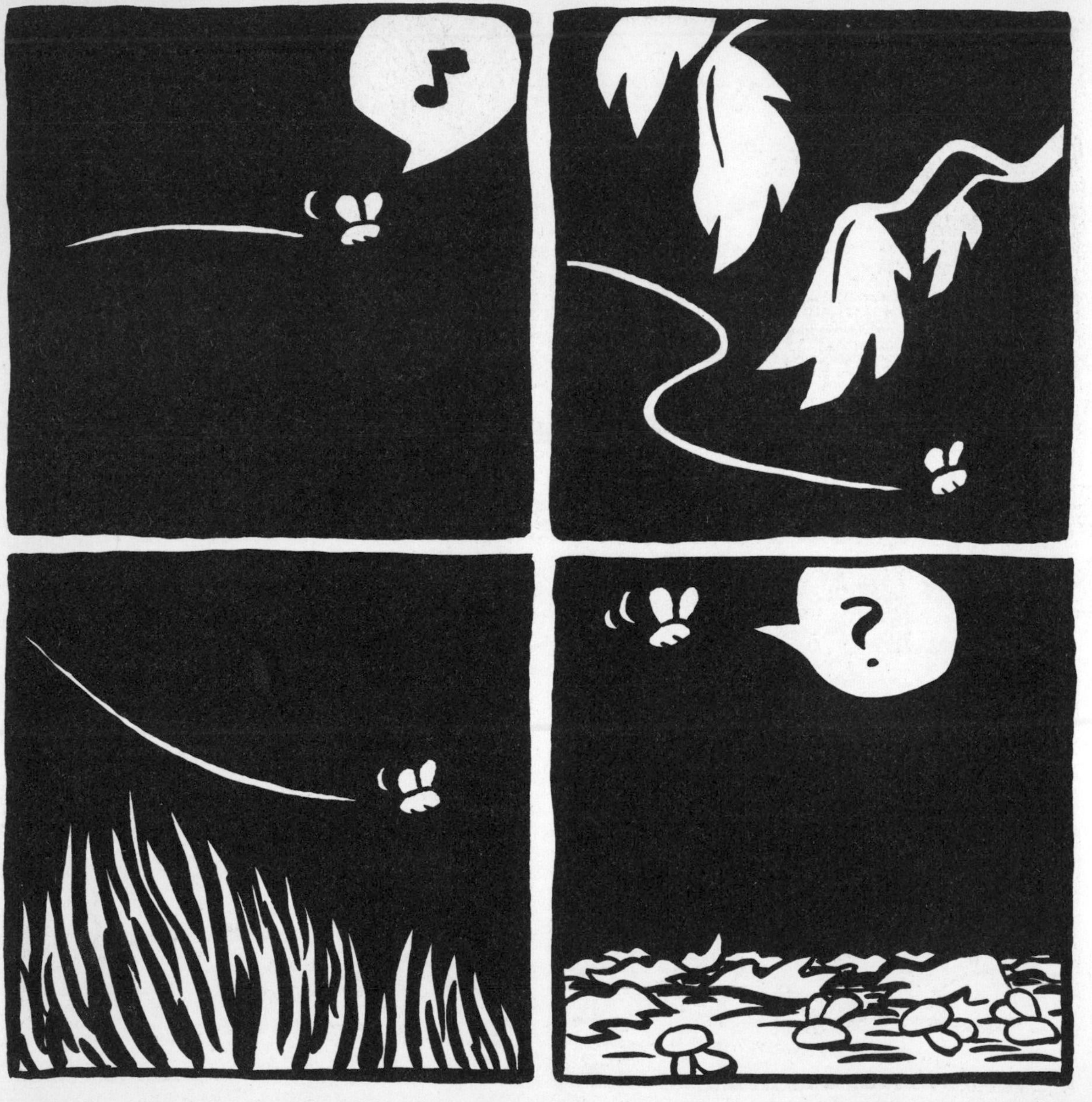
?

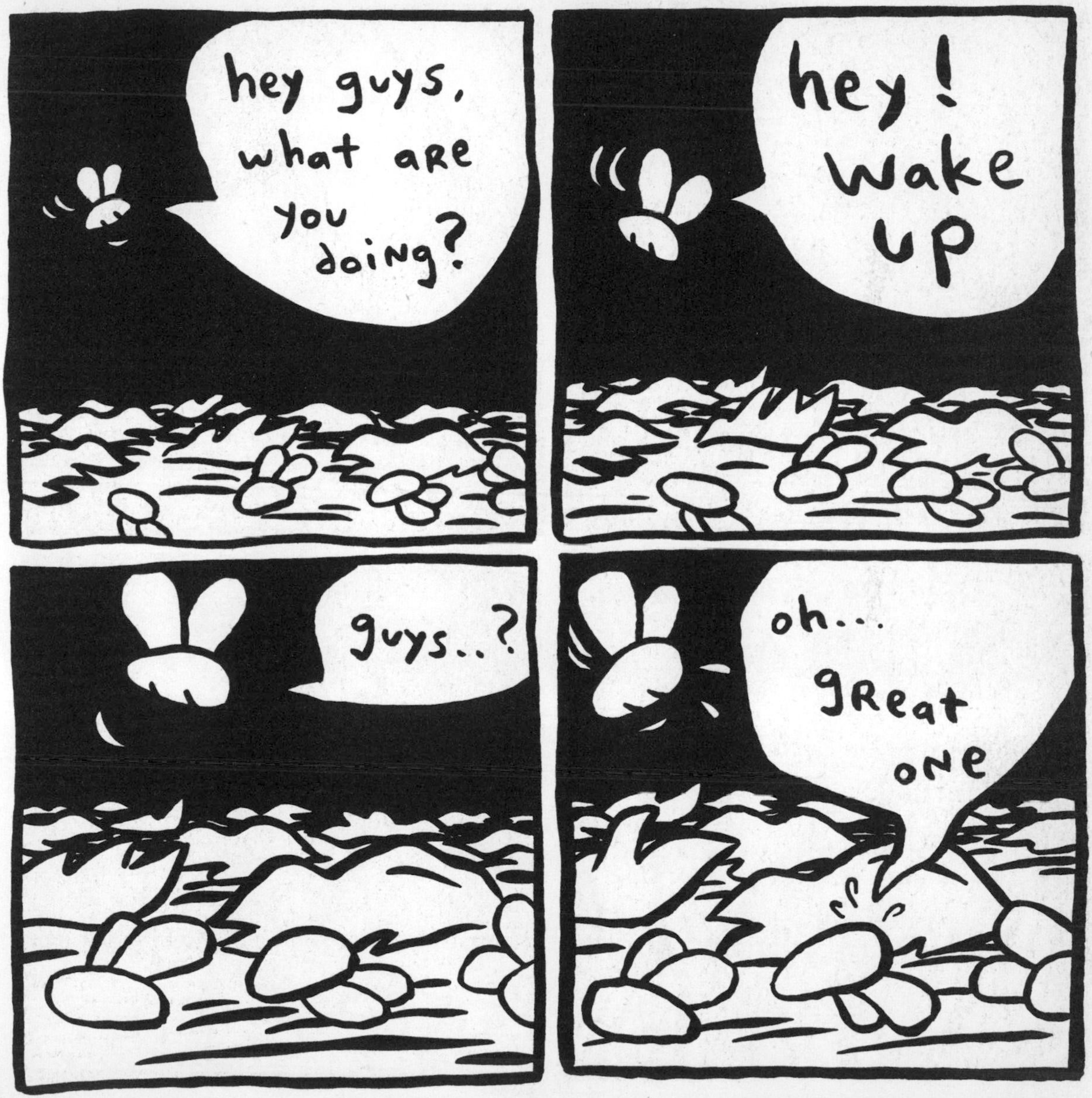
hey guys, what are you doing?
hey! wake up
guys..?
oh... great one

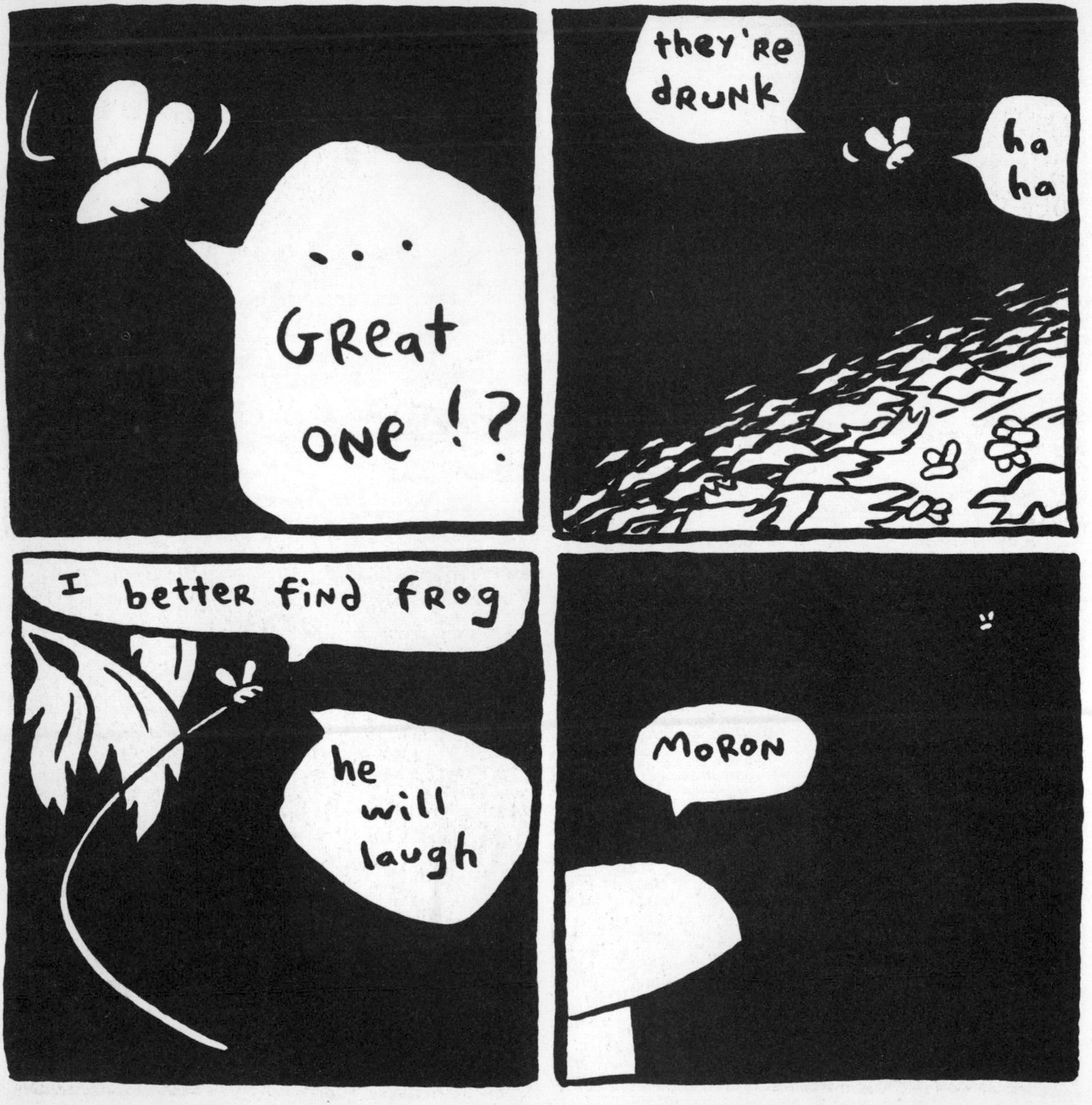
... GReat ONE !?
they're dRUNK
ha ha
I better find fRog
he will laugh
MORON

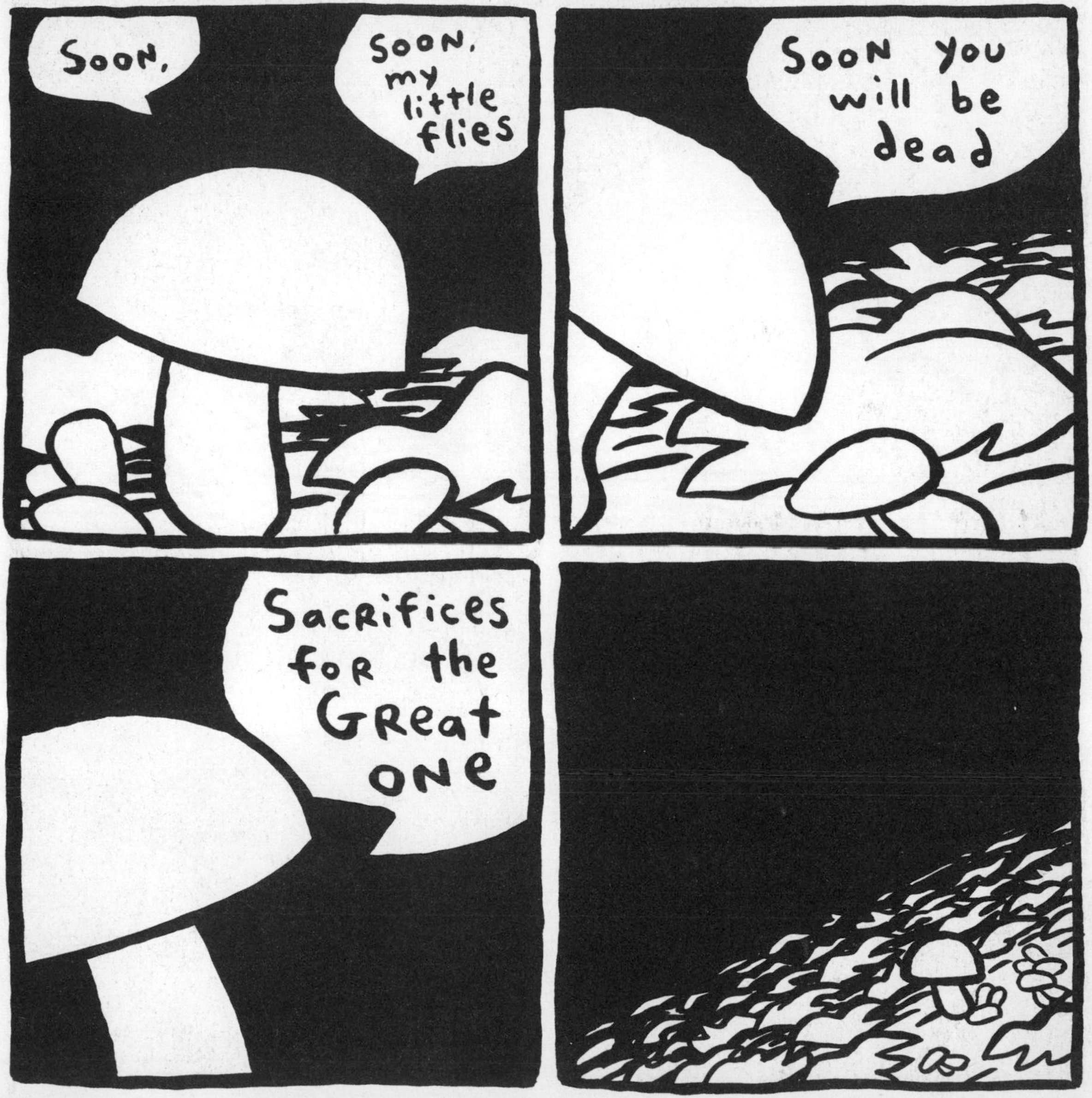
Soon,
Soon, my little flies
Soon you will be dead
Sacrifices for the Great One

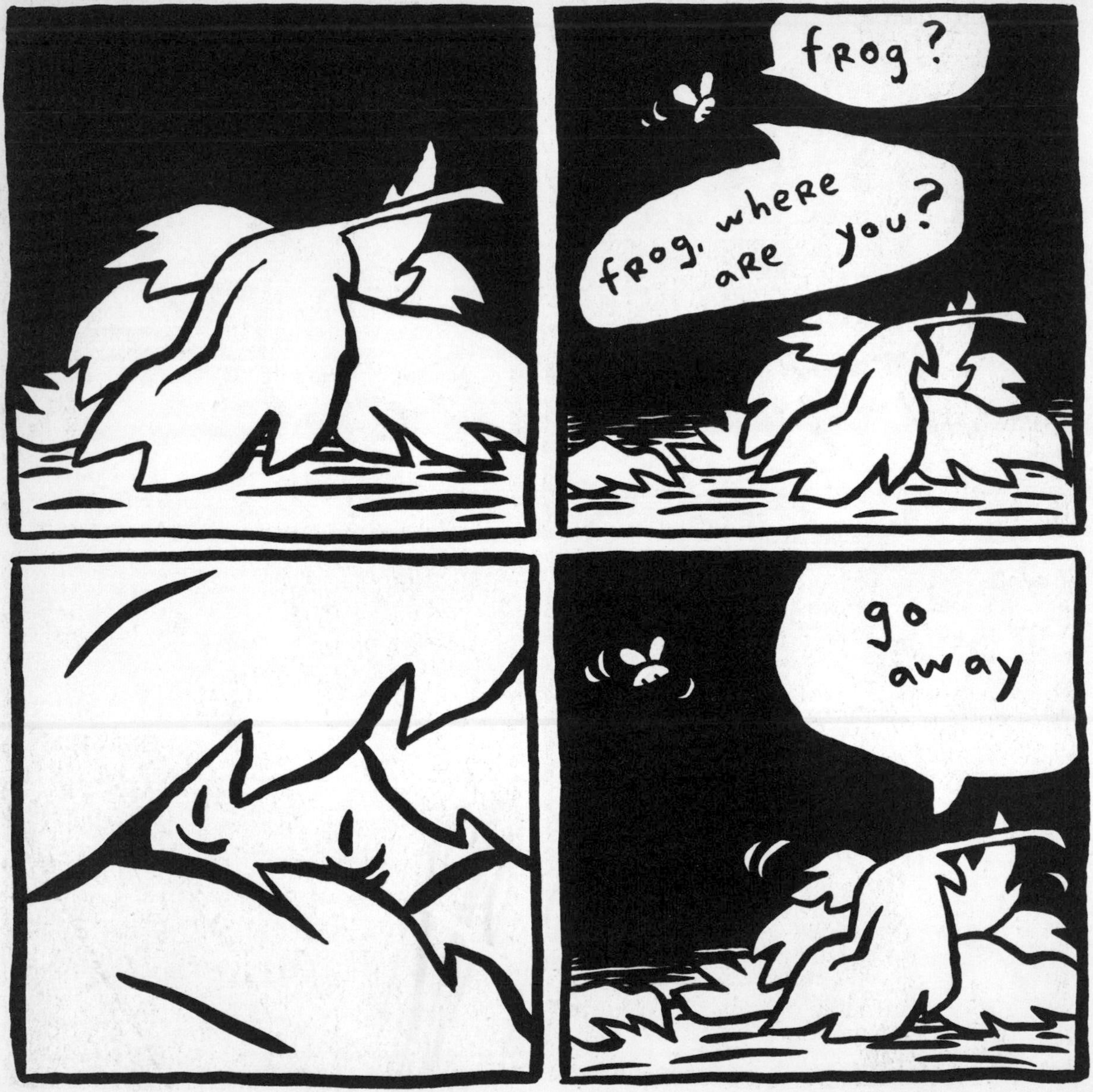
frog?
frog, where are you?
go away

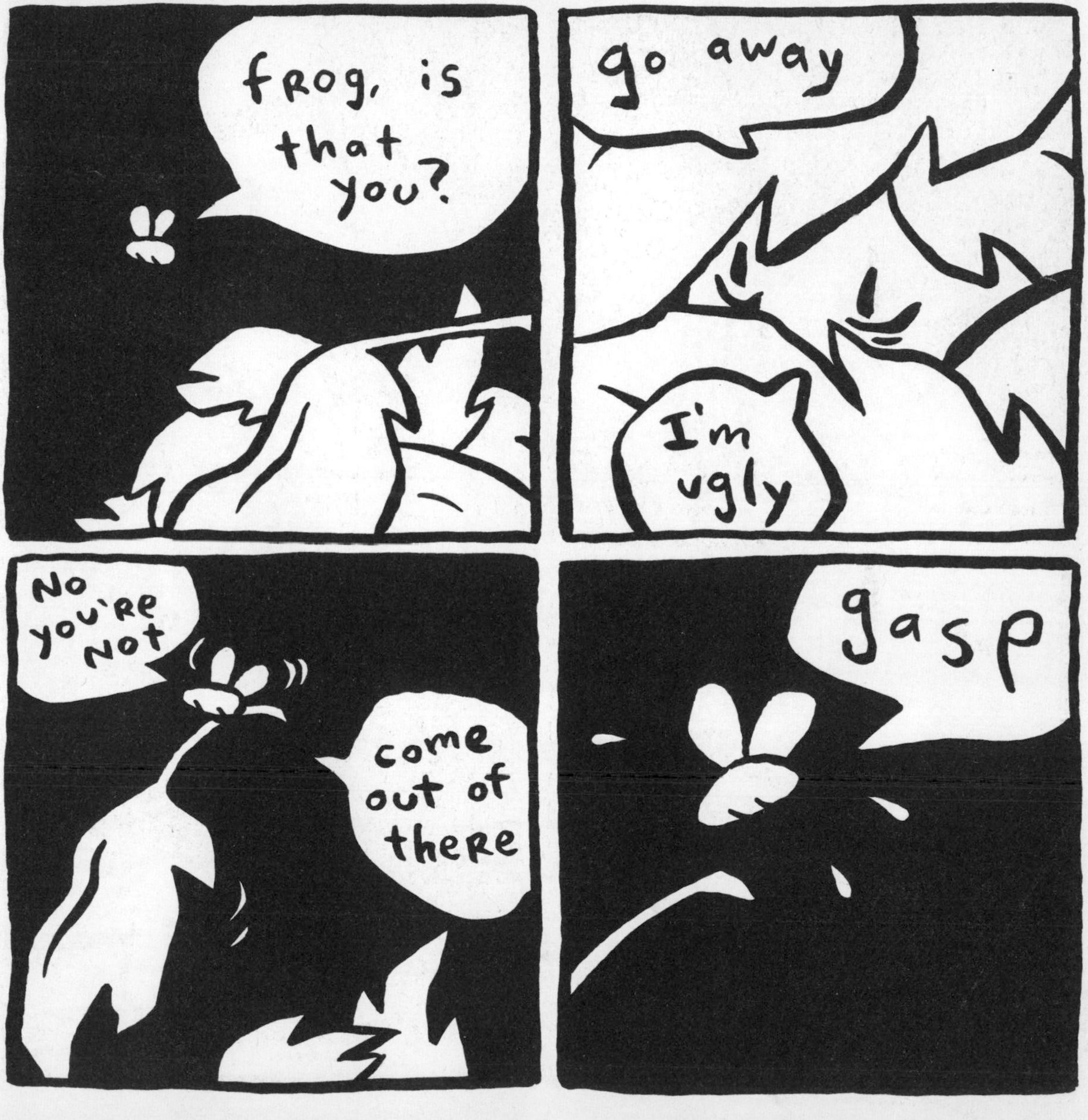
frog, is that you?
go away
I'm ugly
No you're Not
come out of there
gasp

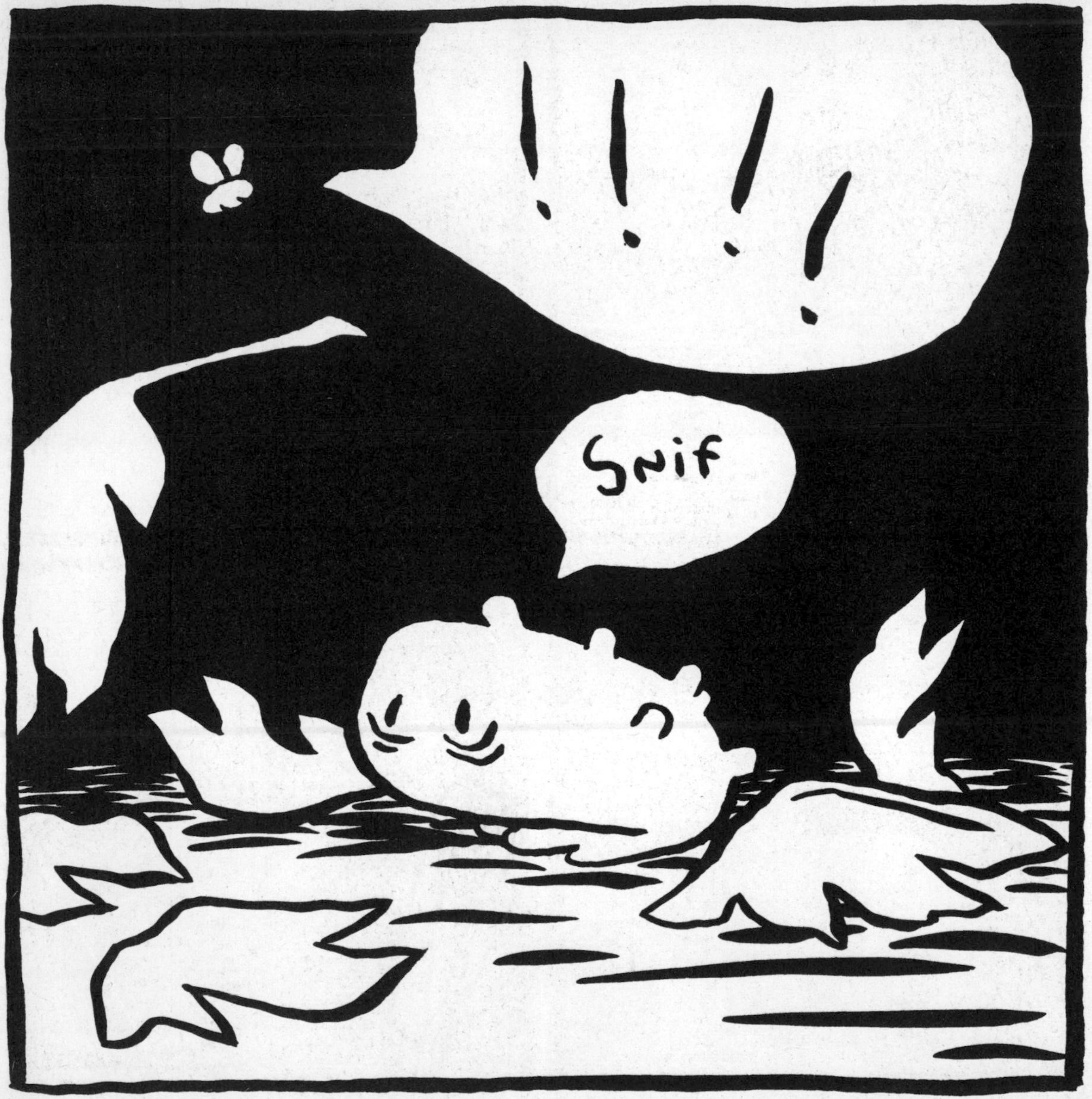
!!!!
Snif

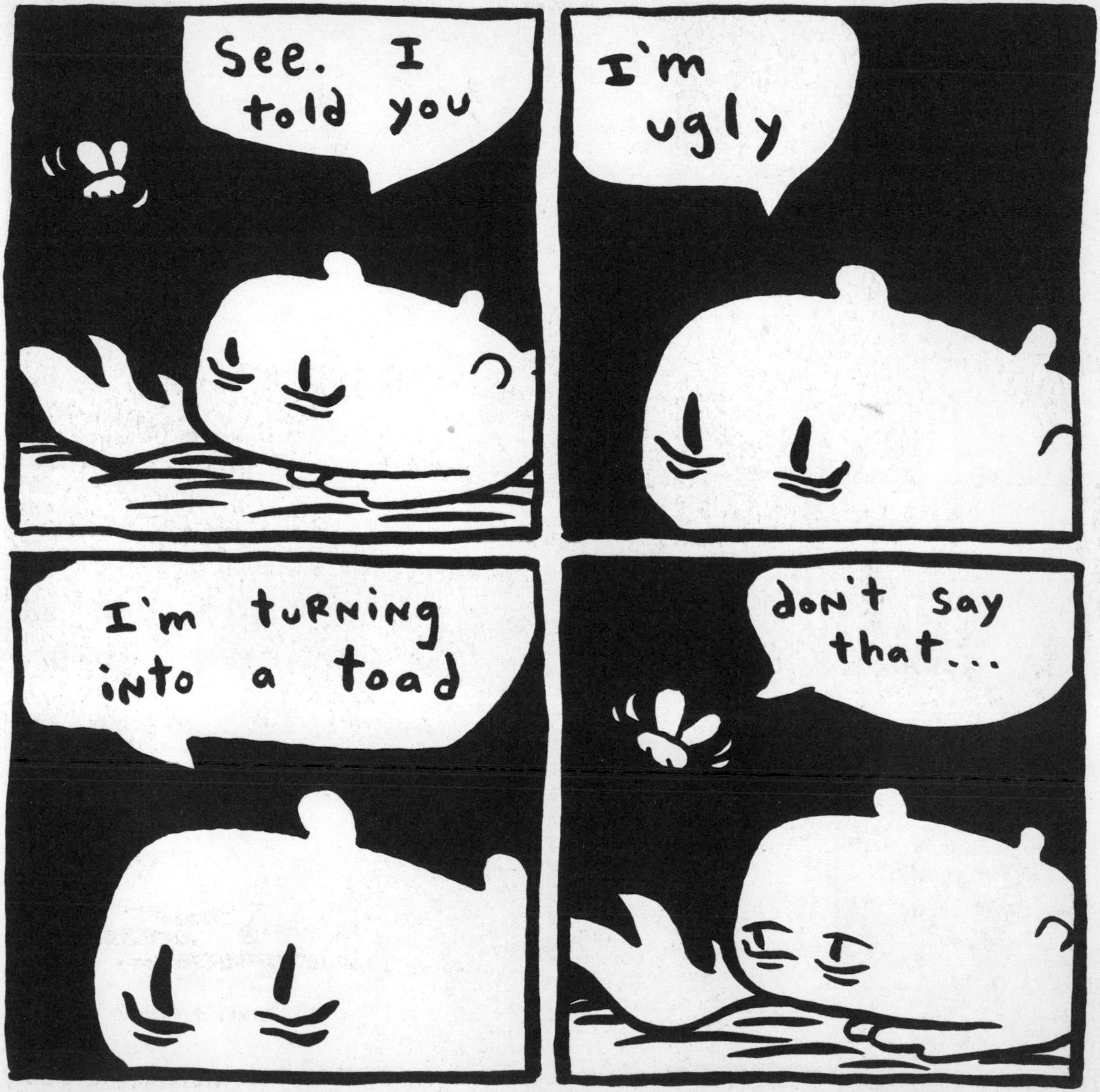
See. I told you
I'm ugly
I'm turning into a toad
don't say that...

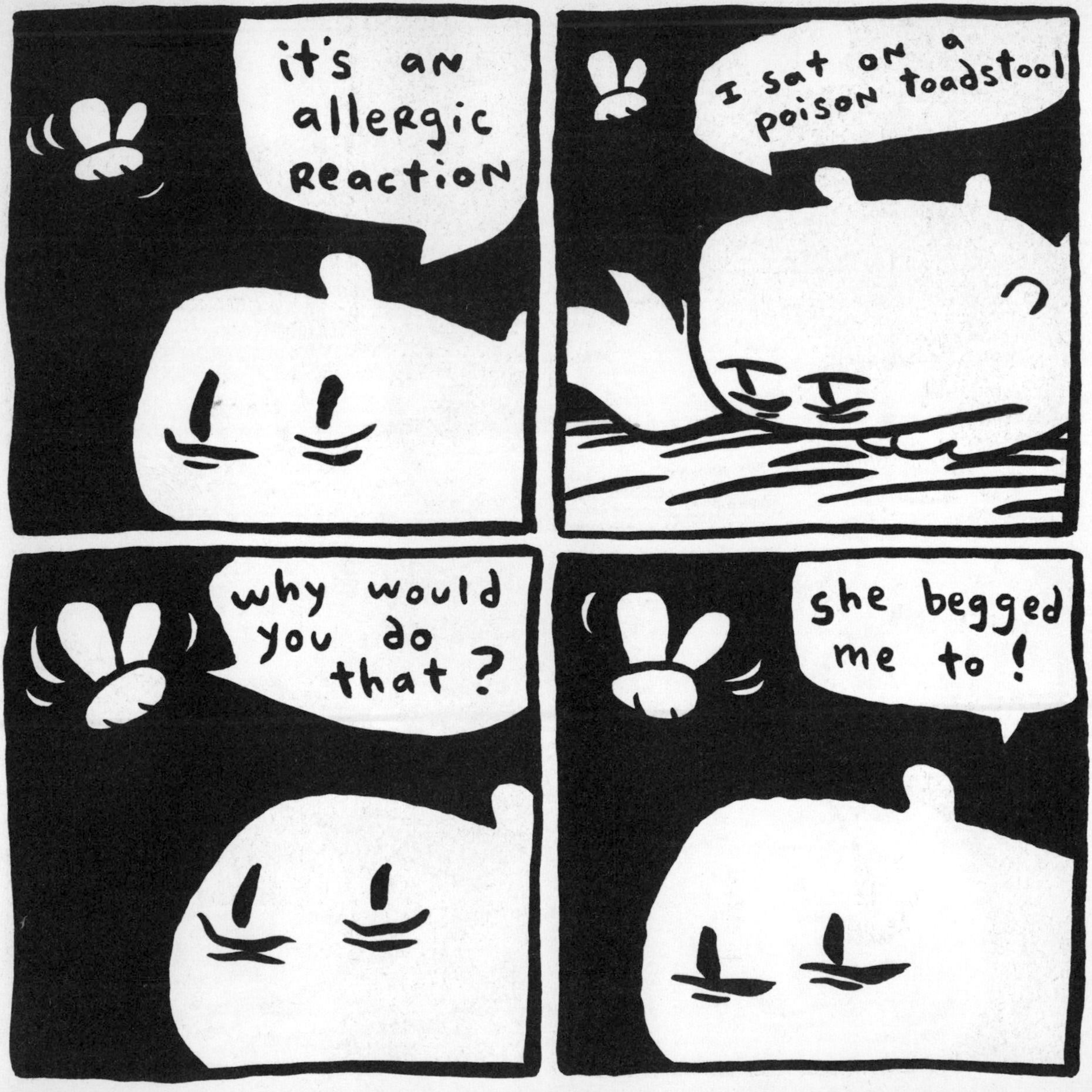
it's an allergic reaction
I sat on a poison toadstool
why would you do that?
she begged me to!

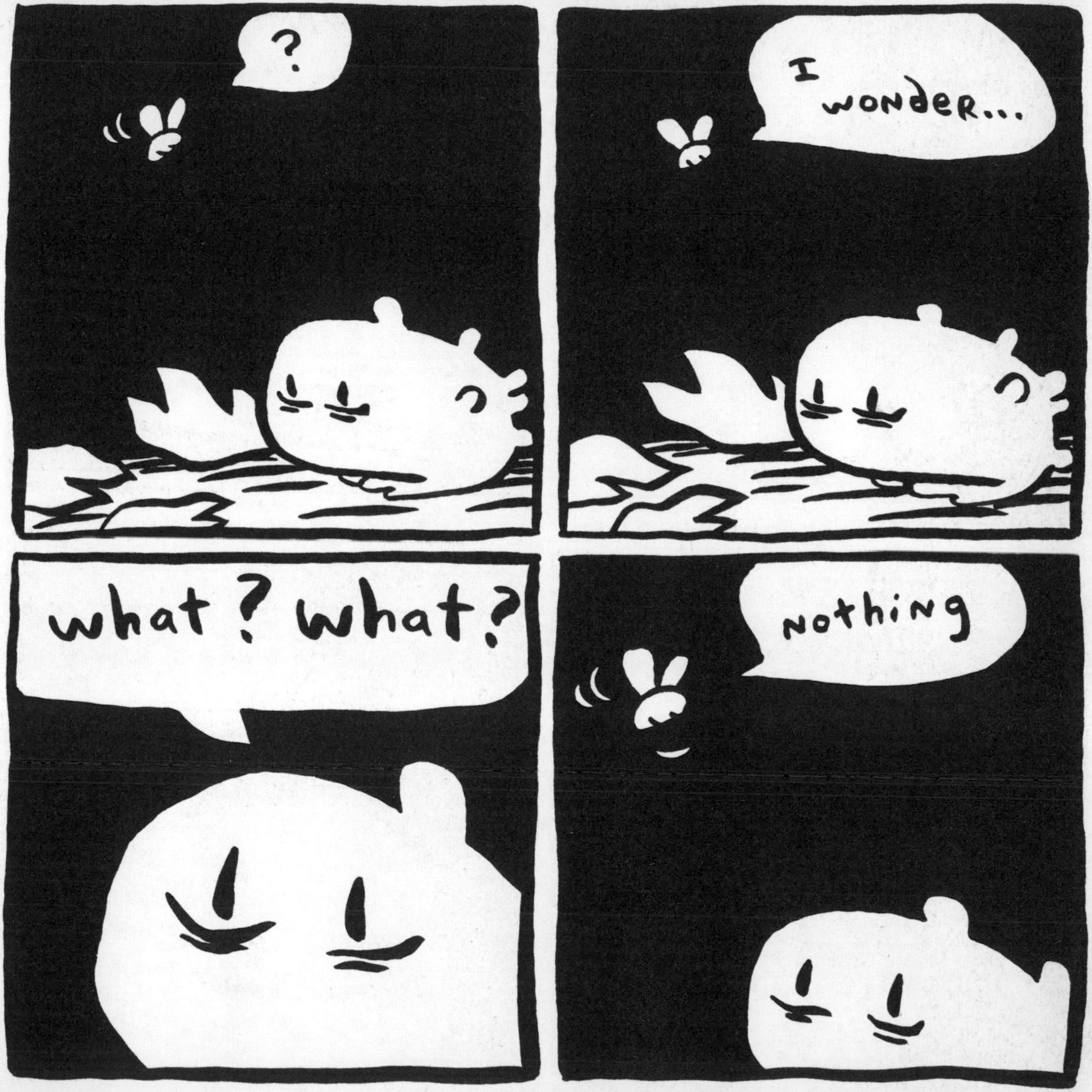
?
I wonder...
what? what?
nothing

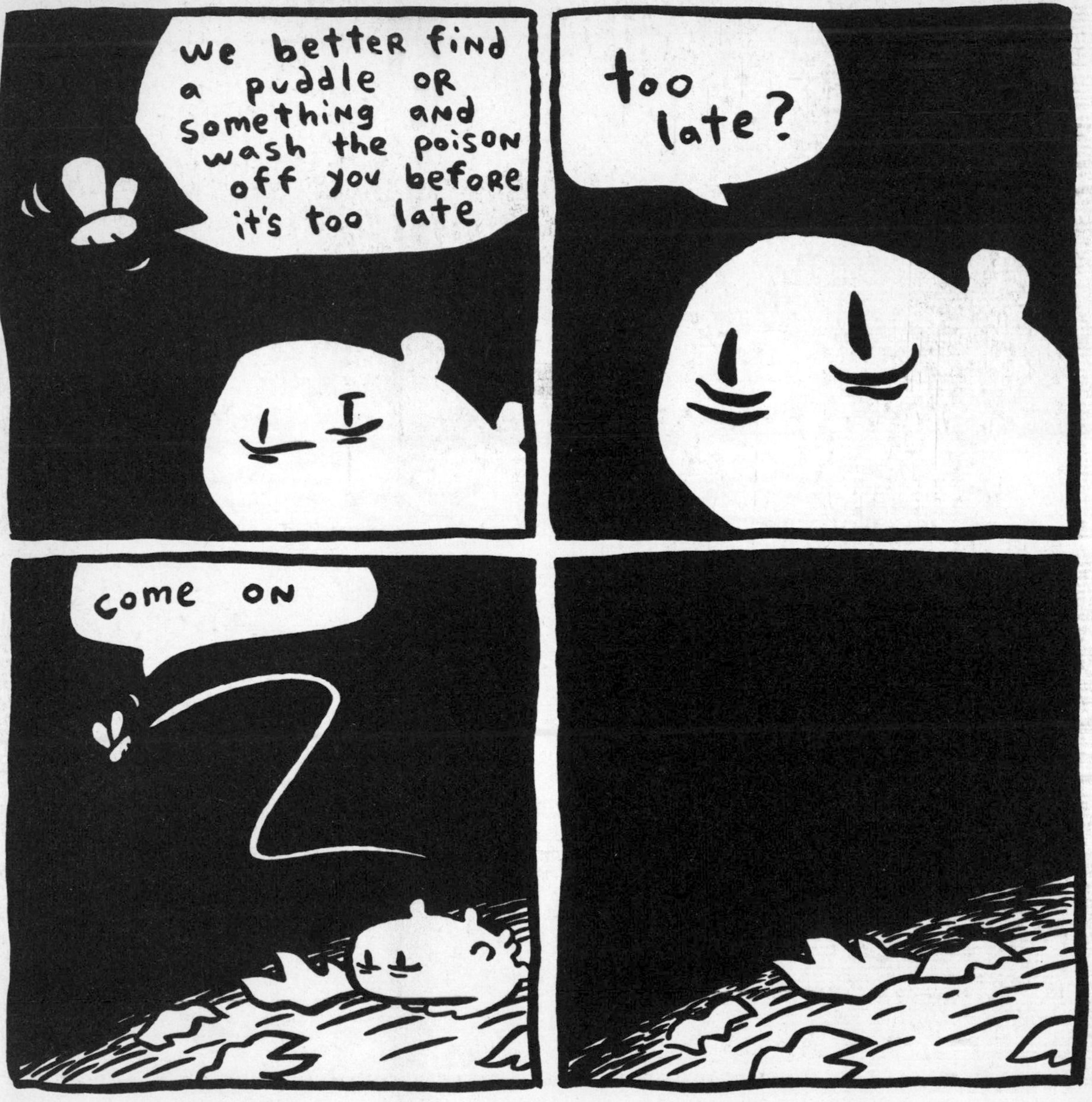
we better find a puddle or something and wash the poison off you before it's too late
too late?
come on

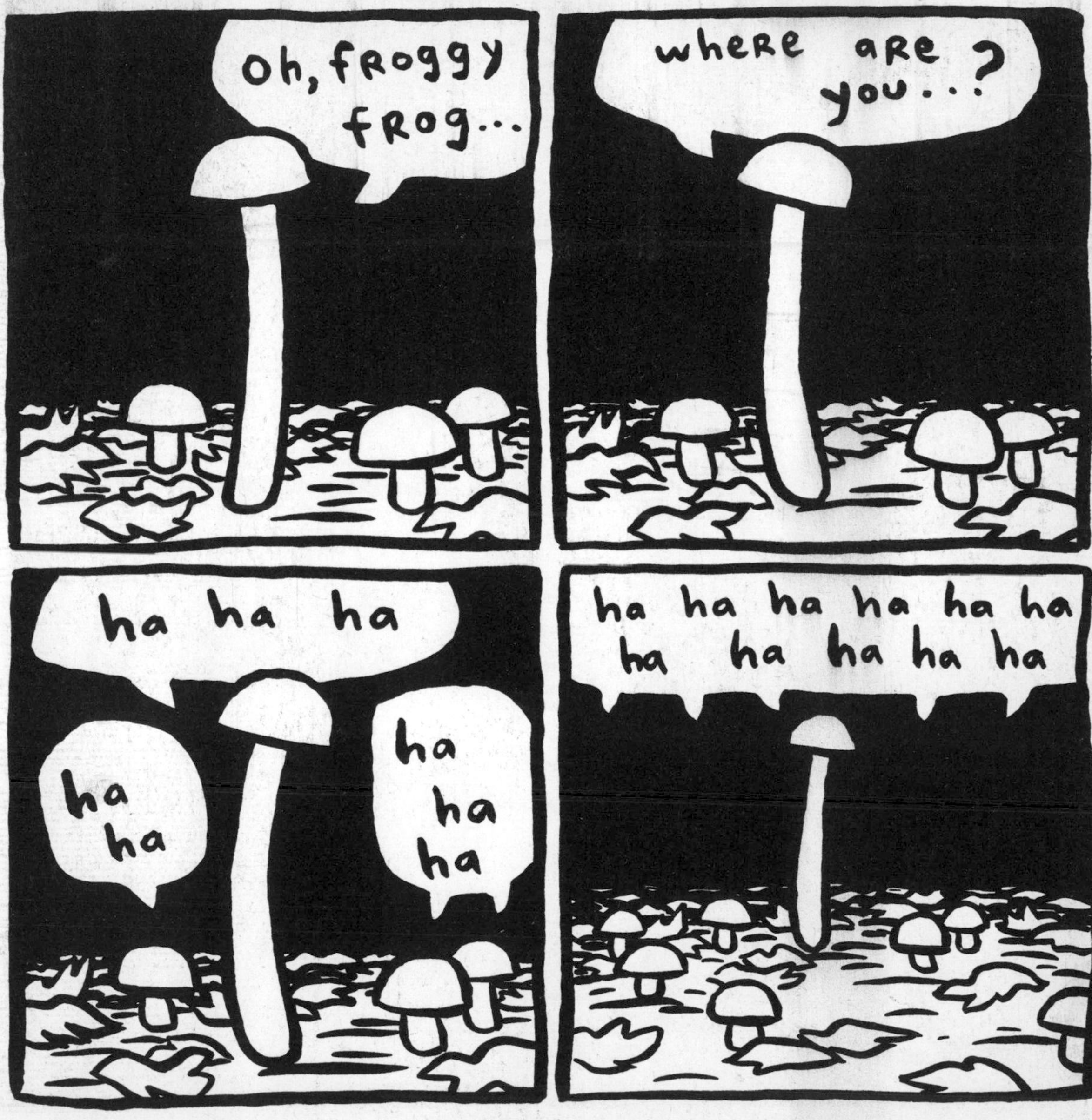
Oh, froggy frog...
where are you...?
ha ha ha
ha ha
ha ha ha
ha ha ha ha ha ha ha ha ha ha ha

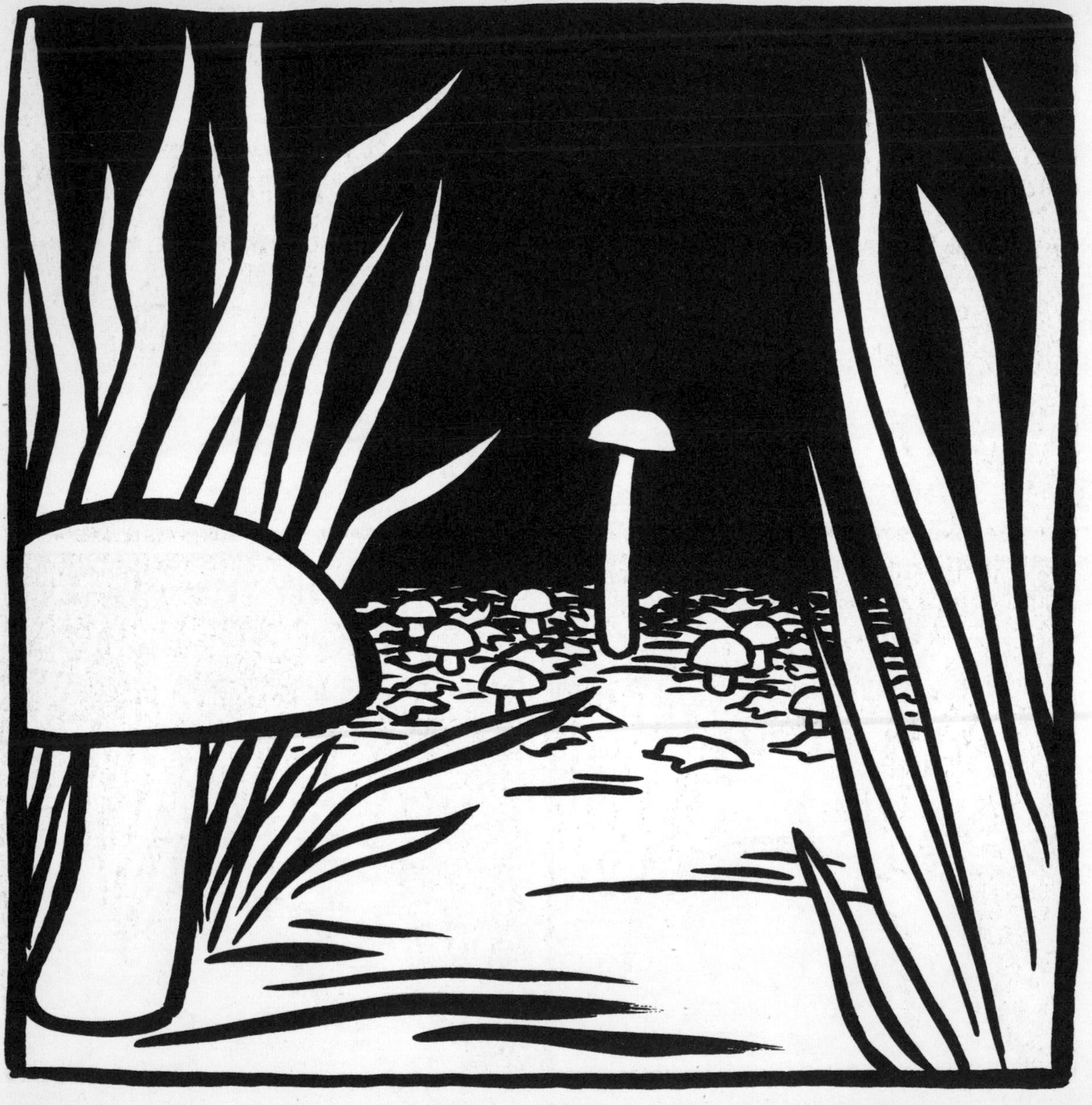

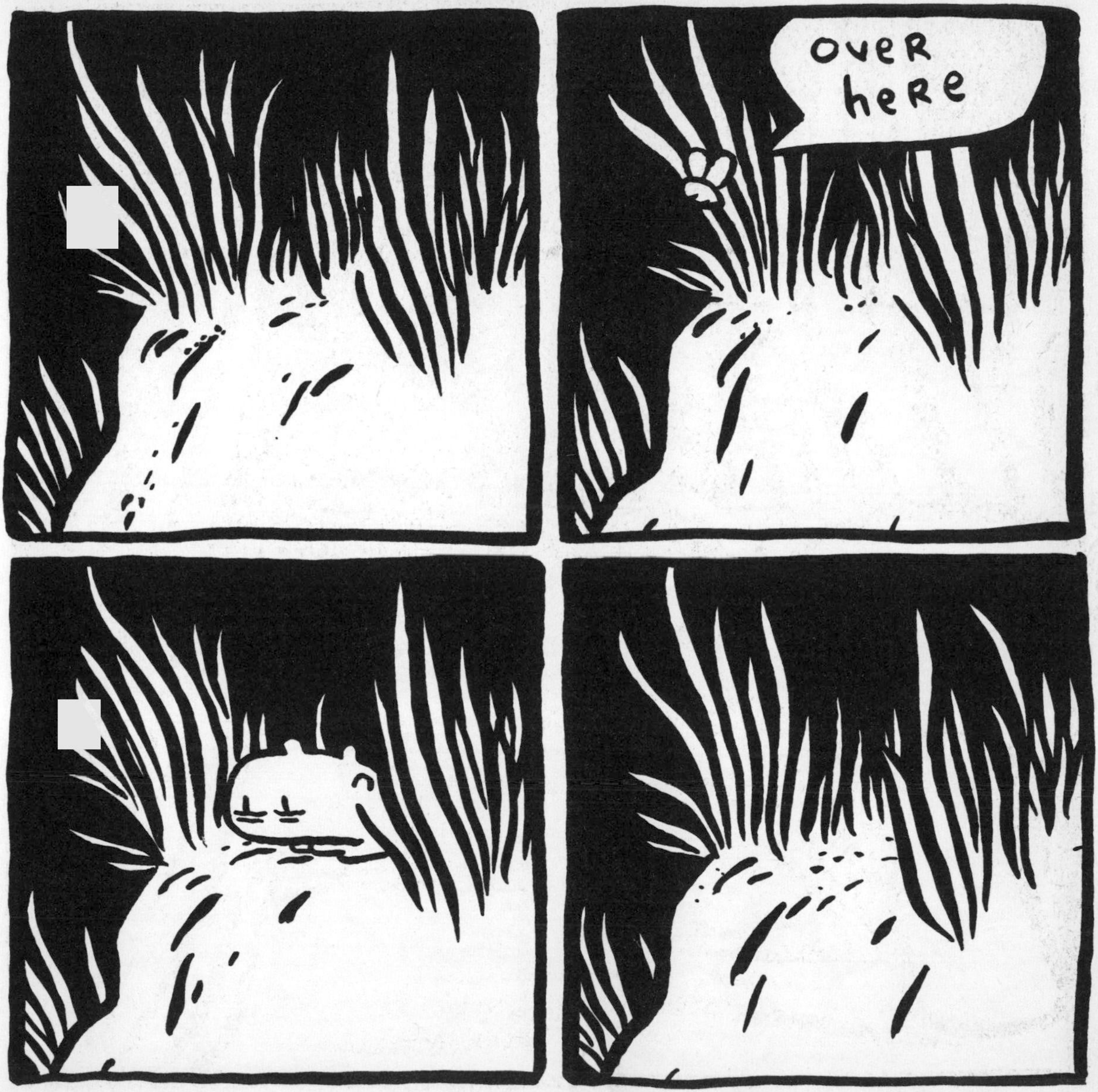
over here

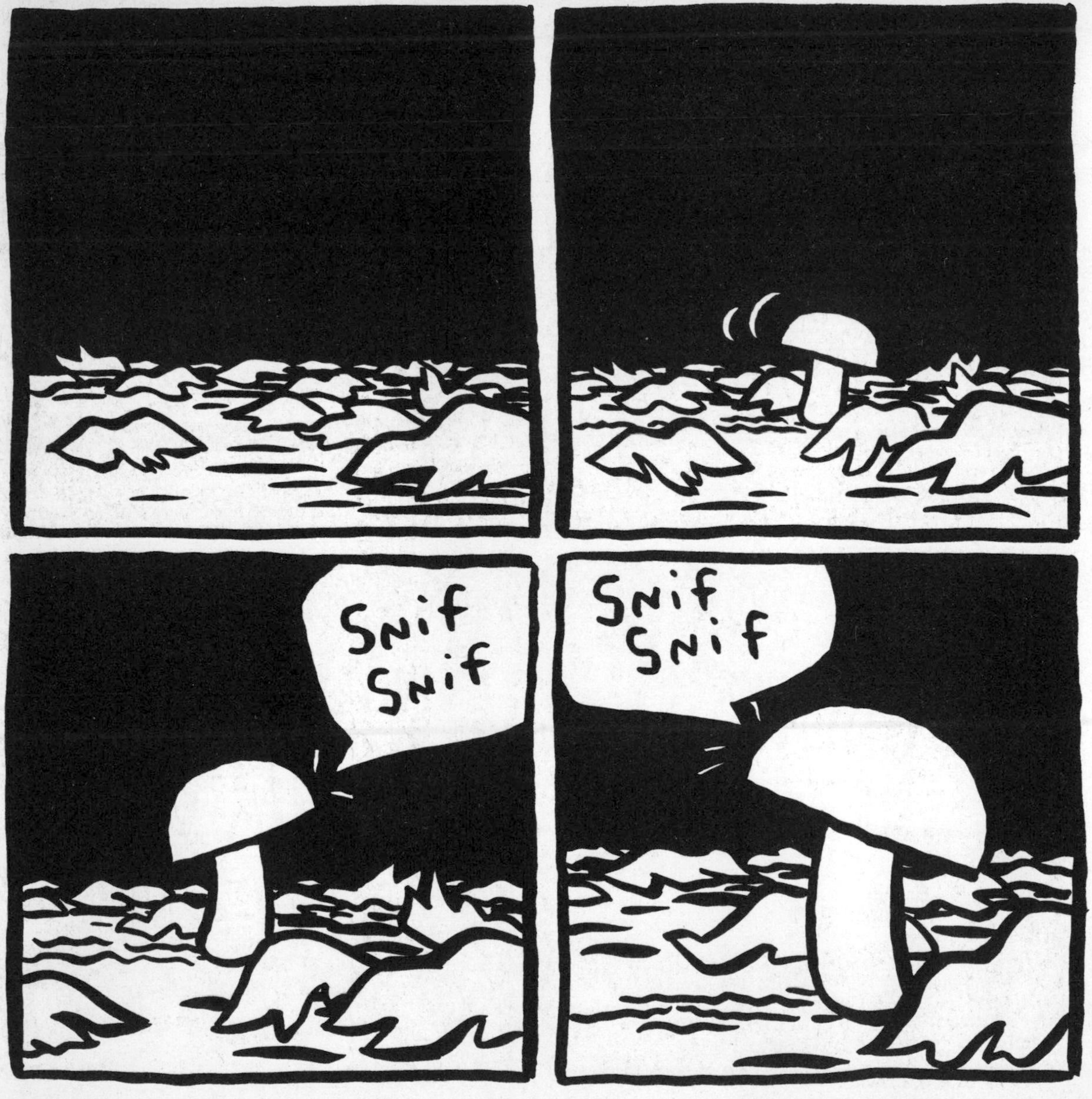
Snif Snif
Snif Snif

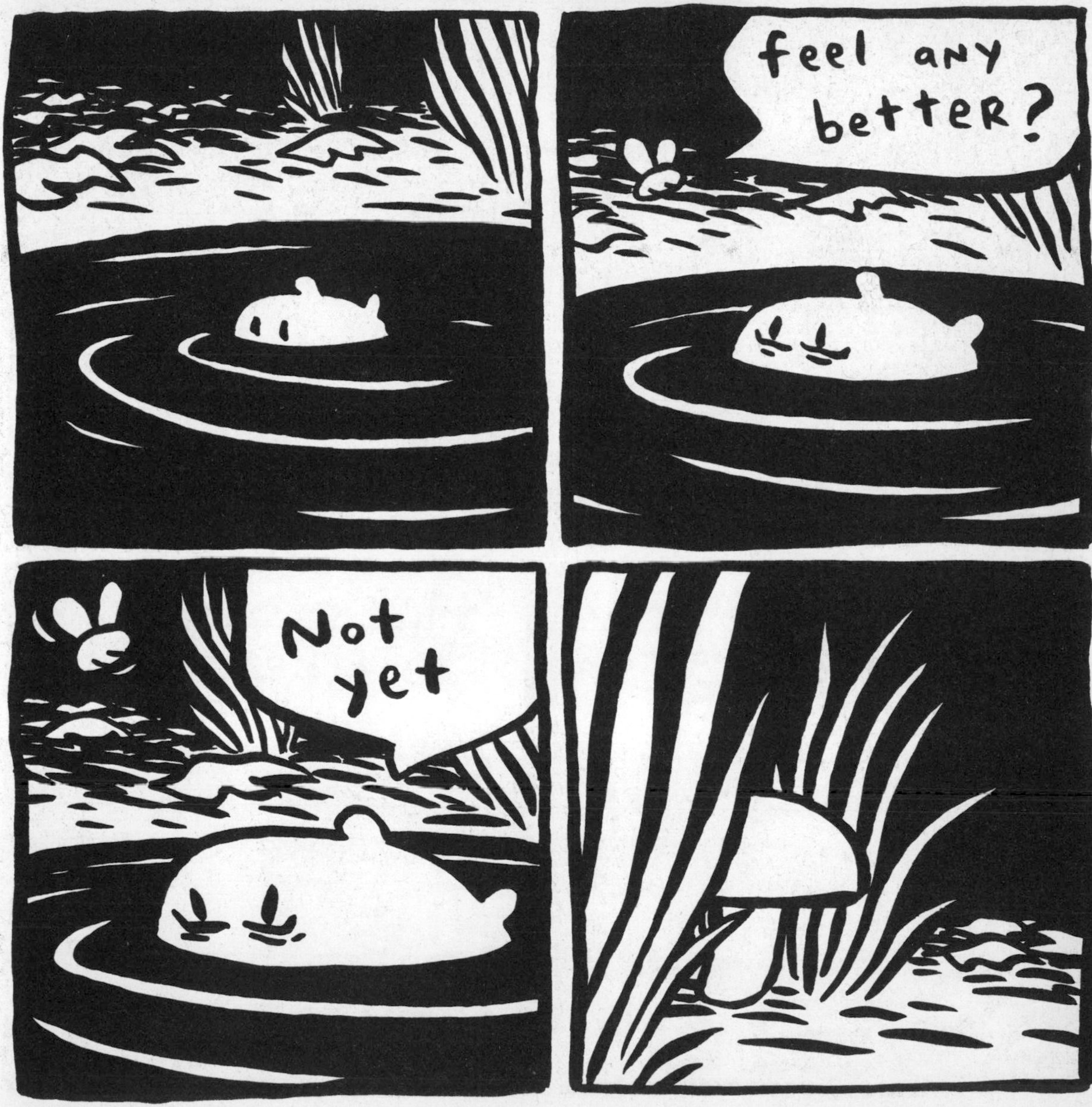
feel any better?
Not yet

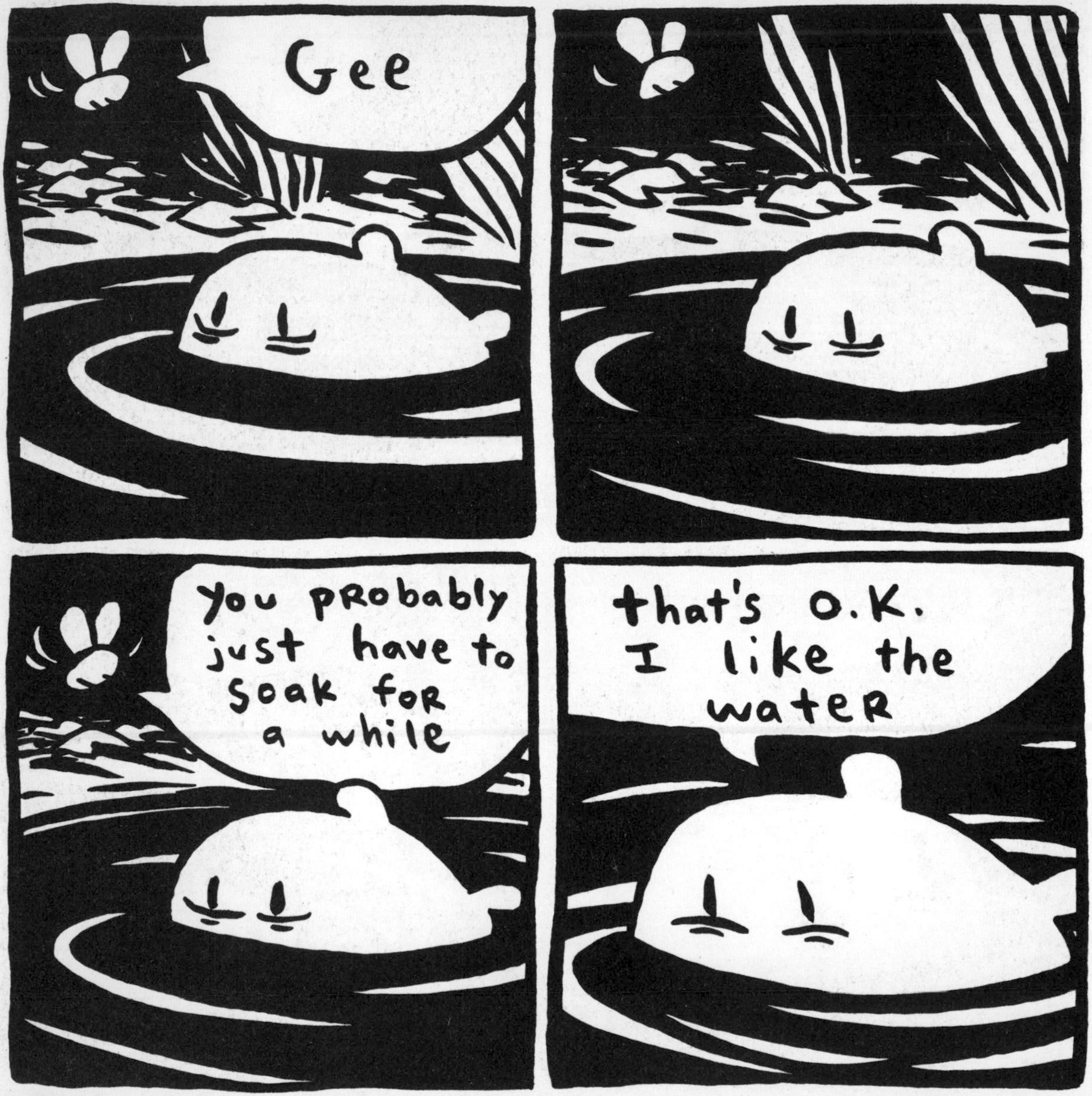
Gee
You probably just have to soak for a while
that's O.K. I like the water

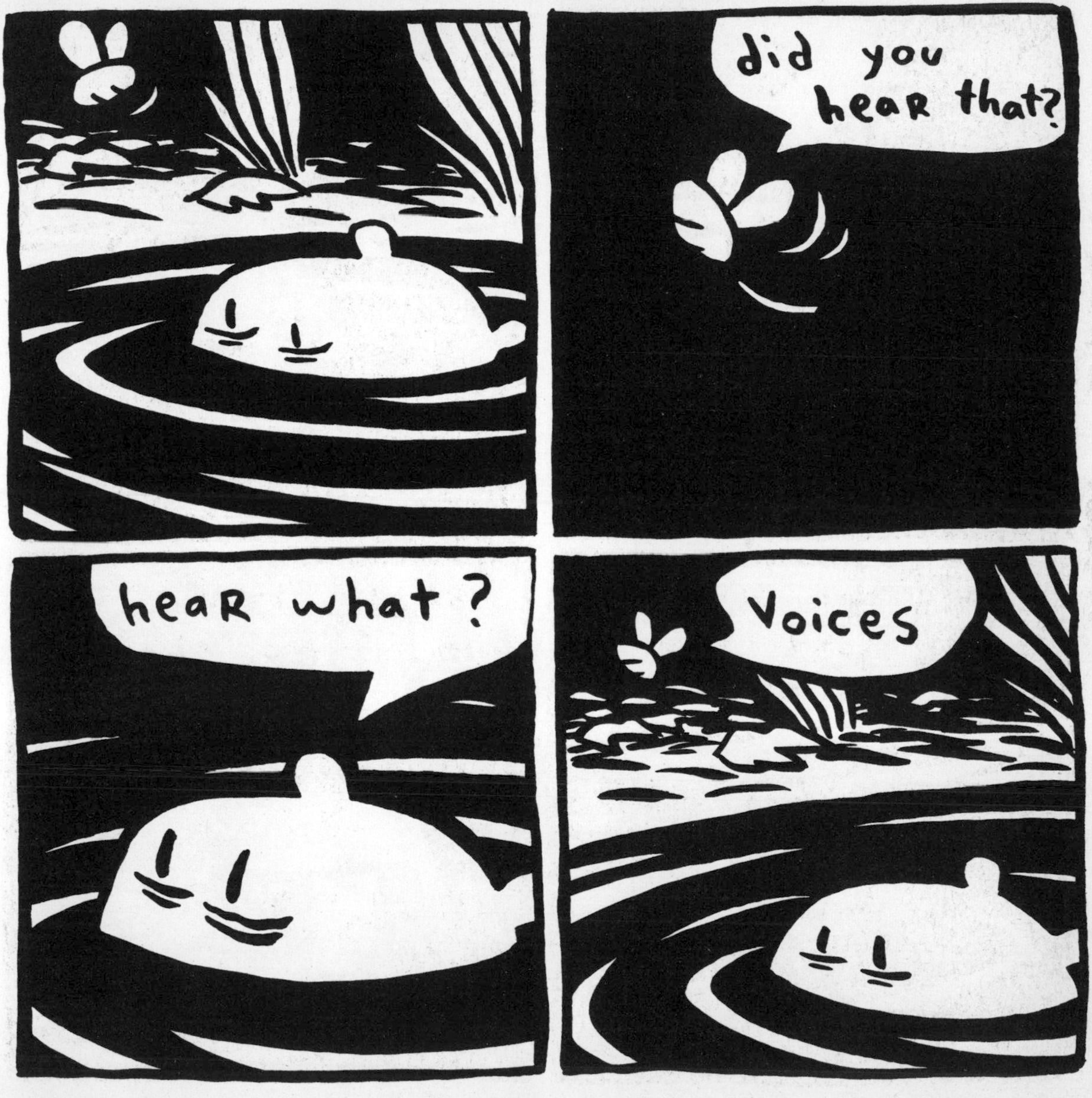
did you hear that?
hear what?
Voices

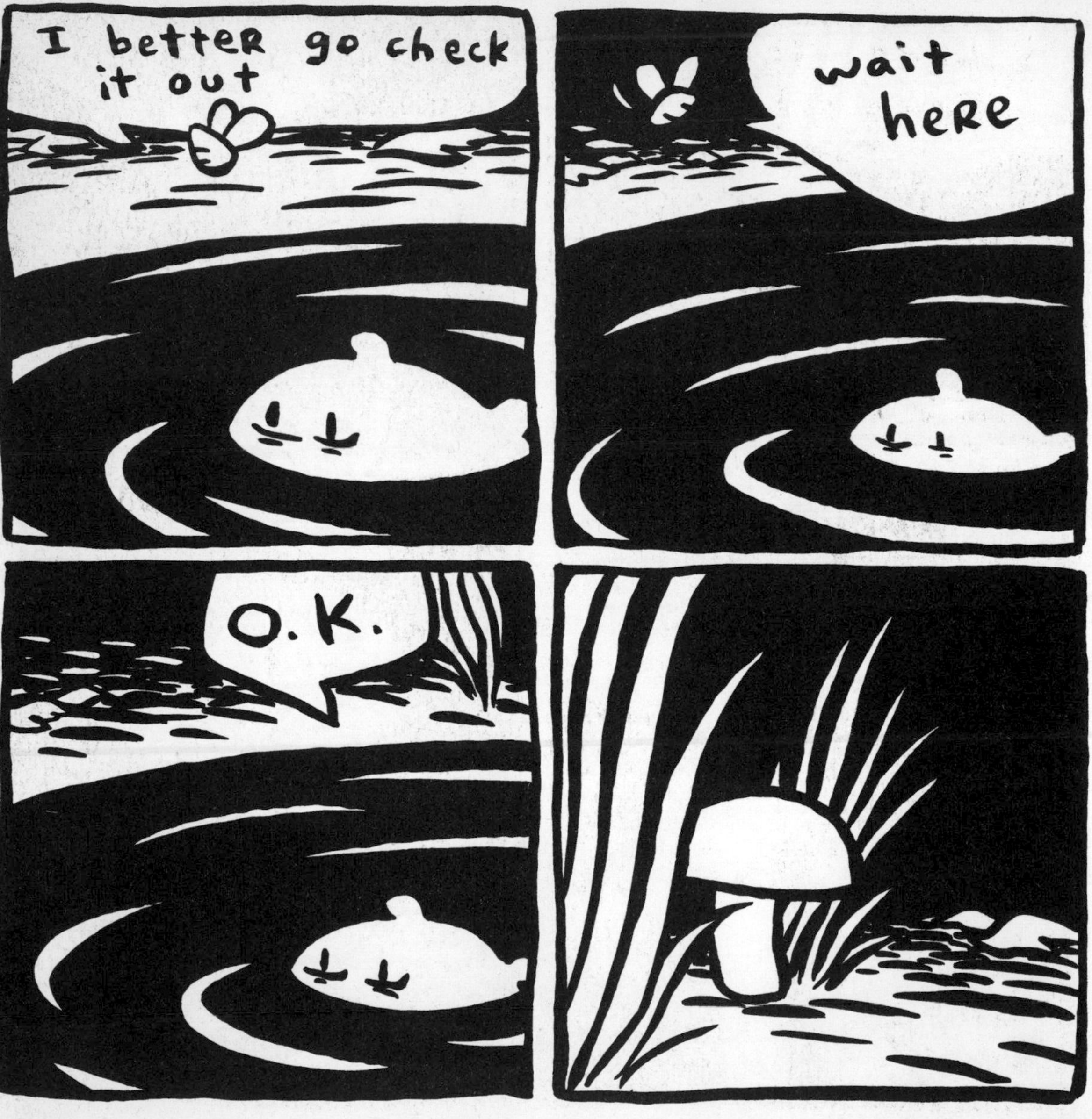
I better go check it out
wait here
O.K.

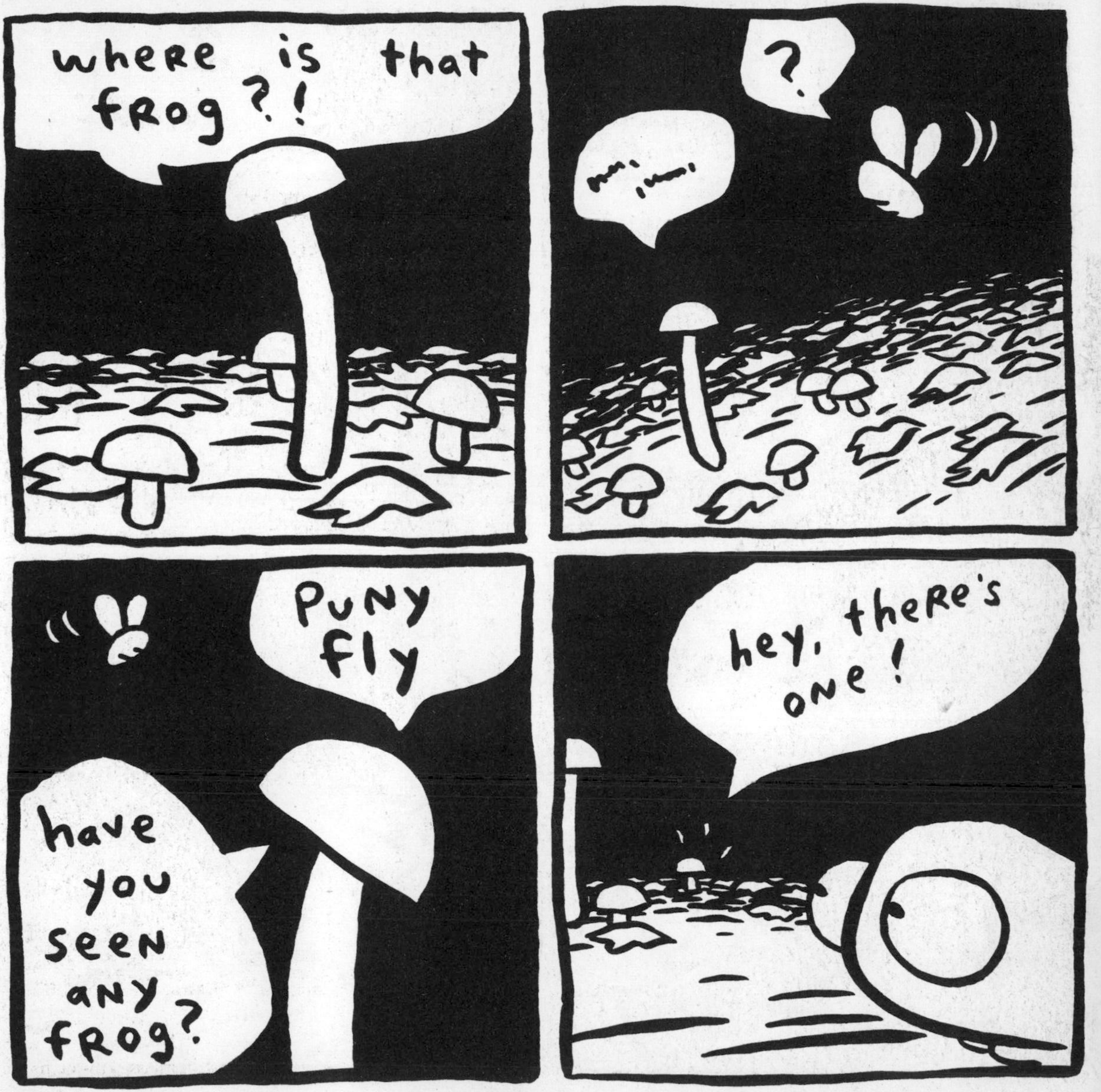
where is that frog?!
?
puny fly
have you seen any frog?
hey, there's one!

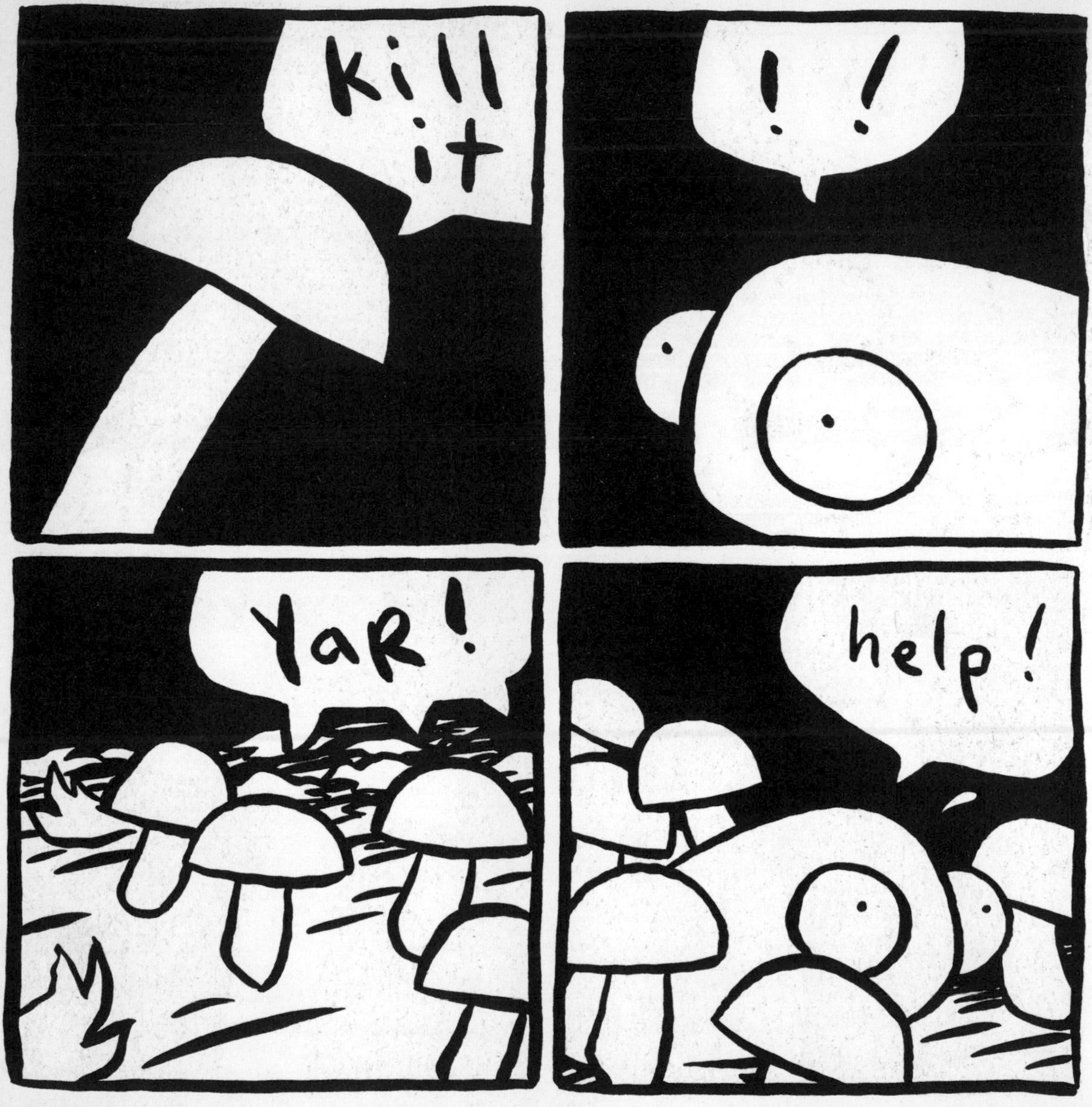
kill it
! !
Yar!
help!

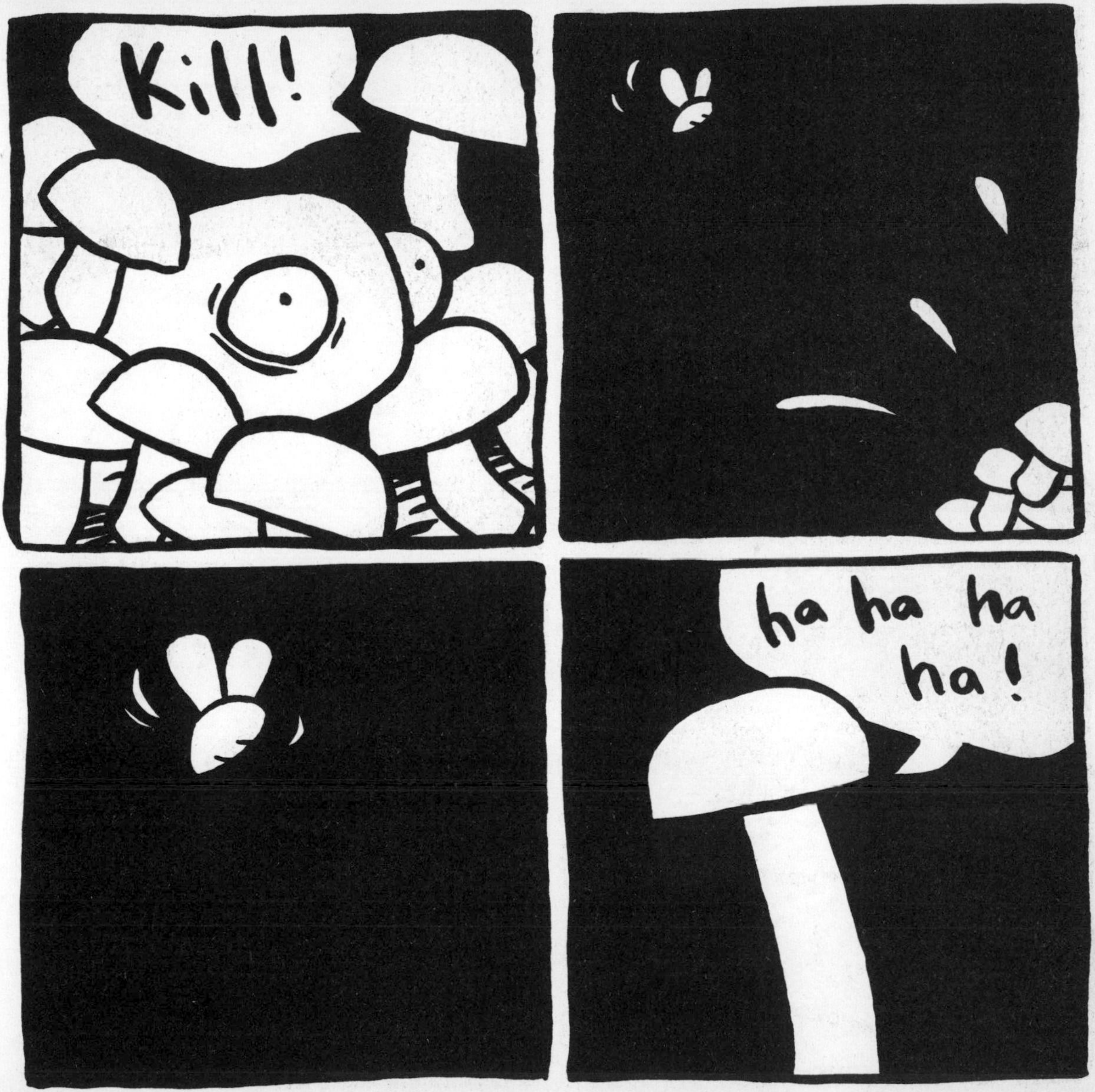
Kill!
ha ha ha ha!

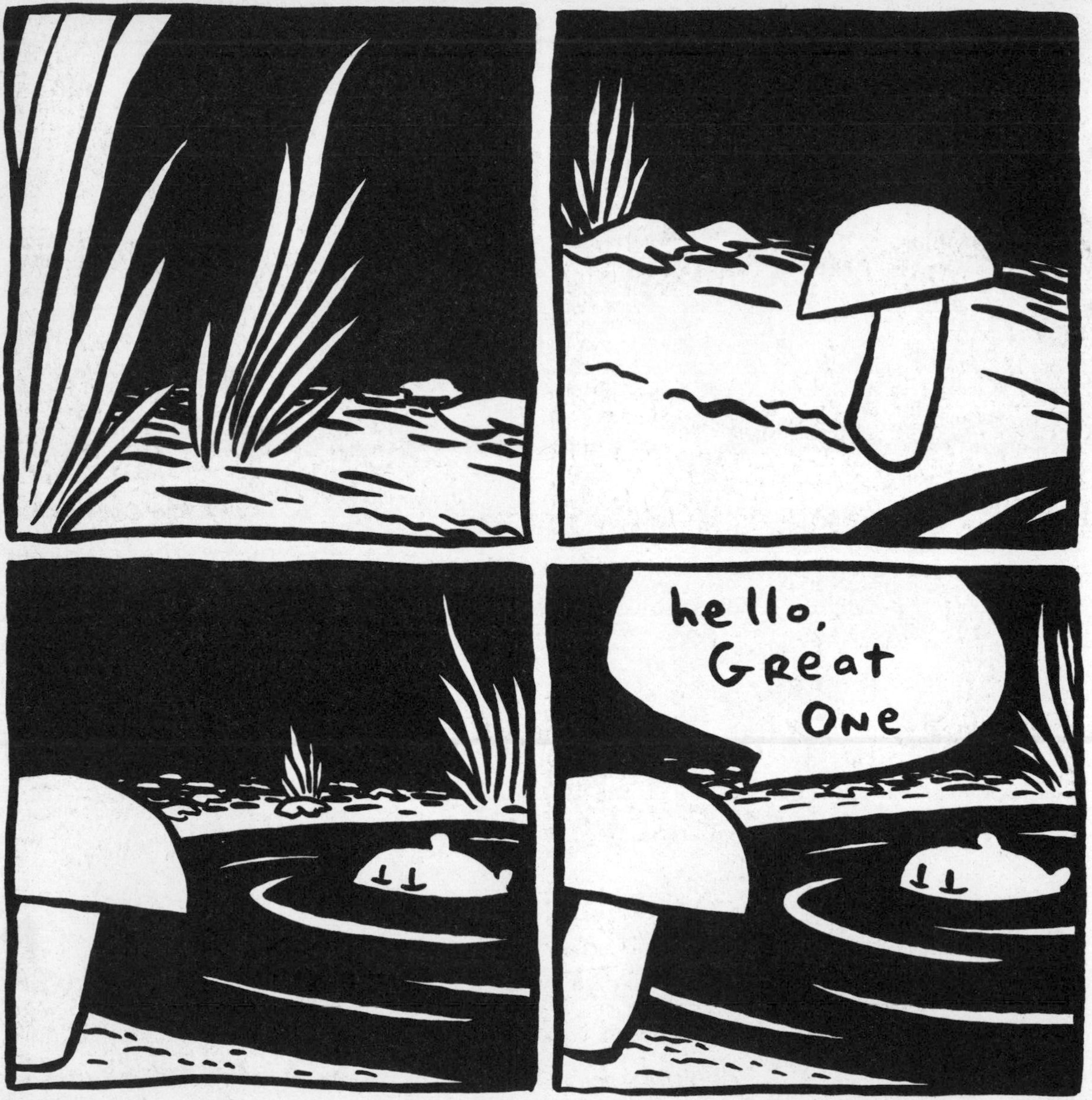
hello, Great One

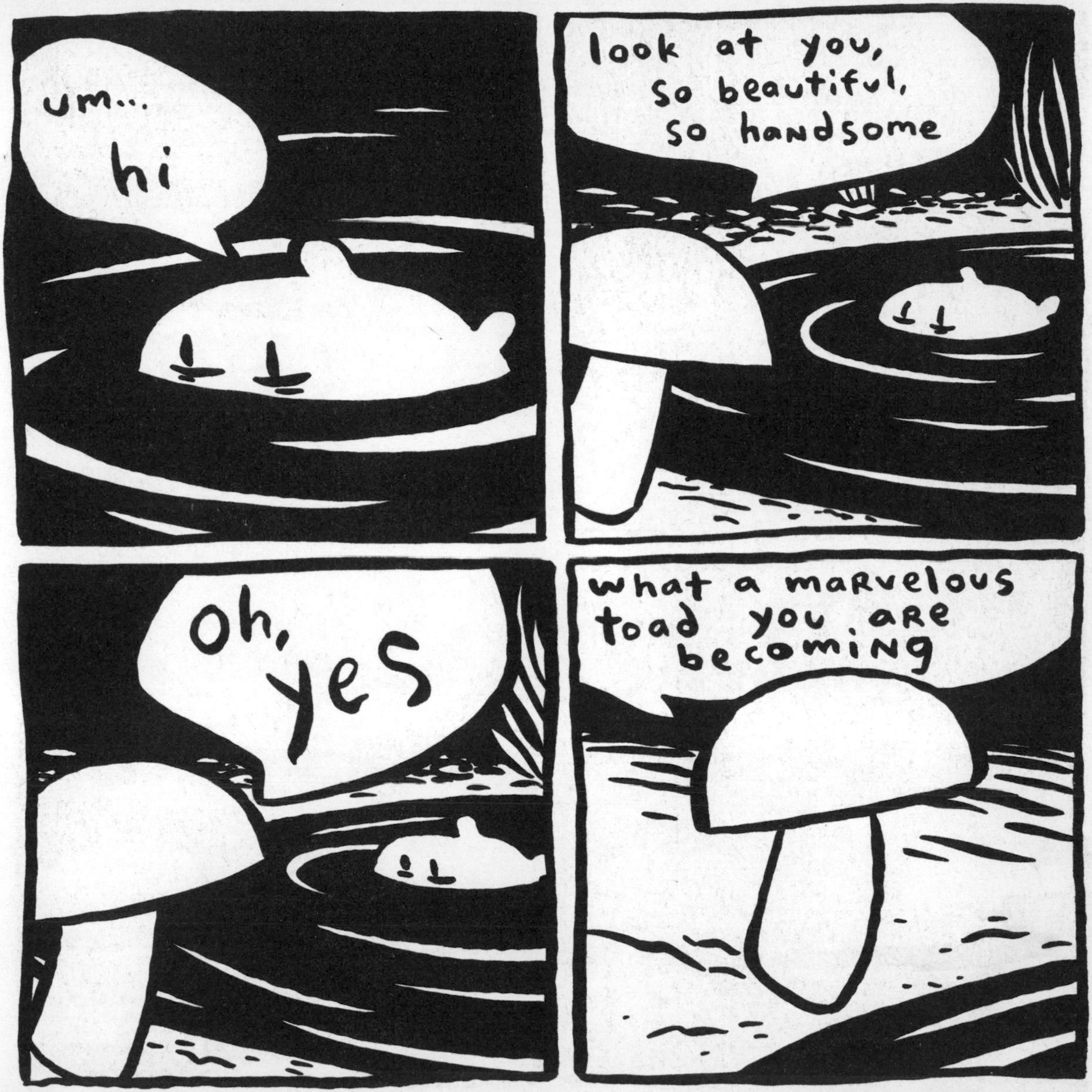
um... hi
look at you, so beautiful, so handsome
Oh, yes
what a marvelous toad you are becoming

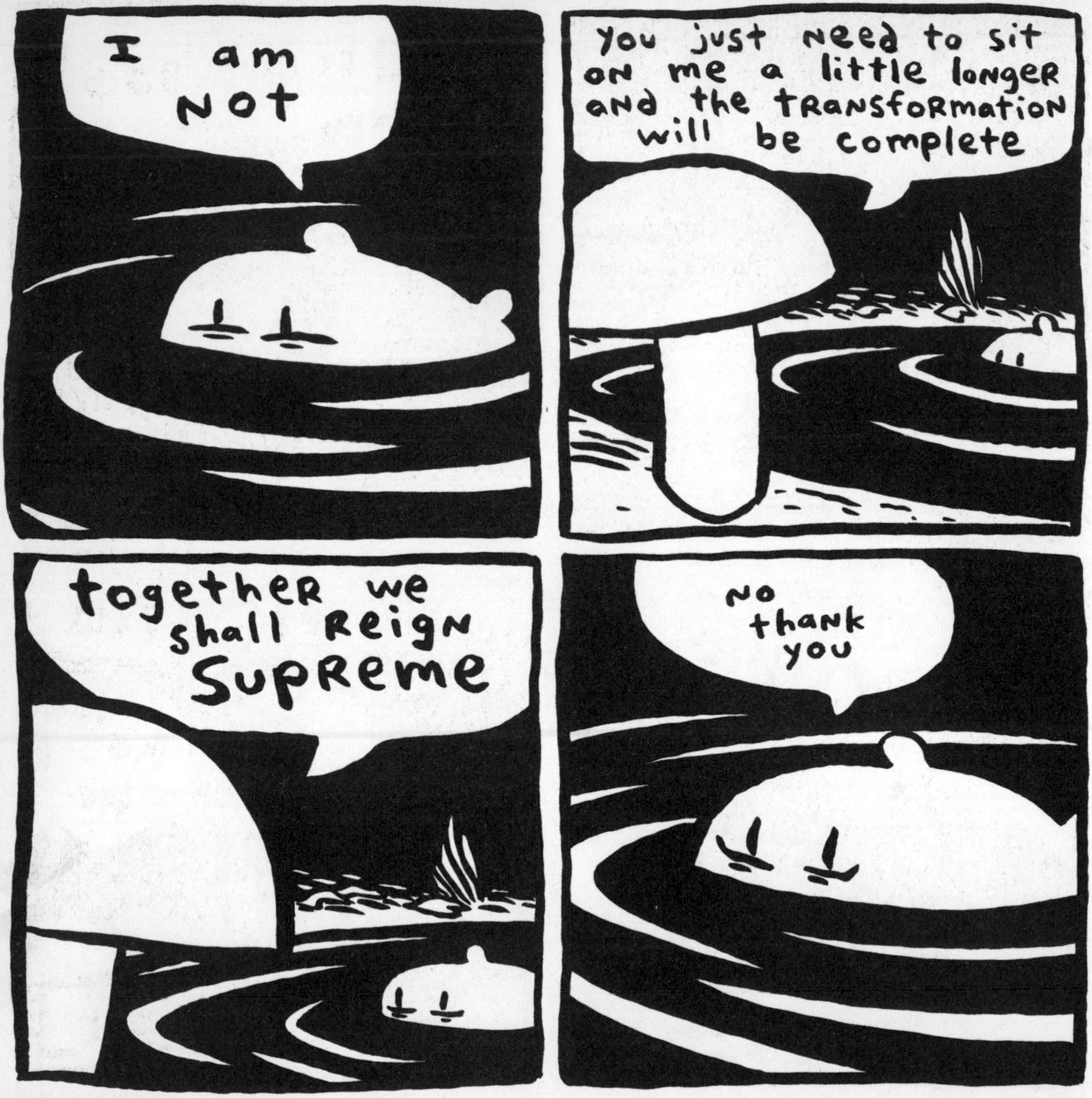
I am NOT
you just need to sit on me a little longer and the TRANSFORMATION will be complete
together we shall Reign Supreme
No thank you

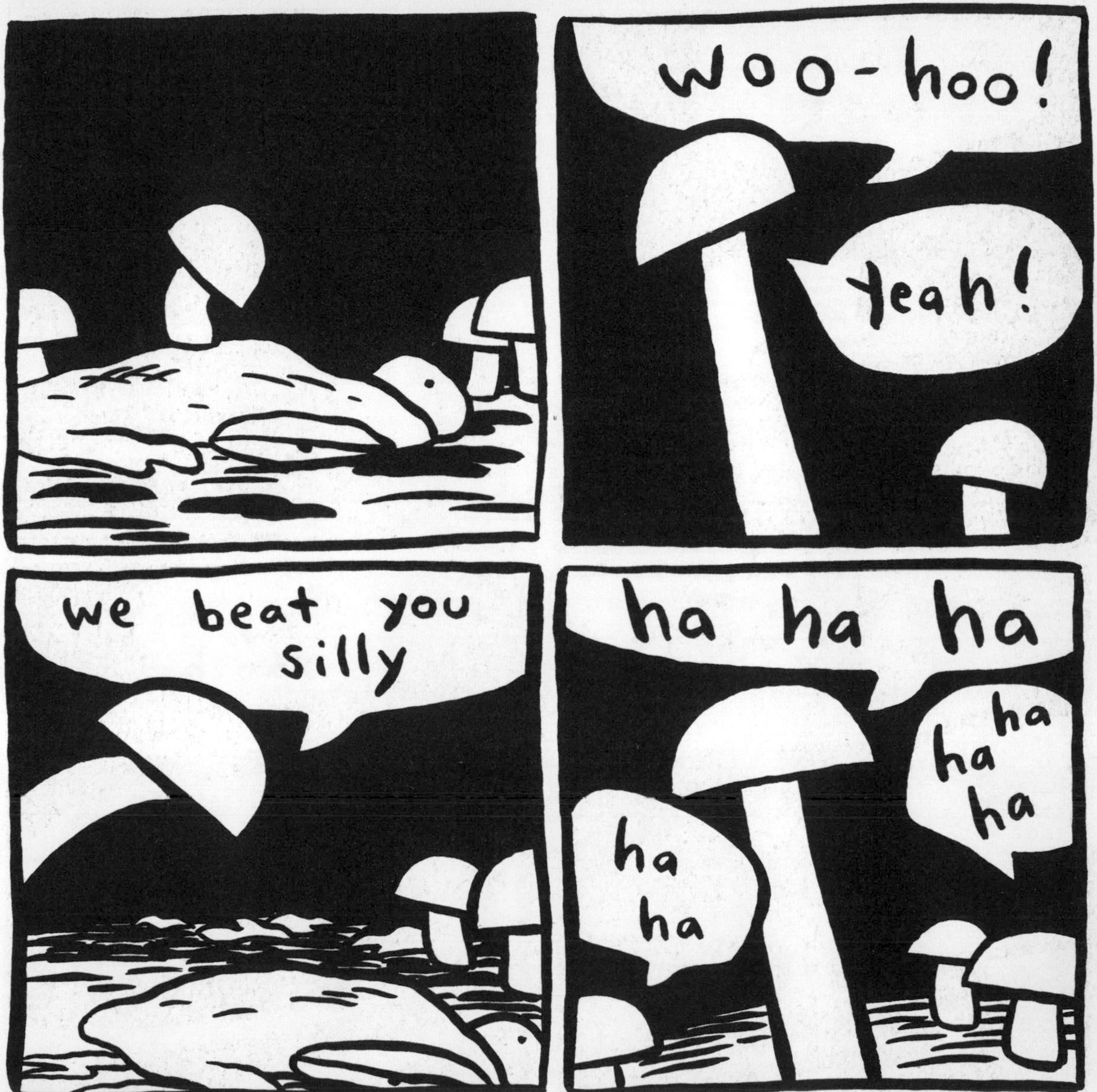
woo-hoo!
yeah!
we beat you silly
ha ha ha
ha ha ha
ha ha

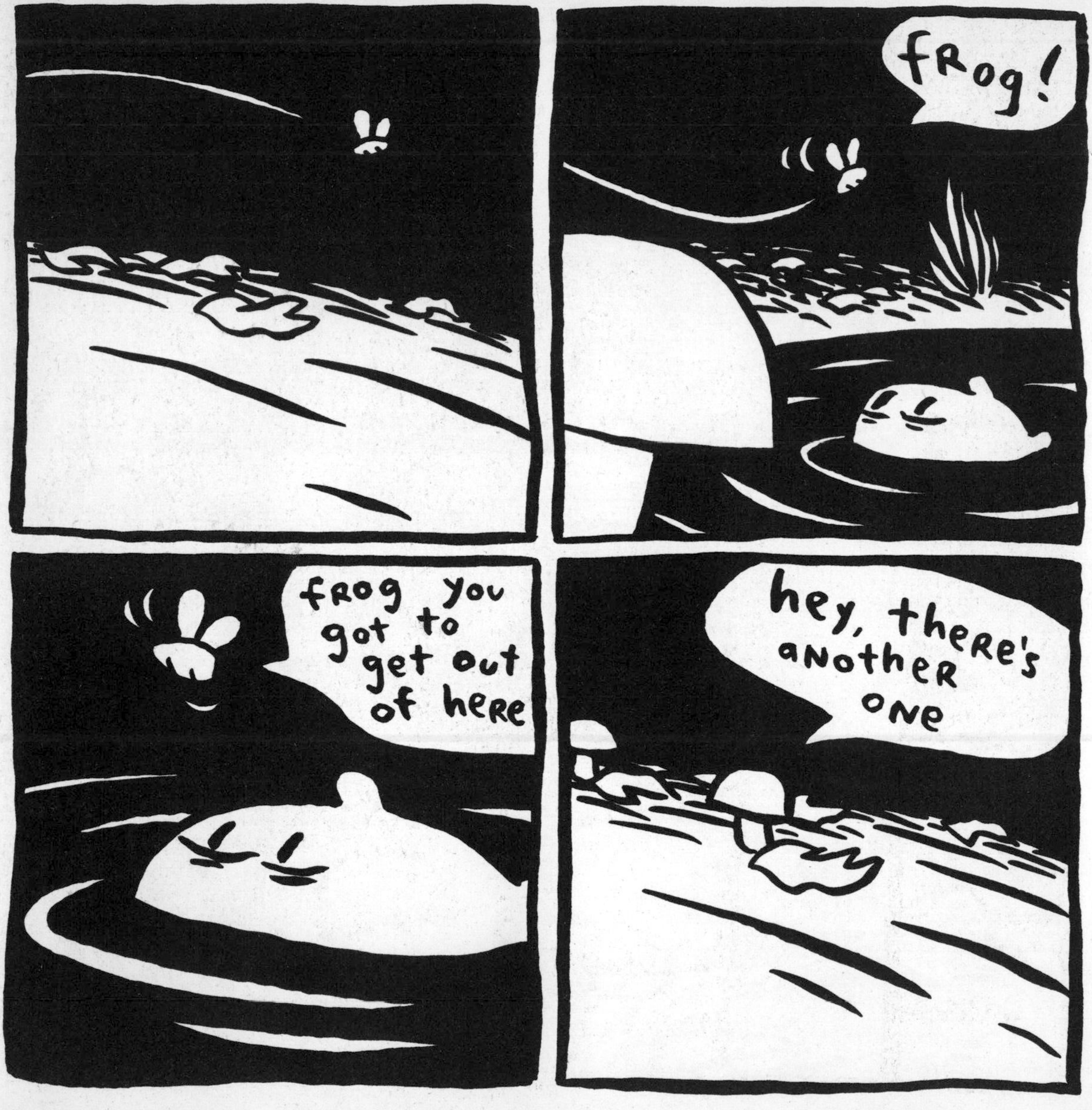
frog!
frog you got to get out of here
hey, there's another one

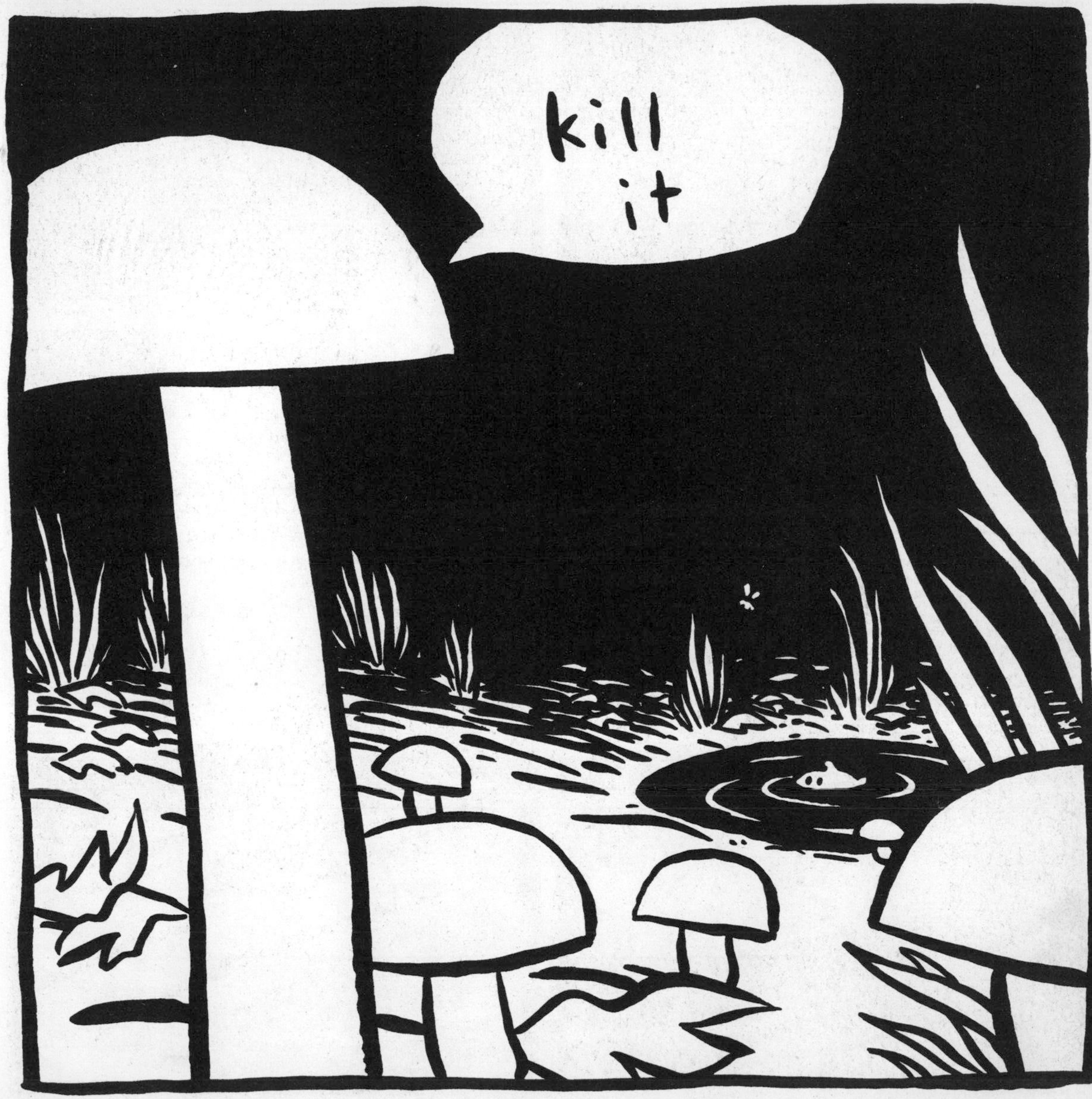
kill it

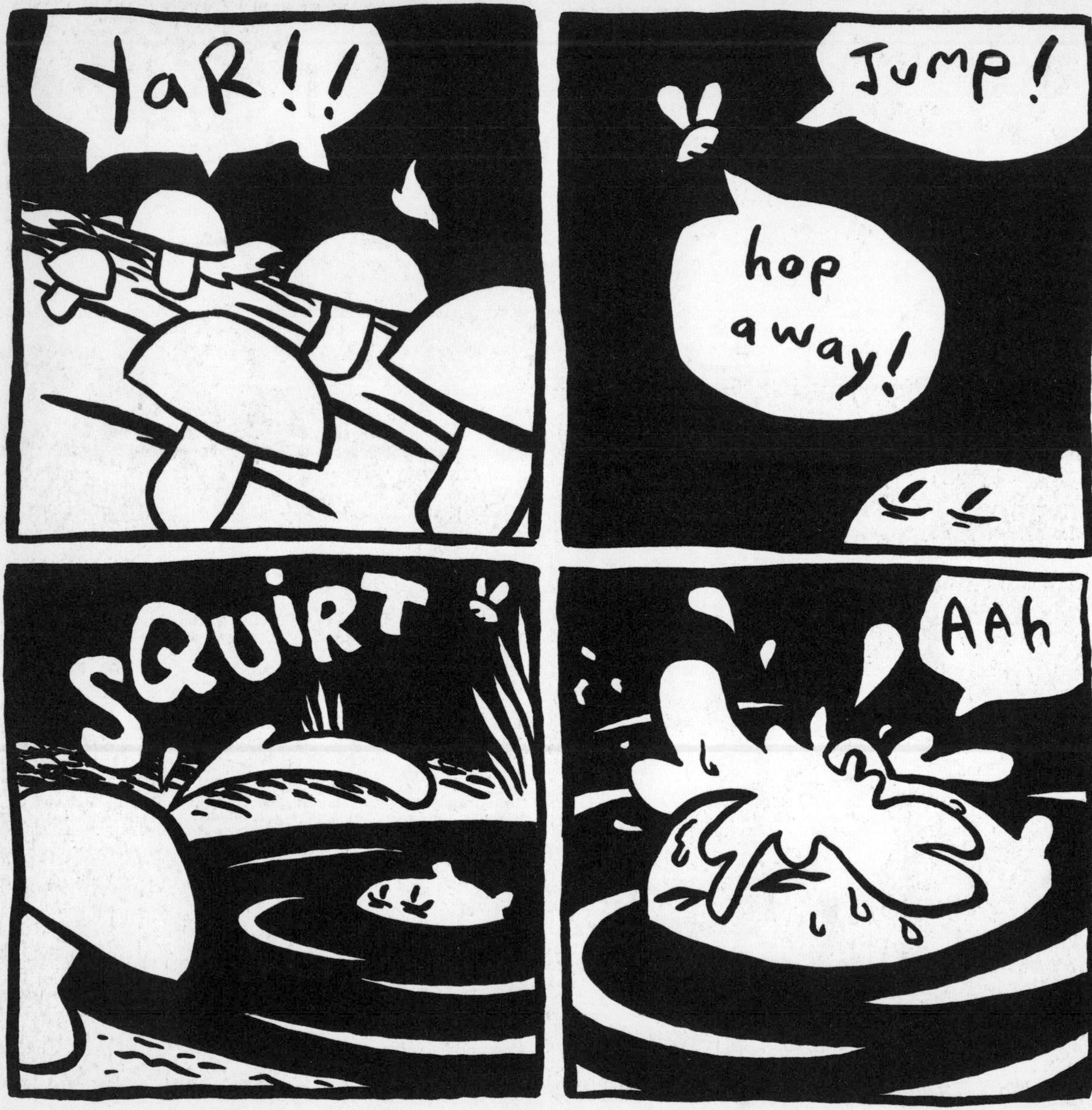
YaR!!
JUMP!
hop away!
SQUIRT
AAh

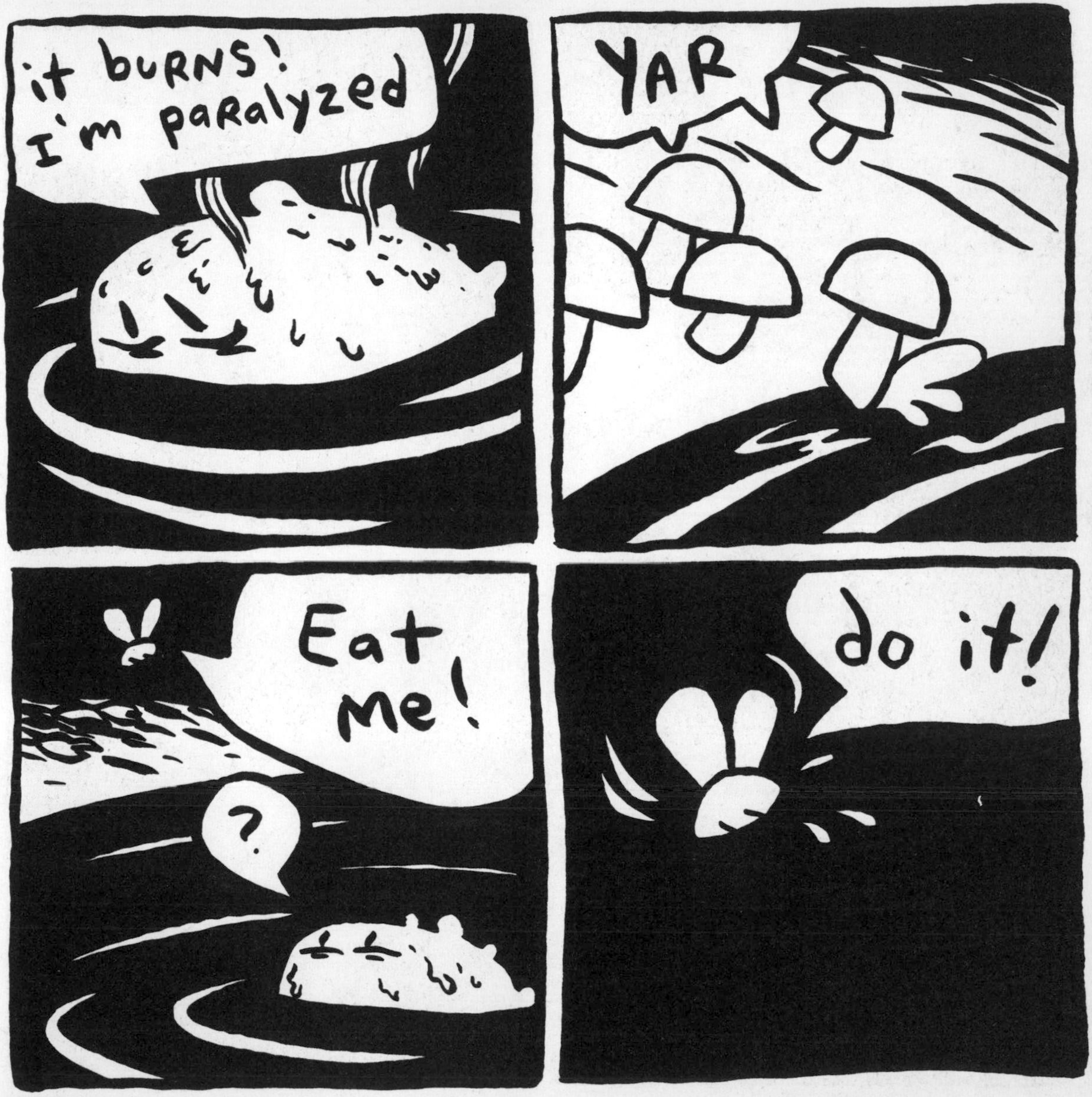
it burns! I'm paralyzed
YAR
Eat Me!
?
do it!

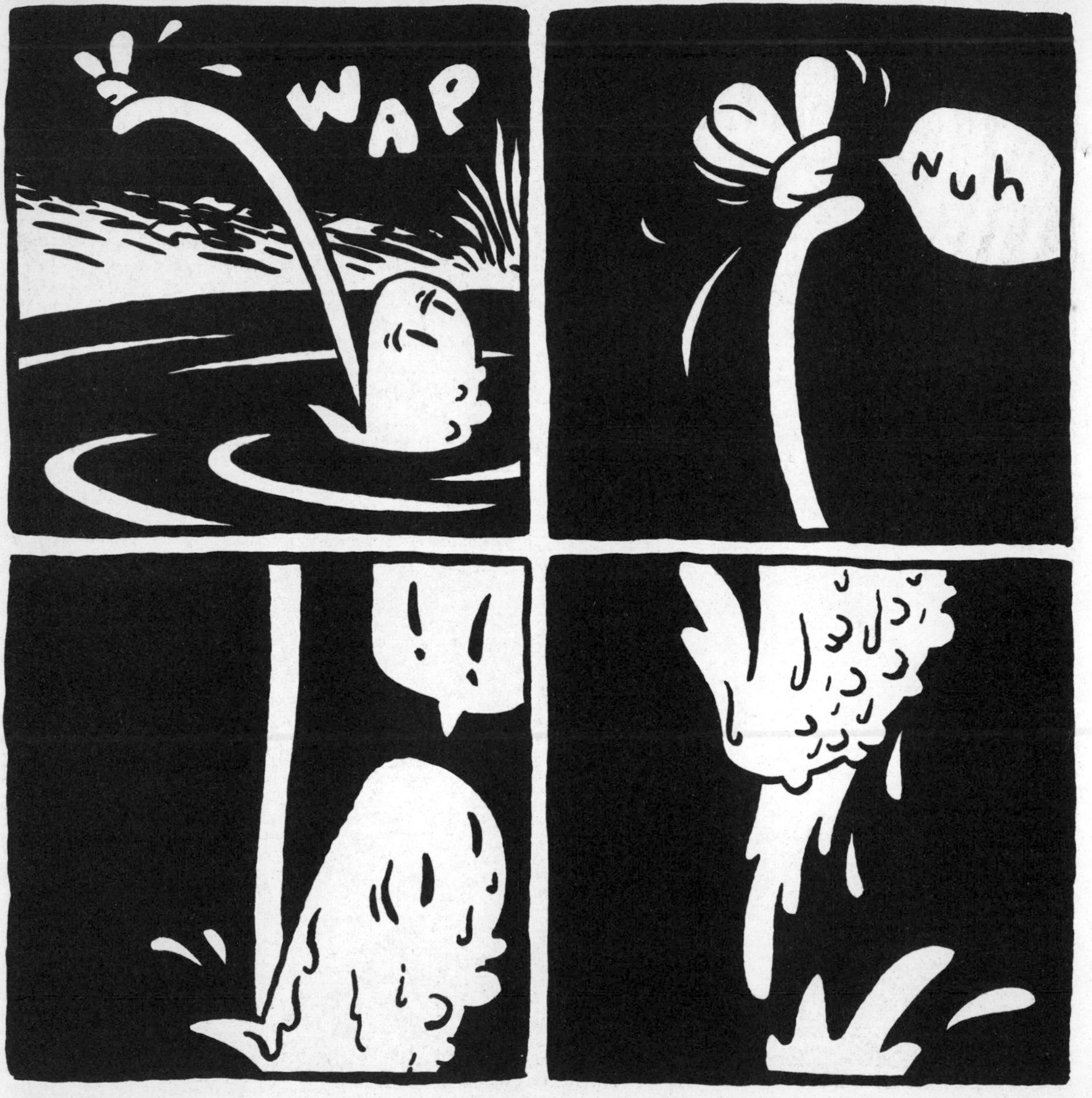
WAP
Nuh
! !

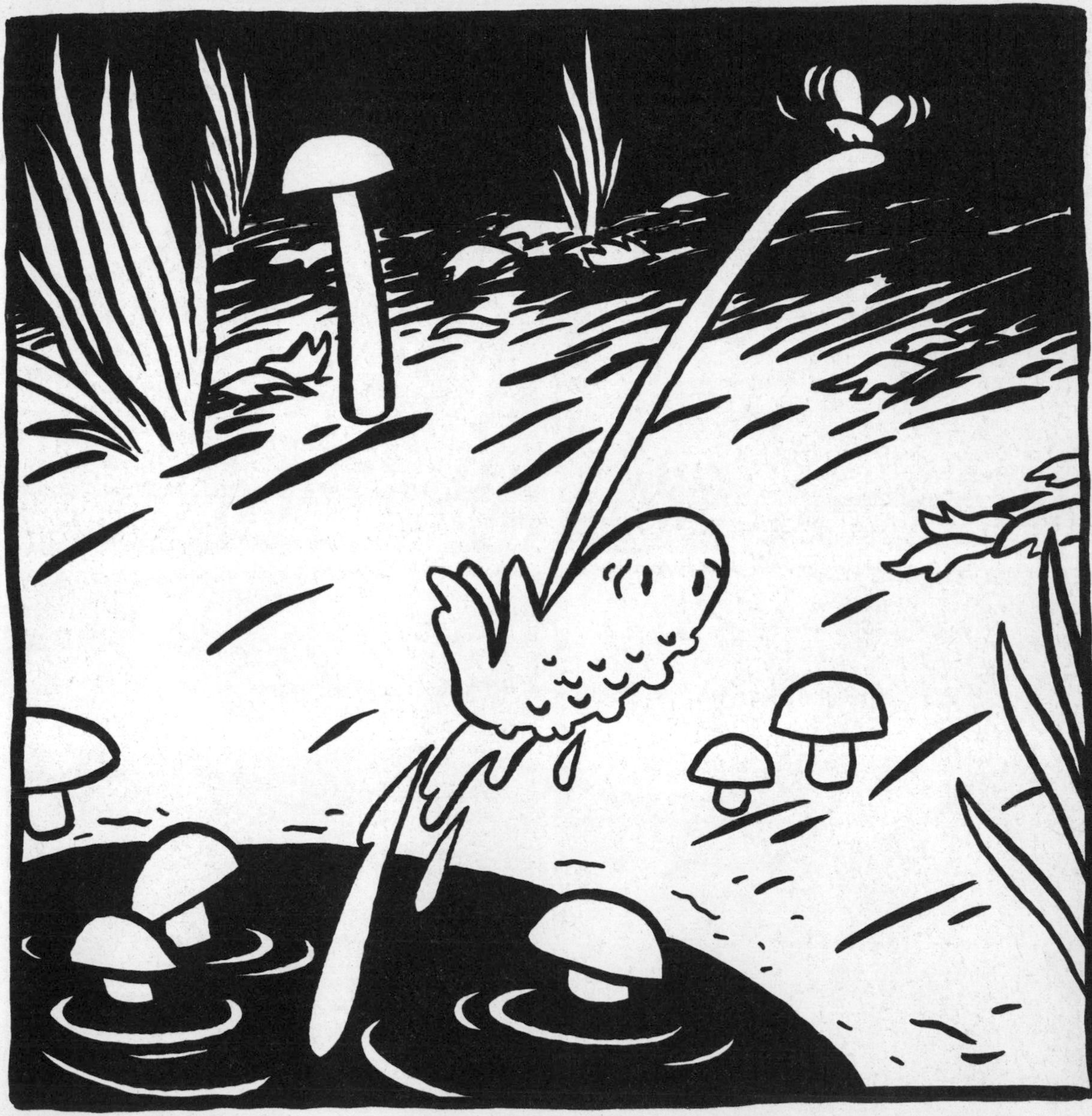

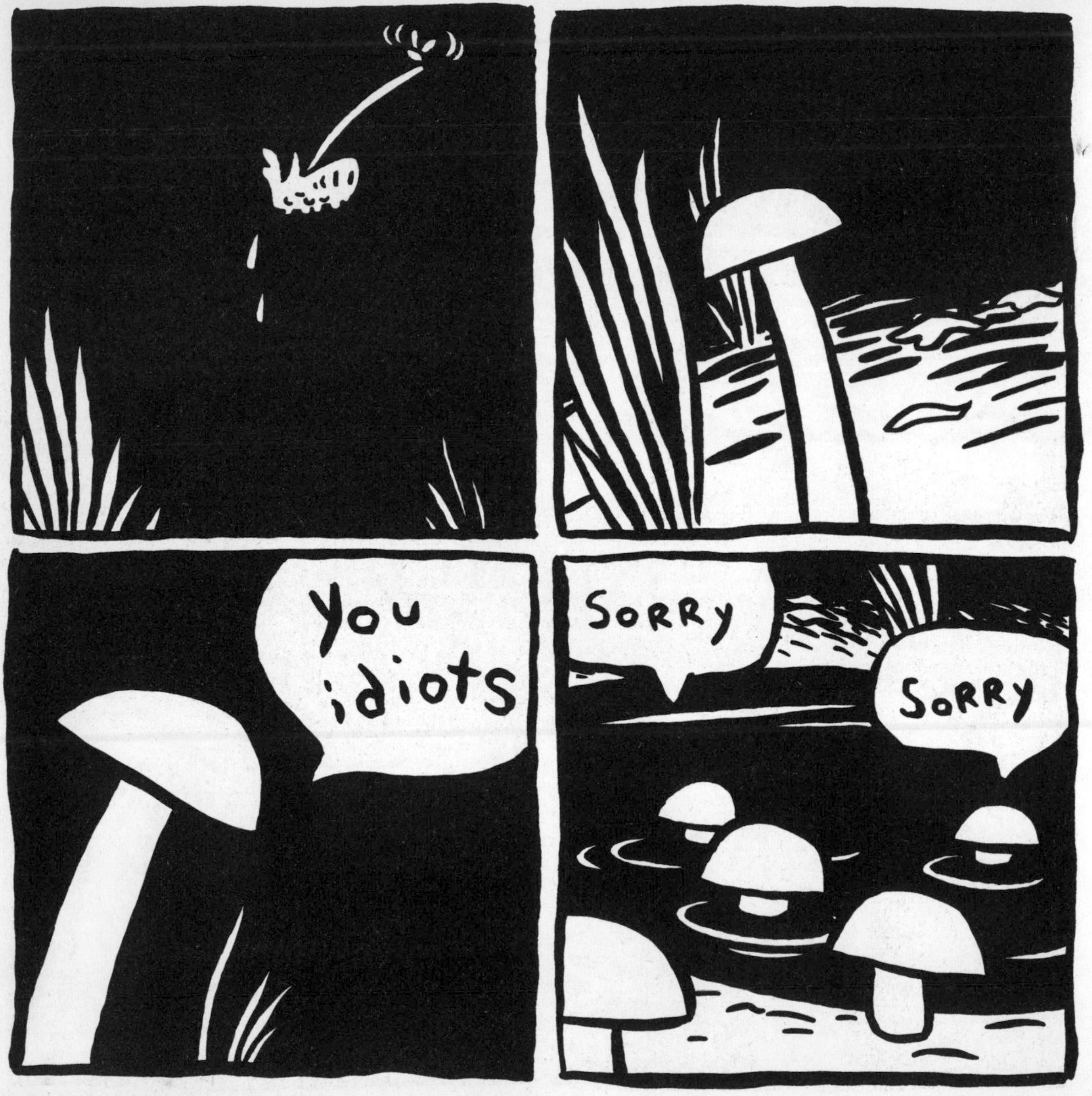
you idiots
SORRY
SORRY

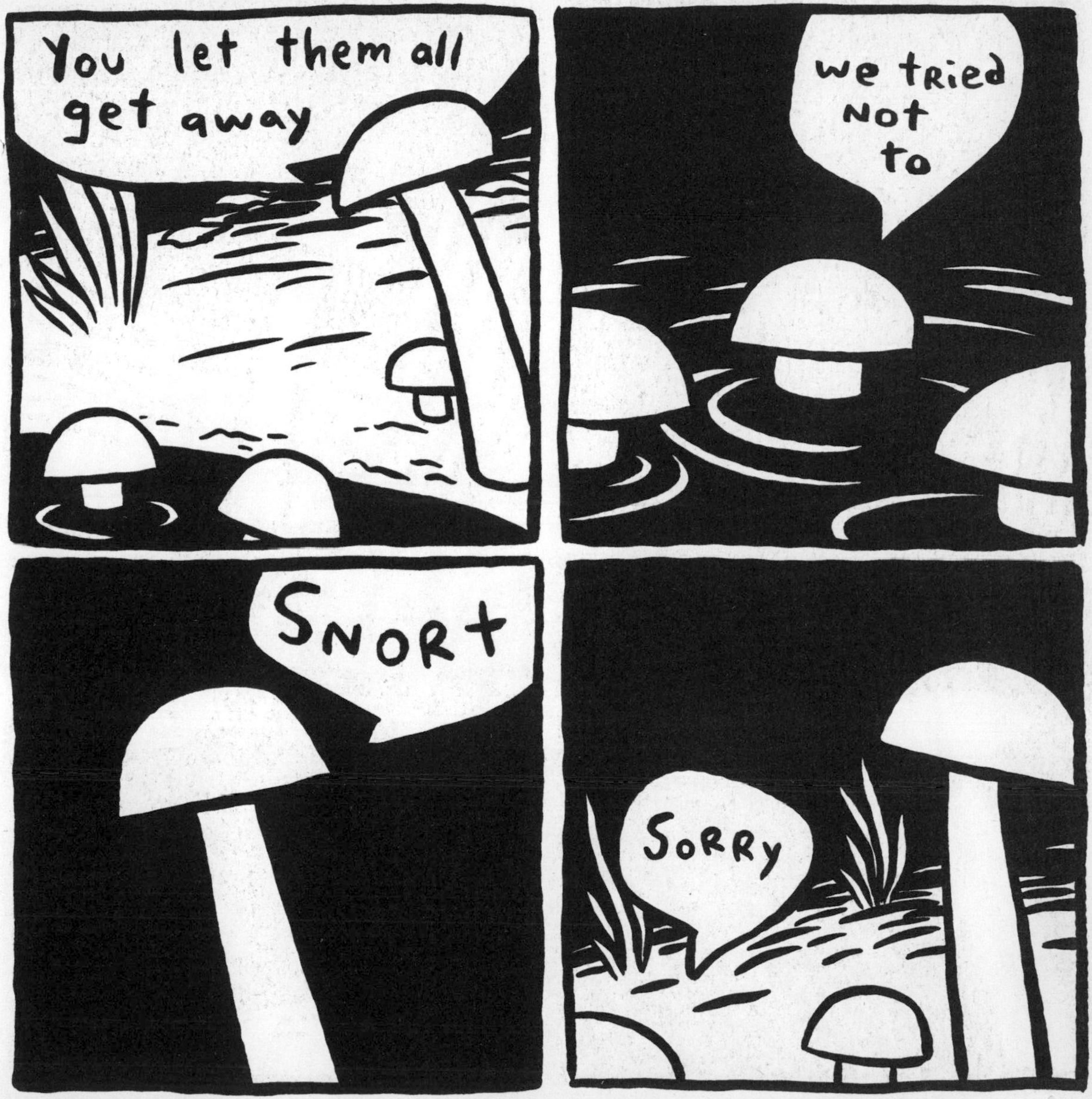
You let them all get away
we tried not to
SNORT
SORRY

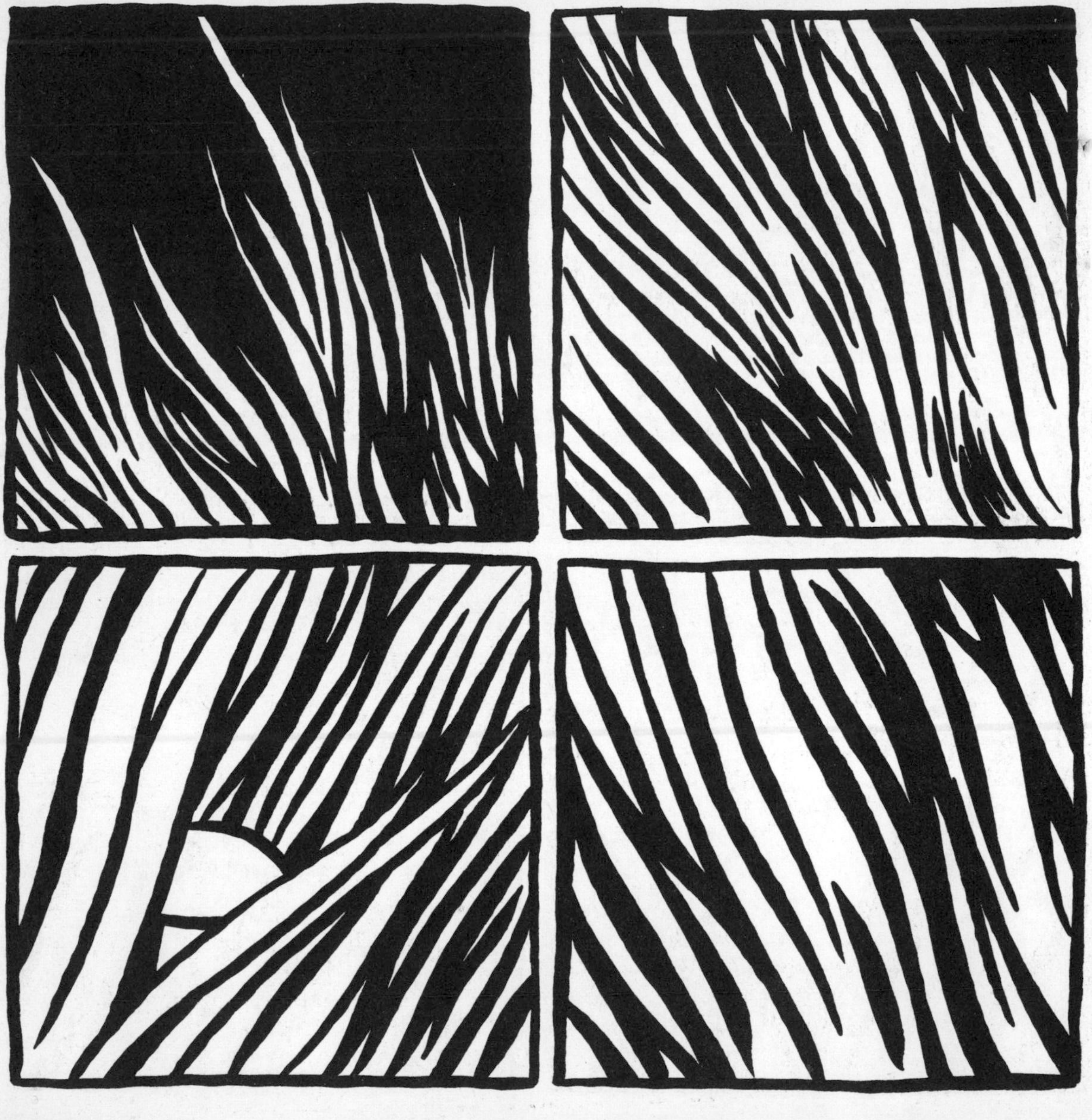

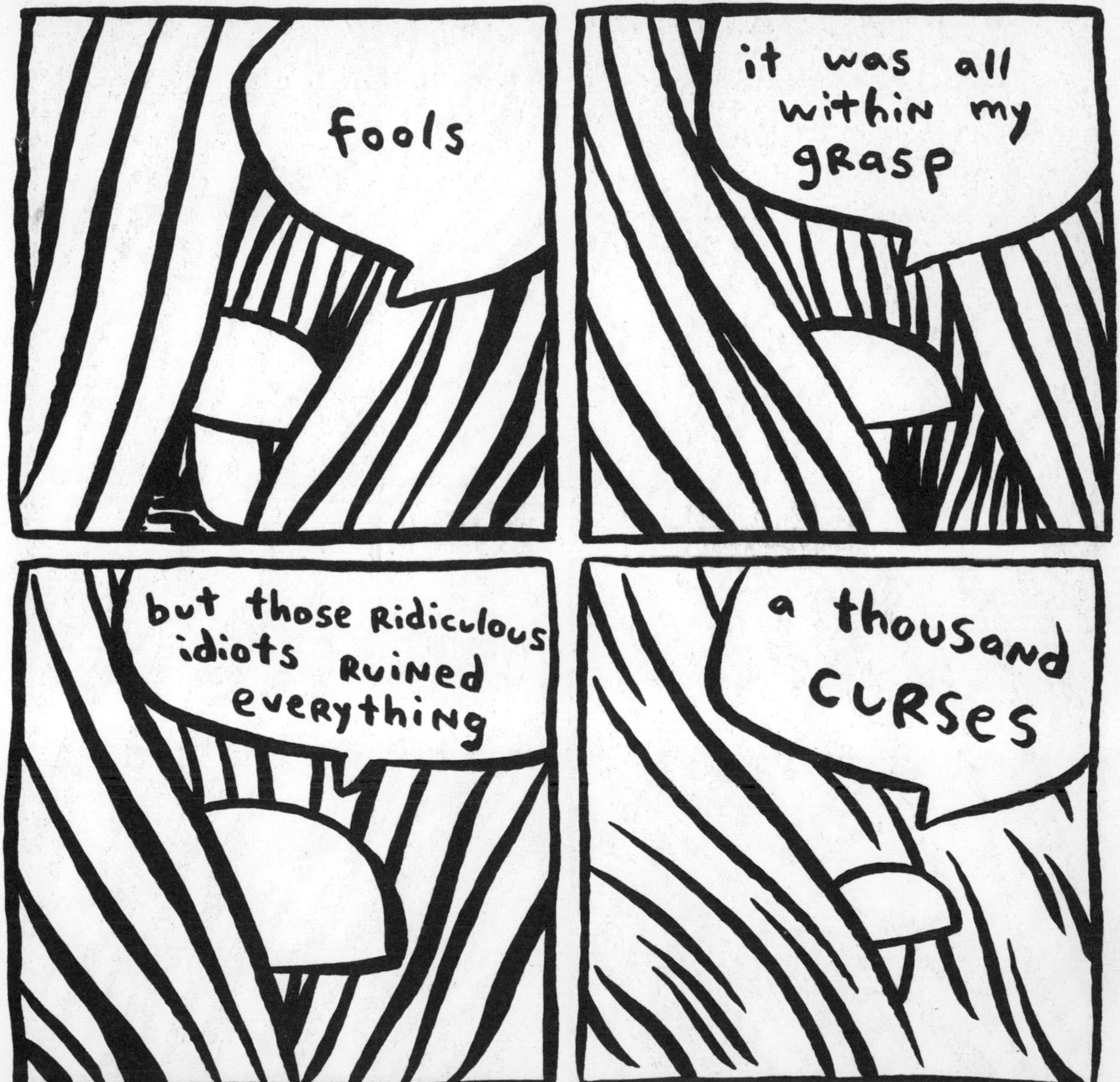
fools
it was all within my grasp
but those ridiculous idiots ruined everything
a thousand curses

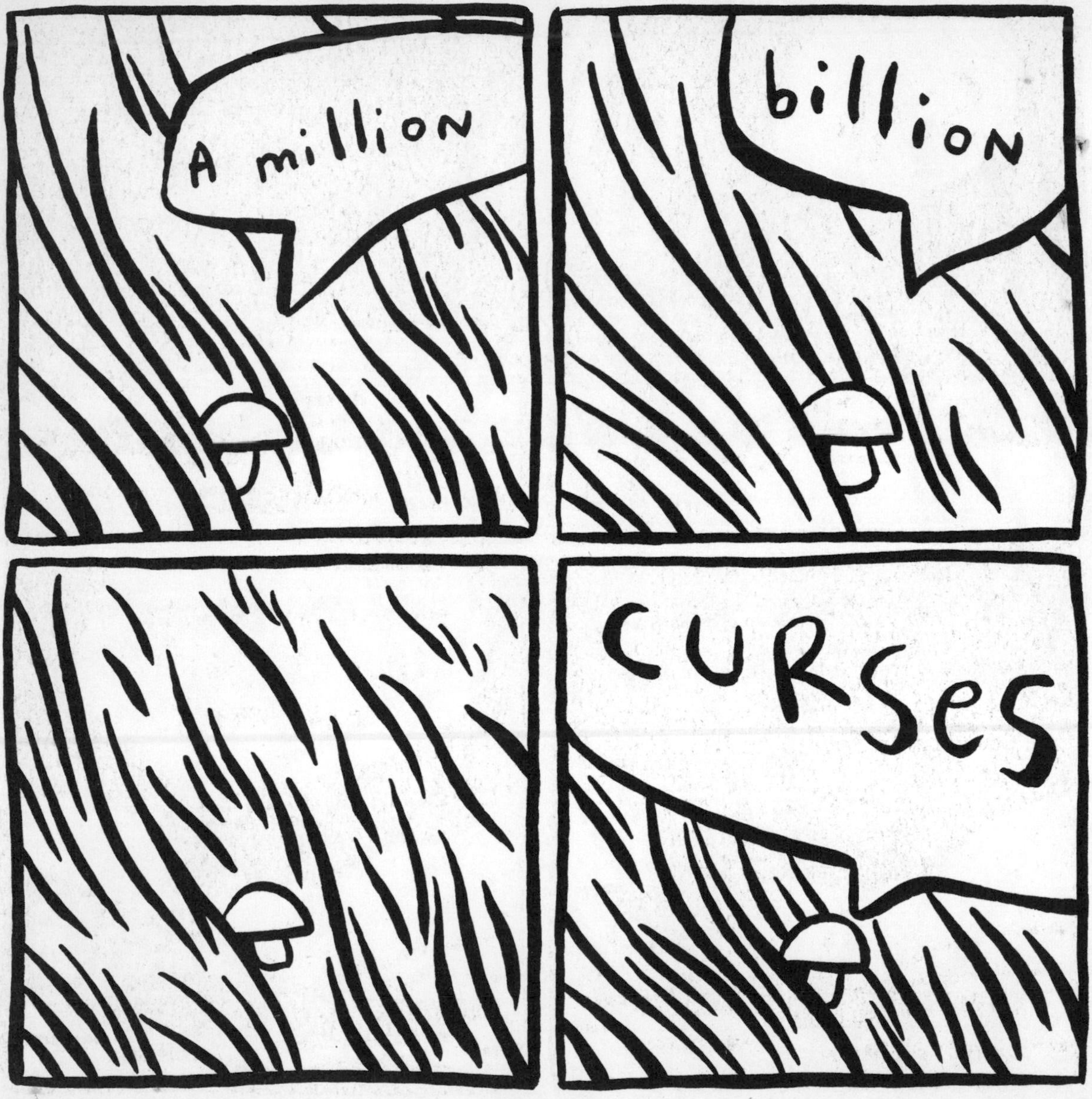
A million
billion
CURSES

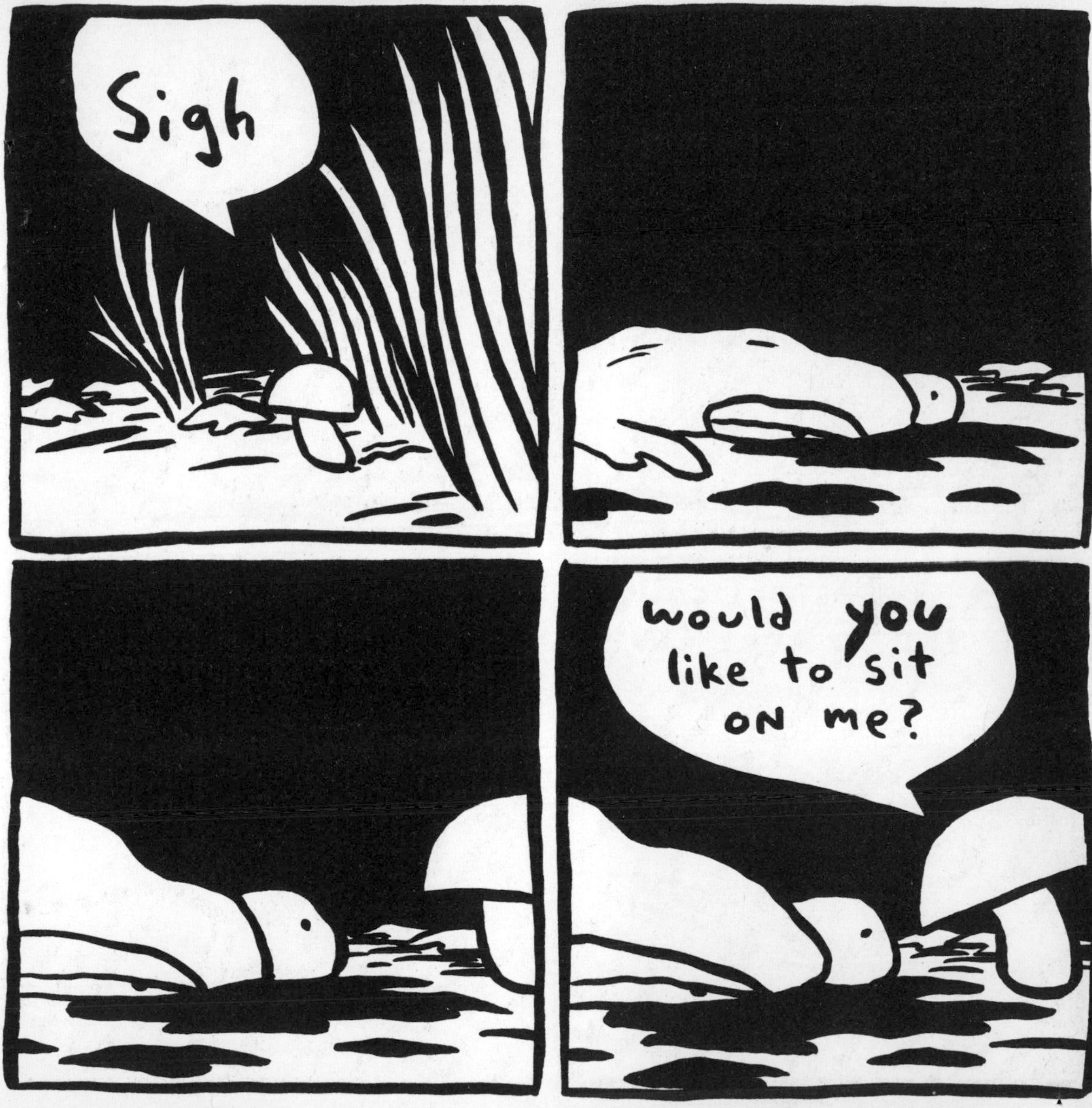
Sigh
would you like to sit on me?

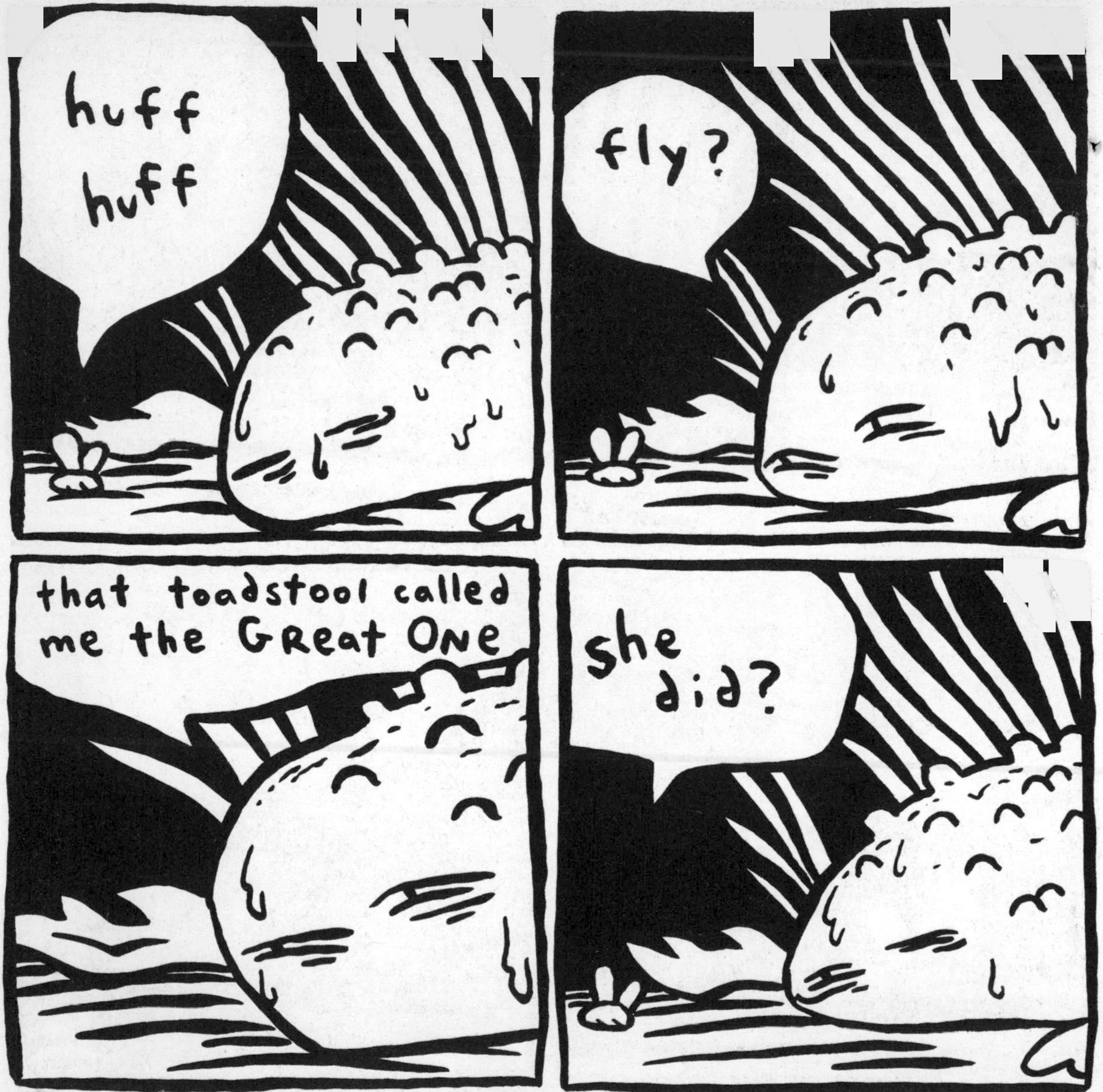
huff huff
fly?
that toadstool called me the GReat ONE
she did?

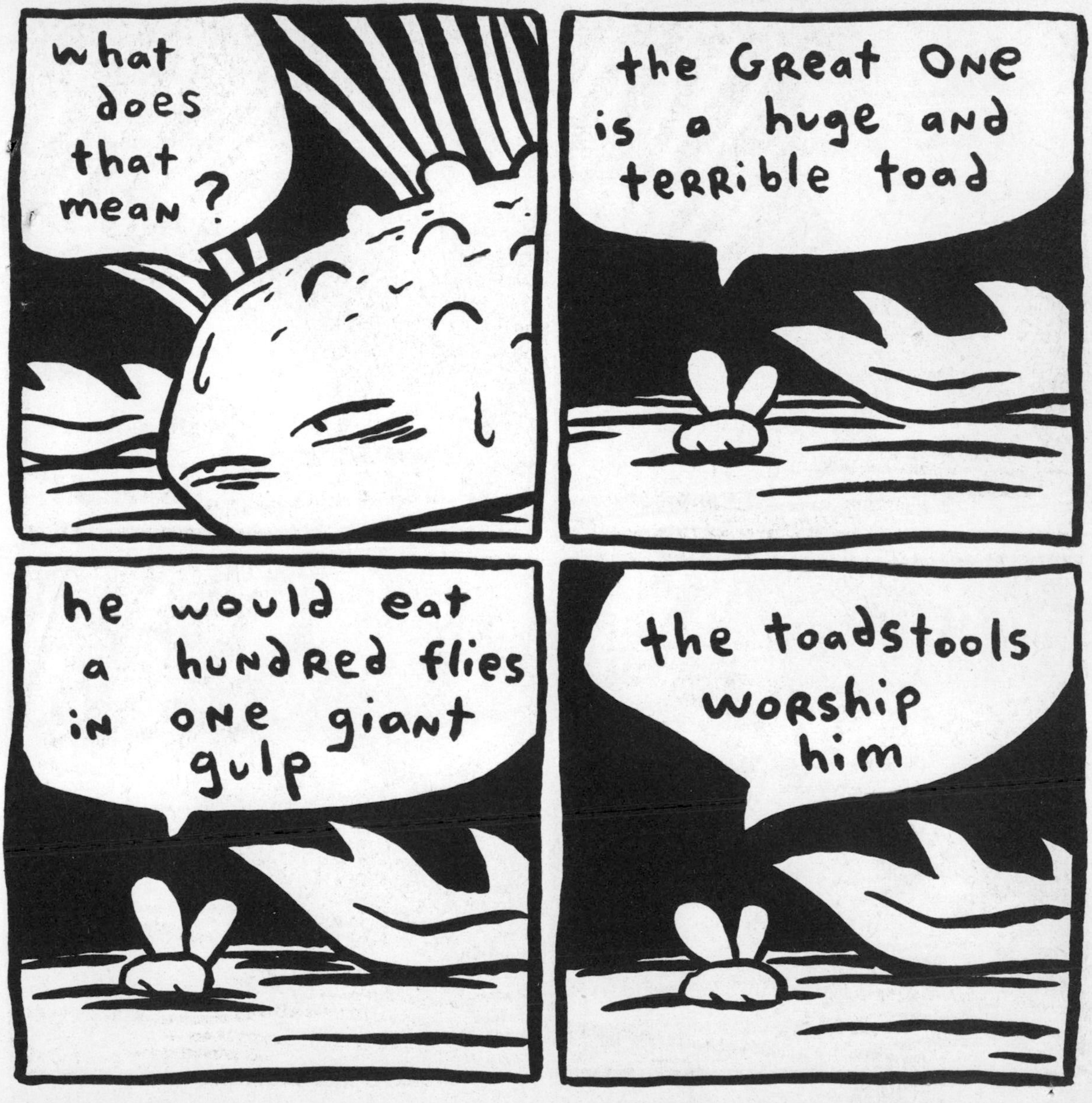
what does that mean?
the Great One is a huge and terrible toad
he would eat a hundred flies in one giant gulp
the toadstools worship him

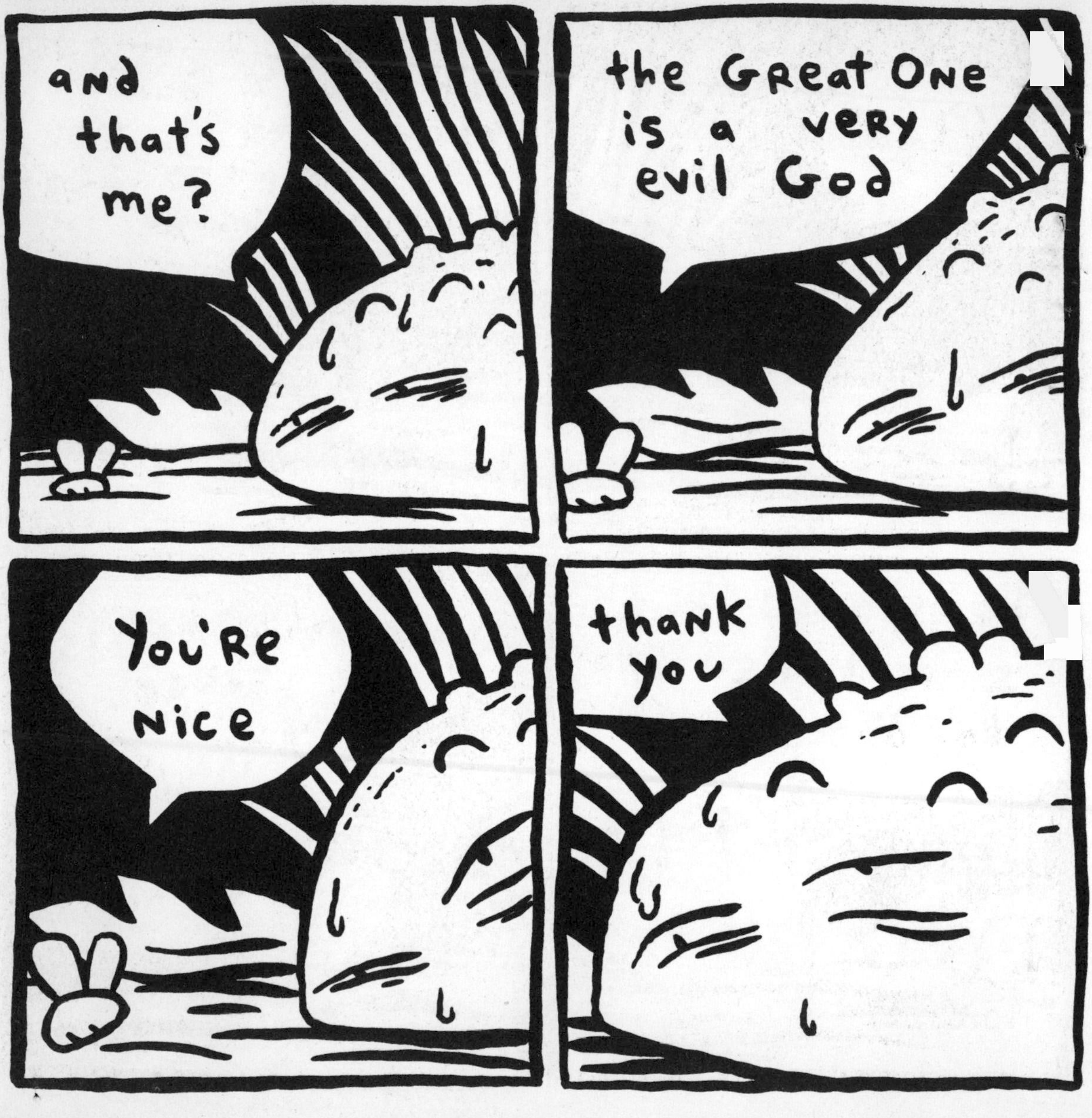
and that's me?
the Great One is a very evil God
You're nice
thank you

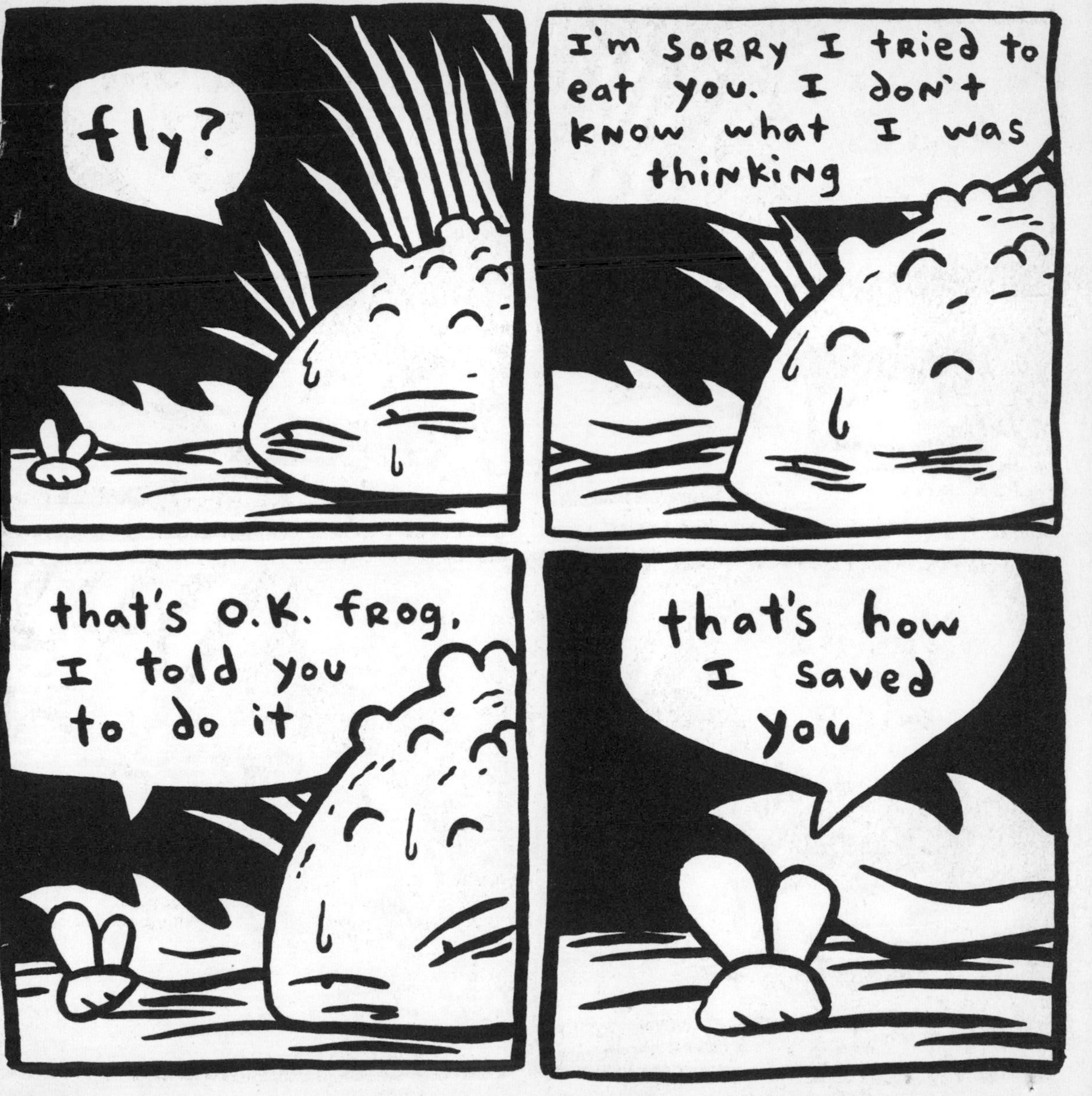
fly?
I'm SORRY I tried to eat you. I don't know what I was thinking
that's O.K. frog. I told you to do it
that's how I saved you

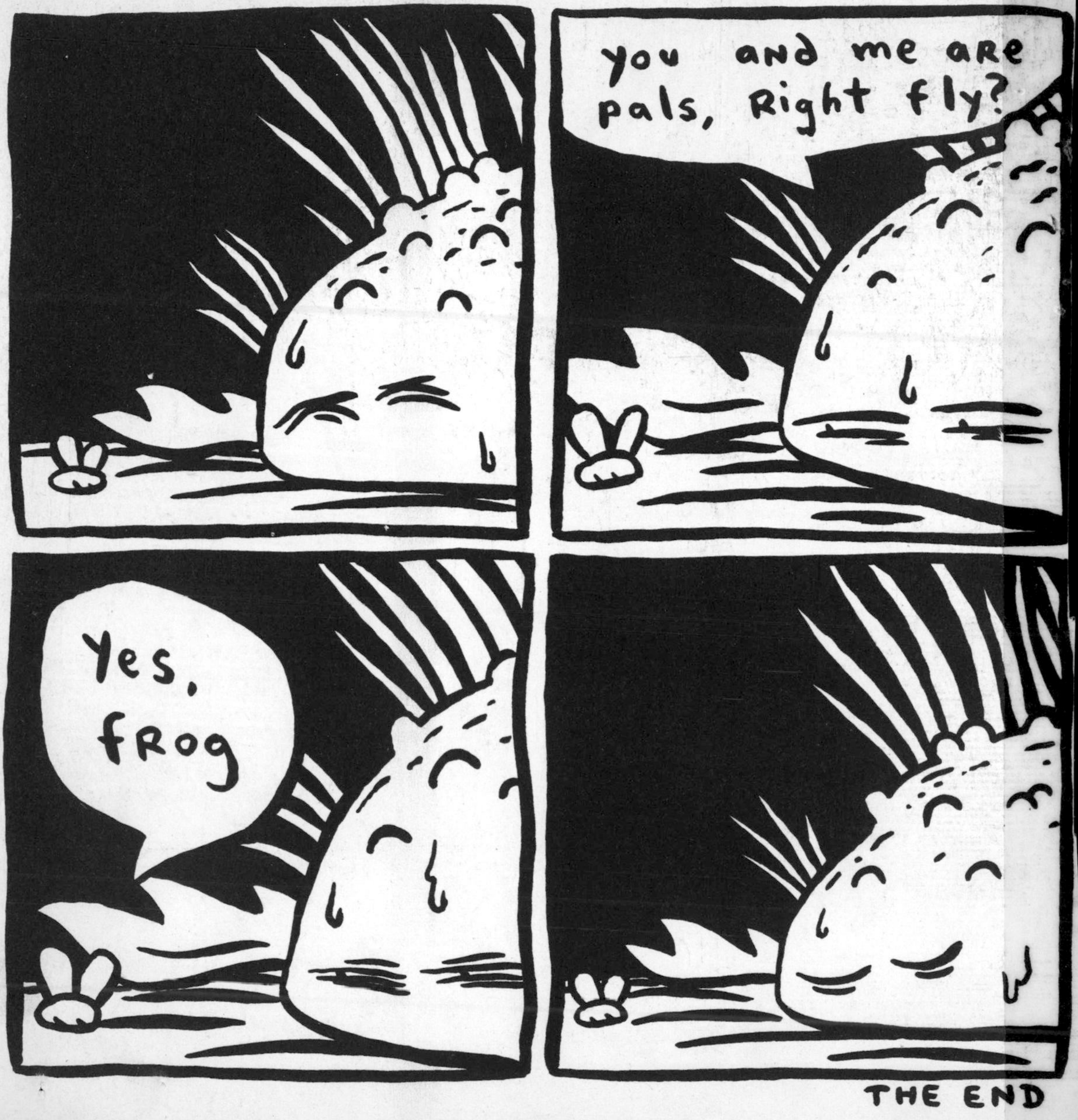
you and me are pals, Right fly?
Yes, frog
THE END